Caroline Chanter

A Life with Colour
Gerard Wagner
1906–1999

Gerard Wagner, 1983

Caroline Chanter

A LIFE WITH COLOUR

Gerard Wagner
1906–1999

RUDOLF STEINER PRESS

Rudolf Steiner Press
Hillside House, The Square
Forest Row, East Sussex RH18 5ES

www.rudolfsteinerpress.com
www.goetheanum-verlag.ch

Edited by Matthew Barton

Published by Rudolf Steiner Press 2021
© Copyright 2021 Verlag am Goetheanum, CH – 4143 Dornach
All rights reserved

A catalogue record for this book is available from the British Library

Typesetting and Cover Design: Sven Baumann, Rheinfelden
Print: Beltz Grafische Betriebe, Bad Langensalza
ISBN 978-1-85584-595-4

‹… I am convinced
that Gerard Wagner's time
is yet to come.›

From a letter of 15 June 2001
from Sergei O. Prokofieff
to Sonja Vandroogenbroeck

CONTENTS

FOREWORD

Gerard Wagner was a lone wolf, living and working in
his studio. He was like a Russian monk with his pale
face, fine head and black clothes: 'painting for God'.

INGEBORG MARESCA

His whole being bowed before the mystery of colour in a loving,
joyful yet serious way, full of devotion and dignity. His life and work
itself became a living metaphor of the creative power of colour.

CHRISTIAN HITSCH

Recent decades have seen the publication of noteworthy studies by anthroposophical authors of the brilliant painter Gerard Wagner (1906–1999) and
his distinctive art. These range from single essays to the catalogue of the Hermitage exhibition in St Petersburg (1997), and the book-length monographs
by Peter Stebbing. The latter explored Wagner's work on Rudolf Steiner's
Goetheanum cupola motifs (2013) and his studies of "The Art of Colour and
the Human Form" (2017), as well as shedding extensive light, for the first
time, on Wagner's teacher in Dornach, Henni Geck, and her studies of Rudolf
Steiner's training sketches. (In: *Conversations About Painting with Rudolf
Steiner*, 2008.) Nine years ago, painter and painting therapist Caroline Chanter
(born 1950) presented Wagner's early artistic biography up to the point when
he moved to Dornach in her valuable book, *His beloved St Ives. The Painter
Gerard Wagner at the Cornish Art Colony 1924–1925*. Wagner himself, partly
in collaboration with his colleague and wife Elisabeth Wagner, published
several books between 1968 and 1996 that very carefully detailed his artistic
principles, the method of his work and its aims (including in the volume *The
Individuality of Colour*, 2009).

In the present work, based on research extending over several decades,
Caroline Chanter – who studied firstly at Exeter Art College and Leeds Pol-
ytechnic, and then at the Margarethe Hauschka School for Artistic Therapy –
offers the first complete survey of Gerard Wagner's biography and his artistic
intentions. Her documentation highlights the many stages and details of his
development in so far as this is possible for a reticent and retiring, indeed

even hidden and enigmatic figure such as Gerard Wagner. At one place in her introduction she writes:

In the figure of Gerard Wagner one is reminded of Rudolf Steiner's description of an initiate of the Middle Ages – one who had no name and no rank and was called a 'homeless man'. In this regard an interesting occurrence: a visitor at the painting school introduces herself to Gerard Wagner with: 'I'm just a visitor here.' And he answers 'So am I.'

After the early death of his father, who came from Germany, Gerard Wagner spent most of his childhood and youth in England, his mother's native country. He was an extraordinarily sensitive child, with fine perceptive faculties, in fact a remarkable capacity for observation and an outstanding sense of colour, form and metamorphosis which developed in him at an early stage. Towards the end of his schooldays, when he was 16, and having as yet no knowledge whatever of anthroposophy, he read in the *Manchester Guardian* of the destruction by fire of the wooden double cupola building in Dornach. His spontaneous thought was, "Now I'll never see it" [the Goetheanum]. In February 1924, as the Class Lessons and karma lectures were starting in the Joinery Workshop in Dornach, Wagner began his training with the landscape painter John Anthony Park in a remarkable artists' colony in St Ives, a village of painters and fisherfolk in Cornwall. Park already asserted the primacy of colour above line and form in painting, an emphasis that spoke to Wagner, and one he later pursued in a uniquely consistent way, supported by methodological indications from Rudolf Steiner. At Michaelmas 1925, six months after Steiner's death, he began his studies at the Royal College of Art in London, and during this period encountered anthroposophy through another artist, the illustrator Hookway Cowles. By 1926 already, Gerard Wagner had not only joined the Anthroposophical Society but also, on the way to a painting trip in France, had attended the "English Week" at the Goetheanum (31.7.–7.8.1926) with Cowles. Caroline Chanter describes the unforgettable atmosphere he found there – and Wagner's decision not to continue his trip but to stay, forever. During this same English Week, participants were shown Rudolf Steiner's studio, the Group with the "Representative of Humanity" but also the "sublime" room envisaged for its location in the Goetheanum – as "heart" space of the mighty building, which Wagner saw in its unfinished state, with all the scaffolding still in place. He attended significant lectures, watched performances of eurythmy and scenes from the mystery plays, and, at the tender age of twenty decided there and then to work on the Dornach hill, to become a co-worker at this centre of science, art and religion, which, as he believed, was of a kind that existed nowhere else in the world. He witnessed the topping-out ceremony of the building (Michaelmas 1926), the transfer to it of the sculptural group (Michaelmas 1927) and the opening of the second Goetheanum (Michaelmas 1928). He lived from hand to mouth in very impoverished circumstances, and yet continued to school himself in art, as well as in sculpture, eurythmy, drama and speech formation (wih Ilja Duwan). He took to the stage in *Faust,* and the fourth mystery play. But the nine months in 1928 that he spent with Henni Geck in her new painting school in Rudolf Steiner's studio, with Steiner's original training sketches on the walls, were of central importance for him. Then the sketches were taken from her, and Henni Geck ended her teaching work in one of the countless tragedies that Wagner experienced at the Goetheanum. "What time and energy were lost for the important things!" Nevertheless he pursued his continuing development as a painter, described here in detail by Caroline Chanter, through to his first exhibitions, the opening of his own painting school (1967), his expert work also in the field of pedagogy and painting therapy, and his scientific ability and interests. He helped design the second Goetheanum building, with wall paintings in the English Hall and the Foundation Stone Hall, and with the ceiling paintings. Chanter describes these and many other aspects of Wagner's work, often as reflected in the painter's correspondence and in the memories of his pupils and colleagues. He was always concerned with the inner consistency of his work, and its esoteric foundations. For Gerard Wagner, schooling through colour was a path toward one's true humanity ("and whoever notices this cannot help but continue on the path") – a path also to a "different mode of consciousness" as the prerequisite for any future that art might have. In his close to complete immersion in colour as a "language" he had very far-reaching and profound inner experiences. As he once said, this was also an immersion "in the objective world of human feelings" and in "the forces working in nature".

As Sergei O. Prokofieff wrote in his notable obituary for Gerard Wagner, art and science had attained in his work a new and great, Rosicrucian "synthesis". Among other things he highlighted how, during his last illness, Wagner had studied his own body from within as the "great artwork of the gods". Prokofieff also pictured the painter's new beginning in the world of spirit: "How the spiritual world rejoiced to receive this soul is something we can only intimate – a soul which on earth was devoted so selflessly and in such purity to the beings that are revealed here in forms and colours. He helped them to utterance and manifestation in this world of ours."

With her book, Caroline Chanter has not only accomplished a great and seminal study that illuminates the life and work of Gerard Wagner, but has done a great service also to the Goetheanum and its School of Spiritual Science, within which, as he always saw it, his work was embedded.

General Anthroposophical Section   *Peter Selg*
Goetheanum. Dornach, 7 June 2021

INTRODUCTION

*Our life is no dream –
however it should and
perhaps will become one.*

NOVALIS[1]

When embarking on writing a biography of the painter Gerard Wagner one encounters a kind of paradox – for Wagner claimed not to have had a biography. It is true that events in his life were not particularly dramatic and he hardly travelled the world. Few artists have so wholeheartedly spent most of their adult life before an easel as Gerard Wagner did. The journey of his life is written in his paintings. As Gerard Wagner described in his biographical sketch, those inner journeys to different lands of colour are no less significant than outer journeys:

> When one is a painter and one stands before your easel and paint, one goes on 'journeys' during which one has experiences. These 'journeys' lead further, and the experiences penetrate deeper, than anyone could otherwise have. If one wants to know something about a painter's life, therefore, look at his paintings. On these 'painter's travels'– if he really is a painter – more than he can initially comprehend or consciously intend unites with the work he executes.[2]

The experiences the painter has on these 'journeys' belong to him. The pictures are visible for all to see, they are an 'open secret'. But few of us can plumb the depths of these visible colour journeys in their entirety and follow the painter on his path. On the other hand, the paintings are art, and art has a language of its own which speaks to every human heart. So even if the mysteries of colour do not immediately reveal themselves to us, we can roam through at least 70 years of painterly works – through the 5000 pictures in his archive – beginning with those of the 1920s, then through the 30s, 40s and 50s, right up to the end of the 1990s – and attempt to live into the visible changes and developments in style and subject matter. Not an easy task!

Some may be surprised at the quality and subtlety of his early colour compositions, executed in oil during his student days in Cornwall and at the Royal College of Art in London. Being accepted into the Goetheanum painting school was, according to Gerard Wagner, the real beginning of his artistic schooling. None of his student work remains from that time but in his archive one can see some rough attempts carried out a few years later, in which the high standard of his abilities in painting and drawing learnt in Cornwall and London have seemingly disappeared. The young painter consciously left behind the old and started anew, and one can have the impression of an absolute beginner when looking at these rather primitive early works.

Moving on to the pictures of the 1930s and 40s, painted more than a decade after the beginning of his artistic schooling in Dornach, one notices how the paintings invoke motifs which might be called 'Christian'. These include unusual imaginations of the being and deeds of Jesus Christ. The large and dramatic paintings of the 1950s, dominated by the Jordan Baptism, are painted in many variations like a recurring vision of a distant past. Thereafter paintings often arise in response to a question from a school-teacher or a pupil: animals, plants, fairytales, for instance. Gerard Wagner once commented that his subject matter would have been quite different if such questions had not come towards him.

Motifs of the late 1960s and 70s depict occurrences deeply rooted in spiritual-scientific research: birth and death, human beings at the mercy of ahrimanic powers, and further themes of evil and redemption. These subjects were often approached in series depicting development and transformation within a theme. The painter's large, light-filled 'cupola motifs' of the first Goetheanum, showing the evolution of mankind, must also count as a high point of his work in the 70s. The painter Gladys Mayer called these 'a resurrection' of the Goetheanum cupola paintings. The 1970s also marked a new phase in terms of the painter's materials. Windsor & Newton watercolour paints gave way to newly produced plant-based pigments made at the Goetheanum, which the painter used exclusively from that time onward, and which gave his paintings a new quality of colour.

The eternal archetypal motif of the 'Madonna and Child' weaves through all these different periods. We are inevitably reminded of the series of Madonna motifs painted by Raphael; but now, instead of the three-dimensional aesthetic beauty of the Renaissance, the motif arises out of the all-encompassing 'mothering blue' in its archetypal gesture: 'out of colour' as Rudolf Steiner showed in the two versions of the motif that he painted. Gerard Wagner was not averse to repeating this tender motif in manifold variety and mood, finding recurring joy in, as it were, meeting an old friend again, and learning continually from Rudolf Steiner's colour insights.

The delicacy and subtlety of the work of the 1980s reveals further secrets of Creation. In one image from nature's workshop, the rose has become the heart of the Madonna. And then comes a longer stride to new territory in the late 1990s, when a fresh, dynamic rhythm of light and movement signals the last period of the artist's work. Here motifs give way to colour itself or, one could say, the paintings are colour symphonies in themselves whilst motifs as such recede into the background.

Wagner's whole journey could be described as a passage from space into time. Individual paintings focus us more on the motif, on the subject. In the series of paintings, on the other hand, it is as if we enter the world of processes, of movement and life. Through evolving discoveries in the field of metamorphosis, the painter found a thread running through all Rudolf Steiner's painted motifs that allows one motif to transform into another. Step by step, painting by painting, one motif can change into another quite organically. The 'Easter' motif, for instance, can change into the 'Archetypal Plant' and this, in turn, changes into the 'Threefold Human Being'. This is a revelation. Only a *living* thing such as a plant appears in such a variety of form. In this sense Gerard Wagner, accompanied by these 'blueprints' of Rudolf Steiner's as his guide, was led into the mysteries of *life* in colour.

What else can the paintings tell us? They can reveal the interests and the subject matter close to the painter's heart. And one can surely learn something about the painter in other ways: the dramatic works reveal a dramatic element in his temperament; the soft graduations of colour tone a softness and gentleness. Purity of soul and clarity of vision seem present throughout.

In attempting to follow the movement and events of Gerard Wagner's life, a leitmotif reveals itself that has been chosen as the motto of this book. It seems appropriate for this painter's life, for one can see in phases of his biography an increasing drive towards an unfolding inner life. Expressed in the words of the German poet Novalis in his *Fragments:* 'Inward leads the mysterious path'.

> *[...] We dream of journeys*
> *through the universe –*
> *Is not the universe within ourselves?*
> *We do not know the profundities of our spirit –*
> *Inward leads the mysterious path.*
> *Within us, or nowhere*
> *eternity lies with all its realms*
> *of past and future. [...]*

Inwardness was there from the very beginning in Gerard Wagner's life. He was a silent, reflective, thoughtful child whose rich inner life was full of colours. The happy middle years of childhood were decisively cut short when he was 12; and from then until the age of 17, his surroundings offered him no support for unfolding his gifts. Then, shortly before he was 18, he found a place where he *could* blossom – the art colony of St Ives where he took up the paintbrush and his artistic talent was nurtured.

Two years later Gerard Wagner was once more in a new place – in Dornach, Switzerland, at the Goetheanum, where he felt at home. At the same time, doors closed on a possible future life as a successful artist with recognition and fame. He began a new life studying anthroposophy, engaging in its artforms and, most importantly, in a new way of painting. About seven years later he found himself in his studio alone with the challenge Rudolf Steiner had given him – to discover 'form from colour'. This was the real beginning of his inward path. He had to call up life from within, by his own will: a pioneer in an unknown world. He was driven to focus his energies on painting. But ultimately, it was not painting in the usual sense but something more like meditation. It was inner life to the full.

But this was not the whole of his life. The subject of 'balance' was central to Gerard Wagner's work and person and it showed in the configuration of his life. The intensive inner work he was engaged in was balanced by connections to a growing circle around him. His paintings brought a large group of people to him. He was asked to teach, something he felt he wasn't suited for. The first painting course he gave in Biel was, in his own words, 'dire'. He was asked to paint murals in public buildings; asked for advice on the subject of handwork and clothing, and asked to help therapists and educationalists; and pupils flocked to him who wanted to learn from his insights. Overall a picture emerges of a point within a circle: the point is where the painter stands in solitude before the easel, and the circle around him is made up of everything else he was called upon to take part in. And the most important thing – his paintings – found their way into the wider world, enriching the lives of others.

This rather simple image of point and circle only fully struck me when I was well into writing this book. It is quite astounding to see how much Gerard Wagner actually did apart from his own artistic work, which he carried out at home. The peripheral activities all connected with his work – the painting school, the exhibitions etc., reveal a great deal of labour; also a great deal of physical work in some instances.

*

Quite a bit has already been written about Gerard Wagner's work and life, yet much about him remains hidden. The hiddenness is partly due to the painter's own modesty – he said little about himself and what he thought. What he did say was usually in a quiet moment with one other person or a small group, away from the centre of an event. He didn't announce his thought and opinions. In the figure of Gerard Wagner one is reminded of Rudolf Steiner's description of an initiate of the Middle Ages – one who had no name and no rank and was called a 'homeless man'.[3] In this regard an interesting occurrence: a visitor at the painting school introduces herself to Gerard Wagner with: 'I'm just a visitor here.' And he answers 'So am I.'

It would need much more than can be offered here at this time to unravel the mystery of Gerard Wagner's being and the full significance of his art. What the book hopes to achieve is to reveal something more of the person Gerard Wagner through his own words and through the memories and letters of others, and to give an overview of the long 93 years of his life. And a particular wish – for Gerard Wagner certainly the most important aspect of such a book – is to make better known the close affinity of his artistic work and his teaching with the new impulses which Rudolf Steiner gave for painting and for art. Only with this connection in mind can Gerard Wagner's work be fully appreciated and understood.

*

England plays an important role in Gerard Wagner's upbringing. Being English myself, the connection with England naturally colours the book. Other biographies could be written highlighting other aspects and events. The family letters, including Gerard Wagner's own, were written in English. His mother's diary gives limited but still memorable pictures of the growing boy, which fill out the few facts he related himself in very few words in the years I knew him.

Apart from his mother's maiden name of Lange, Gerard Wagner knew very little about his family background. Through family documents provided by his niece Mary Ingham (Wagner) and his cousin Andrew Lang, some biographical background of the Lange and Wagner families came to light, and a rich collection of family photographs has been helpful in forming a fuller picture. Conversations with Wagner-Lange family members – primarily with Mary Ingham, and cousins Andrew Lang, Jennifer Ware and Julie Neild – were invaluable, and it was interesting to discover what a close family they were and how, despite the painter spending most of a lifetime away from England, and from them, 'Gerry' still lived warmly in their hearts and minds.

The detective work needed for the book turned out to be quite exciting. I must thank Marion Whybrow, author of *St Ives 1883–1993. Portrait of an Art Colony*,[4] for putting me in touch with Austin Wormleighton (2.9.1937–31.3.2019), journalist, art historian and biographer of John Anthony Park, and Gerard Wagner's first painting teacher. He was indispensable in my research of the St Ives period.[5]

The Wiesbaden visits were fruitful; and finding the house where Gerard Wagner was born, as well as other houses where the Wagner family lived, was quite an experience. Discovering his father's workplace and business, still in exactly the same place, in Schierstein, where he established it in 1897, also seemed meaningful.

Reminiscences by Gerard Wagner's colleagues and associates – Rex Raab, Anne Stockton, Ernst Schuberth and Hermann Koepke – were essential for giving a fuller picture; and Susanne Wulff gave vital support in many ways. Conversations with others who have lived for many years here in Dornach and who knew the painter, were valuable, as were the memories of pupils that rounded out the picture of Gerard Wagner as teacher.

I thought I might find some notable artistic talent among Gerard Wagner's ancestors, but this has not been the case. Yet it is clear that his parents and especially his mother had a deep feeling for art, and that she was well versed in the history of painting. A marked talent for music certainly runs through the family but most outstanding is a talent for scientific research. Wagner's father Max Wagner, was an inventor in the field of engineering, as was his maternal grandfather Hermann Lange. His first cousin, Professor Andrew Lang (1924–2008), Senior Researcher in Physics at Bristol University, was well known for his pioneering studies in X-ray diffraction physics, for which he developed topographic techniques to image imperfections in crystals. His method (known as the 'Lang method') has been widely used for the electronics, diamond and other industries. A description of the qualities of this work in his obituary could equally speak for the results of Gerard Wagner's research, his artistic-scientific experiments with colour: 'His work showed sustained innovation, craftsmanship in experimentation, and perceptiveness and thoroughness in the analysis of experiments. The topographic images which he produced were of the very highest quality and were often exceedingly beautiful.'

Gerard Wagner was most probably the first, at least in our times, to be simultaneously an artist and 'scientific' researcher. Leonardo Da Vinci was both artist and scientist but Wagner united the two aspects in a unique way: he was a colour-researcher, an artist-scientist. In this unique meeting of art and science, Gerard Wagner's work went beyond the usual concept of painting to create a foundation of knowledge about colour which can render many areas of life fruitful.

*

The final part of Rex Raab's recollections, 'Impressions of Gerard Wagner', is a suitable doorway into this biography of the great painter Gerard Wagner:

> In Gerard Wagner, art and the spirit of discovery, the urge to research and investigate, were united to a superlative degree. Most helpful to the development of higher knowledge is a quiet introspective nature, which Gerard also had.
>
> The result of these two circumstances coinciding in Gerard's character was that he made quite unprecedented discoveries – we might almost say inventions – in the field of colour and painting. Their full value and significance has, perhaps, still to be recognised and acclaimed.
>
> Has a painter before him so been able to create a blue with that glow, like a lake in fairyland? Or such a persuasive pale mauve? Or such flames? – effects otherwise familiar only to the goldsmith and the jeweller, but here created through watercolour!
>
> Such things did not come lightly to this painter. They had to be earned by indefatigable work. It is not unknown that labour is the secret of achievement! But in Gerard's case it was not so much achievement for its own sake that he was aiming at, he wanted to find out how colour works, how colours work on one another, how they can open our eyes to have great experiences and infinitely enriched lives and at the same time make us more harmonious human beings, if we are prepared to give ourselves up to their kindly influence – as he was.
>
> Two influences were brought to bear on him at a fairly early age which proved to be particularly favourable, and he would never have denied it. On the contrary he was clearly grateful for this circumstance, and daily sought to justify and earn it. The two influences, that were really one, were the path of training and Dornach as a place to live and work in.
>
> Gerard Wagner took full advantage of this circumstance in his life by responding unstintingly. He worked day and night at the fulfilment of the goal he set himself already on his first day at the Goetheanum,

which was his home for over 70 years. An obvious source of inspiration for Gerard's painting work was the eurythmy he constantly saw. And there were many other sources.

Gerard Wagner did not preach; he practised. And practice means doing something regularly, rhythmically.

> *Soul of Man!*
> *You live in the beat of heart and lungs,*
> *that bears you through the rhythm of time*
> *into the feeling of your own soul being:*
> *practise spirit contemplation*
> *in balance of Soul ...*[6]

One feels that Gerard had made this a habit for life. It led him into clear depths of genuine mystical experience, true feeling as the instrument of art. In his paintings he has left posterity the message of his experiences for all who want to see and love them.

LINEAGE AND PARENTAGE

In Gerard Wagner's life we see an interweaving of the British and German nations with their different cultures and languages. While he showed a clear consciousness-soul approach to his work, a quality of objectivity and impartiality which was apparent also in his outward behaviour, warm heart forces also shone through his distinctively Central European character.

As a cosmopolitan person in the deeper sense, nationality was not of first importance to Gerard Wagner and he admitted he knew nothing about where his ancestors came from. His parents were German but both had a strong sense of connection to England. 'My father wanted us to live in England,' he said. Gerard Wagner's maternal grandfather, Hermann Ludwig Lange, came to north-west England, to Manchester, during the 19th century emigration of Germans to Britain where, according to his son Ernest Lang, he became 'altogether wedded to English life and ideas, and wished his children to grow up in this milieu'.[7] Thus Julie Lange, Gerard Wagner's mother, who was brought up as English, also possessed a strong German cultural heritage.

Max Wagner, Gerard Wagner's father, was born and brought up in Germany but left his native land in early adulthood, and after travelling widely settled in Hampstead, London. Thus Julie Lange and Max Wagner met in England, and when they married Julie Wagner adopted German nationality. After a few years, Max Wagner's work took them to Germany, where Gerard Wagner was born. Gerard Wagner's first six years of life were spent in Germany. Then the family moved back to England, and Gerard found himself amidst the Cheshire countryside. Fourteen years later, at the age of 20, he was again in a German-speaking country, Switzerland, which he made his home and place of work.

Rudolf Steiner described how our ancestry connects us with elemental nature, elemental spiritual beings, who participate in the development of the physical body. Folk spirits, he says, work through the elemental beings as their instrument. They organize, so to speak, a host of beings which work into the etheric body, and from the etheric body into the physical body so that the physical body can be an instrument for the specific, individual configuration a person needs for their particular mission on earth.[8]

The folk spirits in Gerard Wagner's ancestry are distinctly Germanic. His father and maternal grandfather came from East Germany, from Plauen, a town tucked away in the southwestern corner of Saxony, near the borders of Thuringia, Bavaria and the Czech Republic. The nearby Ore Mountain region on Saxony's southern border forms a natural boundary with Bohemia, and the ancient Bohemian-Czech legends connected to the place are steeped in tales of the elemental life of its mountains, forests and animals. The area has been associated with mining since 2,500 BC: originally tin and later other metals and ores, including silver, uranium and the cobalt blue pigment.

Plauen is the capital of the Vogtland district. In the words of Gerard Wagner's uncle, Ernst Lang, it is an 'elevated and well-wooded region and the stronghold of a sturdy Puritanism which seems to reflect something of the spirit of its austere uplands'. Besides being known as the home of the Reformation and Martin Luther, Saxony was also the spiritual and intellectual heart of Germany, the homeland of notable personalities such as Friedrich Nietzsche, and the poet-philosopher Novalis. Weimar is of course associated with Johann Wolfgang von Goethe: his house can still be seen there, a memorial to his genius as poet and thinker. Saxony's high musical culture includes the musical genius of Robert Schumann, Johann Sebastian Bach and Richard Wagner. At a more mundane level, Saxony is associated with talents of invention and commerce, and was an early force in the development of industry.[9]

The town of Plauen lies in a long, pleasant valley through which flows the White Elster, dividing the town into two, a southern and northern part. The ancient stone bridge, the Elsterbrücke, which crosses the river in the centre of town, marks the historic trade route from the South into Thüringen and Bohemia.

Plauen continued to be a significant centre of trade and commerce and became known for its great textile industry, particularly lace. It grew to be a forerunner in the modernisation of 19th-century German textile manufacture, and its foreign trade dealings had an especially lively connection with North America, as demonstrated by the existence of an American Consulate there in the 19th century. And within Germany itself, an efficient railway system connected Plauen directly to the chief industrial centres of Dresden, Leipzig, Berlin, Munich und Frankfurt am Main.[10]

Max Wagner – Gerard Wagner's father

Into this background of diligence and industry, Max Wagner was born on 28 March 1860, as the fifth child and fifth son of master weaver Heinrich Ernst Wagner and Christiane Luise Gross, also from Plauen. On their marriage certificate Heinrich Wagner is recorded as the owner of the Golden Lion Guest House, and in keeping with Plauen's textile tradition, weavers and bleachers were the chief professions of Max Wagner's ancestors. The inhabitants of Plauen were known to be friendly, non-judgmental people, accepting of strangers; and like Saxons in general, they preferred to exercise their wit and good-hearted humour in the coffee house rather than at the tavern. Despite the emphasis there on material values and the practical necessities of life, Plauen was also known for its cultivation of the arts in family and private circles, especially music, singing and acting.

The only surviving early photograph of Max Wagner, at about the age of ten, shows a boy of delicate build and gentle countenance with an intelligent, open gaze. After completing his school education Max Wagner most likely entered the Commercial School of Plauen and joined a business which took him abroad. He was the only one of five brothers to leave Plauen, probably in his early 20s. In 1888 he was in Melbourne, Australia; he spent some time in New Zealand and may have been in North America. He then settled in Hampstead, the most rural of the suburban districts of London and a focal point for German emigrés. He was 'cosmopolitan and must have been social, judging by the little leather book of American drinks given to him by his friends', a family chronicle tells us. We learn that he was a 'merchant' by profession, and is said to have been a clever engineer and inventor.

Julia Lange – Gerard Wagner's mother

Julia (Julie) Elizabeth Lange was born on 2 August 1868 in Manchester, the second child of Hermann and Stephanie Lange. Appendix 1 offers more background information about them, and about an interesting connection with Caspar Hauser. Julia's birth followed that of a son, Ernest, born in 1867. Julia was the oldest of four daughters: Gertrude, born 1873, followed by Emily and Rose. It was said that Julia largely brought up and cared for her three younger sisters, her mother Stephanie being studious and having 'little understanding for children'. Julia Lange was described by her niece Julie Neild as 'the most outstanding of the Lange offspring'.

When Julie Lange was eight, the family left St Georges Place, Gorton and moved to The Poplars, an old Georgian House with pleasant grounds in Plymouth Grove, where she spent the remainder of her childhood. At the time of this move her father Hermann Lange had been in England 15 years and was in the prime of his life, now chief engineer and co-manager of the locomotive building firm Beyer-Peacock & Co. Subsequently, the family moved to Victoria Park, a high-class residential area with large homes and gardens to the south of Manchester where, due to the prevailing winds, they were protected from the smog of Manchester's cotton mills. Victoria Park attracted the rich and famous and was the home of many eminent Victorians, amongst them Richard Cobden, the free-trader and liberal. Manchester was at that time a place of revolutionary thinking, promoting free trade and new forms of labour organisation.

Hermann and Stephanie Lange were both passionately fond of music, and shared their enthusiasm with their children, all of whom played musical instruments. Julie played the violin but Gertrude, the closest to Julie in age and her confidante in later life, was the most gifted musically of the five children. At 18, she was given a concert-size Bechstein by her father that she kept and played all her life. She took piano lessons with Charles Hallé, the German born pianist and conductor, who founded the Hallé Orchestra, Britain's first permanent professional symphony orchestra based in Manchester. The Lange family were regular visitors to the Free Trade Hall to hear the Hallé Orchestra concerts. Music was not the only art nurtured at home; Julie had a particular love for literature and drama, and an appreciation of the fine arts, especially painting. An able pupil, she attended Ellerslie Ladies College in Victoria Park, and was reported to have spent some time at the Slade Art School in London.

An outstanding feature of Julie's childhood and early adult life was the strong bond she had with her father, who was, as his son Ernest tells us,

> an energetic man with a warm and generous temperament, transparently honest and kind … He emanated a profound spirit of thoroughness and of unselfish, single-minded devotion to duty that influenced everyone he had to do with.

In 1891, when Julie was 23, her father was ordered by his doctor to take a long rest from work, and so father and daughter undertook a six-week journey together to Italy and the Italian Riviera. Julie's diary account of the journey shows her interest and love of art as well as her interest in human character. It also gives a different picture from the one passed down through the family, that her father had been strict with her and made her very repressed:

> We travelled all night through and breakfasted at Basel. We had intended to stop in Lucerne until the next day, but father and I, being both impatient creatures, decided to go right on to Milan. We took a walk through

the Gallery to the Piazza del Duomo – I was eager to show father the lovely cathedral.

And on the first morning at the Palazzo Rosso in Genoa, she revisited some of her favourite paintings 'my dear knight by Van Dyck and the lovely Sebastian by Guido Reni'.

Apart from the art and the architecture of the various places they visited, they enjoyed the scenery and fresh walks, and had an enjoyable time at the Monte Carlo Casino in Monaco as well:

> We looked at the Prince's Palace, quite a small affair, but with very pretty rooms – there is even a throne room which father made much fun of. After lunch we went straight to the casino. I had great luck winning in nearly everything I tried. The next evening I treated father to a small bottle of the best champagne on the strength of my winnings, and we both enjoyed it very much.
>
> The place I liked best in the Rivera was, I think, Monte Carlo – the Casino is a most fascinating place. I shall never forget the curious excitement that came over me when I was watching the play and trying my fortune at it – and I am sure father felt the same – we could not help getting excited – it was all so novel and intensely interesting – the luxury of the place, the people, representatives of all nations, all classes, all types – it is really a place for character study – I could have stood for hours watching the play, and the faces of those who played – very seldom one saw any display of emotion. … After lunch we went to the concert room, and listened to the finest classical music I have ever heard – father and I agreed that Hallé's orchestra is far inferior to it. Father said afterwards, if we ever went to Monte Carlo again we would not play – but I said I was quite sure we would. He said he would be afraid of my becoming a confirmed gambler but he did not mean it – he felt about it just as I did – enjoyed it greatly at the time, and afterwards looking at it in cold blood, felt a little ashamed of it.

This journey was the last Julie and her father took together, and the family was shattered some nine months later, in early 1892, when Hermann Lange died suddenly of a stroke at the age of 54. An obituary stated: 'Mr Lange, it may be said, fell a victim to his own restless energy of temperament. He had naturally a strong constitution, but, as the result of over application to work, his health had been declining for several years.'[11]

Marriage to Max Wagner

Julie Lange's devotion to her father was such that she would not marry while he lived. In 1888, four years before her father's death, she and Max Wagner had become engaged, and they visited Plauen and Max Wagner's family, but sometime after that Julie broke off the engagement. They probably first met at the Lange's home in Manchester, which was also a meeting place for people in the engineering world.

On 6 September 1894, almost three years after Hermann Lange's death, Julie Lange and Max Wagner were married in the German Protestant Church of Greenheys in Manchester. She wrote in her diary on 5 September: 'Tomorrow is my wedding day – I pray that it may be the first day of the happier half of Max's life, and of mine.' She was 26 and Max 34. The couple moved into 53 Belsize Avenue, Hampstead:

> We are both very pleased with our pretty home and in spite of business troubles and Max's bad health we are very happy. I like Hampstead extremely, it is a very pleasant place to live and is convenient on the whole for town.

The next few years were, as Julie put it, uneventful. They enjoyed the social life of London, had many visitors, and spent time with the Lange family in Manchester. It is not known what Max Wagner's work was at that time but an important step in his career was to acquire a patent from the well-known English metallurgist Dr John Stead, for a lead-based alloy – 'malleable yet stable' – that was considered an ideal metal for bearings in machine construction. John Stead named his product 'Glyco'.

In 1895 Max and Julie Wagner made an extensive visit to Germany, including three weeks in Max's hometown Plauen. In Munich they took in the cultural life of the city including a visit to the Succession Art Exhibition. Julie wrote in her diary:

> There are some fearful and wonderful pictures there of the new Impressionist school, all very modern, some interesting, few beautiful; there are such a number of rooms, about forty-five, that one comes away with a very confused impression after a few hours. In the evening we went to a performance of Lohengrin at the Hoftheater – it was splendidly given and we enjoyed it very much.

In 1897, Max and Julie Wagner moved to the Spa town of Wiesbaden, the capital of Hesse in central-western Germany. The town, close to Frankfurt am Main, was free of industry and, with its mild climate and virtually smoke-free air, was a haven for sufferers of bronchial illnesses, who flocked there to take the waters:

> The main spring is the Kochbrunnen, from the shaft of which no less than 15 springs rise, bubbling and steaming to the light of day with a temperature of 68° Celsius, discharging about 100 gallons of water per minute which are conveyed to eight adjoining Bathing Establishments supplying about 400 baths daily. In addition to the main spring, there are no less than 23 other springs. The total number of bathing rooms in the various establishments in Wiesbaden amounts to about 900, in which the superabundance of water permits of 2,500 baths being given daily.[12]

In nearby Schierstein am Rhine, Max Wagner founded the Glyco Metal Company (Glyco-Metall-Gesellschaft mbH) with his friend, the engineer Hermann Leonard, and the owner of the Schierstein metals factory, Heinrich Ludendorf. Dr Stead's patent had not yet been tested in production so a considerable risk was involved, and Max Wagner carried sole responsibility as well as providing most of the finance for establishing the company. He set up his enterprise as a small mechanical workshop opposite the Schierstein railway station. For the first few years the metal was produced at the Neusser Ironworks in Düsseldorf-Heerdt until production began in Schierstein in 1900. Soon the company could guarantee 'Glyco' as a bearing liner 'equal in efficiency to the highest-priced tin alloys at less than half their cost'. Max Wagner patented his 'Glyco' inventions in 1901 and 1904.[13]

Meanwhile Julie Wagner gave birth to their first child, Roland Hermann Ernst, on 4 March 1898. On 17 May 1901, Erich Theodor was born, but survived only for four days. Felix followed on 10 August 1904. On 28 March 1906, Julie Wagner wrote in her diary: 'Max's birthday and close to another – a certain little person, whom I hope will make *her* appearance very soon – how strange it seems!'

Germany:
Wiesbaden 1906–1912

EARLY CHILDHOOD

Gerard Wagner was born at 9 Uhlandstrasse[14] in Wiesbaden on Maundy Thursday, 5 April 1906 in the early morning. At the time of his birth the Promethean planet of Uranus was rising in the dogged sign of Capricorn, and the Sun, Mercury and Venus were in the fire-sign of Aries. His mother was 37, four months away from her 38th birthday, and his father had just reached the age of 46. To begin with no names were recorded for the child on the birth certificate, which, together with the mother's diary entry, seems to suggest that the couple were expecting a girl. The certificate confirmed that 'on 5 April of the year 1906 ... a boy was born and that the child has not yet received his Christian names'. Two months later the names Werner Gerhard Max were added, but even then it took some time for a name to settle. To begin with the child was called Werner, then his name changed to Gerhard when he was about four, soon afterwards shortened to Gerry.

At the age of eight months, on 28 December, Werner Gerhard Max was baptised by a pastor of the Protestant Marktkirche. The late baptism could have been due to Max Wagner's consuming work commitments and his recurring bouts of ill health. Shortly after Werner's birth Julie Wagner writes in her diary how happy she is with her boys, 'big and little, from Max downward – long may we remain together in health, peace and contentment!' She wrote too of the great love her husband had for her and for his sons.

The newborn was clearly a healthy baby. At eleven weeks Werner is described by his mother as a 'healthy, thriving little fellow', and during a stay at Münster am Stein in the Black Forest, she wrote: 'Today Baby Werner completed the first quarter of the first year of his life – and very well and bonnie he looks, especially since we have been here.' The only mention of ill health is in a letter written by his father just over a year later: 'We will not be spending our holidays in England after all but in Belgium. I have rented a small villa in Middelkerke for July and August. It became necessary to change our travel arrangements because our youngest child had a rather severe illness. Luckily he is now a good deal better.'

The future painter Gerard Wagner was born into a cultured, comfortably well-off family in whose home hung fine works of art. He was brought up with both languages, English and German – the father was more at home in German, the mother in English. Both parents were deep thinkers with high ideals and principles, and the mother did not want 'common chatter' around her children. They were both Protestants by religion, and Julie Wagner's journal, 'Miscellaneous extracts etc', collects various profound thoughts and sentiments that were dear to her heart. The first entries were written when she was 18, and they show characteristics which later she wanted to instil in her sons – nobility, goodness, truth and self-sacrifice. These verses from poems by George Eliot and Longfellow are amongst them:

O May I join the choir invisible
Of those immortal dead who live again
In minds made better by their presence: live
In pulses stirred to generosity,
In deeds of daring rectitude, in scorn
For miserable aims that end with self,
In thoughts sublime that pierce the night like stars,
And with their mild persistence urge man's search
To vaster issues.[15]

*

Nay, never falter: no great deed is done
By falterers who ask for certainty.
No good is certain, but the steadfast mind,
The undivided will to seek the good:
'Tis that compels the elements, and wrings
A human music from the indifferent air.
The greatest gift the hero leaves his race
Is to have been a hero.[16]

*

The heights by great men reached and kept,
Were not attained by sudden flight,
But they while their companions slept,
Were toiling upward in the night.[17]

Julie had a warm-hearted, somewhat regal temperament, and Max was a sociable and well-liked man, a romantic with a melancholic disposition. In the surviving fragment of the only extant letter from Max Wagner to Julie, mostly likely written before their marriage and not long after the death of her father, he writes about the picture of *Hope*, painted by the well-known English Victorian artist George Frederic Watts,[18] which later hung in their home. This image of a blindfold woman sitting on a globe with a single star above her, plucking the last string on her harp, was a painting Gerard Wagner later remembered from his childhood. The letter reads:

> In one of my latest periodicals *The Art of our Time*, one finds a copy of G. F. Watt's picture 'Hope'. You know of course its meaning, but it may interest you to read what I enclose here in my own words:
>
> 'A noble figure with eyes bound, rests on a terrestrial sphere, an ear inclined towards her harp, her finger plucking its last string. Above her shines a star – Hope! She reigns over the world that is no longer a veil of tears but a paradise when the sound of her harp murmurs above her. One golden string remains on the harp – the last. Blind to everything around her, Hope bends over her playing, listening to that single tone and all distress, sorrow, anxiety and need are forgotten. This sound alone makes life worth living.'
>
> For who could stand the ridicule and castigation of the times, the pressure of the powerful, the maltreatment of the proud, the insolence of the functionaries, the unworthiness of silent endorsement, if Hope did not offer betterment. She holds us to life more mightily than fear. The clear sound of her last string meets our hearts and a star rises in deepest night. She is already happiness in some measure, and for an infinite number of people she is happiness itself.
>
> I have thought about this picture so often, and often I have asked myself, what thoughts have inspired you, my good angel, when you look at it!
>
> Do you pray again, my darling? I do for you morning and evening; may the Almighty grant us the happiness that we are both so in need of. Sleep well my heart of hearts and do not stop thinking with love about your most affectionately loving
>
> Max
>
> Greet your mother and siblings heartily from me, likewise mine greet all of yours, and especially you!

Max Wagner loved flowers, and he made sure the children's birthdays were made beautiful with them. On their son Felix's first birthday Julie wrote: 'Max had ordered some flowers and a garland of fir twigs dotted with dahlias, and one of greenery and small roses, and decorated his stall very prettily.' Another of the few facts about Max Wagner passed down through the family is how he loved to decorate the Christmas tree.

The Wagner family lived in the centre of Wiesbaden at the heart of the spa district, a short walk from the Warmer Damm, first in Uhlandstrasse, and then in the adjoining Kleine Frankfurtstrasse. The Warmer Damm is a park known for its unusual variety of rare trees and flowers, flourishing on fertile ground created by the overflow of mineral-rich waters from the nearby spring – the Kochbrunnen. Adjoining the park stands the sumptuous building of the Court Theatre and the Schiller monument, and a short distance away the Kurhaus with its famed colonnades surrounded by the Kurpark gardens with boating lake and bowling green. Crowds would gather by the broad Wilhelmstrasse that runs alongside the park to watch the Kaiser as he passed in his carriage or paraded down the street on his white steed.

The pleasant walks on the Warmer Damm's meandering pathways, beside the duck pond and fountain, together with sight of the many elegant villas of Wiesbaden, formed a backdrop to the child's earliest years. An early event remembered in old age with some amusement was seeing a portly gentleman sporting a yellow suit and elegant walking stick whom the enquiring child was told was 'a gentleman of leisure'.

Popular amongst European dignitaries since 1806, when it was chosen as the seat of government of the Duchy of Nassau, Wiesbaden was frequented by nobility, royalty and the wealthy. From the turn of the 19th century, the last German Kaiser, Wilhelm II, was a regular spa visitor and attended the annual imperial festival at the Court Theatre. Wiesbaden's growth was rapid, along with the development of its architectural splendour. In 1905 the population reached 100,000 compared to a mere 2,500 in 1799. Goethe visited Wiesbaden in 1814 and in 1815 to 'take the waters', and remarked on the cheerful and beneficial atmosphere he found there. The city's fame as an international spa, together with its culture of performing arts, especially music, was at its height between 1894 and 1914, coinciding roughly with the period when the Wagner family lived there.

Wiesbaden means literally 'Bath in the Meadows' and the name Wisibada is mentioned by Einhard, the biographer of Charlemagne, in 829. The Celts were early settlers there, considering water with its luminosity to be an integral part of their cult of light. The original Celtic name for Wiesbaden was transcribed by the Romans as 'cives wsinobate', and they in turn gave Wiesbaden the name 'aquae mattiacorum'.

Lying between the Rhine and the richly wooded Taunus – between river and mountain – Wiesbaden strikingly combines the elements of earth and water. As the author of a book on Wiesbaden put it, 'Here in this region, rich in springs ... the mighty forests serve as inexhaustible containers of water with their deep rocky gorges and dark valleys, where luminous water pours into numerous rivulets and brooks ...'[19]

The abundance of water, pure air and vivid light, the 'clean brightness of Wiesbaden' as Julie Wagner described it, surrounded the child – whose destiny it was to paint in the fluid element of watercolour – with an unspoilt elemental life.

The connection between water and colour, and between colour and life, is an essential part of Rudolf Steiner's teaching about colour and painting. He said in a lecture:

> Thus it is a matter of discovering in painting the secret of recreating nature out of colours. For a great part of the reality we survey is in fact born out of the creative world of colour. As vegetation sprouted out of the sea, so everything living grows out of the colour world.[20]

As regards light, Rudolf Steiner proposed this task for artists of the future: 'Art is obliged at some point in time to grasp the essence of light which, through its shining radiance, is the revelation of the spirit that weaves through the world and enlivens it.'[21] One of the chief aspects of the future painter's achievements would be the way he brought a particular and quite new quality of light into the colours he painted.

Gerard Wagner was a quiet child, unusually observant and thoughtful. He recalled an event that took place before he was 18 months old in a letter to his sister-in-law Dorothy Wagner in the 1990s:

> In mother's room at home hung a large photo of our father sitting in a chair on the garden path – that was in Wiesbaden. He is looking at two small boys – Felix and myself. Felix is watering a plant. I am sitting on the edge of the bed behind him. I well remember that moment. We had been told not to move – a photo was being taken; I saw the water coming out of Felix's watering can, flowing in a regular stream. I hoped it would not stop and perhaps spoil the photo. The water was still coming out of

the can when we were told we might move again. What a relief! (I was not quite two years old then.)

Another event of those early years, which remained clearly in Gerard Wagner's memory, was of looking intently and triumphantly at a biscuit his father had just given him, which he had been eagerly awaiting. This moment is also caught on camera and is a beautiful image that shows the buoyant uprightness of the young child not yet two years old, still in a dress and with his hair uncut.

An early experience of self, of his I, was aroused when he was eating an apple and saw the core at its centre. With an awakened feeling of self came the thought: 'I am the *only* one who has seen this.' In attempting to characterise all three of these early impressions one notices the emphasis on sense perceptions with their connection to self-awareness – a theme intimately bound up with Gerard Wagner's future work as a painter.[22]

In the words of Julie Wagner, her husband had 'too little time to enjoy his children'. Max Wagner's work involved a great deal of travelling, and time was also spent away from home convalescing at Badenweiler in the Black Forest. Since arriving in Wiesbaden Max Wagner had been very engaged in the 'Glyco' business, and expended great efforts to build up and expand the company at home and abroad. The company's innovations were exhibited at the Düsseldorf Show for Industry, Trade and Art in 1902, and in the same year rights were bought for Glyco production in the USA, Canada and Mexico. There were affiliated companies in Manchester, Paris, Amsterdam, Chicago and Charkoff. In 1906 railway customers included the Berlin firm Orenstein & Koppel and the Royal Prussian State Railway, which used Glyco bearings for 300 freight and passenger carriages. That year the company had 20 employees. 1907 brought it a gold medal at the Berlin German Army, Navy and Colonial Exhibition, and new tasks were looming along with the expansion of the company.[23]

In June 1907 Max Wagner wrote to a colleague: '... I fear we will gradually be forced to set up an extensive manufacturing plant on our site. I am now getting a few sheds built and also a building for offices. I have in mind to move the offices there early next year'. And in a letter of February 1907 he reveals his high aspirations regarding his profession:

> During the eighteen years in which I have concerned myself with the 'bearing problem' and have learnt a great deal about the technical side of things, I have never been under the illusion that I could do it better than a good, technically-trained engineer. Up until now I have succeeded without a metallurgist but I have now taken one on. I often hear it said

that there is no other firm in the whole world that has worked in this way. This puts us in an extraordinary position and because of it we will be respected and treated quite differently. I believe we will always agree that neither of us serves Mammon but rather we seek honour and respect by achieving excellence and creating something worthwhile.

Max Wagner was also strongly socially engaged and caring of the families of his customers and company representatives, to the detriment of his own health. The letters below, from 1907, reveal something of his hard work and commitment:[24]

I was glad to hear that you have begun the tuberculin cure for Mr G. as I consider myself amongst those who have trust in the same, so long as the cure is applied in the right way. I have already written to the parents and uncle of Mr G. and asked them to use their influence as much as possible to keep any business worries from him. Inner peace and quiet will be essential if he is to return to health. (…) I would have liked to have gone there myself for a few days to present myself to Dr F. but with the 3-week leave of Herr L. and the many visitors I am expecting, it is utterly impossible.

I am expecting many visitors during the course of the month and so I must make my arrangements in good time. As I find speaking for a long time still very tiring, I have to be careful how I use my energy. It would be good if you could find your way to Berlin and see for yourself our products that we are exhibiting at the German Army-Navy and Colonial Exhibition. You will get an idea of the great progress we have made. For my part I have not the slightest doubt that the Glyco flange bearing will be the bearing of the future, not only for machine construction but above all for that most eminent of customers the railway …

I had the firm intention to come to Vienna with my wife towards the end of the month to take part in the annual members' meeting of the Iron and Steel Institute, especially as Mr Stead – who as you know is the inventor of Glyco Metal – and his wife will also be there. But unfortunately during a short business trip in July I had to accept that I was in danger of becoming ill and needed 4 to 5 weeks to feel more or less well again.

Five months later, on 4 February 1908, a few months before Werner's second birthday, Max Wagner fell ill. No sense of alarm was initially felt, especially after the family doctor was called and diagnosed 'the usual thing with Max'. Julie Wagner recorded the crisis:

> Poor Max is just going through what I suppose is one of the worst illnesses he ever had – certainly the worst during our married life. ... Dr Lugenbühl came and said it was the usual thing with Max, bronchial catarrh, ... it was only on Wednesday that we began to feel a little anxious that he got on so slowly and the medicines did not seem to have the right effect. Yesterday after a comparatively quiet night he began to look changed and was very weak so that Dr L took fright and ordered strong coffee and champagne to be given constantly – then for the first time I realised the danger. He dozed off often but in between his mind was quite clear – he thanked the doctors for what they did and altogether was never anything but his dear, loving, considerate self. On Friday Dr L and Prof W decided to give injections – then for the first time we had a night nurse – even then I had no fear that Max would not get well. Yesterday before they went to bed each of the children went to say goodnight. Felix put his hand on his father's and said goodnight, and Max bid him goodnight so nicely, but he called him Werner at first – then when Felix made this little bow on going out of the room, Max nodded his head to him ... I was not in the room when Roland went in but the poor boy came out crying ... My darling died at 8.30 this evening.

Julie Wagner recalled later how in the last few months of her husband's life he was always so absorbed with business, and worried. She wrote in her diary after his death:

> I have the strongest feeling that I will not allow, if I can help it, any one of my sons to start a business of any sort. The troubles that Max went through for years were really awful and I can't make out what was at the root of it unless perhaps he mistook his vocation and ought to have been anything else but a businessman. Well it's too late now.

For the sake of the children Julie Wagner decided to stay on in Wiesbaden and try to further the interests of the business so as to get a steady income from it. Daily life went on much as before and the family continued their usual sojourns in the Black Forest. In the summer of 1908 they stayed at Herrenwies where 'Baby' first showed his zest for walking:

We came here on July 31st, the two little ones and I and the maid. Roland had come with his Grannie a fortnight earlier. We stayed at the Kurhaus. Herrenwies is a lovely little place with a great variety of walks, and the woods, pine mostly, are splendid. The time did us all a great deal of good – Baby became such a good walker, at least as good as Felix who is quicker to say that he is tired than Baby.

Whereas in earlier, happier days the mother wrote regularly in her diary about the early years of her two sons Roland and Felix, virtually nothing is recorded of Werner's early stages of development. Yet a characteristic picture emerges from her few diary entries: it is as if she is gradually getting to know and appreciate her quiet, but obstinate 'Baby'. She wrote: 'Felix is highly-strung and sensitive and will need me most. Dear little Werner with his pig-headedness, will, if he is well and strong, always make his way.'

When Werner was born, Felix was not yet two. His mother described him as an active expressive baby 'with a temper', who sings a little and loves the music box. Roland was eight years old at the time of Gerard's birth. He was a complex child, physically weak, 'very affectionate yet at times cold and indifferent'. A few months before Gerard's birth it was discovered that he was ill with epilepsy and from then on his health deteriorated. It was Felix who most obviously suffered from the loss of his father and often spoke of him:

6 September 1908. Today is our 14th wedding anniversary. A few days ago in bed Felix was asking all sorts of things about his father: whether he has a bed in heaven, whether he has wings, when he will return to us and will he not fall when he comes back down to us. Baby piped up from his bed 'Vater krank!' ('Father sick!') I think Felix will be the most like his father with his loving ways. Baby is like me, and has some of the faults I had as a child – obstinacy etc. Both are very sensitive to blame of any sort.

The move to Neroberg

Despite support from visiting family members from England, worry about the continuing ill health of her first-born Roland ('our little treasure and Max's darling'), overshadowed the years following her husband's death. In the summer of 1909 when Gerard Wagner was three years old, Julie Wagner moved from Kleine Frankfurterstrasse with its 'sad memories' to the airy woodlands and open expanses of the Neroberg where the children could have a healthier and freer life. Their new home with its large garden was at the top of Nerobergstrasse, a street lined with impressive villas. Their next-door neighbour was Princess Elisabeth von Schaumberg-Lippe who was active in social and church parish affairs and was the initiator of philanthropic projects.

A short walk further up the hill stands the Russian Orthodox Church of Saint Elizabeth whose shining golden cupolas could be seen by the excited children from an upstairs window of their new home. The church was built by Duke Adolf of Nassau as a monument and tomb for his young wife, Elizabeth Mikhailovna, Grand Duchess of Russia (1826–1845), who died at the age of 19 in childbirth. It soon became the centre of the Wiesbaden Russian Orthodox community and also a meeting place for Russian exiles further afield. Not far down the hill, the nearby Nerotal – a park landscaped in traditional English style with impressive trees and a cascading brook, the 'Schwarzbach' – made an ideal playground for the children. And at the far end of the valley the little funicular railway offered a merry ride to the top of the Neroberg.

The larger house also meant more space for live-in governesses and nurses, and the children experienced quite a few changes in this regard. Julie Wagner was often disappointed with them. 'Now I can get rid of hateful Frl. Schäfer, and look after little Gerry more myself', she wrote in her diary. Generally the governesses or 'Kinder-Fräuleins', were English speaking, the maids and nurses German.

*

Gerard Wagner's early childhood was full of rich colour experiences. Later in life his conversations often went back to his early childhood impressions of colour and of nature. He spoke of the special feeling that rose in him when seeing cherry blossom through the nursery window; or the mysterious mood he imbibed at the sight of violets. These affected him so strongly that he would not go to the place where they grew without his mother being there. In a letter to his sister-in-law in 1991 he recalled that time:

> How those impressions of nature, before six years old, help to form one's faculties of sense-perception and feeling. One increasingly realises this as one gets older and needs – for the profession of painter – those same early childhood faculties. One loses them later on, at least they become dimmer, clouded, through abstract learning (irregular Latin verbs!), and if one is lucky enough to have to try to develop these faculties consciously, then one realises that 'once upon a time' one *had* them,

without knowing. The first primrose in spring! But even the white of the soup tureen, or the lilac colour of the Cailler milk-chocolate paper – like a fresh drink!

I remember – our father had died before I was quite two years old – how mother used to wear violet blouses, apart from black (or now and then a light uncoloured one, and this was the custom later on also), and what a special feeling was always connected with this violet colour. In a corner, a chair and table was also there, in our garden in Wiesbaden grew violets. I was always shy of going there except when mother came with me.

Rudolf Steiner writes: 'When we ourselves experience the life of colour, we step out of our skins and take part in cosmic life. Colour is the soul of nature and the entire cosmos, and we take part in that soul when we experience colour.'[25] We can see from this that Gerard Wagner's being and consciousness lived strongly in higher spheres, within the soul and spirit world, when he was a child.

Colour experience, moral soul-experience, as Goethe describes it, is, according to Rudolf Steiner, one of those finer inner experiences people today often lack. Generally speaking, in our modern materialistic age we live in a very coarse way, he said, and we do not notice the finer experiences that we have. He goes on:

> This finer element may be experienced if we take notice of the soul-impression made upon us by colours, for instance. We can live with colours in such a way that blue, say, calls to life in our souls a force that resembles a feeling of longing, going forth from us and taken up in a kindly way by the blue itself. In the case of red, something always arises which seems to come toward us, wishing to overpower us. When we feel colours in this way, we have a soul-experience – a moral soul experience.[26]

It was after the move to Neroberg that Miss Ellen Collette, a governess from Canada, was employed to look after the children. She was well-liked by five-year-old Gerry, and it was she who brought about the significant event that he described in his autobiographical sketch:

> It could be seen as a gentle call of destiny for the future painter when one day an English governess was leading two small boys along a path through meadow and woodland, when to the children's amazement she scooped up a handful of frogspawn near the banks of a small pond. She

put it in a large jar in the nursery and tended it until tadpoles wriggled out and gradually turned into little frogs. Finally she painted a picture of this whole process in watercolour on a large sheet of paper which she hung on the nursery wall.[27]

Miss Collette's painting of the developing tadpoles was like a seed laid in the soul of the future painter that later grew into a deep interest in metamorphosis. This was perhaps the most significant aspect of Gerard Wagner's work, fundamental to the artistic-spiritual stream which he embraced. He wrote further about his childhood experiences and their connection to his future life as a painter:

> When limiting the description of one's life to what is significant for the path of the painter, a problem arises at the outset. For going back in memory to childhood and seeing nature as one did then, every single thing takes on meaning. The little child sees the smallest thing large – the violet, the spider, the anemone, the grasshopper … everything that grew and crawled, swam and flew, in the garden, meadow and forest, was of the greatest interest. The child's eye is alive and sees the life within each thing, and this life speaks directly and completely to the child's heart and mind; he is what he sees. Later the artist noticed how closely these impressions of early childhood were related to what he was striving for as a painter.[28]

After two years at Neroberg, and feeling out of her depth with the constant worry and care needed for her now 14-year-old son Roland, Julie Wagner arranged for him to be taken care of by Dr Klein, a doctor in nearby Idstein. He settled down well with the Klein family and remained with them. The eight-year difference between the oldest and youngest brothers made Roland's absence less noticeable for Gerry. He and Felix were only 14 months apart, and were close companions. When visiting his cousin Roland Wagner years later in Idstein, Andrew Lang observed the loving devotion of the Klein family toward Roland.

In the meantime, during a visit from her brother Ernest in 1911, Julie Wagner records some observations of her now five-year-old son Gerry:

> Today a rainy Corpus Christi. I spent a great deal of it with the children and quite enjoyed making a 'zoo' with dear little Gerry. I went for a short, quick walk with him before his bedtime. He is so fond of everything out

of doors and notices all sorts of things – I think he will be a good boy and man. Ernest said he was a splendid little fellow.

Little Gerry had strong likes and dislikes and could express his feelings in his own way, without verbal language. He preferred to be silent, at least with adults. He recalled how once at table after he had answered a question, he thought to himself: 'Now that I've spoken I won't have to say another thing for the rest of the day.'

In a diary entry in January 1912, Julie mentions Gerry's love of flowers and his reluctance to speak:

> I was rather touched by Gerry's wish a few days ago. If you see a chimney-sweep, the children here say, and count 100 white horses, you can make a wish. His wish, I found out with some trouble, was for a bunch of violets, which of course I fulfilled as soon as I could.
>
> The children had a very happy Christmas – today we let the last of the tree candles burn out, and during the last ten minutes, in the dimness of a few flickering ends, Felix sat on my knee watching them. I told him how this reminded me of the old days when Roland used to watch the lights, and how he loved to do it, and how sad he was when the last one went out. Felix said it was 'very beautiful' at Christmas. I said how much nicer it used to be when Father was with us, and he reminded me of how his father had given them all black moustaches and made them walk round the Christmas tree. He added afterwards 'he was a very nice man'– my heart aches for the fatherless boys who have no idea what they miss.

The education of her sons was one of Julie Wagner's chief concerns, and she noted down moments of progress. Of Gerry, nearly six, she wrote: 'This evening Gerry had a paper of some sort in bed – German printed in Latin letters. He pointed out to me with pride 'im' and 'em', the first time the little fellow has done such a thing – a step forward in learning.'

And on his sixth birthday she mentions his quite individual way of seeing things:

> My little Gerry's 6th birthday and Good Friday – of course Felix had to have one or two presents too. They are great friends these two, but want to be as equal as possible in all ways. One day in March when the Zeppelin flew overhead, and we all rushed out into the garden to get

a view of it, Gerry laughed so much – it seemed to him a very funny spectacle 'that we all ran like that *just* to see the Zeppelin'.

Julie Wagner had a strong feeling that after all the uncertainly of the last years she needed a refuge for herself and the two younger boys, and she decided to return to England and live near her family. Also on her mind was the 'superficial moral atmosphere of Wiesbaden from which one can't protect one's children', and she wished her sons to start at a 'good English school'. At the end of June 1912, almost a year after her eldest son moved to Idstein, she left Germany with her two younger boys to start a new life in England.

It is an interesting fact that at the time the Wagner family lived in Wiesbaden Rudolf Steiner gave the only lectures he ever gave there. Rex Raab has suggested that 'salient events in Gerard Wagner's life quietly coincide with the development of the Anthroposophical Society'. Limiting myself to the painter's childhood, I found significant events within the anthroposophical movement relating to new impulses for the arts, which correlate with Gerard Wagner's early life. (See Appendix 2.)

England:
Bowdon, Manchester 1912–1926

BOYHOOD

On 10 October 1912, after spending the summer at Colwyn Bay on the north coast of Wales, Julie Wagner and her two sons moved into their new home in Bowdon, a picturesque village in the Midlands county of Cheshire, bordering Wales to the west and providing a rural haven from the industrial cities of nearby Lancashire. Their large late-Victorian house, 'Westholme', was situated on the Firs, a quiet leafy road near the parish church of St Mary. Grandmother Stephanie, Julie Wagner's mother, moved in with them and Julie's brother Ernest and his three children lived close by.

There is no record of how the boy Gerry Wagner experienced the move to his new home and country, but he soon found himself part of a wider circle of aunts, uncles, cousins and friends of his mother's. He adjusted to English life – played cricket, accompanied his mother to church on Sundays and had holidays by the sea, mostly on the Welsh coast. Along with his brother Felix, he was soon attending the local school as well as having lessons at home. Both took piano lessons. Part of a letter written by Felix aged nine to a former governess reveals a little of the boys' activities:

> On Sunday it was a very wet day here. I also still go to church. I have got a very nice piece by L. van Beethoven, two sonatas one in G Major, and the other in F Major. I like them both very much. At present Gerry has learnt all the scales except about two. He has not learnt the minor ones yet. I have learnt my scales in sixths which I think sound very nice but are very hard until you get into them. Auntie Gertrude came to stay with us for nine days and played to us very nicely. In arithmetic we are doing weights and measures which I think are the horribelest things you could think of but in History we are having the Greek stories told by Homer, the Iliad and the Odyssey which we all think is very exciting.

Gerard Wagner was six years old when he did his first painting. It happened soon after arriving in Bowdon when his mother was away visiting relatives in Germany. It was done on a paper napkin, using some kind of fruit-juice for colour and a matchstick as a paintbrush. It came out of the blue so to speak without previous instruction or suggestion, simply through his own initiative. Wagner touched on the event during an interview given when he was 89 years old:

You want to know how I became a painter. – Well, when I was only about so high, I had a small book and it had little pictures of a bird – that was in England. And I began to read it in my grandmother's room and wanted to paint it. I only had a matchstick – and so I began to copy a little picture of a bird [a robin] on a piece of paper. That was my first painting. My mother saw it when she came home and bought me a small paint box – and that was the beginning of painting for me.[29]

The boy had a creative mind, as well as a precocious wit, and at nine years old he created a kind of riddle in letter-form called 'Pickles', which mixed words and images together. (See plate 61) He was even younger when he composed the two humorous stories below, entitled 'In Lighter Mood by Wagner Barker & Co', framed by a drawing.

A Wonderful Contrivance

A servant maid from the country who had never been used to cooking by the help of a gas stove took a situation in London. Her mistress, when showing her the use of the stove lit the burners to show her new maid how it worked. Then she went – leaving the maid to her own domain. A fortnight later she asked Mary how she liked the stove. Mary beamed enthusiastically 'Oh! Ma'am,' she said 'its [sic] a wonderful stove, you lit it for me when I came and it has not gone out from that time to this.'

Resourceful

An army officer's wife, who was giving a small luncheon party at her home in Madras not long ago, remembers to her horror, that she had forgotten to order any cheese, and that cheese unhappily, formed the stable diet of the vegitarian guest of honour. Towards the close of the meal, she was about to apologise for the omission, when to her surprise, the native servant entered, bearing the required dish. She was amazed at this forethought and after the guests had departed, she asked him how he had managed to procure the cheese at such short notice. 'Ah, Mem Sahib,' he replied with a smile 'me emptied all the mouse traps!'

His sense of humour was well known in later years as well. A former pupil, Christa Donges, recalled the roguish quality in the eyes of her teacher, the 90-year-old Gerard Wagner:

When Herr Wagner looked at you, his light blue eyes always radiated light and joy. They remained young – almost like the eyes of a little boy with a roguish glint that could flash up now and again.

When Julie Wagner was out of the house engaging in her weekly day of social work in Gorton, Manchester, her sons enjoyed getting up to mischief. They played tricks on their rather stern grandmother Stephanie by fixing up some apparatus under her plate so it would move during the meal, and they added grass to her salad pretending it was chives. Their grandmother had once told them you could catch birds by sprinkling salt on their tail feathers. They went out enthusiastically to try it out and when this failed they returned to their grandmother who scolded them for believing her and called them 'stupid boys'. With his deep-rooted feeling for truth, Gerard Wagner recalled how that event was deeply disappointing to him. Another favourite game of the young brothers was throwing mud over the garden wall at people cycling down the Firs, which once caused a local bobby to call at the house to give the boys a serious telling off.

Despite the nearness of family, and especially of uncles as male figures to support the boys, the mother wrote a little anxiously about the task of bringing up her children alone. Gerry was almost seven and Felix was nine when she wrote:

> Five years since my dear one left us and I begin at last to realise what it means to bring up boys alone – and how much it means to them to have a father's hand over them. I miss Max as a father more now than ever. Gerry I think will be alright – he has a good deal of me in him – but Felix is more difficult, he cares less, I think, more defiantly naughty – not so affectionate as he used to be. My poor darling [Roland] in Idstein is an angel in character, and healthwise gets gradually worse.

Gerard Wagner was eight years old when the First World War broke out in 1914, a few days after Julie Wagner's 46th birthday and almost two years after the family moved from Germany. She wrote in her diary on 16 August:

> We are all living under the shadow of this terrible war declared between England and Germany on 4 Aug. It seems incredible even now that such a thing should be possible – it has changed all life – suddenly there is no certainty anymore – ruin and even death may come, the one to me – the other to many friends and relations in Germany. Since 1 August I have had no word from Germany – nor from the business, my men may be all

at the war for anything I know – everyone is affected and full of dread at what may be coming. We shall all have to help each other, that is certain.

The war severely affected the family. Contact with the eldest son Roland and other relatives in Germany became difficult, and the family's financial situation changed for the worse when Max Wagner's company in Wiesbaden was sequestrated. After the war, Julie Lange received a modest amount from the company but the family struggled financially from then onwards. Two nephews of Julie Wagner served in the British Army, and Philip Sugden, with whom Gerard Wagner was close, died from his injuries after the war.

The outbreak of war in August 1914 was assuredly even more devastating for someone like Julie Wagner whose parents were German. Since emigrating to England in 1861, their lives had spanned the two countries harmoniously and naturally. Julie Wagner became German when marrying Max Wagner and after the war, in 1919, she took English nationality again.

In her biography, an English anthroposophist, Eleanor Merry, vividly described the rupture between the two countries:

> … Our present-day picture of the 'British Empire' for instance, was not there in our youthful consciousness. Perhaps because Queen Victoria as a national figurehead drew the lines centripetally towards herself – the Empire was 'hers' – and in Egypt and the Boer War we fought for the 'Queen' rather than for the Empire. And that changed after she died. But the strangest experience was to have lived, as a member of the English nation, having always taken Germany for granted not only as a close friend (whom one visited frequently and joyfully) but *as an indispensable fountain of beauty* in her literature, its wonderful language, and above all in her music which was so inseparable and an intimate part of our natural soul-life; and then to have it torn away, trampled on and despised …[30]

About three months into the First World War, Rudolf Steiner spoke about the special connection and love between the two nations of Germany and England. On 15 November 1914 he said:

> I must also ask that you do not take what I have to say today as a theme for speculative intellectual enquiry. It is necessary to observe these things in the spiritual world, otherwise one will not be able to arrive at the truth. A harmony gradually begins to develop between what is reflected from Central Europe and the British Isles, a sense of accord,

a true spiritual bond that has by degrees been gaining strength to the point where one could say that, from a spiritual point of view, no souls on earth love one another more than those living in Central Europe and those living in the British Isles. These souls, seen spiritually, are united in the strongest love, and this comes to expression in what we see before us now, so entangled have human affairs become.[31]

Meanwhile further diary entries of Julie Wagner's give some small facts about Gerry Wagner and his development. At eight years old the shy boy had become somewhat more talkative:

> I returned from Wallasey yesterday so as to be able to go to my rent collecting in Gorton tomorrow – it will be sad work I'm afraid. I was sorry to leave Wallasey, the children – dear boys – are getting companionable at last. I believe I could do something with them if I could make them feel my influence – Felix is getting much more manly, Gerry is more talkative – though still very shy and quiet.

And in September 1914 she wrote:

> Felix came home quite excited and said 'I've had my first Latin lesson today, it was upping' – and Gerry said in a sepulchral voice 'and I've had my first lesson in rotten old French!'

Books were important in the family and the children read the usual children's classics and enjoyed being read to by their mother. One of Gerry's Christmas wish lists figured three typical boys' books: *The Three Midshipmen, Wonder Book of Ships, With Roberts in Khartoum* and the usual things wanted by boys of his age: a 'Fretwork Outfit' for making models, 'money for more Meccano parts', pencils and so on. His wish for Sunday kid gloves shows his early interest in good clothes.

As she always did, Julie Wagner wrote in her diary on the anniversary of her husband's death:

> To think that Max my dear boy has been gone now seven years. I wonder if he ever thinks of the boys and me – and feels for us in these dreadful troubled times and sees that the business, the work for which he gave his life, has been taken from me by his countrymen. Why?! I cannot fathom their motives, their attitude of mind, the business was German throughout, I had no penny from it since the war began. Now it is sold to Gaebler for a nominal fee of 100,000 D Marks, and who knows how much I will see of that.

On Gerard Wagner's tenth birthday his mother wrote of his purity and goodness and her perception of him as being a 'curious mixture' of herself and his father:

> Just ten years today since my little Gerry came into the world. I have been thinking today of what those ten years have brought – trouble, great sorrow and pain – not so much happiness – they seem so long. The twenty months of war seem like several years … Gerry has been so sweet today, so sort of proud of his birthday. I told him my wish for him on his 10th birthday is that when he is ten years older he will still be as good and pure as he is now. He is a curious mixture of his father and me, reserved, more thorough and accurate than Felix but conservative, unwilling to try new things and ways. Felix is much quicker and more go-ahead …

Despite the tragedies and the shadow of the war, in the first six years in England between the ages of six and twelve, Gerry Wagner seems from his mother's descriptions and from photographs to have been a serene, contented child.

Julie Wagner once again, as ever, remembered her husband on the anniversary of his death:

> Nine years today that my dearest boy was taken from me – sometimes he seems near at others so far away. How he would have hated this war – it is good that he is out of it. Felix grows more like him outwardly – dear boy – I think, though Max must have been more contented as a boy, of course I don't really know. Felix is apt to be moody – he is not so happy as Gerry, my little darling.

Apart from a Christmas card painted for his mother in 1915 when he was 9 and a few other drawings and cards his mother kept, there is one small, harmonious still-life of daffodils, outstanding in its details and colouring, painted in watercolour when Gerry was almost 12. Whether he had painting lessons is not clear but he said later that his teachers in drawing were the illustrators of the weekly satirical magazine *Punch*. The influence of the *Punch* cartoons can be seen in his early drawings as well as in the striking caricatures he did when he was an adolescent of 16 or 17, which were printed in the school magazine. Amongst his favourite *Punch* illustrators were Bernard Partridge and L. Raven Hill.

Gerard Wagner's love of poetry and drama was influenced by his mother who loved literature and had an extensive library. In a letter to Dorothy Wagner he said: 'Mother had such a good library. Scientific works were probably rather scarce – but many very good books – also illustrated – and all the plays of Bernard Shaw, Galsworthy etc.' He recalled a visit to the theatre with his mother to see the *Merchant of Venice* when she whispered to him to take note of Portia's speech. He later referred to this occasion as 'one of the first moments of Shakespeare that I noticed'. The words have an unmistakable affinity with the character Gerard Wagner later developed in himself:

> The quality of mercy is not strain'd,
> It droppeth as the gentle rain from heaven
> Upon the place beneath: It is twice blessed,
> It blesseth him that gives, and him that takes.
> 'Tis mightiest in the mightiest, it becomes
> The thronèd monarch better than his crown:
> His sceptre shows the force of temporal power,
> The attribute to awe and majesty.
> Wherein doth sit the dread and fear of kings;
> But mercy is above this sceptred sway,
> It is enthronèd in the heart of kings;
> It is an attribute to God himself;
> And earthly power doth then show likest God's,
> When mercy seasons justice.

When Gerard Wagner spoke of his mother in old age, one felt his devotion to this warm-hearted and noble woman who wanted to give her sons a good cultural and Christian upbringing.

Her niece, Julie Neild, recalled her aunt fondly:

> Julia was petite with a pointed nose, bright gentian-blue eyes and a low, musical speaking voice. She had a gentle manner and looked venerable but she had a resilience, courage and determination. I loved her dearly. She came to stay with us in Bristol, and my father admired her courage and was always especially friendly towards her. She never mentioned Max, or Roland their first child, although she sometimes mentioned Felix and Gerry. During the years when she came to stay with us I was still a girl at school.

The Wagners were a 'liberal' family, readers of the *Manchester Guardian*, and Julie Wagner had a keen social conscience. After the Great War, she joined, among other things, the Church League of Women's Service and the League of

Nations Union, an organisation founded in October 1918 in Britain to promote international justice and permanent peace between nations. She hoped that 'the League will become a great power for the prevention of war. Also I am now a member of the executive of the Women's International League WILPF (very proud of this)'. The Women's International League for Peace and Freedom was founded 1919, to bring together women of different political views, philosophies and religious backgrounds to work for permanent peace, and to unite women world-wide who oppose exploitation.

YOUTH

Gerard Wagner's adolescence was overshadowed by five unhappy years at Aldenham School, a boarding school for boys in Hertfordshire, 15 miles from the centre of London. Founded in 1597, Aldenham School is one of the oldest schools in Britain. The school was not his mother's choice but that of John Sugden, a brother-in-law of Julie Wagner who supported the family financially during and after the War. She wrote in her diary in December 1917:

> The boys and I were quite alone on Christmas Day which I liked ... we had the presents in the drawing room, mostly books this year, and then went to St Margaret's Church. I have been very sad and depressed these last days, but I shall begin the year with new hope. At Easter the boys go to Aldenham and I shall be lonely and bereft – it seems to me best to send them away, they need more discipline than I can give them. Felix's health has not been good this last term, and Gerry needs to be persuaded to work harder. I hope to let Westholme, perhaps at the March Quarter – I saw a house – No 4 Belfield Rd, Didsbury, which I might take.

Stephanie Lange, Julie Wagner's mother, who had lived with her and the two boys since they moved to England in 1912, had died the previous June.

Gerard Wagner, with his brother Felix, joined Aldenham School around Easter 1918, and were allotted to Beevor's House, which Wagner described as feeling more like a prison than a home. At the same time the family home moved from the pleasant countryside of Bowdon to 'grey' Didsbury, a suburb of Manchester. These two events coming so close together must have given Gerard Wagner a very real experience of the ending of boyhood as described by William Wordsworth in his 'Intimations of Immortality': 'Shades of the prison-house begin to close / Upon the growing Boy.'

Gerry Wagner was just 12 years old when he started at Aldenham, a year earlier than boys were usually accepted but it was thought better for the brothers to begin together. On one of the first days there he was punished because of a simple oversight – for misreading a notice which caused him to arrive late in the classroom. The boy experienced the then British public school ethic of strict discipline and he later told how the French teacher particularly, beat with a viciousness that left a deep impression on him. He recalled how this teacher created such fear in the pupils that the bench they were sitting on shook when he entered the classroom. Once when looking at a portrait of the zealous, fiery-tongued preacher Savonarola,[32] with his piercing and fanatical-looking eyes, Wagner said: 'My French teacher!' The German name of 'Wagner' also drew taunts from some of the teachers there.

Competitive sports, a strong aspect of public school life, was not something Gerard Wagner enjoyed. He won the 'Slow Race' however, which consisted of staying on a bicycle as long as possible whilst moving as slowly as possible – a feat needing a good sense of balance! Sundays at the school were also regulated, with Chapel twice a day, poetry, and walks taken in pairs.

Julie Wagner wrote of the first Christmas in their new home in Didsbury:

> The boys and I have had a very happy Christmas time together and now the first peace Christmas is over and the old year with all its wonderful changes, bad and good, is nearly gone. Today I had a letter from my cousin Lily enclosing one from Roland – he is happy and well it seems. Our family on the whole has had a good year. I feel in better health than for many years, and Felix and Gerry, in spite of influenza six weeks ago, are well now – especially my darling little Gerry – bless them both.

Gerry clearly remained young at heart for a long time. Two years later, when he was well over 14, his mother described his 'girlish voice and sweet little laugh' and said that he 'grows slowly' and was still 'shy and unsociable'. Her entry for Christmas of 1920 conveys a sense of relief when the close-knit family can enjoy their own company.

> This time last year the boys and I were with the Sugdens at 'Blackthorn' for Christmas and New Year. It was delightful being with them but kind as they were, home is best at such times as the boys and I agreed. They want to be quite free in the holidays – very naturally so, after the confinement, the *Zwang* of their whole school life, and they hate the long meals! ... Neither are fond of new acquaintances and unluckily we have practically no young friends here.

The Wagner and Sugden families were close, and John Sugden, 'Uncle Jack', played a fatherly role to the Wagner boys. He was their favourite uncle. It was at the Sugden's home that Julie Neild and her sister met their somewhat older cousins Gerard and Felix:

Gerry was a good-looking boy with very fair hair and blue-grey eyes – he was more solemn than his brother Felix. He was tall and slender and seemed very balanced and self-contained. I found his presence made me feel shy and 'not good enough'. With Felix it was different. Both boys were thoughtful and capable of forming their own opinions. They got on well together and were good companions.

Life at Aldenham School had a strong effect on the sensitive youth, and he recalled feeling nauseous when walking from the train station to the school at the start of a new term. Later in life, in 1989, Wagner referred to his time at Aldenham and the treatment he received there in a letter to his sister-in-law Dorothy Wagner:

> I hope Mathew [great-nephew] has good fortune in his future school – not like what Felix and I had ... I daresay schools are better now than in our time – I can't imagine modern children standing the kind of treatment we were put through, without rebelling. Surprising that one could come through without being mentally and artistically wrecked.

In August 1921 the brothers went on a school trip to France organised by their mother and one of the Masters of Aldenham School. The most interesting outcome of that holiday is a picture painted in Annecy by Gerry Wagner entitled 'Annecy in the Moonlight'. Previously thought to be a painting from his St Ives days, this work painted in oil colour on canvas shows rare talent for a 15-year-old. Some drawings of his were printed in the school magazine two years later and he must have had a reputation at the school for being artistically gifted.

Two amusing letters from this trip to France are quite revealing of the lively, critical character of the adolescent Gerry Wagner. In unusually mature handwriting, the letters show his interest in the sights of Paris and his appreciation and love of the countryside. Also sent to his mother on this trip in August 1921 is a postcard of a motif that would become central to his future work as a painter – a Madonna and Child sculpture in the Grand Trappe Abbey in Orne by the sculptor and Trappist monk Frère Marie-Bernard (1883–1975), entitled 'Mater Misericordiae'.

Dear Mother
I hope you have not been expecting that postcard every other day, because it is really quite impossible to send it. We are nearly always out, we have no postcards at present because it takes at least an hour and a half to get down to Grenoble and the same coming back, also the

postman is the only man who comes anywhere near here who can take the cards and so far I have only seen him come here once. We had an awful journey here, at least I did. I had a most fearfully uncomfortable position in the boat, and then thirteen hours train journey during which Sammy wanted me to have some tea, which, as you know, I do not like, but I only had a few grapes then. In fact for three days, I ate practically nothing at all though I am feeling awfully well now.

Mr Beaumont, uncle Walter's brother, is jolly fine, quiet but very sporting and so is his son Louis who is twenty but not at all reliable, always making jokes and goes about as though he doesn't care a hang for anything. The sister of Louis is also nice and is about sixteen and so is Jack Strong, a Harrow boy who is staying here a month for his French so as to pass an exam. Mrs Beaumont is the only one whom I don't care for, she eats with her mouth wide open, talks the whole time in a high pitched jarring voice and seems as though she does not take the slightest interest in us. There is a large stone bath into which a spring of icy water is always flowing and here we wash and have our cold bath every morning under the shade of some trees a few yards from the Chalet.

We went on an expedition on Tuesday afternoon (Felix, Sammy, Baker, Louis and myself) and climbed up a mountain 6,500 feet high. It was awfully steep and an awfully shagging business climbing through a very thick and sloping wood and also over a great many steep rocks, but on the whole we were very careful. We had not time to get to the top on Tuesday so we slept on the mountain side (which is just at present covered in snow) on the best bit of ground we could find, a sloping piece of grass about 6,000 feet up. We only had one counterpane thing under which we all got, or rather tried to get, as it would hardly cover the outside people at all. I did not sleep more than an hour and a half during the whole time between 9 pm and 5 am when the others lay down. I got up now and then to walk about and try to get warm, a very difficult process, but we started off again at 5 o'clock and reached the top at 7 am. Then we went down the other side to a small house where some French signallers were billeted. They were awfully nice and hospitable and offered us coffee, bread, paté and tinned salmon, the last of which we refused ... The rain started coming down so hard that we were sopping in the first five minutes. We stopped at a café on the way for hot coffee and bread and butter, and the inhabitants stared at us as if they had never seen anything like it before, especially Felix ...

Yesterday just our party went down to Grenoble and had a fine lunch for about 50 frcs. The only disadvantage to all the meals is that we only get one knife and fork for everything we eat. Of course coming back in the evening it poured again so that we had to change for the second time, the consequence being that most of us, except myself, were lacking clothing and so they came in pyjamas and blankets and things like that. I took three suits altogether, the blue for travelling, the grey, and the grey bags and blazer.

Some of the food here is very good, some is very bad, especially the bread which is *horrible!* We get no butter and some of the dishes are awful. We have a cup of coffee or cocoa with a piece of bread and jam for breakfast, and a cup of tea and dry bread for tea. Yesterday night at supper, Mm B. asked Mr Sadler, the clergyman, if he wanted some cheese, – he foolishly said 'yes'. Sometime before we had all had some sour milk (alias cheese) which we had all decided was loathsome and so when this was offered to Mr Sadler we all laughed so much that the others at the table who did not speak English, wanted to know what the joke was; I think I have hardly ever laughed so much in my life to see Mr S. eating that bad cheese which he did not like. I think we are going to Chartreuse tomorrow but we are waiting a day to let the weather settle before we risk being landed without clothes again.

This morning I took a photo of Mr Firbank in his wonderful garb, sloppy hat, pyjama suit socks over his bags just when he looked most idiotic, I only hope it will come out well. Please give my love to Auntie Emily, Uncle Jack and Philip if you are writing to them. Much love from Gerry

Dear Mother
Thank you very much for your letter. When I wrote to you last, I forgot altogether to tell you most of the things which I had meant to, but I am afraid I must leave all that till I see you next time and tell you of our doings today and yesterday.

Yesterday at about 2.30 pm our party plus an old chap from school (Beevor's House) who, by the way, sends you his love, went down to Grenoble by tram, as far as possible, and then we took a steam train to some other place an hour's ride down the line. We passed through gorges, tunnels and went through some of the most wonderful scenery which I have ever seen. Most of the way, there were steep cliffs covered in pines on our side and a deep gorge with water at the bottom on the other, and we could take it all in especially easily as the train went so slowly. When we got out after our enjoyable ride, we walked five and a half miles all the way uphill to Chartreuse. On this walk we had just the same kind of scenery as we had on the train journey but the worst of it was that it was gradually getting darker and darker so that it was difficult to make out our surroundings at all. When we arrived at the Grand Chartreuse Hotel it was about 10.30 pm and we rang the bell. After a few minutes a head came out of an upper window and on being asked if he had a room or two, he said that it was absolutely full up. Braby, who speaks French very well, indigaggered with the man and asked him if he could not let us have some place downstairs, but to all this he answered 'no'. Then we went wandering about and found a big barn with enough hay for about one person to sleep on, but, as it was the best place available, we had to put up with it. We all had our raincoats which we put on with our collar up and then got among the hay with our feet in the middle. (You can imagine the kicking and swearing at the hotel manager). The others used their caps as pillows, only as I had lost mine among the hay, I took someone's pyjamas which we had expected to wear. Nobody slept very well as it was much too cold and uncomfortable and so we got up at about six, after I had routed out my cap and we got someone to open the hotel door for us. We were at last given a large cup of coffee each, some hunks of bread and some jolly fine butter (which we never get down here).

After we had finished this, we were told that we could go into the monastery and get shown around. (This was the real object of the trip). We went out just as it began to rain but the man who looked after the monastery said it was much too early to come in and so, as Mr Sadler was ill, we thought we had better get home as soon as possible. We walked down to the train in the pouring rain, getting fearfully muddy all the way. We had lunch at Grenoble, and, after waiting in some gardens for the tram, we went in it up to Sennacy and then began to walk, which at a normal pace takes one and a half hours. The others, except Mr Sadler, sat down in a field and played nap, during which I took their photo. Later it began to rain again and so we finished this most unsuccessful trip in the wet.

The worst of it was that as we were going to such stunning places I had taken my camera and a spare film, but as it was so awfully dull all the way, I could not take them. The few which I did take will probably not come out. We bought some postcards of the places we passed instead of the photos.

Today we practically made up our minds to go to Milan, stay there a few days, and visit lots of fine towns on the way, but Sammy reckoned out the cost of the return fare, adding in £1 for the visa, and as it came to £3 each just for that, we decided that it was not worth it, though it could have been fine! Perhaps you can come next year with Philip to show us around.

You know that Uncle Jack has supplied us with about 700 francs, well could you please tell me privately, without mentioning it to anybody else, whether that is meant to pay for the whole trip or not. Uncle Jack said that it was just for our own private expenses. If you do not know please do not bother about it.

We are going to visit all kinds of interesting towns on the way back, staying about a day and a night at each. I should very much like to stay in Paris for about two days at least, to see the Louvre, Notre Dame, the Opera House and several other famous places we saw during our taxi drive through Paris. I hope my animals are quite well.

Much love from Gerry

Meanwhile the adolescent Gerard Wagner seemed to be making progress with his studies. His mother was pleased with a favourable school report he received in 1921 but his appearance when arriving home for the school holidays gave another picture: 'Gerry came home white and thin as usual, I doubt if school life agrees with him.'

In 1964, in a letter to his brother Felix in which he described his present interests and the work he was doing, Gerard Wagner wrote about his difficulty with intellectual learning:

I'm afraid my knowledge of science, in the usual sense, and scientific names especially, is very much below the average school-boy or -girl standard. Unless I have seen and smelt and touched a substance, and seen it react when dissolved or heated, until I have in some way experienced it personally, I have no knowledge or realisation of what it is – the name tells me very little …

One positive recollection from his schooldays was the way the chemistry teacher involved the boys in the experiments so they felt they were approaching the subject together.

During the next school term, 17-year-old Felix ran away from school. He kept his promise to return but only long enough to hand over a box of chocolates to his younger brother before taking off again. The mother wrote: 'Jack is very angry with Felix – I doubt if the old kindly relationship will ever be restored – none of us will forget the dreadful scene when Jack came down after Felix's second running away.'

Gerard Wagner himself broke with his uncle when he refused to work at the latter's factory during a school holiday. This moment of destiny, in which the youth chose his own way instead of following family tradition, often came up in conversation with Gerard Wagner in later life, and he wrote about it in a letter to Dorothy Wagner in 1981:

> My uncle had wanted me to inherit his business. But the third time he sent me a wire to appear at his works in Manchester, to work during the last week of school holidays (I had done it twice before), I wrote and said I had something else that I wanted to do more. That was the end of our relationship. Uncle Jack called it the biggest disappointment in his life. One does so much out of one's instinct in a quite naive way – only much later can one survey the way one went and see that one was led surely and rightly.

As Uncle Jack (John Sugden) played an influential role in Gerard Wagner's boyhood and youth, it seems relevant to say something about his life. Julie Neild, Gerard Wagner's cousin, gave this description:

> John Sugden was Yorkshire-born, tough, opinionated and self-reliant. He was the husband of Emily, a sister of Julie Wagner. They had one child, Philip, who served in the 1914–1918 war, was badly gassed and invalided out, but died later. Emily was heartbroken, took to her bed and became a permanent invalid.
>
> John Sugden was 19 when his father died and he inherited the ownership and running of his father's firm which produced Ostrich feathers for the fashion trade. All went well until the fashion changed and John found his firm bankrupt. He then turned to engineering and became involved in an enterprise that produced sand-blasting equipment. The enterprise succeeded and he became quickly wealthy. With the proceeds of his financial success he bought a large house and garden in the country in Surrey, had a large domestic staff and invited friends and relations to stay. It was here that my sister and I met our cousins Gerry and Felix, at that time in their early teens.

Uncle Jack loved young people and was generous to them, and having plenty of servants and a well-run household he was free to spend time with them. In his large garden there was a group of pine trees which were felled and burnt, and when we were staying there he dressed up in an old raincoat and shapeless hat and walked round to the kitchen window pretending to be a tramp asking for some large potatoes and a saucer of butter. The potatoes roasted in the bonfires were duly cooked and eaten then and there – I remember even now how delicious they were … At this stage of his life he was impatient of opposition and eventually withdrew his offer of support to Julie's (Wagner) sons. It did not occur to him that other people had a right to their own feeling and opinions. Later in life he developed cancer and suffered much pain. When I asked him what the doctor said he replied that he wasn't in the care of a doctor, he couldn't afford two doctors' fees. John was innately kind and generous, but very obstinate and determined. How he would have loved having grandchildren.

Almost two years after his brother, also at the age of 17, Gerard Wagner left Aldenham School. It wasn't a dramatic ending like his brother's. It happened during a teatime visit from his mother's closest friend, Hilda Brighouse, who was very fond of Gerry. She asked him if he liked school: 'I loathe it', he said. 'No you don't!' said his mother, – 'I *loathe* it!' he replied. A conversation between the two adults followed and he was withdrawn from Aldenham School forthwith. He left in the summer or autumn of 1923. The way Julie Wagner found out about her son's feelings was characteristic of Gerard Wagner who rarely expressed his own feelings or wishes without an opportunity being presented to him. Years later, in the 1940s, Hilda Brighouse received the present of a beautiful painting sent from Dornach. She wrote about the picture in a letter to Felix Wagner:

When I was all cluttered up in the sitting room wondering what to do next, I caught sight of Gerry's Angel in the full light of the sun, glorious and holy – a great inspiration! I can understand his care about placing a picture with regard to the light. I have hung mine in three positions and I am not fully satisfied but feel I now know the ideal spot in my bigger sitting room. I think the subject is the creation of the garden of Eden – there is a lovely tree in the middle – it is a vague world but there are gleams of rainbow colours in it, and a guardian angel (or God himself?) watches in glory, and, as time does not exist in the realm of the spirit, that creation is ever in the soul of man. (Gerry would say nothing to all that!) I shall enjoy it always.

Like his brother Felix, Gerard Wagner probably also rounded off his schooling in Manchester at Grime's Tutorial College on Oxford Road, where he was coached for exams. When his schooling was over he was able to follow his wish to become a painter. Felix Wagner went on to study farming. Because of his health (pulmonary weakness like his father), which prevented him from working in a city for long, he trained on a farm in Cheshire and later settled in Berkshire with his wife Dorothy where they farmed poultry and later turned to fruit farming of both apples and soft fruit. Felix Wagner was a gifted letter writer and musician and for a short time worked in London as editor of a farming magazine. In May 1949 their daughter Mary was born. In a letter to the author in 2002, Mary Ingham (Wagner) described her father Felix as follows:

> My father was a warm, charming and gentle man, a deep thinker blessed with an extraordinarily happy marriage and lots of interesting friends. He could play anything on the piano by ear with great musicality and had a memorably dry sense of humour. He and uncle Gerry shared an unusual kindness and sweetness.

Roland Wagner, the eldest of the three Wagner brothers, lived with the Klein family in Germany for the rest of his life. Because of the epilepsy he suffered from and the debilitating treatment given at that time he was not able to pursue a profession. In his youth he expressed the wish to be a gardener and was very fond of flowers. His mother wrote in her diary when he was four years old '... we picked some violets and daisies too ... he loves that – he says "Oh look at the *dear* little daisies, or violets"; he can say "dear little" with such a tone!' Roland Wagner was fond of his sister-in-law Dorothy Wagner, who wrote to him and sent him flowers. In the 1930s and 1940s they occasionally exchanged letters which testify to his gentleness and sensitivity.

APPRENTICESHIP AT ST IVES

It is unclear exactly when Gerard Wagner decided he wanted to become a painter. We know however that his mother discussed with her son Felix whether she should allow Gerry to follow this profession. Here, as later in life too, Felix supported his brother, and so the die was cast.

It was most likely his mother's idea, encouraged by her close childhood friend Edith Skinner, for Gerry to begin his painting training in an art colony rather than at a conventional art school. Edith and Edgar Skinner were embedded in the cultural and social circles of the St Ives Art Colony in Cornwall, at that time the most vibrant and well-known art colony in Britain, and knew all the painters there. So with the Skinner's help, Julie Wagner's son was able to visit the artists' studios and see their work. There was no art school there at that particular time but some artists took private pupils, and soon arrangements were made with the Post-Impressionist painter John Anthony Park (1878–1962) to take Gerry Wagner as his only full-time resident pupil. His apprenticeship began in the spring of 1924. John Park was more than a teacher; he took care of his young apprentice also in the evenings, which were spent mostly with Park and his wife Kitty at their home up at Bowling Green.

John Park had a long association with St Ives. In 1902 he became the star pupil of the painter Julius Olsson, and in 1923 he and his wife made their home there. Park was 46 when he took on Gerard Wagner as a pupil. He was a warm and kind person and well liked amongst the St Ives fishing community. According to Austin Wormleighton, Park's biographer, he is still talked about by 'ordinary' people of St Ives in the most loving terms. In a letter to the author in 2004, Wormleighton wrote: 'One thing for certain is that John Park's Catholicism would have placed Gerard in the safest and kindest of hands.'

John Anthony Park's paintings were popular and he was considered by many to be the most talented of the St Ives painters. Julie Wagner liked Park's work and a painting or two of his hung in the Wagner's home. He also had admirers amongst the later abstract artists of St Ives, the painter Patrick Heron for instance, who wrote, 'Despite his lack of recognition I always thought Park stood out a mile. You must go back to Constable's sketches to find one of the sources of his freedoms.' (John Constable's sketches are known for their dynamic elemental feel and loose colouring – and as forerunners of the Impressionist style.)

Harold Sawkins, editor of the periodical *The Artist* wrote in the September 1935 edition:

> There is nothing of the so-called modern about Park. He never plays tricks with nature; we see no distortion in his work. He has too great a respect for nature. He goes for the spirit of what he paints, and endeavours to get the last ounce out of a scene. Park is never satisfied to stand still. He is always striving … he is a true artist, sincere in everything he sets out to do. He is out to learn, and therefore everything he undertakes is a problem to be mastered. I have heard many famous artists speak highly of his work.

Austin Wormleighton characterised Park's work as follows in his biography of the artist, *Morning Tide:*[33]

> John Park's art has to be judged in the context of the older St Ives tradition, just as the crabbers, herring and pilchard boats that appear in much of his work are part of another way of life that has largely disappeared. His pictures, painted almost exclusively in oil colour, were often small and intimate, domestic in scale and informal, but always comfortable to the eye and easy to absorb. He painted off and on at St Ives for almost 50 years, rooted there by the magic of the place – the warmth especially suited his languid temperament – but it was the special quality of light and colour that suited his art.
>
> He was more expressively French in his vision than almost any artist then working in Cornwall, one of the survivors of a generation that had been in Paris at the turn of the century at the same time as Monet and Cezanne, and after his studies under Eugene Delacluse, Park was able to express light and water in paint much in the manner of the Impressionists themselves.
>
> But Park was more than a painter of Cornish scenes. He worked across Britain in Devon, Wales, Berkshire, in his home county of Lancashire, and in Kent, London, Essex and Suffolk and on the continent of Europe, painting not only the harbour subjects for which he is best remembered, but landscapes and rivers, townscapes, portraits and still life, exhibiting 72 pictures at the Royal Academy in London. He also showed at the Royal Institute of Oil Painters (ROI) and the Royal Society of British Artists (RBA) – bodies he was elected to join – and other leading galleries in the United Kingdom, and in Paris, New Zealand, New York and Toronto. In the peculiar way that Britain sometimes fails

to acknowledge the brightest of its creative talent, Park never received in his lifetime the acclaim he deserved. He seldom earned more than £ 200 a year from his painting, and it is tempting to speculate the scale of recognition he might have received had he grown up in, say, France or Belgium, or almost any country other than his own. Partly as a result of his Britishness, therefore, and partly of his own unworldliness and lack of interest in fame, John Park was destined to end his days unjustly neglected – but never entirely forgotten. The lack of recognition was perhaps the cause of a 'curious sadness' detected in him by his friend the sculptor, painter and writer Sven Berlin.

Park was anything but academic and as a *plein air* artist he worked out in the fresh air in all weathers. With his pupil Gerry Wagner at his side he painted in the winding cobbled streets and alleys of St Ives or on the wharf or harbour. Park sought colour 'on the streets, on the harbour wall, on the fishing boats and washing lines' but his favourite subject was undoubtedly water: 'I don't think I could live away from the sea or a stream. I am fascinated by the movement of water and the light on the water. Water brings the sky down to earth,' he said.[34]

Gerard Wagner described the Cornish locality in a few telling words in his autobiographical sketch (where he often speaks of himself in the third person): 'Rocks and water, but especially the changing play of light; the entire power and beauty of the elemental life of a seacoast formed the surroundings of this first apprenticeship.'[35]

Wagner's loft studio was on the granite sea wall of Porthmeor beach. It was part of the Piazza Studio complex, a ramshackle wooden building not in the best of repair, now demolished. It was here – a room previously used by fishermen for drying herring – that Wagner also painted portraits of the oldest fishermen. John Park occupied one of the Island Studios at the north end of the sea wall at that time. Many of the artists' studios were previously sail and net lofts used by the fishermen before painters first flocked to St Ives towards the end of the 19th century.

With landscape and portrait as the central themes of his painting, Gerard Wagner was in all senses a pupil of the St Ives school, absorbing within the colony all aspects of an artist's work in the traditional manner. The light and intense colour of St Ives is legendary – the white peninsular light coming from the Atlantic, free from pollution, highlighted everything in absolute clarity. Park's teaching, which introduced Gerard Wagner to the value of light and colour, influenced Wagner for the rest of his life. And the way John Park taught his pupils to take in the colour of an object before its shape or form, no doubt helped Wagner to adjust quickly to the mode of painting he was to meet in Dornach. Wagner said of his teacher: 'He was a good colourist who did not emphasise drawing.'

In the spring of 1925, following in the footsteps of the French Impressionists, the young painter went with John and Kitty Park on a sketching tour of Provence in the South of France. They painted in the harbour of St Tropez and in the surrounding villages. The three surviving oil paintings by Wagner from this trip show views of Gassin, Grimaud and Martigues, the 'Venice of Provence', and are subtle in their colours and colour balance. What stands out in the harmonious colour compositions is the equal value the young painter gives to colours and their harmony; no single colour seems more important than another. Already then, Gerard Wagner must have been practising subtle colour balancing. Also noticeable is how he uses every inch of the canvas in creating a full organism of colour.

At Gassin the little party met up with a fellow artist, the celebrated Californian painter Euphemia Charlton Fortune (1885–1969), who had painted at St Ives and was now exploring the warm sunny colours of Provence.

It is not hard to imagine just how meaningful the year of apprenticeship at St Ives must have been for Gerard Wagner. After five years at a regimented boarding school, how wonderful for him to be free and independent and out in the open air in beautiful surroundings with a warm-hearted teacher and guardian. And what it must have meant to live in such a fishing community as St Ives with good-hearted fisherfolk. Wagner kept fond memories of St Ives all his life.

An American artist Wilson Henry Irvine described the St Ives fishing community in his 1923 journal:[36] 'They are all civil and kind, as all people seem to be who follow the sea. They are extremely poor here and many are being helped. … I have not heard an oath or near it, or an obscene word or remark, or seen a drunken man.'

He also described the fishermen there as being helpful and scrupulously honest.

When Gerard Wagner began his apprenticeship at St Ives he was almost 18 and close to his first 'moon node'. Signifying an important juncture in biographical development, the moon node is when the moon, sun and earth are in the same configuration as they were at the time of birth, and anthroposophical teaching draws attention to this as signifying a new experience of birth, defining for a person's further destiny and task. It is characterised as a moment of awakening which points towards the approaching birth of the I at the age of 21. The exact date of this first moon node is calculated by adding seven months and ten days to the 18th birthday, although the date can be flexible depending on the individual biography.[37]

In Gerard Wagner's case the first moon node, calculated from his 18th birthday on 5 April 1924, would have been in November, about half way through his apprenticeship with John Park.

When considering Gerard Wagner's time in St Ives as the 'birth' of the future painter, a certain parallel is apparent between his early childhood, when he had such a strong inner and intuitive experience of nature and colour, and this first apprenticeship in painting as a more conscious activity of perception. John Park challenged his pupils to look carefully for the finer nuances of colour. He would say: 'What do you see?' and not being satisfied with the answer, he would say: 'Look again!', until the pupil began to describe more thoroughly the colours they saw rather than the object in front of them. Another parallel can be found between the 'clean, clear light' of Wiesbaden and the legendary 'white peninsular light' of St Ives. The contrasting elements of earth and water are also found in both places: the mountains and springs in Wiesbaden and the rocks and sea at St Ives.

To appreciate the appeal of St Ives it is best to approach it by train. The journey from London westwards is a preparation of sorts: gradually 'civilization' is left behind and you begin to relax as vistas open of field and furrow. Entering Devon and passing Exeter, the train hugs the cliffs of red earth and allows an open view of sea and sky. The train heads back inland again, and entering Cornwall the first distant sights of harbour and boats soon fade as the journey continues. Walls of green rise up either side of the train as it heads on in the direction of the most westerly corner of England. It stops just short of Penzance at the quiet station of St Erth. Here the little footbridge leads over to the waiting St Ives train. Now, for twelve minutes, you glide slowly along the Hayle estuary, past sand dunes and on between high rock and trees with an intermittent view of blue sea. The ocean broadens out and in the distance the well-known sight of the harbour of St Ives appears! It is as if you have arrived in another country, another land.

Leaving the platform you can look at the long wind-swept expanse of Portminster beach far below, but instinctively you may head in another direction, down some narrow steps into cobbled alleyways, past the church to St Ives harbour. At the far end a narrow lane leads up and around into meandering side lanes (it's easy to get lost here) to the other side – to Porthmeor beach, where once a line of artists' studios stretched all along the sea wall. A few remain, just enough to give an idea of how it used to be in 1924 when Gerard Wagner, aged almost 18, would have taken the ten-hour journey to St Ives from Manchester by steam train.

But the colours may not have changed very much. The 'legendary light' of St Ives really does exist. Striking colour is everywhere: magical shades of blue in the rock pools; the grey and black of rocks standing out against the bright orange and yellow-coloured lichen partly covering them. The colour of the sea changes constantly: it can be a grey-greenish blue in a warm, pink light, changing to gold as the setting sun reflects upon the water, before dusk gives way to the deepest black and a universe of glittering stars.

North of St Ives, on the same stretch of Cornish coast, lies the village of Tintagel where King Arthur's Castle and Merlin's Cave are to be found. On 17 August 1924, when Gerard Wagner was painting at St Ives, Rudolf Steiner visited Tintagel and spoke later of the invisible forces behind the wonderful drama of water and light there:

> Standing on this promontory by the meagre remains of the ancient castle of Arthur and looking out to sea, one sees something quite remarkable. The sea here is filled with soul in a striking manner; one sees a continually changing picture. While we were there sunshine and rain alternated comparatively quickly – and that is how it was also in ancient times. Today it is quieter – the climate has changed there. One looks into this wonderful interplay of elemental light-spirits, playing into one another and interacting with water-spirits raying up from below. And the appearances of these spirits is very special when the sea surges onto rock, struggles free and is thrown back again, or when it curls up upon itself. This particular vital weaving activity of the world's elemental beings is found nowhere else on earth except here.[38]

Words that Rudolf Steiner wrote from Tintagel on a card to his close colleague Albert Steffen during his visit in August 1924, express well the elemental forces in the surroundings and the spiritual powers behind them:

> My dear Herr Steffen,
> We come from eloquent castle ruins
> where once lived the ancient conquerors of demons,
> strengthening their leader's power through the starry Twelve.
> Ruined is the castle,
> the astral world is dumb,

yet still spirit-forces surge around the Mount,
and soul-configuring power storms from the ocean.
Light and air wrestle in magical interplay
still striking the soul as forcefully today
even after three thousand years;
we send you now these memory pictures of the elements
along with our heartfelt, loving greetings.

Compared to the more dramatic and isolated setting of Tintagel, the St Ives landscape is open and friendly, yet similar dramas of sea and rock (which Gerard Wagner liked to photograph) play out along the nearby coastal path. Here, the high, dark austere faces of rock contrast dramatically with the white foam of the crashing waves below. The elemental life there remained a fount of inspiration for Wagner. One could say that the elemental life and astral atmosphere in certain places in Britain, as described by Rudolf Steiner, had a powerful influence on his future work.

Rudolf Steiner in Britain

It is an interesting fact that the places where Rudolf Steiner visited and stayed during his 1922–1924 visits to Britain are mostly in the same area where Gerard Wagner lived. The correspondence is quite striking (See plate 94):

From 14 to 23 April 1922, Rudolf Steiner was in London and visited Kings Langley in Hertfordshire. Gerard Wagner was at Aldenham School, also in Hertfordshire, and only about eight-and-a-half miles away from Kings Langley. Between 8 and 12 November 1922, Rudolf Steiner was lecturing in London, and eurythmy performances took place there. November was term time at Aldenham School so Wagner was again in the same area. Aldenham School, or rather the nearby village of Elstree, is roughly 12 miles from the centre of London. (During Rudolf Steiner's summer visit to London and Oxford in August 1922 Gerard Wagner was not in the neighbourhood, but in Penrhyn Bay very close to Penmaenmawr, on the north Wales coast where the Wagner family spent time in the summer.) From 4 to 31 August 1923, Rudolf Steiner was in Ilkley in Yorkshire, giving lectures on education, and in Penmaenmawr lecturing at the International Summer School. He was in Ilkley until 18 August, after which he travelled by train to Penmaenmawr, staying there until 31 August.

Gerard Wagner was in the Manchester area in August 1923, roughly 32 miles away from Ilkley. Steiner mentions Manchester briefly in a report he gave of his 1923 visit to Britain:

Ilkley is a place which can perhaps be taken as a kind of summer resort. But it lies in the direct vicinity of towns which in fact set one deeply in the industrial and commercial culture of our time. Leeds and other places, Bradford for instance, lies in the immediate neighbourhood, and Manchester is not far away either.[39]

(He also tells an amusing anecdote during a discussion with teachers in Stuttgart, about an experience he and his party had with their luggage and a delayed train at Manchester station on their way back from Penmaenmawr to London on the 31 August.)

One can get a feeling of the atmosphere of the different landscapes which Gerard Wagner absorbed from an article written by Marie Steiner about Rudolf Steiner's teaching activity in England. She describes impressions of the journey from London to Ilkley and the journey from Ilkley to Penmaenmawr when the train passed through the county of Cheshire, 'a friendly, light-filled area' – where the Wagner family lived until they moved to nearby Manchester. Marie Steiner goes on to say that the Celtic past played strongly into the special atmosphere still experienced at Ilkley, but most strongly at Penmaenmawr:

One travels through the blackest of industrial regions: Leeds, Bradford, enormous black dwellings, monstrosities worthy of a Strindberg-Hell. Ilkley is a friendly town at the foot of the Yorkshire moors. The ancient past spoke to us there, in the Druid stones and dolmens carved with signs speaking the language of that inwardness which linked the culture of those times with the spirit. Such things are experienced even more strongly in Wales, the legendary land of Merlin, clothed as it is in the sighing of the wind in the trees and in the ocean's foam. The train from Ilkley travels along railway lines that pass through an over-populated, black industrial region crammed with factories of Manchester, finally arriving in a friendly light-filled area. The medieval battlements of Chester draw one's attention, as do the blue bays as one approaches the Irish Sea. Flocks of seagulls and other ocean birds proclaim the beginnings of their undisturbed realm. Mighty castles rise up, splendid in their shapes, lording it over the wide valleys and cliffs. The realm of the barons, unconquerable by any king or church, impressively dominates one's soul. Up above on the cliffs the heroic epic; down below the idyll of gentle herds of grazing sheep. The peaceful movement of their backs swaying side by side reminds one of the gentle ocean in which the universal pulse of worlds is trembling.[40]

On the same stretch of coast on the Irish Sea, separated from Penmaenmawr by the Great Orme headland, are the two small seaside towns of Colwyn Bay and Penrhyn Bay, where the Wagner family stayed in the summer holidays. Colwyn Bay and Penrhyn Bay are both roughly eight miles from Penmaenmawr.

As to the choice of Penmaenmawr for the 1923 Summer School, Rudolf Steiner said there could not have been a better choice of location for 'this anthroposophical undertaking':

> The astral atmosphere there may be directly experienced as having been shaped by emanations of Druid worship, traces of which can indeed be sensed everywhere. It is situated directly on the sea coast, close to the island of Anglesey ... On the other side of Penmaenmawr, hills and mountains rise up, on which are found scattered remains of ancient, supposed sacrificial altars, cromlechs and so on ... These things are of course not recorded in what knowledge of today tells about these temple sites. But it is in fact something which can here be directly beheld, for the potency of impulses emanating from the work of Druid priests in their heyday – the might and power of the impulses – was so strong that even today these things are still absolutely alive there in the astral atmosphere.[41]

During Rudolf Steiner's tenth visit to Britain, from 11 to 23 August 1924, he was in Torquay and Tintagel. Torquay, on the south coast of Devon is roughly 90 miles from St Ives, where Gerard Wagner was painting. Tintagel, on the same stretch of Cornish coast, is around 45 miles north of St Ives.

Summing up, one could say that Gerard Wagner also participated in the special etheric and astral configurations at and near the places where Rudolf Steiner was. Rudolf Steiner felt that Britain was especially open to spiritual science, and is known to have given some of his deepest esoteric revelations there. George Adams remembered Steiner speaking in a more intimate circle in the rooms of the Zarathustra Group in South Kensington, on Easter Sunday 1922, about spiritual history and the dangers threatening mankind. He recalled: 'I can still see his dark penetrating eyes at that moment, looking as if down long avenues of time.'[42]

Marie Steiner began the article mentioned above with the words:

> Rudolf Steiner much enjoyed frequent opportunities to speak about spiritual science in England. There is a degree of tolerance in England towards accepting the truths of spiritual science: people are more open

to the unlimited range of possibilities. There is less anxiety regarding the loss of one's own hard-won cerebral knowledge; antagonism toward what is new or unfamiliar is less ingrained; one is less embedded in one's own intellectual vanity. People are bolder in their willingness to set out on a quest for unknown worlds.

The young Englishman Gerard Wagner possessed this willingness and one could say that on a certain level ground had been laid, through the presence of Rudolf Steiner in Britain, that helped him to absorb spiritual science so deeply and so immediately when he first came to Dornach – also in visual form, which according to Rudolf Steiner is an appropriate doorway for persons of the West to come to anthroposophy. In one of his addresses given before a eurythmy performance in London, Steiner mentioned the fact that the English-speaking people of the West can come to an understanding of anthroposophy through art, while Russians and the East can best approach anthroposophy through its scientific impulse.[43]

Gerard Wagner himself would point out to his pupils that anthroposophy in England must be *seen,* in other words it should be there in an artistic form. And he felt that the subject of metamorphosis, with its artistic-scientific character, would interest the English particularly.

STUDENT AT THE ROYAL COLLEGE OF ART

At the end of a year of painting at St Ives with his intuitive mentor John Anthony Park, the young painter was ready to start off on his own. First, though, it was thought that Gerry Wagner should 'catch up on his drawing', and arrangements were made to enrol him at the Royal College of Art in London with the help of a friend of his, the St Ives Potter, Bernard Leach. In September 1925, Margarita Lucins, a St Ives friend who was attached to the Leach Pottery at that time, wrote to Tsuronosuke Matsubayashi, Bernard Leach's kiln maker: 'Last week I spent a day in London with Mrs Wagner and Gerry. He has done good painting at St Ives for a year with Mr Park, and has hopes to continue his studies in London.'

The academic year at the Royal College of Art began at Michaelmas 1925. As Gerard Wagner could draw well he had no difficulty with the classical life-drawing lessons that were taught at the College. The students there also worked on their own a great deal. Wagner spoke little about the training, but he did say years later that as his approach to artistic work changed, he needed to forget what he learnt at the Royal College: 'It took me ten years to get it out of my system', he said.

There is only one signed painting by the gifted art student remaining from those art college days. During the first term the students were told to go out into nature and paint the theme 'autumn'. Gerard Wagner went to nearby Hyde Park and found his motif of down-and-outs sitting on a bench. His striking oil painting, 'Tramps', with its spontaneous, expressive brushwork, is reminiscent of the style of Vincent van Gogh whom Wagner greatly admired. Austin Wormleighton, Park's biographer, said of it: 'The painting of the sleeping figures is stunning. It reminds me of John Park's drawing "The Land of Nod"; I wonder if Gerard was encouraged by Park to paint sleeping figures.' The College Principal William Rothenstein,[44] who was Head of the School of Painting and Drawing, and was himself a celebrated painter, was impressed with young Wagner's talent, and he was offered a scholarship for a further year of study.

Wagner's painting at that time was considered by his artist cousin Julie Neild to be 'strongly impressionistic, resembling the style of Maurice Utrillo'. Whilst one could hardly think of a stronger contrast between Utrillo – with his flat, hard-edged paintings of buildings and streets – and van Gogh's vital colouring and movement, a few street scenes done by the young art student in Provence are somewhat reminiscent of Utrillo. And a tendency for defined outlines tallies with what he said he liked to do as a child – keep the various foods on his plate separate from one another.

During his year at the Royal College of Art Gerard Wagner lived in Notting Hill and enjoyed London. He wrote in his autobiographical sketch:

> London offered many opportunities to study the great masterpieces of past centuries. One delved into the ancient worlds of the Assyrians, the Persians, the Egyptians and the Greeks; there was no end of inspiration to be gained in the sphere of painting, from the earliest beginnings to Raphael, Leonardo, Rembrandt, Turner – through to Van Gogh, which until then had only been known from reproductions.[45]

During lunch breaks, Gerard Wagner used to go through a connecting door from the Royal College of Art into the Victoria and Albert Museum where he found a wealth of colour and motifs in Raphael's cartoons, which hung in a special room there.

The ten Raphael cartoons are designs for tapestries which hung, on important ceremonial occasions, in the Sistine Chapel, the Pope's own chapel in the Vatican in Rome.[46] Although he used only the simplest range of pigments, Raphael contrived from them a series of exquisite and harmonious colour combinations.

In 1981, Gerard Wagner gave a few glimpses of his life in London in a letter to his sister-in-law. The last sentence is especially interesting in relation to the artistic path he eventually chose:

> Dear Dorothy
> A little note from Mary came the other day. She tells me of her new flat – that must be a joy to have. I wonder what life in London is like now. I used to enjoy it tremendously, even without a flat of my own. Along the Embankment at night – where people who seem to have no homes sleep under the bridges – and round St Paul's early in the morning without a soul about. I am still sometimes surprised, or more than surprised, at the poor level of 'ambition' I used to have in London. I used to see myself as a pavement artist (I often passed them by with their caps at their sides – for pennies), but I had my serious doubts as to whether I would be able to draw well enough on the pavement – especially with the passers-by looking on! And I got a sinking feeling at the thought of Uncle Jack coming by and seeing me there! One did not realise in

those days what one was looking for – or that one would need to give up all that seemed fascinating about an 'artist's life' and lead an existence more or less of a recluse, to work at something which no one else could teach one.

It was in London that the art student became interested in the work of Rudolf Steiner and with the help of a friend, the well-known illustrator Hookway Cowles (1895–1987), he found his way around the anthroposophical world there. Rex Raab (see Appendix 3) wrote:

> Lecture readings or other occasions in the Cowles' lofty London studio always bore a festive note. Surrounded by Hookway's own varied pictures, man's participation in the life of the spirit was celebrated. Although Hookway and Kitty Cowles were perfectly at home in the rest of the world, and had only a smattering of German, a visit to the Goetheanum and their Dornach contacts seemed to be their safest port of call, the harbour nearest the home of their heart. Albert Steffen[47] was a pillar in their spiritual temple and Hookway would make brush sketches from memory of Steffen's dramas. Hanging on Hookway's studio wall was one of his attractive plant studies, meticulously but not pedantically executed: myriad wild flowers. On a London visit, Steffen stood before this picture and proceeded to recite the names of all the many flowers represented in it.[48]

During a visit in 1926 to the Anthroposophical Society Headquarters at 46 Gloucester Place, Gerard Wagner was asked by the then secretary Miss Frances Melland, whether he wanted to become a member of the Society. He asked her permission to think it over – and joined the next day.

The college year ended on 16 July 1926, and at the end of the month, as part of his summer vacation, Wagner joined Hookway Cowles and his wife on a painting trip to France; but first the Cowles wanted to attend a conference for English-speakers at the Goetheanum, the international centre of the Anthroposophical Society, in Dornach, Switzerland.

Dornach 1926–1949

THE GOETHEANUM –
A NEW IMPULSE FOR THE ARTS

Gerard Wagner came to Dornach in late July 1926, a little more than a year after Rudolf Steiner's death and almost four years after the first Goetheanum building burned down. He arrived in the company of Hookway Cowles and his wife Kitty who had taken him under their wing when he came to London, and now accompanied him over the English Channel to Dornach in the northwest corner of Switzerland. They came to attend 'English Week', a Goetheanum summer conference that took place between 31 July and August 1926. Afterwards they planned to go on together to France for a painting vacation.

On the Dornach hill, the second Goetheanum building was under construction. Bernard Crompton-Smith, one of the conference participants from England, wrote a review in the weekly *Das Goetheanum*:[49]

> As one toiled up the Dornach hill luggage-laden to the lodgings assigned, the stark tall bulk of the new Goetheanum suddenly loomed without warning overhead, still swathed in an intricate mass of scaffolding from top to bottom. This first impression coloured all that followed, in the writer's mind, during a crowded, bewildering week of pure anthroposophy.
>
> Formerly there stood on this splendid site a beautiful building, with shining domes, a complete and finished thing, standing there as though clad in shining armour, a creation of one man, a being itself one with him. Today the man has gone, the building is no longer visibly before us. On the site of the building there stands this new massive structure, stern and incomplete, obscured by scaffolding. Within, busy workmen, labouring early and late; without, the masses of material ready for the completion of the great work. And what have we to replace the man?
>
> As day followed day, lecture, eurythmy and Mystery Play unrolled in symmetrical, balanced sequence the truths and applications of a philosophy new in our day and time. As the writer, himself no longer young, sat and listened to these young speakers, and watched the eurythmists and the players, one and all inspired by an enthusiasm which rendered their expositions at times flame-like, but always trained and restrained, he felt the hidden presence of the man who has gone, just as in the sanctuary

of the studio the figure of Christ fills the narrow, sacred space with an extraordinary life. The view of the studio with its haunting presence and sense of sanctified peace, of Dr Steiner's paintings, the Schreinerei [joinery workshop] itself, was hallowed by the memories of so many lecture cycles delivered there.

Dr Wachsmuth, leading us over the new building, brought us to the lofty room in which he said the great group of Christ, Ahriman and Lucifer was to be placed, and which was thus to become a sanctuary, a heart of this great, stern, busy building.

Amongst the lecturers at the conference were prominent anthroposophists: Dr Friedrich Rittelmeyer, Elisabeth Vreede, Daniel Dunlop, Caroline von Heyderbrand, Zeylmans van Emmichoven, Karl Schuberth, Guenther Wachsmuth, Günther Schubert, Dr Hermann von Baravalle. The mood, a little more than a year after Rudolf Steiner death, was full and vibrant. There were visits during the conference to Rudolf Steiner's studio, performances of eurythmy, and scenes from the Mystery Plays. As the second Goetheanum building was not yet completed, the conference took place in the 'Schreinerei', the wooden joinery workshop next to the Goetheanum.

The atmosphere around the Goetheanum had such a compelling effect on Gerard Wagner that he decided to remain in Dornach, and when the conference was over the Cowles continued their journey to France without their young friend.

He settled into a room in the same house as Gladys Mayer (see Appendix 4), the English painter who had had such a close connection with Rudolf Steiner and had remarkable spiritual encounters with him, also in relation to her painting. In 1924 Gladys Mayer had sold all she possessed and moved from England to Dornach to be near Rudolf Steiner, 'to spend all the time which was possible still with my teacher, for I could see it might not be long'.

The two painters, Gladys Mayer, 18 years his senior, and Gerard Wagner, read Rudolf Steiner's books and lectures together, and in this way the young painter began to learn the German language. He found the help he needed in settling into the Dornach community, and in meeting the artists who had known and worked with Rudolf Steiner. These were initially Steiner's co-workers and assistants who were busy working towards the completion of the second Goetheanum building: Oswald Dubach and Carl Kemper with their sculptural models; the architect Albert von Baravalle who was working specifically on the design of the building's west façade; and the artist Assja Turgeniev who was engraving the coloured glass windows. He also saw the architectural and sculptural models by Rudolf Steiner himself, and his sketches for the cupola painting of the first Goetheanum, as well as his other art works. And he described how, being a stranger to the German language, all visual impressions were intensified: the unique configurations of a new living art of architecture, sculpture, and painting were impressed indelibly upon the young painter's senses. He felt instinctively that all these different fields of art 'arise from the same wellspring'.[50]

In 'The Goetheanum and the Ten Years of its Life',[51] Rudolf Steiner likewise described the new art impulse and the ideas of anthroposophy as arising out of the same wellspring:

> Friends of anthroposophy took the initiative to build the Goetheanum. Their initiative could only truly be carried out, if, in every detail of its form, the building could arise from the same living spirit from which anthroposophy arose. Often I used this image: Consider a nut with its shell. The shell is certainly no symbol of the nut, yet it is formed out of the same laws and principles as the nut itself. So too the building must be the outer shell, revealing artistically in its forms and pictures that spirit which lives in the spoken word when anthroposophy uses the language of ideas.
>
> In this sense every style of art was born out of a certain spirit, which also manifested ideally in a world conception. And so, in a purely artistic way, there arose in the Goetheanum an architecture which had to make a transition from symmetry, repetition, and the like, to that which breathes in the forms of organic life. The auditorium for instance had seven columns on either side. The forms of each capital were different, save always for corresponding columns right and left. Every succeeding capital was an evolution in metamorphosis from the preceding one. All this resulted from artistic feeling, and not from any abstract, intellectual element. It was not possible to repeat typical motifs at various positions, but every shape was moulded quite individually at its place – in the same way that in an organism the smallest member is individual in form, yet such that it appears of necessity just as it is, at the actual place it occupies.

Gerard Wagner had read about the catastrophic fire on the Dornach Hill in the *Manchester Guardian* of 9 January 1923, when he was 16, in a front page article entitled 'The "Goetheanum". Dr Steiner's Headquarters burnt down'. At that moment he had thought: 'Now I will never be able to see it.' This meeting with the second Goetheanum could be perceived as partial compensation for having missed the experience of the first, that unique 'total artwork' which had taken ten years to build. Now aged 20, Gerard Wagner could begin to absorb the new artistic impulses initiated by Rudolf Steiner in a quite different form and situation. Instead of a harmoniously rounded building created out of the warm living material of wood, he found an unfinished building of concrete more like a fortress in character. In a report by Ita Wegman of Rudolf Steiner's intentions in creating the model of the second Goetheanum, the building is characterised as follows: 'It had to be fortress-like, ... artistic and beautiful, but strong and austere in its forms and lines.'[52]

If one thinks of the Michaelic character of the bold artistic work Gerard Wagner was yet to develop, it seems fitting that the young artist should arrive at a time when he could be a witness to the construction of the second building, and become a member of the community present around this work. Could he have had any inkling that in the future he himself would be painting murals inside the building as well as being involved in the ceiling-painting project of the Great Hall 70 years later?

The intended function of the second Goetheanum, and the artistic connection between the first and the second building, is described by the architect Albert von Baravalle in an article in the weekly *Das Goetheanum*:[53]

> When Dr Steiner spoke, a year after the burning of the first Goetheanum on New Year's Eve 1923, about the rebuilding of the Goetheanum, he began by setting out the architectural brief. He sketched the special arrangements based on the requirements that arise from the vibrant activities and functions of the Anthroposophical Society. He announced that the construction material had been chosen. In order to give the building the greatest possible protection from destruction, following the experience of the fire, he had decided on reinforced concrete. The next day, as Dr Steiner spoke about his approach to the outer artistic treatment, he developed a portal motif, which everyone recognised as a metamorphosis of the West Portal of the First Goetheanum. With this, the continuity between the First and the Second Goetheanum was established. The form of the new building was to be fashioned out of the same inner artistic-spiritual impulses as the first Goetheanum, only now in the new material of reinforced concrete.

At Michaelmas in those first three years of Gerard Wagner's life in Dornach, significant events of the life of the second Goetheanum building occurred: in 1926 the topping-out ceremony; in 1927 the monumental wood sculpture created by Rudolf Steiner was moved from the joinery workshop to the Goetheanum, to take its place in the special room built for it; and at Michaelmas 1928 the official opening of the Goetheanum took place. In 1928 Gerard Wagner, aged 22, took the decision to become a member of the School of Spiritual Science. His membership card, dated December 1928, was signed by Albert Steffen, Dr Ita Wegman and Marie Steiner.

In 1928 Gerard Wagner became a pupil of Henni Geck[54] at the Goetheanum painting school. She was teaching on the basis of training sketches for painters which Rudolf Steiner had given her at her request. In his essay on Henni Geck, Walter Roggenkamp described how the sketches came about:

> A small group of students who also worked as watchmen guarding the Goetheanum grounds, wanted painting lessons with Henni Geck. After a few lessons, however, it was clear to Henni Geck that in view of the grandeur of Rudolf Steiner's artistic intentions, she was not qualified to lead her students into a new contemporary approach to colour exercises and to a painting training based on anthroposophy. To 'paint out of colour', as Rudolf Steiner formulated it, was a difficult task to fulfil.
>
> So on 1 June 1922, when Rudolf Steiner visited Henni Geck in her studio, she asked him for advice – for indications for a painting training corresponding to an academic training.
>
> Henni Geck often vividly described how Rudolf Steiner looked around, found a piece of brown wrapping paper and, using coloured chalks, drew a sketch. Out of spiral-like forms, radiating forms and hatching, in yellow, red, and blue-red colours, a characteristic motif arose. 'Try something like this,' he said, and gave instructions for transposing the sketch into watercolour. This she did at once with her students …
>
> Despite their beauty, the sketches were given only to further and support artistic work, merely as stimulus for artistic elaboration: 'Pastel is inartistic' replied Rudolf Steiner to one who admired such pastel drawings, 'it lacks the process and transparency necessary to the creation of colour if this is to work artistically!'
>
> In irregular intervals up until winter 1922, nine nature moods arose, drawn from our surrounding world in simple, elemental forms: sun, moon, clouds, earth, trees, in various aspects. The rising and setting of the heavenly bodies, light and heavy earth shapes, dark and light, positive and negative cloud or light formations. These were tangible and detailed configurations, yet not naturalistically created; through their

proportions and structure a new and original framework for creating pictures emerged.[55]

The classes took place in the studio of the joinery building, Rudolf Steiner's former work place where the great sculpture 'The Representative of Humanity' was created. Henni Geck and her students were surrounded by works of art created by Rudolf Steiner: the great wax and plasticine model of the sculpture, and, on the surrounding walls, the originals of the 'training sketches' for painters by Rudolf Steiner's own hand. The pupils were instructed to observe the sketches carefully and transpose them into watercolour. Wagner remembered:

> In following an indication given by Rudolf Steiner, we were directed to transpose the pastel sketches into watercolour and in so doing to observe the forms and their relation to one another – down to the smallest detail. Henni Geck gave us the order of colours.[56]

What initially drew Gerard Wagner to Henni Geck were the posters she painted for the artistic performances. They were large watercolour paintings carried out in line with original picture motifs by Rudolf Steiner, and they hung every weekend in the joinery workshop to the left of the stage. The young painter was instantly and deeply interested in

> the fullness of colour, the quality of light, the concreteness of their configuration; motifs which were not taken from the world he had known up until then. They were unique, complete in their formation without a trace of naturalism – an entirely new art of painting.[57]

Gerard Wagner's training with Henni Geck lasted only nine months, however, as the painting school closed shortly before Easter 1929 after the training sketches were removed from the painting school.[58] Wagner recalled in his biographical sketch:

> After nine months – due to tragic circumstances – this form of teaching stopped. Later the sketches were made available for students and other interested persons at the Goetheanum. But that short period of learning had lasting value for all following years.

It is both ironic and significant that the initiative that led to the training sketches being taken from Henni Geck bore the date of 5 April – Gerard Wagner's birthday.[59]

After the abrupt end of his learning period with Henni Geck, Gerard Wagner continued his involvement in other arts – he took sculpture classes with Oswald Dubach, and eurythmy lessons, but his chief focus became the art of speech. Now at 23 he became part of the community around the Speech School and the Goetheanum Stage. He had a natural feeling for drama and a love of theatre, and had been particularly impressed and motivated by what he heard and experienced during rehearsals under Marie Steiner's direction, and what he had seen on the stage. In his autobiographical sketch he wrote: 'It was wonderful when one could experience from the stage the quality of sound spoken with such inner activity and true selflessness. One could imagine at such moments that one was experiencing the future aims of humanity.'[60]

Ilja Duwan,[61] one of Marie Steiner's most important pupils, was Gerard Wagner's teacher in speech and drama. Duwan's special talent was the art of gesture.

In his own teaching many years later Wagner often brought his pupils' attention to how the creation through colour of a certain form was like creating a gesture out of a feeling or mood of soul. And he once demonstrated an exercise he had done as a pupil of Duwan's but now reinvented as a colour exercise. Ilja Duwan had also trained in painting; and perhaps it was this, along with his interest in different nationalities and their own characteristic tendencies that helped to give the Russian teacher and English pupil a fruitful and warm relationship.

During Gerard Wagner's early years in Dornach, the powerful atmosphere around the Goetheanum – still pervaded by Rudolf Steiner's presence – made such a striking impression on him that he always felt unable to speak about it in a way he felt would do the place and the people justice. So he said and wrote very little. However, when interviewed some 40 years later by his pupil and colleague Ernst Schuberth, his passionate feelings can be heard in the fervour and excitement of his voice:

> Life in Dornach was very different at that time. There was a tremendously strong atmosphere! I was a night watchman for a short time when there was only scaffolding in the 'Great Hall'; something dropped from above – one heard it after a while as it landed below, a tremendous sound deep in the night. I was mostly a dawn watchman and slept up in the joinery workshop as I had to get up at 6 am and be there until 10 am. I could, of course, go into all the rooms. I went always to Dr Steiner's Atelier [studio] and to Frau Dr Steiner's rooms. *The mood there!* Dr Steiner's bed was still just as it had been: his table with his

writing things, everything just as he had used it was still there. The wooden statue, Lucifer and Ahriman, and the wonderful plastiline head [of Christ] were still there.

And then the rehearsals, the people there – the air was full! The whole of Dornach was there. Everyone came to the readings at that time – Zuccoli, Savage were there, one knew them, not that one spoke [to them] but there was simply atmosphere, a tremendous mood. And what happened on the stage, and in the rehearsals – that was really something extraordinary. There were of course far fewer people then, perhaps 300 or so; no stranger was allowed on the premises at that time. There was the little guardhouse where Kemper stood, and Trapeznikov and others.

I was present at the rehearsals for eurythmy and for the dramas. How I was able to be there I'm not sure, I believe it was through a friend of mine perhaps, Frl. Wicher ... But I simply went there and she [Frau Dr Steiner] didn't throw me out. I sat right at the back and watched. It was really interesting, really exciting. I was at Henni Geck's school at that time and had spare time. The fact that these things were being done for the first time was unique, – the Mystery Dramas, the rehearsals; it was not as if something already learnt was being performed yet again – but something quite new. And she was exceptionally strict, Frau Dr Steiner. And then Albert Steffen – he read the words of Rudolf Steiner's lectures aloud as if they were his own. That was something *enormous* – I understood everything although I was only just beginning to learn the language. One simply understood it ... [62]

Wagner's involvement in speech and drama and other arts did not mean he had abandoned his own painting work altogether, as a letter from his mother to her son Felix shows:

This morning's post brought letters from you and Gerry, also a remarkable pencil drawing carefully packed round a roll, which Gerry did in 1929 and which I am to send back. He did not say when but he says vaguely it is not to be shown. If it is his own conception entirely, it is rather wonderful.

Gerard Wagner visited his mother every summer after moving to Switzerland, and because of family connections they met in various places in Germany as well. Before the outbreak of the Second World War in 1939, Julie Wagner was in Germany at least once a year visiting family, always in Wiesbaden, and in Baden Baden and Munich. She also went to Switzerland, visiting her cousin

Lily at Figino, and on her way to and from various destinations, mother and son could meet briefly at Basel Railway Station. She visited Dornach on at least one occasion.

In 1930 they met in Munich and afterwards Julie commented on her son's appearance in a letter: 'Gerry is cheerful – pale and thin – but his eyes are bright with rather a steadfast expression – and he holds himself well. He looked nice in his English suit.'

With his promising artistic career seemingly abandoned, some members of the wider family circle looked upon Wagner's new life in Dornach with bewilderment and non-approval; and apart from the regular visit to his mother he had little connection with England or with the extended family there. Once he had come to Dornach, so wrote Wagner's colleague Rex Raab, 'He never looked back.' At times during the 1930s and 40s he also reverted to the original German version of his name – Gerhard. He became a member of the Goetheanum Branch of the Anthroposophical Society at the end of October 1931 and regularly attended lectures there.

The enthusiasm Gerard Wagner had for anthroposophy, so readily accessible in all its forms in Dornach, occupied him completely. Feeling somewhat shut out from his world, Julie Wagner, who always kept in close touch with her sons by letter, was feeling anxious about her youngest son, his future and the effect his 'studies' were having on him. In letters from 1930 and 1931 to Felix she shares her concerns:

> I believe I gave Dorothy [Felix's wife] the impression that I wanted Gerry to have stayed at home, or at any rate near me for my sake. You know that was not so. I only felt I had lost the, let us say, spiritual or mental or human contact with him when he lost all interest in everyone and everything not connected with his studies. I was never one who made physical nearness a condition of affection. Some people do. Some day of course Gerry may come back to the natural, normal world again of human relations. I hope for his own sake he may.

> I am so glad you are to meet Gerry's friend on Sunday. I had forgotten his name. Perhaps he might give you some explanation of the anthroposophical views on earning one's living. Gerry seems more vague than ever on this point and ignores my questions. He does not seem capable of answering clearly unless it is the simplest thing, such as the price of the coat he had made. He is so vague and queer that I wonder now and then if his brain is not a little turned from all his abstract study.

You will have my hasty note of yesterday about Gerard. He is much in my thoughts and I feel really anxious about him – not only as regards the money question – it is his whole attitude to life and the world that worries me. Ah well, I cannot get rid of the feeling that it is my fault, in a measure, for making it possible for him to live there all these years without duties of any sort. I hope I am wrong. Still you would say it's not my fault, Gerry must do what he feels impelled to do and we (you and I) must trust that the future will prove him right, and leave him – as we can't help doing – in 'higher hands'.

The special connection between the two brothers Gerard and Felix, which was strong in childhood and youth, continued throughout their lives. Felix supported Gerard when he first decided he wanted to become a painter, and his support for his younger brother never wavered. The mother wrote:

I am glad of what you say in regard to my responsibility towards Gerry, you are very reassuring and comforting. I shall try to be less anxious for him if only he keeps his health. A very sensible letter arrived from him this morning, evidently carefully written. I will send it to you when I have answered it. There is not much German in it. He always expresses himself much more clearly when he writes in English.

In 1931, now a student of speech and acting, Gerard was planning a move to Berlin to follow up an opportunity of work there:

Now Gerry writes with a request for money to go to Berlin. This may be the chance of paid work he has been waiting for. He did not say which day he travels – he says he has 'one or two' good friends in Berlin and hopes to make many more.

And about three weeks later:

He travels to Berlin today (9 March) in this weather! Berlin has terribly cold winters I know. Aunt Lily looks upon his plan of becoming an actor as absolutely hopeless … He is sure to meet hindrances – and only time will show whether he is doing right. His motives are of the highest – that is a comfort. The most serious practical obstacle I see now is that he will not be able to earn a living in Germany or Switzerland unless he becomes German or Swiss.

During the late 1920s and 1930s, particularly, the Goetheanum Stage performances produced and directed by Marie Steiner were important events for

Gerard Wagner.[63] He trod the boards himself at least twice, in Rudolf Steiner's fourth Mystery Play (the Egyptian Temple scene) and in Goethe's *Faust*.

Gerard Wagner felt a strong connection with Albert Steffen's dramas and poetry, and motifs from Steffen's work appeared in Wagner's paintings. One of the special events at the Goetheanum at that time was when Albert Steffen gave readings of his latest plays. Wagner recalled:

> And Steffen's dramas – he read them to us before they were performed. That was the greatest thing altogether that happened in Dornach. And one was always a little disappointed when they were staged, as his readings were so much more characteristic and alive. His dramas had an effect on the atmosphere of course. Also his poems, that was one of the chief things that brought one to oneself at that time. The poems in the Goetheanum and the mood – these motifs were simply in the air and one took them in. One didn't search for them, they were simply in the whole surroundings as motif. In any case the atmosphere brought them out – and one painted them. In that way they came into what I painted.
>
> I think when one reads Steffen's poems one has the feeling they are not only fantasy. One needs fantasy to paint them perhaps, but they are true. They are simply true happenings, and therefore they can work in one. Also out of a certain etheric feeling probably. I don't know how one paints a poem. But I would say they [the motifs] are fitting, they are right.[64]

Wagner was deeply inspired by the drama *Hiram and Solomon*, and later in life – evidently moved – he described the moment when Hiram rises up from the centre of the earth onto the stage after the casting of the brazen sea: 'It was the most dramatic thing I saw in Dornach!' he said. The image of Hiram painted in the costume and colours Albert Steffen gives him in the play, appears ever and again in Gerard Wagner's paintings right up to his final creative period. He saw the première of *Hiram and Solomon* on 25 December 1933 during the Goetheanum Christmas Conference, when he was 27 years old. In the words of Ernst Uehli, this play bears 'witness to a deep transformation undergone by the poet … in the magnificently fashioned scene in which Hiram carries out the casting of the brazen sea, Steffen raises the word to ritual significance'.[65]

Gerard Wagner used also to mention Rudolf Steiner's comment that *Hiram and Solomon* 'belongs to us' [to the anthroposophical movement]; and Wagner himself added that 'the drama is relevant to us all today'. Albert Steffen describes in his book 'Meetings with Rudolf Steiner'[66] how he presented his play to Rudolf Steiner some five weeks before Steiner's death on 25 March 1925:

> On 14 March I gave Rudolf Steiner my play *Hiram and Solomon*, which I had completed on the 6th of that month. I brought it to his studio at five in the afternoon. He opened the manuscript, read the dedication, 'To Rudolf Steiner, with deep respect', and was visibly moved with pleasure.
>
> The next day I was fortunate enough to visit Rudolf Steiner once again. He told me that three developmental aspects of the legend could be identified: one, where Hiram continues working after completing the brazen sea; the second, when he is murdered before its completion; and the third, where his deed, offered for the good of humanity, results in his death. The third, said Steiner, is the synthesis of the two others. Thereupon he gave instructions for the play to be printed in the weekly journal *Das Goetheanum*.

THE INNER PATH

Inwards leads the sacred path

NOVALIS[67]

Gerard Wagner's intended move to Berlin did not materialise, and the involvement with speech training and the Goetheanum Stage continued until a conversation with Albert Steffen changed Wagner's direction once and for all – as he related to the author:

> I was walking along the road with Albert Steffen when he asked me what I was doing at the Goetheanum. When I told him I was involved in the speech training and the stage, he began to talk about the typical attributes of actors, and described – with emphasis – their grand statures and powerful voices. At the same time he began making movements with his hand on the nearby hedge as if he were painting. The next day I went up to the Speech School and told them I would not be continuing.

This meeting, which led Gerard Wagner back to painting and to his actual task, most probably took place in 1932 or 1933 when Wagner was 26 or 27. The biographical significance of this moment in life is assigned special meaning by Rudolf Steiner.[68] He describes how up until the age of 27 the human being finds support for his soul-spiritual development from life itself, but then these natural developmental forces end, and we require for our further development an inner spiritual impulse arising out of our own initiative. This difficult period of inner crisis and drama lasts roughly from 27 to 35. In Gerard Wagner's biography this would relate to the years 1933 to 1941, an incubation period for the development of his painting – 1941 being the year he first exhibited his work at the Goetheanum.

This significant moment of change around the 27th year takes on a special colouring when we consider Gerard Wagner's biography and the task he had set himself. What he was about to embark upon had to come entirely from his own initiative. The path he had chosen had not been trodden by anyone else before him. Wagner touches on this aspect in the previously-quoted letter to his sister-in-law about his student days at the Royal College of Art in London: 'One did not realise in those days what one was looking for – or that one would need to give up all that seemed fascinating about an "artist's life" and lead an existence more or less of a recluse, to work at something which no one else could teach one.'

Having taken up the paintbrush once more, Gerard Wagner began, in solitude, to investigate the challenge Rudolf Steiner had given to painters to 'find form through colour', a task Gerard Wagner devoted himself to entirely. 'The teacher,' Wagner wrote in a letter to a pupil many years later (1994), 'is Dr Steiner, the colour and oneself.'

Gerard Wagner's developing work with colour became meditative life for him. His atelier was his hermitage, in which he researched the question of how form could arise out of colour. Over the years, communion with the soul of colour became a *terra firma* of experience and knowledge, the focus and wellspring of his inner life.

In his autobiographical sketch Wagner describes how he set about approaching the riddle of how form arises from colour. He had pondered this question already as a pupil at the Goetheanum painting school:

> The teaching had left me with a great riddle. Rudolf Steiner always said that form should arise out of colour, and one can assume that this happened in his own pictures. With Henni Geck we had begun the first three sketches by applying vermilion red, first in the form of a rising sun, then in the form of a setting sun, and in the third sketch as three crescent moons. And the question arose in me as to how, when starting with the same red colour on white paper in all three sketches, the different motifs had come about. How could these differences in form be reconciled with the requirement to find the form out of the colour?
>
> I began to look for answers. I asked myself if, in building up a training sketch (the initial ones were painted with only three to four colours), I were to change just one colour slightly, how would the form change? In this I followed a suggestion of Rudolf Steiner's to colour the paper, or to imagine the paper already coloured, before painting the motif.
>
> Experimental series were begun with one or with two colours, one of which changed in minute steps from one painting to the next (e.g. from blue-green to yellow-green; from cool red to warm red and so on), and with each change in colour the question arose as to the corresponding change in form.
>
> I attempted to participate in the life of colour through my own experience. So the goal was set …
>
> This method of practice evolved in order to train one's own colour feeling. The sketches of Rudolf Steiner teach one relatively soon that the

life in which the colours are always steeped, and which is brought to form and made visible by means of those colours, can be grasped only by feeling which has cast aside the 'merely subjective'. One sought entry into the sphere of the living, into the world of formative forces. This is only possible by starting out from a higher principle.

So one stood at that time at the beginning of a long journey. Many years passed in seemingly unending practice. To anticipate how long one would need to arrive at the 'beginning of painting' so as to be able to paint a picture in the sense striven for, was naturally impossible – perhaps twelve to fourteen years.

The question of how form arises out of colour, and to what extent it can be answered, depends on how one is able to have the colour – as objective experience – so strongly in oneself that it can supplant the mental image. Only later does one know why it is so difficult and what it means. In isolated moments a *real* experience – like a flash – seems to take hold. One tries to catch it so it can repeat itself – this goes on for years, until the experiences build up. At some point it must be possible for it to become a continuous stream.

But even if one should never reach the goal of finding form out of colour – of lifting the 'Veil of Isis' – the process, the practice itself, is a path towards becoming truly human, and whoever notices this cannot help but continue on the path.[69]

Two or three years after Gerard Wagner returned exclusively to painting, the architect Rex Raab first met him and was impressed by what he saw. He sensed that this modest painter had found a path of inner training that was already 'bearing him along'. He wrote in his essay 'Impressions of Gerard Wagner':[70]

At Easter 1935, a week after my twenty-first birthday, I was on my first visit to Dornach, in order to experience the Goetheanum building, which I had wanted to see ever since starting to study architecture in London four years before.

Whilst stormy sessions were going on in the Great Hall during the critical general meeting of the General Anthroposophical Society of 1935,[71] I walked each day around and around the building at terrace level. The effect on me was that it altered my sense of balance in life. The immediate experience was like disembarking after a longer ocean voyage – the building stands firmly on the earth, and yet in its form overcomes the gravitational pull that makes most buildings so earth-bound.

It was in this building during those Easter days that I first met the young painter, Gerard Wagner. A mutual friend, Cathleen O'Donnell, an Irish colleen and half a pixie introduced us to each other. It was in the 'Wandelhalle' of the Goetheanum, at that time – seven years after the opening of the building at Michaelmas 1928 – still raw concrete: floor, walls, ceiling, besides quantities of sculpted concrete radiator screens saved from the original Goetheanum that had been destroyed by fire.

We met near the inner wall. I found myself in the presence of a smiling, friendly, unassuming, even self-effacing older brother. Gerard was 29, eight years my senior, and had been in Dornach nearly nine years. He told me he was working with the sketches Rudolf Steiner had made as an aid in learning to paint. Cathleen suggested that he show me some of his own paintings too. At a second meeting, on the same spot, Gerard then obligingly brought a sheaf of sheets under his arm, and showed them to me, accompanied by an occasional explanation or comment, but more frequently punctuated by enthusiastic ones from Cathleen.

From the studies based on Dr Steiner's example, one could sense that Gerard had found an approach to consistent work; he had found a path of colour and inner training that was already bearing him along. It was too early to say but one could guess where and how far his devotion and wonderful tenacity were going to take him.

His own work at that time in many ways contrasted strongly with the gentle quality of Steiner's studies. There were sometimes even wilful, sudden changes in colour and strengths of colour, making a 'hot' impression. In some of his later work what is refreshingly, even excitingly, dramatic, had at that time not yet achieved the maturity that made it completely acceptable. It was not always harmonious. But in contrast to much that was being presented as 'anthroposophical painting' (and still is, seventy years later) it was 'interesting'. One instinctively felt: This man is grasping for something of his own; something will emerge from these struggles! It was good to know Gerard Wagner, a mild, gentle soul with artistic devotion, founded on a well-hidden resolve.

Rex Raab's impression of this 'mild gentle soul' who had a found a path of inner training through colour finds an echo in Gennady Bondarev's perception of the artist:

After Gerard Wagner had begun to copy Rudolf Steiner's originals he was able to develop new levels of his personality. This in turn enabled him to delve more deeply into their esoteric depths and discover through them the secrets of artistic metamorphosis. This is equivalent to the progress of an esoteric pupil on the schooling path. Thus did Wagner's life become transformed after his move to Dornach into a life of constant meditation on the nature and being of colour through the 'colour mantras' that are the training sketches of Rudolf Steiner. In this connection he reminds us of the early icon painters one of whom was Andrei Rublev, the 'pious monk', whereas in his dynamic creative potential he is more like Michelangelo. There is nothing exaggerated or incredible in this if we understand that the true nature of the synthesis achieved in the Rudolf Steiner-Gerard Wagner School involves uniting the mastery of the painter with the pupilship of the meditant.[72]

Complete devotion to painting did not improve Wagner's financial situation. He lived in very modest circumstances, in various small rooms which also served as studios. For lack of money he painted on both sides of the paper, and survived at times on a cup of milk a day. After an initial two years living in Reinach, the painter moved to Dornach, and by the end of October 1934 had moved from Haus Ditzler to Haus Thomann, later known as Haus Eckinger, at Blumenweg 3. His mother wrote: 'I hope you are well and as happy as can be in your new rooms. Can you keep warm or have you no cold weather yet?'

Gabrielle Kaiser Day (1925–2009) remembered seeing Gerard Wagner almost daily as a child in the 1930s. Her family moved to Unterer Zielweg in 1932 when she was seven, and she and her siblings often saw the painter walking past their house. She recalled:

> Our window looked out onto the narrow lane and in the lunch hour we saw an unusual-looking gentleman walking down past our house. He wore black clothes and looked pale and melancholy. We had many opportunities to meet him. He made a strong impression on us children, he was friendly and we respected him.

Frau Kaiser thought he was probably returning home after the midday meal offered to the actors free of charge at nearby Haus Haldeck.

Ingeborg Maresca (1929–2018), a student of the sculptor Oswald Dubach from about 1935, recalled the impression she had of Gerard Wagner, and the occasion when she invited him for a meal during wartime:

Around the Goetheanum we were all one big family who met at the canteen not necessarily to eat but to have a cup of coffee, smoke, play chess or whatever. Gerard Wagner was a lone wolf, living and working in his studio. He was like a Russian monk with his pale face, fine head and black clothes: 'painting for God'.

I invited him for a meal, for which occasion I saved my ration of butter; and he showed me his paintings in his studio at Eckinger House (Blumenweg 3). Louise van Blommestein also invited him and he took along his paintings to show her.

A close friend of Gerard Wagner's at the Goetheanum Speech School during this time was Annamarie Michaelis, later Brons (1901–1980). Her daughter, Angela Koconda, remembers the painter coming to their house when she was a young girl in the 1940s, and waiting on the doorstep as her mother fetched food, and other supplies for him. She thought the beautiful paintings from different periods of Wagner's work that her mother owned were in part offered in gratitude for the help she gave him.

FIRST EXHIBITIONS

The four main Goetheanum conferences at Easter, Summer, Michaelmas and Christmas were usually accompanied by group exhibitions of the 'Dornach painters' and other artists. The earliest recorded exhibition of Gerard Wagner's work at the Goetheanum took place in the summer of 1941, although there was apparently an earlier show of his work in the autumn of 1939 mentioned in a card dated 3.10.1939 to Wagner from R. Haas, who wrote: 'How is it going with the exhibition. Has it taken place yet? I could not find out anything about it until now.'

Gerard Wagner's work was mentioned in a review of the 1941 summer exhibition:[73]

> In deep chasms, colours, like wild animals, are subdued by other colours – purified in the service of knowledge. From such regions, the paintings of Gerald Wagner, reminiscent in their character of medieval times, shimmer and gleam out, at the same time conveying the utter dread that sets the universe a-tremble wherever beauty seeks to work into the future. This penetrates every surface, every farthest nook and cranny, so as to seize upon what cannot yet shine forth as beauty by its own power. These pictures gain striking impact by making this drama visible.

In the Goetheanum Christmas exhibition of 1942 Wagner's work was again shown with a group of painters that included Louise van Blommestein and Assja Turgenieff. Karl Heymann wrote the review:[74]

> The work of Titian and his pupils show how coloration can be lost on such a journey toward another sun. But once colour has faded from sight, the soul can distinctively reshape itself so as to relinquish altogether the attempt to discover new colours in sunlight. The soul then turns, as we find in El Greco with astounding consistency, to the moonlight. His colours and forms, in fact whole compositions, are created purely out of moonlight.
>
> One is reminded of this singular source of coloration in painting when looking at the pictures of Gerhard Wagner. Again colour seems to be lost initially because painting itself seeks another sun. The artist

turns to the colours woven by the silvery light of the moon. As he tries to grasp and embody forms with this light, he must gather together the different aspects from infinitely distant regions. He then also introduces the crystal hardness of cosmic realms of ice.

At Michaelmas 1943 and 1944, works by Gerhard Wagner were included in exhibitions in the joinery workshop. In a sensitive review of the 1944 Easter exhibition, Ursula Schulte-Kersmecke draws attention to the inner quality that comes to expression in human uprightness – the intuitive sense of spirit which is at the core of the quality of balance that Gerard Wagner continually sought in his work:

> … The pictures of Gerard Wagner give quite a different impression. These glowing, shining colours could work bewitchingly or have a dispersive, evaporating effect if they did *not* abide lawfully by universal principles. The fact that these colours, in obeying these principles, weave together to create form cannot necessarily be detected by someone not well-versed in painting. Yet the observer feels neither fixedly spellbound nor dispersed, but rather wonderfully strengthened and moved in his centre. What streams toward us in dynamic tranquillity is not the painter's expertise in applying the laws of colour; that is self-evident, not brought to consciousness, and disappears completely into the background as the medium of colour revelation. So what is it then that these flowing colours, and the forms that arise out of them, leave behind as an essential feeling? It is very remarkable, but one would like to describe it as follows: 'I must and will be an upright human being. And I *can* be.'[75]

In 1945 Gerard Wagner took part in group exhibitions in St Gallen and in Bern. The summer exhibition at Bern was entitled: 'Artists affiliated with the Goetheanum' and a review was printed in the August 1945 issue of the anthroposophical newsletter:

> The Goetheanum artists are not bound by a rigid programme but rather are united in a common striving which fulfils and guides them. Observing the primacy of colour, their preference is for watercolour, which, having little corporeality has all the more luminosity. Jérôme Bessenich, Theodor Ganz, Gérard Wagner, Maria Strakosch-Giesler and Lili Wadler-Bosshard are the artists who each in their own way conjure forth luminous colour symphonies, the unusual effects of which – especially in the case of Gérard Wagner – would be hard to ignore.

FIRST EXHIBITIONS

At Michaelmas and Christmas 1945, Gerard Wagner exhibited once more in group exhibitions in the joinery workshop, and did so again in the summer show of 1946 along with a group of painters that included Liane Collot d'Herbois, Hilde Raske and Hilde Boos-Hamburger. Wagner was a consistent exhibitor throughout the 1940s and beyond, and having started more or less as an unknown – his name alternating between Gerald, Gerhard or Gérard; Gerard Wagner then figures consistently in these shows whilst other participants seem to change more frequently. A review of the 1952 Michaelmas exhibition says this about his work:

> One must observe and meditate on Gerard Wagner's pictures for a long time. One should only really look at them when one has time for it. His deep brown tones do not allow one to disperse into the light. One should experience worlds of spirit in the limbs, right down into the experience of weight.

It is clear from Margrit Engler's letters referring to the shows in Bern and St Gallen that Gerard Wagner already had a growing following. She was an enthusiast who corresponded with him and helped him out financially. Others did the same. The impoverished artist received two pairs of socks and a jar of honey every Christmas from Berthe Naef, and Helen Hoch also provided a lifeline with gifts of money. Margrit Engler wrote to the painter regularly in the 1940s, and a few excerpts from these letters are given below:

> 20 June 1944
> Dear Herr Wagner
> I wonder if you can imagine the wonderful surprise and great joy you have given me? I thank you from the bottom of my heart for that wonderful light-filled painting, and for your thoughts! Your priceless letter was forwarded to me as I have recently moved to St Gallen to be near my mother who is ill. How excited I am to be able to show her the picture in a few days. Perhaps I may add that Herr Uehli, when he visited me, saw your paintings and admired them very much. He has already seen a lot of your work in Dornach. I would like to express once again my heartfelt thanks and wish you all the best for your work.
> Yours truly
> Margrit Engler

2 January 1945

Dear Herr Wagner

I thank you from the bottom of my heart for the wonderful Christmas greeting! Once again – quite undeserved – you have given me such happiness. Daily I am able to experience the joy of being surrounded by this beautiful living world of pictures. Please accept my heartfelt greetings for the New Year. May the wider world find ever more interest and love for your great language – painting.

Yours truly,

Margrit Engler

15 April 1945

Dear Herr Wagner

Can you forgive me that I always want to turn my feeling of thanks into deeds? In any case, I entrust this spring greeting to you and to its destiny. It comes with my best wishes.

I have great respect for people who tread a spiritual path as a path of sacrifice, and I want to do my bit for this 'soldier'. To have a role to play in this manner, however small, is my deepest wish.

Yours truly

Margrit Engler

22 April 1945

Dear Herr Wagner

What joy you have given me! I can hardly conceive of having something so wonderful – and even to own it. You have made me eternally rich. What fullness of colour and spirituality comes towards one. Every one of your pictures is so new, and ever more radiant.

It's good to hear that pictures from Dornach painters will be exhibited in St Gallen. I am so happy about it – and now I had a thought … Herr Uehli is giving a lecture next Saturday in St Gallen. Would you feel like hearing it and then the next morning visit the exhibition? … As I know there is no question of you being able to afford it, I would, with pleasure, like to send you the means to make the journey if you should decide, as a 'Dornacher', to risk an excursion into the world. And now you can imagine that I await your response almost with impatience!

With grateful thanks

Yours truly

Margrit Engler

10 May 1945

Dear Herr Wagner

Only today have I found a quiet moment to thank you for your letter – I well understand that you were not able to come.

The lecture by Herr Uehli, an introductory lecture about the anthroposophical view of Christianity, was as ever so human, and drew on a deep understanding of the problems and questions which people carry with them. The audience included many young non-members, and one felt how their attention was held right up to the last words and how much gratitude they felt. At 70, Herr Uehli has such a strong connection to youth! He visited me briefly and we admired your 'Butterflies', which flew here to me somehow.

When looking at your summer picture, an old saga came to mind. Perhaps you know *The Sunset of Old Tales* by Fiona Macleod? This book contains wonderful pictures.

I was very happy with the exhibition. On leaving these rooms you carry a whole world with you. I knew some of the pictures already, but sometimes you look at things again later with quite new eyes. I have to admit that the picture of yours that impressed me most was 'The Apprentice of Nature'. It is a picture that takes one back into ancient times. And one sees the picture so clearly when no longer having it before one ...

The letters from Margrit Engler are revealing in more ways than one. They tell us what books she discussed with Gerard Wagner, and those either lent to her by him or *vice versa*. They include *The Sunset of Old Tales* by Fiona Macleod, *Green Dolphin Country* by Elizabeth Goudge, *Life Everlasting* by Marie Corelli. He also lent her his much-loved *Letters of Katherine Mansfield*. To save him the money for postage she insists that he need not return her books by post. Without Gerard Wagner's own letters to Margrit Engler to hand, one can read between the lines of hers something of what he has said about certain important aspects of his own work, and about painting more widely. She also makes significant comments of her own about Wagner's art and the role of the painter in general – such as: 'The artist is someone who continually gives.'

23 August 1945

Dear Herr Wagner

It is wonderful what you say about painting and the world ether. For me it is putting into words a truth which I have felt rather than thought.

In relation to those who have died, one is allowed to experience that for a spiritual connection one no longer needs words and bodies. It is a much more undisturbed connection – of light and warmth – than is possible during earth life.

I wish sincerely that the exhibition in Bern will go better. It is anyway certain that Bern is more receptive than St Gallen, which in this regard is rather hopeless …

I will gladly send you the Fiona Macleod book when winter comes in case you are not able to get it at the library. – I must admit that the English language is especially beautiful. You have described its character so well in your letters – I noticed this particularly when reading a book by Marie Corelli (*Life Everlasting*) – it is written in wonderful language. One could ask if this author knows anthroposophy – she often comes very close to it. Dr Steiner held lectures there at that time. The description of the path of initiation she underwent, though, has more to do with her own personal wellbeing.

You find it unfortunate that your group has the name Goetheanum in the [exhibition] title. Certainly, whoever thinks this is most serious in their striving to realise and understand Dr Steiner's indications. I cannot but love and admire your painting. That some pictures speak to one less, and others more, is natural. It is as you say – people expect something they can't understand in art inspired by anthroposophy, already thinking they will fail to understand it before they even see it. And the name 'Goetheanum' calls up prejudices immediately. Nevertheless it is good when they know what seeks to speak to them.

Please accept my heartfelt wishes and greetings

Yours truly, Margrit Engler

November 1945

Dear Herr Wagner

I wonder if further exhibitions of Dornach artists will take place in Switzerland? I have not read anything to suggest this. In Dornach itself there are always opportunities for exhibitions during the conferences although the visiting times are somewhat limited, are they not?

Now the days are shorter, and you will be putting down your brush earlier than usual. In this regard a thought came to me: the painter who lives with nature, in so far as he experiences the twilight consciously, not banishing it with electric light, is more creative during daylight.

I look forward to seeing new works when I next visit – in the meantime I have your painting of the Three Kings near me – which is so alive at this time.

Once more heartfelt thanks for everything.

Yours truly

Margrit Engler

New Year 1946

... Incidentally what you say about the colour atmosphere that you experience when reading *The Sunset of Old Tales*, and all that lives in your pictures, is a confirmation of my feelings, though I could not put this into words.

Your plan for England sounds to me just wonderful! If your stay there can be to some extent pleasant – in post-war times – the journey must surely be meaningful and valuable for you in more ways than one. And am I mistaken to believe that England is more receptive to spirituality than Switzerland? But then I only know England from books and from what my mother told me. And because of this I should think that your colours would speak to the people there I am especially pleased to hear you will be giving lessons there! By the way do you know that Herr Ratnowsky will be giving a sculpture course this year in St Gallen? There seem to be quite a few registrations already, and I ask myself if this might also be true for a painting course ...?

Dornach friends

Gerard Wagner, a friendly and courteous man with a good sense of humour, had many contacts and friendships. Cathleen O'Donnell who studied eurythmy in Dornach from 1934 was one of the English contingent in Dornach with whom Wagner had a lifelong friendship. Her letters of 1938 and beyond give insight into Gerard Wagner's circle of associates there.

In a letter of April 1944 she writes:

Dear Gerhard ... I must thank you for bringing about the meetings with your mother, also for the memorable and pleasant visit to her home. One is allowed to keep the picture clear, without clouding ... it might have been the same with yourself, had I been an independent person when arriving in Dornach. Instead there is always the struggle for independence. Others have been single from childhood, and follow the path of their own clear choosing, without diversion; these are related, and naturally find one another, forming invisible bonds of understanding and sympathy, yet becoming ever more single each for himself.

At one time I used to get awful fears that you could be taken in by people who were not of this order – just because of some sort of decorative capacity that certain Dornach people used to flaunt (less of late, since the world is become dead serious), but then seeing the people of your choosing, and often dreaming of you all together in very radiant and joyful dreams, I recognised that my fears had been idle ones, that you belonged with your mother, the Wedgwoods, the Reimanns, with Herr Steffen, and all in different ways, creative, quickening; others too would come later, of whom I would not know, but the trust was established.

Ethel Bowen-Wedgwood, one of Gerard Wagner's English friends, first came to Dornach with George Adams in September of 1919, after corresponding with Rudolf Steiner and with Edith Maryon. They came to discuss the English translation of Rudolf Steiner's newly published book on threefold society, (now published as *Towards Social Renewal)*. With the subject of social change and justice close to her heart, and with her strong conviction that the book should be made available to English-speaking readers as soon as possible, Ethel Bowen-Wedgwood, with George Adams's support, was keen to take on the translation. During their stay in Dornach they had several meetings with Rudolf Steiner who then gave permission for the translation, which was published soon afterwards in London.

When Ethel Bowen-Wedgwood came to Dornach to live is not clear, but she lived in one of the 'eurythmy houses' during the 1930s/1940s, and supported Gerard Wagner in various ways, especially it seems during the war years. In turn she, like others, received a collection of his paintings and drawings given as thank-you presents.

Dear Herr Wagner
Please call in at your convenience and collect a pot of home-made apricot jam (Spanish apricots), made with grape sugar. Affectionately, E. B-W, Saturday evening.

9 August 1944
Dear Herr Wagner
The sketch is really charming and I simply love it. I have displayed it for now and when we leave I will put it away with my collection. For

the holidays I wish you good working hours – and also that you find the opportunity for a few pleasant walks under an open sky. Before the summer leaves us we must take in enough impressions of nature to last us through the winter.

Thank you. With heartfelt greetings and I look forward to meeting you soon again, Ethel Bowen-Wedgwood

30 September 1944
Dear Herr Wagner
Thank you so much for your so loving and charming 'greeting'. This and the last one delight us every time we look at them! It is wonderful that simply from the depths of one's heart, and with a few paints, one can bring so much joy to one's friends!

How is it going otherwise? I would very much like to know, especially as we haven't seen each other for so long. If you feel like it, come by on Tuesday[76] when you are anyway up here – not too late. Julian will bring something of the bread variety from town for you. I am very grateful for the coffee coupons … but! … It might be better for you to make use of them yourself and buy Ovalmatine or Cocoa with them. Don't you think? With sincere greetings until we meet again!

Yours, Ethel Bowen-Wedgwood

And two longer letters in English from Ethel Bowen-Wedgwood, in July 1945, give insight into Gerard Wagner's life and activities at that time, including an intriguing reference to an event of his childhood relating to his drawing, and other thoughts of the painter's relating to art and to the quality of the English language.

15 July 1945
My dear Herr Wagner
It was really a great regret to me to have to leave Dornach, after all, without seeing you again, and without seeing the pictures. Each day I hoped to come next day; and each next day again there came a hindrance through something unexpected, and twice I was working – against usual habits – till midnight, in order to get necessary things finished.

Perhaps there may be a chance again in the autumn or winter; and, meanwhile, do please let me hear from you, and please tell me all the details about the exhibition and so on.

It must be most terribly hot for you and everyone at Dornach, since even here, well over 1000 metres up and gazing straight into the snows and glaciers of the Wetterhorn, we are only able to go out walking in the early morning or evening. The sky is so blue as though it never rained, and the white clouds only collect to take the shapes of the mountain range along which they lie for a while and then vanish away into nothing again.

How very much I wish that you could be in this beautiful place too and getting the fresh air and the cold clear Quellenwasser [spring water]. Opposite is a cataract, and, alongside, a little foaming stream going headlong into the valley. The people are very 'sympathisch' [friendly], peasants of the better sort, very hard-working (our landlord carried up all our luggage and our friends'– including food-stores and books – a quarter of an hour over a stony path uphill on his back, and is just on 70 years old!) They are also quite astute and know the wants and the paying-possibilities of the season-visitors! – Even the desolation of Europe acquires a certain distance in this atmosphere.

Julian sends much love with mine. We really want to know how you are getting on, and what motif you are working at, and whether you have any new pupils ... in short, everything you can tell us about yourself! Affectionately yours, Ethel Bowen-Wedgwood

29 July 1945
My dear Herr Wagner
Many thanks for your letter and for the most convincing picture of you bicycling round the Wetterhorn. I am *delighted* to hear about the new suit; it was really time you had a good substantial one for the cold weather, and one to your make and liking. Also I am very glad it is grey. [...]

I hope all will go well with the exhibition, and that some intelligent persons will buy a few pictures! Wouldn't it be well for you to go over to Bern yourself for a few days, so as to meet the other exhibiting artists and make acquaintances with outsiders? Miss Wetherall's account of London very 'durty' (I agree this spelling fits best!) ... and perhaps also she is right, that at present Bern affords a better public for pictures of a new kind, than London would.

It is really a beautiful place where we are now. ... I don't remember being in any place where one was made more conscious of the connections between the different worlds of nature. The hard mountains are obviously born out of the soft clouds that cuddle their tops and assume their shapes, and then they get fixed tight, while the clouds detach themselves and go circling round the heavens in a gigantic ritual-procession of nascent horses, lions, cows, charioteers etc. It is hardly possible not to see, when one watches the blue, white, orange, lilac butterflies over the flowers, that the flower itself has taken breath, turned its stamen into antennae and little legs, its petals into wings and flown off into the air.

The first fortnight was one of glorious weather; with the full moon came thunderstorms, and now rain and fog, so that the whole landscape – rocks, trees, grass, sky – everything – seems built up of innumerable layers of shifting, coloured mists. The great thing however is, that the crops are saved, both for us here, and let's hope, for the greater part of Europe too.

And in Dornach you will be cooler! The heat must have been terrible, and we thanked our stars every day that we were in a privileged position, 1100 metres up! In Dornach you are better off for food: everything here is dearer –and rather less good – vegetables and fruit very difficult to get at all, and the milk – the cow's milk – instead of flowing into the rustic pails of milkmaids are being delivered creamy and warm … However there is excellent goat's milk which we get sometimes from Frau Thöni – a dear women – who explains to us that the goat's milk is so much more wholesome because the goats browse the fine little herbs close to the earth.

I have been able to work pretty steadily every day and get on with my translation of the Doctor's wonderful cycle of the summer of 1921, *Human Evolution, Cosmic Soul, Cosmic Spirit* [GA 205/206], which itself alone, if he had spoken and written nothing else, would, one would think, be epoch-making for whoever studied it, quite apart from the extraordinary epic beauty of many passages in it. It really is a great privilege to be able to try and give such a work again in the English language.

I think you are right about the English language: *pictures* arise out of it very easily – especially 'soul-pictures'. That in itself is rather a snare of Lucifer – for the pictures carry one away, and one easily gets into rather a '*word-sham*' – a sort of 'Wort-Schein', and can only keep it in check by rigid thinking and a determination to destroy one's best 'soul-picture' if it is not quite spiritually (I mean mentally and actually) true. You remember how someone – I think it was Jowett – gave the advice to a brilliant pupil, 'Go through the thing again, and strike out all the passages you are particularly pleased with!' And I think you yourself told me once that directly a painting got pretty, you hasten to alter it!

After all – and that is the conclusion I have very clearly come to in this unusually beautiful place – Nature as Jehovah made it is wonderful, even to look at, but still I won't say human art is better (though it may be, hereafter), but at any rate one can only be contented to a certain degree with Nature; and, to live with, for full satisfaction, artistic work is necessary, – one's own, *faute-de-mieux*, but especially other people's artistic work.

And here I must tell you that one morning I looked out and saw a dark-haired boy of about 14 with sunburnt arms standing alone in the 'Matte' and drawing with intensest zeal in a drawing-block. He paid no attention to anything else; first he drew rapidly – then he turned the drawing on its head and a bit round to see the effect, then hurriedly, a dash sideways to get in the mountain, then the chalet again – evidently in fear his mother would call him to breakfast before his work of art should be completed ... which alas! of course happened! It was such a refreshing apparition, and I thought of you, and what you had told me of yourself as a boy ...

By the way, you were interested in what we told you about an uncle-in-law of Julian's sister, who was in Theresienstadt (the Jewish concentration –camp there) and of whose fate we were uncertain, so I'm sure you will be glad to hear that we have heard (by telegram) that he is alive, though likely to be still in the Russian zone.

Julian joins me in affectionate good wishes. Do write when you feel inclined! Yours ever, sincerely Ethel Bowen-Wedgwood.

Gerard Wagner had a special connection with Martha and Hugo Reimann and their son Johannes (whose tragic death by drowning at the age of 18 in 1952 deeply touched the Dornach community). In a letter written to his sister-in-law Dorothy Wagner in April 1978, his 72nd birthday, Gerard Wagner's wrote:

One of my oldest Dornach friends was cremated this morning. A rather special person who lived in the flat below me – a Frau Reimann.[77] She brought together a few of us – musicians too, school teachers – who became very good friends, till today. It was rather a special thing all of us meeting again today at the cremation, which in our circle here is always treated in a very special way, from the moment of dying to the cremation at the end ...

(Among the 'very good friends' Gerard Wagner mentions here were the musicians Josef Gunzinger and Joachim von Frankenberg.)

Martha Reimann's letters embody the deep love of nature that Gerard Wagner and some of those close to him had. Reading letters written to Gerard Wagner generally one is struck by the warmth and sincerity but also by the respectful formality of address which reminds one of how the characters in Rudolf Steiner's Mystery Plays address one another. In June 1944, Martha Reimann wrote:

> 6 June 1944
>
> Dear Herr Wagner
>
> Here we are in our little mountain-pine-panelled apartment on the attic floor of the house with a view of the lake, forest, green meadows and mountains with everlasting snow. Below us live a family, the parents are members, with three charming children, of about 6, 4 and 1. The boy, almost 6, is so quiet and full of wonder, that speech is not forthcoming. The girl has large dark eyes in a delicate oval-shaped little head with dark, straight, fine hair, held together with a little white headband, wonderful little graceful hands, a silver-bright laugh that can sound very mischievous; she loves to play with Johannes. He tells them fairy stories, moulds clay with them, romps about, jokes and laughs with them, builds mountains and tunnels in the sandpit, then they dream away on the swing or go to the little one, who is just learning to stand on his little legs and is glad of cheerful company ...
>
> The area is unusually stimulating – crystal clear streams everywhere, many, many trout in the lake, which shimmers in a wonderful play of colours – different at each time of the day, marvellously inspiring for a painter!
>
> Then the light green meadows and woodland glades with the chalice gentians, which I like to call 'Lord God's eyes', between them the yellow sulphur anemones, which Johannes has christened 'moonshine anemones', the violet, perfumed mountain pansies and the reddish primula.
>
> Then the bright larches and the dark-green mountain pines. There are some spots known to be places where deer have eaten; an archetypal memory of the Ancient Indians rises up, yes, even of the Garden of Paradise – imagine the snow-covered mountains that look down onto such pastures where no human foot has trod. And under the living eye of the sun, the lake with the rainbow shining over it.

So here we live, and gradually I rise out of my tomb and feel the wings of the eagle and tell Johannes about Elijah. Johannes has not had one single headache, grows strong as a mountain tree, can rampage like the wind and be gentle with the flowers, today he asked again and again about Dr Steiner, and wants soon to send Herr Steffen flowers. Now I've told enough. How I'd like to hear about your pictures or better see them – you're smiling. Well, I like that smile and send a loving greeting.
Your M. Reimann and Johannes

18 June 1944
Dear Herr Wagner
Your paintings brought me so much joy. It is as if they are embedded in and at the same time rise up out of our present sphere of experience. We take our early walk in the clear light of morning and midday and the sun sparkles on the surface of blue beside us; we ascend on a lovely, little winding woodland path, passing emerald green meadows over which butterflies flit in the sunlit air; through the larches and forest pines we hear the mountain wind rustling and in the distance see the snow-covered mountains shine; Johannes discovers an ancient pine growing upwards straight as a die, its wonderful roots anchored in the granite ground beneath, and the child caresses the roots with such inwardness, and, standing beneath the protective mantle of the trunk, looks upwards with pleasure and lets out a triumphant cry; there, on sunny meadows surrounded by woodland, the deer eat and taste the herbs fresh with dew, and we hold our breath and absorb the fragrance of these sacred wonders – of sun, of resin, of herbs all mixed together; and we feel the holy spirit celebrating a resurrection in nature and in its elemental beings: 'The human being only redeems the elements when the holy spirit burns within him.'

Children, born of nature, are the kings of this sacred world. Grown-ups can become so through the awakening of the spirit. As the present unites past and future, so future aims grow clearer and more definite. I would not know how one could contemplate a trumpet Gentian without being guided by living thinking, with I-understanding, so to speak, with awakened eyes of spirit, and by an 'easy' leap arrive at discovery of the archetypal plant. The plant is surrounded by this purple-crimson colour. Even the gnome-world is astounded, and strange feelings arise in them.

Oh – what I say to you are only stumbling words, meagre bits and pieces from a realm of experience and knowledge, which, to begin with, finds its rebirth only in a certain inner creativity. …

Hearing about your work or seeing it, is always a pleasure. Do I need to say more? Heartfelt greetings, also from Johannes. M. Reimann

The six years of war (1939–1945), with little interaction between Dornach and the 'outside world', could be seen as an incubation period for the development of Gerard Wagner's work. Rex Raab met the painter at the end of the war and was impressed by what he saw:

I believe I was about the first English visitor to Dornach after World War 2. I was on a mission to the Red Cross 'Commission Mixte' in Geneva, and had to rest in Switzerland for a fortnight before the things for refugee camps in Austria were ready for me to fetch. I stayed in Dornach of course until I had to return to Austria.

On the snowy evening of my arrival, mid-December 1945, I went to Desmond Armstrong, the next day I looked up Gerard Wagner. It was wonderful to see the quiet progress he had been making during those six long years of war. I found him in a room and observed that this artist almost always had the curtains drawn. It was like being in the half-light of the forest the whole time. I was therefore fascinated to recognise something similar albeit unintentional, in the 'Hubertus' motif that had recurred a number of times during the intervening years. I continue to be very fond of the way in which Gerard has introduced this motif in such an unconventional way into his work. Unstintingly Gerard showed me the many and varied watercolours from his ceaselessly productive workshop. One picture particularly struck me, an upright format with many smaller figures, light against dark, towering above one another.

We got to talking about the task of painting walls, of creating a meeting between architecture and painting, as I believe Rudolf Steiner, in keeping with all true artists, intended us to. Suddenly Gerard exclaimed with an unexpectedly choleric tone: 'I would like to paint a mural with that motif, where the figures are three times natural size!' My rapid assessment: the wall would have to be at least 25 metres high! Then I recognized what a towering artist was active in Gerard's unassuming exterior. My parting remark was this: when I got back into architectural practice I would like to create some walls for you to paint such murals on! It was eleven or twelve years before I could offer Gerard a wall, although it was not 30 metres high, but only a tenth of that height. But from this arose a good picture, one that brought a melancholy businesswoman much solace.[78]

*

In Florian Roder's interesting research into biography,[79] including the lives of well-known artists, he observed that the period coinciding with the 2nd moon node at 37–38 years of age (37 years, two months and 20 days to be precise), is often characterised by change and upheaval, sometimes dramatic and painful, which can mean a breaking up of the past and the beginning of something new. Or in some cases it can signify the breaking out of an illness, or even the end of life, as was the case with the painters Raphael and van Gogh. On the other hand the moon node can coincide with a breaking out, a blossoming of something that has lain dormant and can now emerge into the world.

In the life of Gerard Wagner both these aspects are apparent. In April 1943 he was 37 years old. Three years earlier his long-dormant work began to be publicly exhibited in the Goetheanum exhibitions. The influence of his work was initially felt in the immediate surroundings of Dornach, then in other places in Switzerland. And through the international participants at Goetheanum conferences, which brought visitors from far afield, it then began to reach further into other countries.

At the same time, despite the appreciation of a more intimate circle, his work was generally met with little understanding or recognition. This had an inhibiting effect on his reputation and the sale of his paintings, which in turn increased the solitary, inner nature of his work. In time, small communities of people interested in learning from him grew up. The *way* he worked became something he was led to share with others; and through the pupils who would find him and come to know him personally he would find recognition of a different kind.

Connections with England

In the mid-1940s and in the immediate post-war years, Gerard Wagner was looking toward England for exhibiting and promoting his work. In the summer of 1946 he made the first post-war visit to his mother, and in January 1947 he was in London with his brother Felix, showing his work to Ernest Brown of Leicester Galleries, who exhibited works of modern British and French painters. For Ernest Brown though, Wagner's work was 'too religious' and the paintings were rejected.

Ella Wetherall, a teacher at Michael Hall School in Sussex, and former pupil of Wagner's, wrote in October and November 1943. She suggested Wagner might exhibit at the Archer Galleries in London, and give a painting course in England. Her letter also shows that in her eyes the 37-year-old artist was already recognised as the significant instigator of a new impulse, even though his work had as yet met with little understanding. In her second letter below, she hints at the depth of his research in painting (see italics):

22 November 1943

Dear Gerry Wagner,

It was so very nice to get your long letter, sometime in June it arrived. Hearing from you always fills me with the great hope that someday it will be possible to have more lessons with you. What you will find to correct may give you cold shivers. Often, I wonder how you manage about the material things of life in these days and hope you get enough of the real necessities …

Your account of your own studio is most interesting, I think you may well be one of the very few who will attain to a true knowledge of the new impulse in this life. I shall not, at most I shall only prepare the way for the future. That you will find very little understanding is inevitable, but it seems to me, we cannot estimate what the present world tragedy will develop in some people. To be alive to this development seems to be our especial task, and 'oh ye gods and little fishes' no one in England seems aware of it. I can well believe that signs of a new age are showing in the younger generation in Dornach. You perhaps know old Dr Morris? She has a picture gallery and would certainly welcome anything you could bring over. It is what she longs for and can never get.

The house at Hampstead has become a sort of art centre, Val Jacobs teaches speech, and Waltraut Offerman has several classes and private pupils for eurythmy, but to live in that huge house without domestic help is a hard job and needs great physical strength. It becomes a question, as everywhere today, of the survival of the fittest.

This may reach you round about Christmas so I send you greetings and thoughts for Christmas and join you all at Dornach for what we long for in the New Year.

Yours

Ella Wetherall

1 October 1944

Dear Gerry Wagner

It was extremely nice to get your letter and more than kind of you to spend a brief holiday in writing it. I have read it with the deepest interest. … If you came to England, and I hope you will for a bit, you would find it worthwhile to restrict your teaching to people who could really benefit by it and make use of it. A place of your own is essential, Jean understood, as one simply cannot work anywhere else. I shall be very glad to help you find a place, though it may not be easy. It would certainly be immensely worthwhile to bring work for exhibitions and I am certain old Dr Morris would exhibit everything you had, at the Archer Galleries. She opened the galleries especially for work from Dornach, then the war came and she has had to depend on work which makes you ill to look at.

It was most interesting hearing of your teaching experiences, and your young friend Johannes [Reimann] sounds a gifted little person …

What you said about colour leading to an understanding of the laws which work before birth and after death is true, I feel, and those who can develop through such study are fortunate, but there are people who seem to need the shocks of war to break down their hard mental outlook. Even though one is aware of the calmer way of growth, the experience of imminent and great danger can have a strangely awakening effect. …

This is an unpardonably long letter and there are still things I should like to write, but it will be better to leave them until such time as it is possible to talk in freedom. When I get depressed about the state of things here your letter will give comfort and inspiration; and I shall remember that you too must have had, and still be having a rottenly difficult time. I pray that more people will want to buy your works.

With all good wishes for your continued success, Yours Ella Wetherall

P. S. Michael Hall teachers asked me to give them lessons in the early spring. It was the best class I have ever had, they were much cleverer than me and Mr. Darrell was a wonderful pupil. He would certainly send you his greetings if he knew I was writing.

In a post-war letter in September 1945 from Julie Wagner to her son Felix, she writes:

Gerry's account of conditions in Switzerland is most interesting, and his reflections on character too. I enclose his letter now as you will have more time in Mullion to read it than in Bethel Orchard. I hope to reply to it this weekend.

And a 1946 letter from his mother likewise gives the impression that her son was looking to renew his contacts in England. She also refers to her eldest son Roland who had died three years earlier, in 1943 in Wiesbaden.

Dearest Gerard

Today, 4 March, is a date indelibly engraved on my memory – the birthday of my first-born Roland, that tragic child. He was a lovely baby – too good and quiet – but I, being quite ignorant of the usual noisy ways of healthy babies, did not realise that it was a virtue in my opinion only.

Many thanks for your letter, postmarked Feb 27th, which came on Saturday – quick work – almost pre-war now. I sent a Red X letter on Feb 21st to Gretel Breslich, as she was the only one in Wiesbaden who had managed to get a letter through brought by an Englishman to London – it was written in October. She said Dr Lugenbühl and his wife, were staying in her home in the Dambachtal, their home having been destroyed in the bombardment, so I asked her to get a message of greeting through to them from me, also to Kleins and Daelens; the Red X form allows only between 25–30 words – so I could not say much. We are told now that in April ordinary letters to Germany will be allowed – so of course I shall write to my Wiesbaden friends then, and trust that they have not moved from their old addresses. *Do* write *now* and say I shall write when allowed.

I am most interested in what you say about the Waldorf schools – what an opportunity is theirs now to counteract the hateful Nazi doctrines forced on young people for so many years. It is a very good sign that after all, the spirit of goodness and truth can never be killed, however much its outward signs are hidden. I shall write and tell Miss Norbury about it – also ask her whether Frances Melland – who has her home in Stroud, Gloucestershire, is ever in London; also, who the secretary of the Anthropop. Society in London is now.

April is too soon for England – the earliest you should come over is May, not only because it may be warmer then, but because before and during Easter week and the following few days the railways will be crowded with holiday makers, I certainly don't intend to travel before May – which will be a quieter month than April or June.

I wish you could have seen the Matisse-Picasso pictures, shown here from Feb 21- March 6, and have given me your opinion and comments on them. Never have we had such crowds, 5000 the first day! Lectures going on throughout the day there. I can see the beauty? and genius? in most of the Matisse works there – also the fine colouring in Picasso, but some of Ps are simply horrible – perverse-ugly, all painted in war time, 1940–45 in Paris. I will keep the catalogue to show you. I am trying to understand Picasso's aim in these works – have been twice and I shall go again tomorrow if I get to town. Have you seen any of his? French art is a subject for itself, I wish I had a good book on it.

I won't begin another sheet, as I was just about to do. Will send this off now and write again soon. It is like you, my dearest, to send food to starving Germans, but I'm afraid it will mean you starving too! We are not allowed to send food out of England.

Much love and every good wish,
Mother

After giving a donation to a child refugee in Basel, Gerard Wagner received this response in February 1944:

Dear Herr Wagner,
Many thanks for the loving consideration which you gave our child refugee and which we received through Miss Wedgwood. The nice little picture added a special personal touch to your donation. That in itself would have been enough to convince me of your friendly feelings towards the little homeless one.

Respectfully
Bella Prijs

Anthroposophical painters in England and their connection with Rudolf Steiner

Letters written to Gerard Wagner show that developments within the Anthroposophical Society in England interested him deeply, and he would have been aware of painters developing the work there who had had a connection to Rudolf Steiner. Three of the better-known anthroposophical painters in England had received personal instruction from Rudolf Steiner and this gave their work particular relevance. They were Arild Rosenkranz (1870–1964), Eleanor C. Merry (1873–1956), and Gladys Mayer (1888–1980).

During the 1940s, Eleanor Merry, together with Maria Schindler, ran a painting school and exhibited in London galleries. In 1953 the painter Gladys Mayer founded the Mercury Arts Group which organised art classes, exhibitions and publications. The illustrated text book *The Mystery Wisdom of Colour* presented fundamental exercises of rhythmical metamorphosis in seven pictures developed by her – see Appendix 4.

Baron Arild Rosenkranz was one of a team of artists who painted the small cupola of the first Goetheanum according to Rudolf Steiner's suggestions, and was given the all-important task of painting the central motif – the 'Christ figure between Lucifer and Ahriman'. Gladys Mayer wrote of the support Rosenkranz gave other painters in England after Rudolf Steiner's death:

> It was characteristic of his really noble character of quiet modesty and dignity that Rosenkranz, though having a far keener and more intimate experience of what had been achieved in the destroyed cupola – paintings accomplished in plant colours in such amazingly colourful, transparent and harmonious weaving forms – did not set himself up as an authority as to how we should continue. He confined himself to making helpful suggestions as to how we might work individually on an agreed theme, and met from time to time to compare our work. ... I met him next a few years later in London, where he commented helpfully on work I showed him, and soon began to send me pupils, treating me as a fellow-artist collaborating in this immensely difficult new task.[80]

Arild Rosenkranz was a dedicated pupil of Rudolf Steiner and recognised his greatness as an artist. He wrote in his important essay, 'Rudolf Steiner, The Artist':

> Rudolf Steiner always spoke modestly about his work as an artist and ever reiterated that the Goetheanum was but a small beginning. He looked for co-operation from artists to help him by their technical knowledge and experience, and one of the saddest points in connection with the loss of the old Goetheanum is that the art world gave no assistance, no encouragement when the building was still there. He was left alone to battle for the regeneration of art, assisted by only a handful of pupils. Little or no understanding for what he arrived at was formed in those quarters where his help could bear most fruit for art. Like the work of all great pioneers, his art was ahead of his time.[81]

Eleanor Merry met Rudolf Steiner in England on various occasions and was instrumental in the organisation of two summer schools there: in 1923 at Penmaenmawr, North Wales, and in 1924 at Torquay, Devon, during which Dr Steiner gave two significant lecture cycles. Unfortunately the instructions he gave Eleanor Merry for a new painting technique have not been documented. She recalled the Penmaenmawr conference as follows:

> ... As I had a good deal to do with the arrangements I saw Dr Steiner every day, and with a few others went with him when we had an excursion to visit the Druid circle in the mountains above the little town of Penmaenmawr ... He made a remarkable sketch afterwards, representing the interior of the earth during a Druidical act of worship. Below the surface of the earth worked and brooded elemental spirits, above them Druid priests conducted their ceremonies at the altar under the sun's rays; and a sign, representing the guardian of the threshold, guarded the approach to the altar, as if to keep the heart of knowledge from antagonistic beings ...
>
> When I returned to London I decided that among my many and various activities I would be able to find time to continue my painting, introducing as well as I could the new technique which Dr Steiner had explained to me at Penmaenmawr ...
>
> Already in May of that year I heard he was in Paris, so I decided to go there ... I told him about my efforts at painting according to his methods, and as I meant to exhibit some of my work at Torquay, I wished so much he had seen them beforehand. He replied: 'I have seen your paintings' and I said, 'No, Herr Doctor. You haven't seen them; they are all in London.' He said again, 'I have seen them.' I contradicted him, and for the third time he repeated that he had seen them, looking at me with his intense dark gaze. Then for the first time, I realised that he had indeed seen them, but not with earthly sight.[82]

Gladys Mayer, as already mentioned, came to Dornach in 1924 and was able to guide Gerard Wagner when he first arrived there in 1926. Like Eleanor Merry, she also had remarkable experiences with Rudolf Steiner in regard to her painting. She described how he began teaching her – but spiritually. When meditating on one of her own paintings she asked herself how it might look to her teacher. She recalled: 'I saw immediately my own picture, looking hopelessly muddy and grey. "How should it have been?" I queried. I saw my picture transformed into radiant transparent colour.'[83]

Through his personal contact to Gladys Mayer, Gerard Wagner was given a direct line back to Rudolf Steiner as artist, and being of the following generation he was in a position to be able to begin from scratch with the indications Steiner had given as a training for painters. In this sense his work can be seen as a continuation of those earlier artists and the 'English' painting stream.

The painter Raphaela Cooper, once a pupil of Gladys Mayer, described her impressions of the artist and her first meeting with Gerard Wagner in a conversation with the author in 2009:

> I first met Gladys Mayer at her home in Scarsdale Villas in Kensington when I was only 18 and my art teacher Norma Weller had encouraged me to look up things to do with the Anthroposophical Society and its artistic impulses. A person at Rudolf Steiner House, London, told me about Gladys Mayer and I decided to visit her. She invited me to visit her and see her paintings. My first impression was that she seemed almost transparent, with shining deep-set eyes and her beautiful white hair was swept back from her brow and held with a silver headband. She was tall and slim, with very expressive artistic hands. She wore a 'Steiner-crafted', 'anthroposophical' ring on her fourth finger.
>
> I later joined her Sunday afternoon painting classes in her own studio and attended the Mercury Arts festivals. She also produced a regular newsletter called by the same name, Mercury Arts Newsletter. When teaching she spoke in a living and colourful way about the nature of colour and we would do exercises based on one, two or three colours. There were plant motifs, sunsets and sunrises, and themes we might bring ourselves.
>
> Rudolf Steiner was her personal teacher. She had been suffering from asthma all her life (and tuberculosis) and Steiner gave her a special breathing exercise which involved standing by an open window and breathing in while counting up to 30. She wasn't allowed to meet Steiner (he kept putting her off) until she had seen his true being. She had experiences one night in which Steiner visited her spiritually and she saw his light-filled radiant aura, and then he allowed her to visit him in his study and talk to him.
>
> I met Gerard Wagner in 1968 when I came with an English group to see the Mystery Plays. Gladys Mayer took me along to meet Gerard Wagner in his studio. He began to show us little painting exercises of many different sorts of motifs and talked about them, telling us about all his research into colour. When he showed us the metamorphosis paintings

I exclaimed 'How beautiful!' but he replied, 'I am not concerned about it being beautiful, it is more important that it is true.' Gladys Mayer said 'I am a Jack of all trades but Gerard Wagner has taken painting much further than I have or anyone else I know because he just concentrated on painting.' They were deeply fond of each other and had deep mutual respect even if her approach to colour was slightly different in some ways.

Dornach 1950–1969

A TEACHER OF PAINTING

The early 1950s were a turning point for Gerard Wagner and his work; and one reason for this was undoubtedly the arrival in Dornach of a 27-year-old sculptress named Elisabeth Koch (see Appendix 5) who in 1950 hitchhiked to Dornach from Hannover to see the Mystery Plays at the Goetheanum. There she saw some of Gerard Wagner's paintings in an exhibition and was immediately so moved by them that she decided to find the artist and become his pupil.

Unknown to her, he lived very close to where she had made a nest – accessed only by ladder – up in the loft of the joinery workshop at Eckinger House. As she later recalled, she saw the name Wagner on the Eckinger House front door and rang the bell. He showed her his work and she asked for painting lessons which he refused. She asked again on a second visit. On the third occasion her strong will prevailed, and he agreed to teach her. As payment she gathered food from the meadows, cooked for him, darned the socks she found in a large basket, 'all with holes in them', and helped in any way she could.

In his studio she discovered 'under the bed' numerous paintings and sketches which needed putting in order, and she used her talents to help present his work by making mounts and folders. She also helped prepare the surfaces for his large paintings on wood. In time she became Gerard Wagner's most ardent spokesperson and representative, and her confidence in the importance of his work was something that sustained him through the years.

A talented artist in drawing and painting herself, Elisabeth had studied and worked with the well-known sculptor August Waterbeck in Hannover.[84] Whilst still at school she joined her aunt, who had herself studied with the sculptor, on a visit to Waterbeck's studio and while the adults were conversing Elisabeth quietly busied herself with some clay. Waterbeck saw what she had done, recognised her talent, and said she should come and study with him. She was his pupil for seven years, from the age of 17, and subsequently took independent commissions, mostly of portraits and headstones, and exhibited her own work. Her wish to find the right person to teach her painting remained unfulfilled until she found Gerard Wagner.

Another significant event in the early 1950s for Gerard Wagner was the death of his beloved mother. Julie Wagner died on 27 February 1952 at the age of 83, at her home in Didsbury, Manchester. Gerard Wagner was present together with his brother Felix, and Gertrude Neild, the sister closest to her.

It seems as if Julie Wagner felt able to conclude her earthy life once the person who was to support her son and his work had come into his life. Gerard Wagner's sister-in-law Dorothy Wagner wrote to him many years later: 'Whenever you mention Elisabeth, I think of your mother, and how thankful she would have been to know that Elisabeth was with you.'

With the money left to him in his mother's will being 'more than I expected', as he wrote to his brother Felix, the impoverished painter now found himself on firmer ground financially. Requests for painting lessons came from various quarters. A painting course in Zurich began at some point in the 1950s, and he also taught at the Goetheanum, where a painting school was officially inaugurated in January 1953 under the direction of the painters Theodor Ganz, Emil Schweigler and Lili Wadler-Bosshard. Painting courses given by Gerard Wagner also accompanied conferences at the Goetheanum.

Jocelyn Walsh (1923–2013) was in Dornach for six months in 1955 and took lessons with Gerard Wagner at the Goetheanum. She recalled:

> Painting took place in the North Roof studio, and there were three teachers at that time – Ganz, Schweigler and Wagner – each allocated two days for their teaching. They all based it on Rudolf Steiner's sketches but each had his own method. I worked with Schweigler and with Wagner. The painter Georg Meier was busy with filters and smelly substances in his 'kitchen corner' on the landing outside the studio, making a start with plant-colour production.
>
> I stayed at Eckinger Haus, on the same floor where Gerard Wagner lived. On the big landing you could cook; the bathroom was downstairs. In the very early days Gerard Wagner had very little to live on; he sometimes tended peoples' fires and did some gardening work. He was left food at the door. When Wagner's mother visited Dornach someone told her how little money he had for food.
>
> When I returned to Dornach in the early 1960s with my daughter Fiona, Ganz had died, Schweigler had retired and Wagner was teaching on Saturdays in the Sketches Room, where I took lessons with him.

The Sketches Room is where the original sketches and drawings by Rudolf Steiner were made available for those wanting to copy and work with them. Jocelyn Walsh recalled how daylight was kept out by long blue curtains which one was allowed to pull back on cloudy days, and in the middle of the room were showcases of pencil sketches. The training sketches done in pastel were hung on the wall and at the bottom edge of the frames one could see how much pastel dust had fallen from the pictures, which gave an idea of the strength of the original colours. When not being viewed, the sketches were covered with thick drapes.

In 1954, the first request for Wagner to teach outside Switzerland came from two teachers of the Engelberg Waldorf School, near Stuttgart – Ilse Molly, the handwork teacher and master dressmaker, and Rolf Adler, the craft teacher. They wanted help with developing the handwork impulse Rudolf Steiner had included in the Waldorf curriculum. Gerard Wagner and Rolf Adler had met earlier in Dornach when Rolf was studying at the Goetheanum Sculpture School, where he played a major role in the development of craft-teacher training.

The courses took place initially in 1954, 1955 and 1956, and according to Elisabeth Adler, Wagner's way of teaching took some getting used to:

> We sat rather close together at tables in one of the classrooms and began to paint on small boards with stretched paper. There were no introductory words – we simply had to begin. That was it – and it was not easy for some. Only during the process of painting came the instructions – out of a 'feeling-seeing'. That is how I would describe it today.

Rolf Adler (1922–1995) and his wife Elisabeth (1925–2014), a eurythmy teacher at the Engelberg School too, were both gifted artists, and dedicated to the new artistic impulses in various forms. As quiet, modest seekers of art and the spirit, they lived wholly with their questions and convictions, and in Gerard Wagner they found a kindred spirit. Wagner stayed in their small flat in Engelberg, enjoying their company and Elisabeth's home cooking when he visited Engelberg. At the end of the course he was always given a jar of honey. The course for teachers at the Engelberg School grew to be a regular and well-attended event with Wagner teaching there for a period of eight years.

On 9 September 1956 he wrote to his brother Felix about teaching at the Goetheanum during the Summer Conference and his teaching work at Engelberg. An exhibition of Wagner's work was also being organised:

> Dear Felix
> I need not say that I am not a good letter writer, but I had meant to write to you for your birthday a month ago. My time was very taken up just then – the Summer Conference was on. Goethe's Faust was being performed three times, unshortened, each performance lasted a week, with a few lectures in between. Not that I attended all that – Faust was sold out and I had seen most of the dress rehearsal – also in former days I've

seen it, and as a Dornacher one doesn't go when it is full up, but I was giving a painting course to a number of summer visitors, and though officially it lasted about two hours a day, I spread them over the greater part of each day as well. It isn't possible to teach sixteen people anything worthwhile in painting if one has them all together for only two hours a day. I'm more accustomed to having single pupils, and then for only two or three hours at once, and if one has them for a few years and they practice a lot, and if they are gifted, one can attain to something. These flying courses are of little value, – I jumped into this one because there was nobody else who was not either ill or away. It was not unwelcome practice for a much more satisfactory course which I gave immediately afterwards to a group of teachers near Stuttgart. They had asked me to work with them during the last week of their holidays, and had kept their whole time free for painting – about fourteen of them.

The school – for about 300 children – lies fairly high amongst wonderful country – wooded hills and overlooking wide plains with villages here and there. In the immediate neighbourhood only very few houses, a very peaceful, shielded atmosphere, and, one felt it at once, very much healthier air and soil than ours in Dornach. And the people very nice – some I had known before I went. To the great surprise of most of them, we painted for a week for seven or eight hours a day – they had not thought they could hold out for even half as long – but in the end they only stopped working because the daylight went, and would have liked to go on – next year I am going there again for a continuation.

For the near future – end of October or beginning of November – I am to have a small show in Rome of about 20 paintings in a very good gallery which I can use rent-free. The owner was here a few days ago to see what I was sending (he had seen three paintings in Rome which a friend showed him, and on the strength of which he invited me). Even without rent, the expenses are pretty big – a catalogue with a coloured reproduction, publicity etc, seven hundred francs, then transport, and then myself, whom I hope to take to Rome also while the show is on – and a visit to Florence and perhaps one or two other places also – my former pupil Elisabeth Koch, who is independent of my teaching now and paints very well, is coming too. I'll let you know how it goes. I'm very much looking forward to seeing Raphael and Michelangelo in the Vatican.

The exhibition of Gerard Wagner's painting took place in Rome at the La Medusa, Studio D'Arte, and showed works from 1945 –1956. Elisabeth Koch meanwhile, after five years as a pupil of Gerard Wagner, was already producing her own impressive paintings and had begun exhibiting her work; her paintings were first shown at Goetheanum exhibitions in 1956. She had also begun to study eurythmy.

In 1956 Gerard Wagner celebrated his 50th birthday. His paintings of the Great Baptism, a central theme of his work around that time, marked the high point of his artistic oeuvre up until then. The large paintings of this 1950s period are strikingly dramatic. In the dark, intense colours and clear-cut imagery, the works tell of inner trials and mysteries, and of battles between the powers of light and darkness. And in different versions of the theme of the Baptism in Jordan, the esoteric significance of this defining event in world history is portrayed.

Theodor Willmann, (see Appendix 6), Wagner's close colleague, wrote in the monograph on the artist about the background and significance of the Baptism motif within the esoteric truths of Christianity, and aptly characterised the dramatic mood of these Baptism paintings:

> In a different way, standing between Egyptian past and Greco-Roman future, the consciousness of the Hebraic-Israelite Yahve religion became manifest, creatively integrating the depth dimensions of the geological forces of the earth itself from Mosaic initiation in Egypt and finding in Palestine's geological constitution something like an imprint of the most significant evolutionary stages in earth's history.
>
> Desert and salt lake characterise the stern circumference. The verdant paradisiacal nature of Galilei at Lake Genezareth in the North, the temple-hill sites of Jerusalem, the Jordan valley lying 100 metres below sea level, deserts of soul-loneliness, characterise the field of tension in the mood of the Hebraic mysteries: expectation of redemption, the trials of temptation, prophecy of sun mysteries within the darkness of the soul. 'The Jordan between the Lake of Life and the Ocean of Death is an image of human incarnation that unfolds between the pre-birth realm and the salt-bearing element of death.' (Emil Bock)
>
> Here, Gerard Wagner's art of colour takes up the theme of the Jordan baptism, the cosmic birth (Gospels of Mark and John) in dramatic, painterly contrasts.
>
> This, after all, relates significantly to the midwinter threshold of the morning sun's resurgent ascent, in the period between Adam and Eve

Day on 24 December, the midwinter solstice point, to the sun's renascence on Three Kings' Day. The figure of John is the prophetic midpoint of the geologically determined mystery of the earth's depths between the heavenly revelation and annunciation to the shepherds, and the kings' offerings of 'gold, frankincense and myrrh': the prophetic words of the Baptist, 'Change your ways', the baptism itself, like an initiation immersion below the deep surface of the winter water element of the Jordan, and the retrospective vision thus kindled in souls of the paradisiacal innocence and the culpable Fall of humanity is sanctified through the prophecy of the fire-sun revelation of the I AM: 'Illum oportet crescere, me autem minui' (He must increase, I must decrease).

In his own death by decapitation, the Baptist suffers at first hand the question of the death mystery of the 'place of the skulls', Golgotha. The destiny question of rebirth kindles to unique expression in his figure, as if from the sphere-aura of the fire chariot of Elijah: he was Elijah. He is the prophetic seer of the Christos, the son of God now come to birth through the Jordan baptism.

Through the cosmic life of the three years of the Christ, from the Jordan baptism to the death at Golgotha, the curtain of the temple is rent: death becomes the birth of the I! In the revelation of the resurrection within death, the midpoint achievement of the earth as cosmic world cross – eagle, bull, lion, waterman – appears anew before the consciousness of humanity as the light that shines in the darkness.[85]

At 50 one might think an artist would be near reaching maturity in his work and goals but this was more like a beginning for Gerard Wagner, who went on to develop at least three more decisive periods of work, the final period spanning the last six years of his life between the ages of 87 and 93.

A TEACHER OF PAINTING

PATRONAGE AND CURATIVE COMMUNITY

The year 1956 was also significant for Gerard Wagner in that it brought a meeting with Frau Frida Lefringhausen (see Appendix 7) who would become the painter's most abiding and significant patron. She took part in the 1956 Michaelmas Conference at the Goetheanum and found herself a participant in the painting course Gerard Wagner was leading. His teaching impressed her as did his paintings, and she returned home to north Germany with about half a dozen small works as her first purchase. The paintings were duly framed in natural unstained wood, as Gerard Wagner preferred, and hung in a row in the 'Haus Arild' community music room. From then on Gerard Wagner's paintings became part and parcel of life in that community.

Haus Arild is a 'Curative and Educational Institute for Children and Adolescents with Special Needs' which developed from work with traumatised children and orphans undertaken by Frida Lefringhausen and co-workers at a home in Hamburg's Bergedorf district during the Second World War. When the war ended they moved with 20 of the children to Bliestorf, a small rural village not far from Lübeck, and settled into an old forester's lodge. Before long, further homes were built to accommodate the growing number of children and teenagers; then a school with hall and stage were added, a farm came into being, then a kindergarten and a training course for curative education. All this constituted the 'Haus Arild' community.

A significant aspect of Frau Lefringhausen's initiative was the inclusion of art and the value she attached to it. And so the buildings and the grounds were made beautiful, not for aesthetic reasons in a narrow sense, but with Rudolf Steiner's pedagogical suggestion in mind that children between the ages of seven and fourteen should experience the world as beautiful.[86] A parent of a special needs child at the school there wrote in the anniversary booklet '50 Years of Haus Arild':

> Frida Lefringhausen had a great deal of fantasy, energy, and zeal for achieving her initiatives. She gave particular importance to beautiful surroundings in which her charges could grow up, and in time building after building appeared, in whose rooms all the arts were nurtured, particularly music and eurythmy. No one could escape when Frau Kistenbrügge gathered anyone who happened to be there to join in the

choral singing! Everything that happened in these rooms breathed the spirit of anthroposophy, which for the founder and her closest co-worker, was what it was all about.

The co-worker Susanne Wulff composed the following mottos as 'leading thoughts' for the practice and experience of art at Haus Arild:

> When everyday life is fashioned and irradiated by art, one can experience the human being's source origin in the spirit.
>
> Practising the fine arts tends to lead people to themselves, while the musical and literary arts enhance the community.
>
> Encounters with art raise the human spirit. Essentially it is not so important whether one creates art oneself or whether one experiences art by looking and perceiving.
>
> Through repeated observation and participation in the colour and form of a painting, or in the configured motion of a sculpture, one's being is enlivened, ordered, stimulated or focused.[87]

Susanne Wulff recalled how Frida Lefringhausen was inspired by the correlation she found between communal life and painting. During painting courses with Gerard Wagner she had learned how one colour behaves in relation to another, how the addition of a new colour causes a change in the colours already present on the page and so on. She said to him 'I am looking for this in the life of society – how a person changes what others have already done, and how something new can arise between them.' Wagner responded by saying: 'That's a difficult path – my paper is patient!'

The co-workers at Haus Arild regularly visited Dornach. Frau Lefringhausen was keen that her co-workers should attend conferences at the Goetheanum, and take part in a painting course with Gerard Wagner or with Elisabeth Koch. Susanne Wulff was one of those co-workers:

> Four of us were sent to the 1956 Christmas Conference at the Goetheanum, and those of us who were not members of the Anthroposophical Society and could not attend all the events, had free time and were able to paint with Elisabeth Koch. This took place in her small, narrow room at Haus Wundt. We walked up a dark flight of stairs to one of the top floors. There were no easels so we put our painting boards on the bed and lent them against the wall. We began painting yellow, from the centre, raying out into the periphery. That was a long process – a 'moral'

experience which only became clear to me much later. Blue followed with the question as to where it could be most effective in relation to the yellow. As it was my favourite colour at that time, I remember very clearly how the relationship to yellow came about through ever more transparency at its border with blue. I was quite content with these two colours but we had a teacher who encouraged us to take red as well! The 'mission' of red was to come to the assistance of yellow, and that could only be effective if it came to the centre of the picture, and in the places where yellow allowed entry. Some of the lovely meetings between yellow and blue had to be sacrificed to the red. That was also a 'moral' process.

As relaxation between our intensive work, we were able to look out of the window westwards towards Landskrone Hill and further to Mont Sainte-Odile. I don't know any more how many hours the painting lessons took, but after the final lesson we were dismissed with hopeful wishes and an invitation to continue another time. With thankfulness we left the little room in which we had experienced so much.

It was also usual during the 1960s and 70s for almost every co-worker from Haus Arild to attend a Goetheanum conference during the year, and a painting course with Elisabeth Koch was always a part of this visit.

During the 1956 visit, the Haus Arild co-workers also visited Wagner, the master painter, in his studio. Susanne Wulff remembered:

We visited Gerard Wagner in his studio next to the joinery workshop in Eckinger House. It was a small room with a few chairs and an iron stove, and many pictures were stacked up against the wall. He showed us rows of plant metamorphosis sequences, pointing out the changing form of the plant emerging through the different coloured backgrounds of each sheet of paper. None of us had ever come across anything like this before so we reacted with silent awe. After Gerard Wagner had asked Frau Lefringhausen in a telephone call why we had remained silent, we could only say that words failed us as we sat in reverence before these wonderful images.

In the summer of 1958 Gerard Wagner, assisted by Elisabeth Koch, created murals in the music room at Haus Arild. They were painted on specially primed boards that were attached to the walls. Susanne Wulff remembered how well and lovingly the two painters were looked after by Frida Lefringhausen, who had the sense they both needed it.

There was good food there, fresh vegetables and fruit from the garden and someone was sent to Lübeck to the renowned confectioners 'Niederegger' to get a number of the supremely delicious cakes from there, after Frau Lefringhausen noticed how much Gerard Wagner enjoyed them.

Thus Gerard Wagner's work was placed in a curative setting for the first time. This was due to Frida Lefringhausen. From the beginning, when the first pictures were brought back from Dornach, her complete trust in his practice of the art of painting led her to include the children in appreciation of his work. After gathering together for the evening song, they were led silently past the paintings in the music room.

In anticipation of a new batch of eagerly awaited works, Frau Lefringhausen wrote to Wagner in January 1972: 'We are extraordinarily happy that your pictures will soon be hanging here. The children will be prepared – I have already begun to create stories around them.'

Twenty-four years later, in 1982, the two painters were again at Haus Arild for the opening of the 'Gerard Wagner House', the only house there to bear the name of a person, in acknowledgment of the community's close association with the painter. Susanne Wulff recalled:

> They celebrated with cake, and the co-workers' children were invited as well. Gerard Wagner spoke with the children and asked them questions in a way that was so appropriate and understandable for them. They looked with wonder at this painting teacher, whom they did not know, but who showed so much warm interest in them.

A painting method for teaching special needs children was developed by Dorothea Kistenbrugge (1928–1995), Frida Lefringhausen's closest colleague. From 1956 she took part in painting courses in Dornach with Gerard Wagner and Elisabeth Koch, and later when preparing a thesis as part of her pedagogical training, she went to Dornach to research her subject and take painting lessons with Gerard Wagner. Her thesis, which was well received by Lübeck officialdom, was entitled: 'Painting with Special Needs Pupils Based on Rudolf Steiner's Anthroposophical View of the Human Being.'

Pupils gather

In 1959, during a festive performance of Goethe's *Faust* at the Goetheanum, a 20-year-old German mathematics student came across Gerard Wagner's work. This was Dr Ernst Schuberth (see Appendix 8) who later founded the Mannheim University for Waldorf Pedagogy. He recalled:

> As other young people at the end of their school education I met personalities who had meaning for my whole future life. Two of the most important people for me were the painters Gerard Wagner and his later wife Elisabeth Koch. To put their influence on me in context, an experience I had in Class 12 in the Wuppertal Waldorf School – a moment of destiny – is relevant.
>
> During an art lesson we were given the task of doing a watercolour copy of a painting by Monet, 'Pine Tree, Cap d'Antibes'. I worked hard but had the feeling I was getting nowhere – the colours just got stronger and stronger. Finally I was in total despair and asked Herr Donges for help. He looked piercingly at my picture, dipped his brush in the darkest blue and added a vivid brushstroke to the sea. Is that better? he asked. The whole painting changed: what before appeared too dark and lifeless had been brightened, and I was able to complete the picture to my satisfaction.
>
> Through this experience it was immediately clear to me that a painting is not essentially an imitation but is a wholeness in itself and has its own laws. Whoever wants to paint would need to learn the laws of pictorial space. From now on I had a new relation to painting. I bought painting material and started to paint. What I produced didn't satisfy me at all. I remained in rigid abstraction rather than producing anything alive or authentic. So it remained until summer 1959 when, with my friend and future wife Erika Seidel, I attended a cycle of the complete Faust performances at the Goetheanum in Dornach.

Having just arrived at the Goetheanum and been offered a free ticket for *Faust* in exchange for work, Ernst Schuberth took a stroll around the interior of the building:

> … I walked through the 'Wandelhalle' and came across an exhibition of pictures by anthroposophical painters. This was at the as yet unopened west entrance of the Goetheanum. The 'gallery' which was separated off by a black curtain, showed works by Jérôme Bessenich, Emil Schweigler, Karo Bergmann and other painters. I was somewhat surprised at the different styles and motifs; each seemed to be an artistic cosmos in itself. What united them was perhaps the use of watercolour as a medium, the vividness of colour and the predominate use of rainbow colours. In

style the pictures were more varied than I'd expected and I came to the positive conclusion: here is broadmindedness, openness for differences. But I had the question: What is anthroposophical about them? Where is the anthroposophy in them?

As I left the 'gallery' I saw further pictures on the grey concrete walls of the west staircase which made a vital and very different impression on me. From further away I saw the pictures simply as colour compositions and as I moved closer I recognised motifs and read the painter's name 'Gerard Wagner'.

I was deeply satisfied as I saw in these works an understanding for art and a discerning capacity. Openness for everything is acceptable, I thought, but the Goetheanum building itself called for an equivalent spirituality in painting. (I thought at the time that the pictures hung permanently along the staircase.) Wandering further I read an announcement for painting lessons with Gerard Wagner at Eckinger House in Dornach. That interested me. When asking the way to the artist's house I was told he was not teaching at present, but that there would be a painting class with Elisabeth Koch, a pupil of his, in the North Studio at 2 p.m.

There I met the course leader, a small, slight person, who appeared older than she probably was. I think we began with the archetypal exercise of yellow-blue-red with the three colours painted in that order. As the lesson progressed a discussion arose about the objectivity of the colours and their relation to each other. I seized the moment and tried to explain what the teacher wanted from us. Much later I heard that Elisabeth said to Gerard Wagner afterwards: 'We have a new pupil.' The long painting association with the Wagners began during that conference in 1959, and in the following years I took part in many courses in the North Studio of the Goetheanum.

The intensive meeting with Gerard Wagner's work led me some time later to seek out as many people as possible with whom I could talk about its significance. I sought out the painter Jérôme Bessenich, Albert Steffen, and Louis Locher-Ernst, the director of Wintherthur Technical College and leader of the Mathematics and Astronomy Section at the Goetheanum. I showed him two sketches of animal metamorphosis. I will never forget the intense way in which he looked at the pictures and said: 'That is also higher mathematics!' With Bessenich I had an interesting conversation about Rudolf Steiner's suggestion of 'painting into the light', a theme which I later came across through Gerard Wagner. Albert Steffen was reserved: I could not perceive a particularly deep connection to Wagner's work. Gerard Wagner told me Albert Steffen once said to him he painted in 'too hard' a manner, and from then on Wagner started to bring softer colour transitions into his paintings.

Henceforth I came into closer contact with Gerard Wagner. In the holidays and university lecture-free periods I was in Dornach painting and earning my way by cleaning at the Goetheanum. In the summer of 1960 I was invited to join him and Elisabeth Koch for a two-week holiday in Graubunden, on the Heizenberg, in a small holiday flat in an old farmhouse. We took daily walks further into the mountains and read a cycle of lectures by Rudolf Steiner.

This contact with Gerard Wagner intensified when, between 1964 and 1966, I was in Dornach for a year and a half – first working with Georg Unger in the Mathematics and Physics Institute, and then as a student at the Dornach Teachers' Seminar. In my free time I painted either with Elisabeth Koch or with Gerard Wagner. Many conversations took place over this period. Wagner was well-informed and always showed a keen interest in current events and problems, so our conversations also included politics and the spiritual forces behind world events.

It was unforgettable how Gerard Wagner greeted visitors. If I had unexpectedly rung his bell and opened the front door, he would often appear at the top of the stairs and, as he recognised you, would make an open gesture of wonder and welcoming affection. A warm soul light shone down upon you.

His astoundingly healthy constitution can partly be ascribed to his rhythmical day, which went as follows: after breakfast some shopping (when necessary); painting until lunchtime; from about 2 p.m. teaching in the painting school; and afterwards, if the light allowed, further painting, or otherwise conversations with visitors. In the evenings he read or took part in courses and lectures at the Goetheanum.

Gerard Wagner had a calm, steady temperament. I never heard him express anger or agitation. If he was not happy with something it showed in his face. Only once when I asked him how he had experienced the difficulties within the Vorstand of the General Anthroposphical Society at the Goetheanum in the 1930s, he exclaimed with a certain sorrowful vehemence: 'What time and energy were lost for the important things!'

Susanne Wulff, who studied eurythmy in Dornach between 1960 and 1963, a period during which she also painted with Elisabeth Koch and Gerard Wagner, recalled how she perceived the artist at that time:

> Gerard Wagner made a striking impression when you saw him striding with others towards the Goetheanum for evening events. He was always dressed in dark clothes, and radiated an aura of 'elegant tranquillity'. His gait was rhythmical, consciously connecting with the ground and at the same time aiming uninterruptedly for his destination. When meeting someone on the way, a friendly greeting would be exchanged; I can't remember having a conversation with him or seeing anyone else in conversation with him on the way.
>
> In the Goetheanum, during events in the Great Hall and in the Foundation Stone Theatre, his seat was in the back row, the last seat on the right. If I remember rightly he stayed there during the intervals as well.
>
> His speech was very lively and for a German the British accent was quite charming. When teaching, he used few words but what he did say was to the point and understandable. Ultimately his corrections were given with the paintbrush, not through speech. His figure was delicate, his movements harmonious and purposeful. It was astounding to see how he used his brush, always finding the right 'tone' like a pianist, cellist or violinist.

PEDAGOGICAL IMPULSES

After his niece Mary was born in 1949, Gerard and Felix Wagner sometimes discussed the subject of pedagogy in their letters. It was a subject close to Gerard Wagner's heart. With concern for his young niece he introduced aspects of Waldorf pedagogy to his brother, in this letter of August 1962 in relation to drawing and painting:

> Dear Felix
> It would be a long job if one were to go into the subject you touched upon as regards education, even if one did so only from the angle of drawing and painting; but it's such an important one, that some time it should be tried.
>
> It is a question often in my mind, as I see a certain amount of teachers' work and what they do with pupils, and cannot help feeling how teachers should be trained – to become a teacher at least in painting – so as to produce the right effect on their pupils.
>
> There are so many theories and methods … I'm inclined to agree with the aim of working for a general all-round development of the faculties, artistic, practical and mental for as long as possible. But there does seem rather a 'helplessness' amongst teachers as regards artistic education, or rather the use of artistic activities as a means of educating; one doesn't want to make artists out of children (one might take away the forces which they need for growing if one tried to make them use them for 'art', which cannot really come before a grown-up consciousness is there).
>
> I'm quite sure that a great deal depends on the teacher whether a child produces good or less good-quality painting or drawing at school, and the effect on the child in later life, whether he or she develops thinking, feeling and will harmoniously, or becomes over-intellectual, at the cost of feeling faculties, or goes off the deep end in his will system and moral life, effects which can be influenced more than anything almost by artistic work of the right kind and at the right time.
>
> I know a young schoolteacher in Munich who is industrious and serious, he brings me his children's work to show now and then. One gets the impression that all his pupils, about 8–9 year olds, are very gifted artistically. They almost certainly are not all above the average,

and they certainly have not copied from their teacher; the secret is partially just that he has thought about the educational value of either letting his children work with line, or with surfaces of colour, of letting the children draw outlines, which they fill in with colours, or letting them develop a picture by using surfaces of colour from the start, and such simple things. One might draw something like this:

and I think one can observe that in the first case, one will probably say to oneself straight away 'that's an apple', in the second, and more still in the third, one will not come to such a conclusion so quickly. That one jumps to the conclusion with the first, has a lot to do with the outline, one feels especially one's head and intellect in activity, whereas where colours meet each other, to form boundaries, but without outlines, one stays more in one's feelings (with watercolour even more so). The latter is much truer to nature than the former – there never is a line where the horizon is, but green of a field meets blue sky etc. One's intellect is more engaged in doing no.1, one's feelings more in the last – and this includes the whole of the person doing it more than the first one with the outline does.

That is the kind of elementary thing that it would be good if teachers began to get a feeling and understanding for. They are there, after all, to help their children to develop themselves into as complete human beings as possible, into people who keep their feelings alive through their whole lifetime, to help them engage actively with outer nature as well as the inner nature of things and humans. And precisely because of this, they have a magic means given them in colour, if they care to look for it and use it – it is the inner feeling nature of ourselves, and, if one learns to experience it in its objective nature, it is the inner soul of outward nature too. That isn't what a child has to learn, as long as it

PEDAGOGICAL IMPULSES

is still a child, but if it is brought into contact with colours properly, at an early age, when its instincts are as yet unspoilt, it will have a good chance of gaining these faculties which we need as scientists or artists if we want to penetrate into the inside of things. And that is after all the possibility which education has to strive for, if it's to be of any good. But those are things which one needs to go into great detail with, and illustrate very fully. (Books one ought to paint and write ...)

In another letter to Felix in August 1963, Wagner mentions the work he is doing with teachers on the theme of fairytales. Always thorough in his preparation, the new tasks that came towards him through teachers' questions opened up new areas of investigations for Gerard Wagner which he incorporated into his own work:

> Next week I have a course to give in Germany for school teachers, their problems as regards painting I find myself having to make more and more my own. It helps me to get onto new ground, brings valuable contacts too.
>
> One particularly interesting problem which school teachers, and working with them, has brought, is the painting of so-called 'fairytales'. If they are genuine 'fairytales' they lead one to the same sources: to stages in human development to which one tries to come in quite a different way through the colours, which are in a way the inner 'substance' of the human being – spirit substance which becomes soul and outer 'substance', right down into nature – into visibility. The laws one finds in colours are the same as those of human evolution. One finds them in fairytales too. A pity we were brought up more on Hans Christian Andersen than Grimm – the former are not genuine ones. Hope you are all right. I wonder how the crops are doing. Love to all three from G.

Ernst Schuberth and his wife Erika worked with Gerard Wagner when preparing their painting lessons, and Ernst recorded a few interesting suggestions they received:

> In 1963 Erika Schuberth took on a Class 1 in the Rudolf Steiner School in Munich and prepared her painting lessons with Gerard Wagner and Elisabeth Koch. Following requests from Erika, Elisabeth offered suggestions that the former subsequently used when teaching at the Dornach Teachers' Seminar; and the play she wrote for Class 1 also came about in this way.

Along with basic colour exercises, they worked on the different main lesson themes of fairytales and fables, a main lesson on trees in Class 2, the Bible story of Creation in Class 3, and Man and Animal and Botany main lessons in Classes 4 and 5. Erika remembers Gerard Wagner painting a scene from *Sleeping Beauty*, and never forgot the moment when the prince appeared on the scene and the hedge opened. Gerard Wagner said: 'And now comes the Prince!' He dipped the brush in a bright strong red and made the hedge blossom. The red was the power of the prince. A figure appeared only later.

One day Erika decided to paint a large picture of the Star Child and described her idea to Gerard Wagner: 'Would the size of a door be big enough for you?' he asked, and they both laughed heartily. Ursula Heinzer-Seidel, the younger sister of Erika and a teacher in the Rudolf Steiner School in Basel, prepared her painting lessons over an eight-year period with both Elisabeth Koch and Gerard Wagner.

Erika Schuberth recalled visiting the Alte Pinakothek art museum in Munich with Gerard Wagner. They went slowly from picture to picture with Wagner making diverse comments about them. He pointed out the splendid red of a cardinal's gown which expressed so well his nobility and self-assured appearance. To Erika's surprise Gerard Wagner looked long and intensely at a painting of Rubens (which she personally disliked) and pointed out the unusually nuanced tones of crimson on the various figures – comparing for example the two crimsons of a mother and her child. And so they lingered in appreciation before many of the great works.

In 1968 I took over a Class 6 in the Munich Rudolf Steiner School, and during those years as class teacher I prepared my painting lessons mostly with Gerard Wagner. I will never forget preparing with him for a European Geography main lesson. How can one express in colour the character of a particular country with its particular geography and special culture? I chose three characteristic countries: Norway as a Germanic country, Russia as Slavic and Italy as representative of Romance cultures. The first question was: what would be the best colour with which to tone the page as a first step, to prepare the mood of each country? We also considered the folk songs of these lands, as they often give the soul character of the landscape and people more strongly than colour. We chose a light grey for Norway, a light violet for Russia and yellow for Italy.

Then for the ground colour, we mixed a colour we thought appropriate with black. For Norway, to my surprise, Gerard Wagner suggested mixing a carmine red with black. It gave firmness and strength below. Blue mixed with black for Russia gave a softer ground which gave little strength below. A brown ground in its atmosphere of yellow sat well for Italy. When I began the geography main lesson, it was remarkable to see the assurance with which the children chose the colours and then completed their paintings, largely by themselves.

For Class 8 we chose the 'portrait' motif, as Rudolf Steiner had presented it to the teachers of the Friedwart School in Dornach. In the same way as Rudolf Steiner suggested drawing maps, the head in profile arises through the meeting of two surfaces of colour – of yellow and blue – without any preparatory outline drawing.

In Class 6 or 7 I asked Gerard Wagner to lend me a picture for my classroom. I chose the picture 'Easter'. I showed the painting during a parents' evening and everyone approved. A frame was made with a protective wooden cover that could be opened and closed, and in this way the natural look of the colours was not disturbed by reflection from the glass. Every month the parents donated 30 Marks to rent the painting from Gerard Wagner, and so by the end of Class 8 the picture belonged to us and hung permanently in the classroom.

THE SCIENTIFIC ASPECT

Gerard Wagner's interests were by no means restricted to the area of art and pedagogy. He regularly attended lectures and courses at the Goetheanum on the most varied subjects. They included lectures on the categories of Aristotle with Günter Schubert; courses on mathematics and projective geometry given by Louis Locher-Ernst or George Adams; the study weeks given by Walter Donat on the history of culture; and van Goudoever's wonderful courses on Rudolf Steiner's Mystery Dramas and Calendar of the Soul verses.

And in direct connection with his own work he had fulfilling contact with scientists of various kinds including the mathematicians Ernst Schuberth and Georg Glöckler, who both had a particular interest in the meeting of art and science, and were appreciative of Wagner's way of working. Ernst Schuberth brought his questions and had conversations with the painter on the subject of geometric metamorphosis and colour, inspired by a suggestion of Rudolf Steiner's that colour should be included in mathematics, one example being that a red triangle would be smaller, and a blue triangle larger. Always practical, Wagner drew geometric shapes with different-coloured pencils in the presence of Ernst Schuberth as he attempted to answer his question.[88]

As a pupil of Gerard Wagner's one noticed his grasp of the dynamics of life and movement in plants and animals, and since childhood he had been deeply interested in the working of nature (as he described in his autobiographical sketch: '... everything that grew and crawled, swam and flew, in the garden, meadow and forest was of the greatest interest'.[89])

Back in 1934 Wagner had briefly expressed his intention to write about the inner organisation of plants and animals.

This card was written to his brother in the needy days of the 1930s:

> Dear Felix,
> Can you lend me a pound note for, say, nine months or so? Don't mind my asking, or saying no. How goes your farming, and the biolog-dynam. preparations if you use them? Your problems preoccupy me a good deal only from a rather different aspect as yet from how they do you – animals and plants, their inner organisms and relationships to man and each other. I intend to crystallise out a book, or at least a series of longer articles on these subjects. Greetings to Dorothy, love from G.

Gerard Wagner's plan was not brought to fruition and it is noteworthy that, as his work developed, he was compelled to abandon writing and concentrate on knowledge acquired in engagement with colour, through this medium seeking to verify the truth of certain matters within himself, as his own experience, including matters of science. ('It is a subject which I busy myself with a good deal – professionally – as colour is one way in, but perhaps more of that another time …'.) Felix Wagner's profession of fruit-grower and Gerard Wagner's interest in natural history meant that their letters contain many references to nature, the seasons and, in typically English fashion, the weather. They also, at times, touched on more scholarly subjects. A book by Pierre de Chardin called forth a detailed response from Gerard Wagner as to the origin of life and questions of evolution. In the letter below, of 1961, which gives insight into his preoccupation with the laws of nature, and with ways of approaching organic rather than only inorganic life, he writes: 'The tiny bit which one learns gradually to test oneself – through painting – gives one a trust in what, in other branches, one cannot for a long time realise out of oneself as being true.'

Dear Felix

At long last this letter begins – perhaps I may jump over the apologies. What a good thing that I do not need to write a weekly letter. Forty or fifty years do not necessarily improve one's faculty for letter writing, unless one wilfully does something towards it, which I have not. I do not think the less, even if words seldom fit the thoughts.

The long pause this time is, in small part, (quite small), due to your very interesting book, for which many thanks. I read it in little bits, but regularly, in so far as nothing interrupts me – the only method for me of getting through a book.

As I am now at page 91, somewhere in the first chapter of book 2, you can gauge how short the reading hours are daily. I mark it continuously, sometimes rather violently, and at first, if I were somewhat different, I would often have exclaimed loudly at thoughts, at a way of thinking, which are so very different from and opposite to mine. But just the difference makes it so interesting.

Many years ago I read Darwin's *Origin of Species*, since when I have not taken more than a very superficial side look at what the natural scientists have to say, much as I would like to. It's a question of time, and choosing what is most important to do. About them and their views I hear pretty often – I go regularly to three or four lectures or lecture readings a week, at periods far more, on the most varied subjects, scientific, mathematical, social, artistic, historical, in the light of the fundamental truths of anthroposophy. Statements, you may say, like any others, many of which one is not near to being able to verify oneself, but which I find bring clarity to the problems of life, if one takes enough trouble to think them through, and which one's feelings also can live with and say yes to. The tiny bit which one learns gradually to test oneself – through painting – gives one a trust in what, in other branches, one cannot for a long time realise out of oneself as being true. To read someone on subjects on which one is more or less always thinking, someone who does not know the world as it is for oneself, that is one of the first and strongest impressions when reading the book. I keep on saying that he will probably answer his own questions which he raises in the beginning, later on in the book, and before commenting at all, it would be better to read right through and then start again, in order not to have to correct myself in what I say. Huxley, a materialistic thinker, nicht wahr?, speaks in his introduction of evolution as if there were a straight-line development from matter, life, consciousness, as though the later arose out of the former – life and consciousness as developments of matter. The author, who says he believes in science, whose aim is to 'see', seems to think on this same line as Huxley, if I see it rightly. There is a moment where he first takes the step from the inorganic to the organic, the latter as a development of the former – to me it is as though he had a black-out there. Later on he says for life to have developed later it must have been there somehow before too. His jump from matter to consciousness causes me the same kind of qualms, but he very probably will get this question clearer when later on he speaks of consciousness, there where he is really in a position to observe it accurately, or at least intimately – in himself – which I would have thought should rather have been the starting point when one writes on the phenomena of man. To start with atoms of matter, which one cannot observe, and to which one has no conscious access, in a time where man's consciousness was not, surely runs a danger of pure speculation.

If one starts from what one can observe of man today, one will, I think, realise that life does not develop out of matter, but comes to it, grips, penetrates it, as a new element, matter becomes inorganic matter again when life leaves it (pull a blade of grass out by its roots and watch what happens); and that consciousness, i.e. feeling consciousness, thinking consciousness etc, do not result from matter or life, but come to these, penetrate or direct these, or else are directed by them. The individual human being, spirit, who directs his thinking, develops his feelings consciously towards a higher morality, instead of being led by his feelings, is independent within this consciousness, of all three stages.

Matter, life, feeling, spirit have different origins, work together in the physical world. Question is how? I shall be extremely interested to see how Pierre de Chardin treats these subjects (how would he explain sleeping and waking? dying and being born?) too intricate for the moment to embark on, I will wait to hear him first. Maybe he will eventually correct the impression that he is evolving spirit out of matter. (One can make interesting observations re the connection between consciousness and 'matter (living matter)' when one is not tired, but listens to a lecture which does not interest one, which sends one to sleep, whereas one is at once wide awake if something is said that awakens one's interest.)

In daily life one knows, from inside, this life, more conscious or less, without thinking, and then so often, when someone begins thinking about it and saying what he thinks, one is prepared to believe all manner of thoughts about this life which are quite wrong and which experience in every moment contradicts,* which means that an exact observation of our own state of consciousness, of thinking, feeling, will, if they can be brought under our observation, is a surer foundation to start from when one studies man and nature, human nature.

(* There are thoughts that one can live with, and cannot live with. But I must wait with these subjects, and rather get into their details when I have an overview of the whole book. I have borrowed an introduction to modern chemistry and physics – atomic physics etc. – and hope to get just a slight inkling on the subject of atoms and molecules which P. d. Ch. speaks of.)

Very many thanks to Dorothy for her letter ... a rare one. It sounds almost as though you were planning a Swiss holiday? ... let me know when your plans get a bit definite. End of August I have my week with the school teachers near Stuttgart – end or middle of July for nearly 4 weeks is packed full here, so not such a very good time for even a fleeting look at Dornach, because within a short distance of the Goetheanum there is not a room to be had. Then it empties quite till toward the middle of September. Will you please thank Mary for her letter too – how

THE SCIENTIFIC ASPECT

well her handwriting has developed. I'm glad she likes her school so much still, and does not learn too much. Are the arts practised much there? And handicrafts. Do they learn botany and mineralogy, and geology and something about medicine in a simple way? Not too much Latin grammar, I hope. And do they have studies there, or live in large numbers in a few big rooms?

On page 92, Pierre de Chardin: '... Surely it is natural that life, *as it just emerges from matter*, should be dripping with molecularity.' That is the kind of sentence I find disturbing. Just before he says '... as we get as near as we can to the threshold of life, it manifests itself to us simultaneously as microscopic and innumerable'. Although later he agrees with Pasteur, that 'protoplasm is no longer formed directly from the inorganic substance of the earth' yet it is as though he thought about life with a thinking suited only to inorganic matter. He goes into the infinitely small – invisibly small, to look for (but not see) where life starts – and in that invisible he theorises as to this beginning. But one cannot see life or think about it with the same faculty with which one perceives and thinks of inorganic matter. No doubt he will answer this later on too to some extent. But I feel he turns things upside down in trying to put matter at the origin of things – of life and consciousness, instead of the other way round.

Goethe was one of the first – the first perhaps – in modern times, to show how one can learn to think properly about organic life, *think* it, with his metamorphosis of the plant. Nowadays one treats life, plant, animal and human often in such an abominable way, really as though it were no more than inorganic matter, that it is very important to try to find a way of approaching this problem of the living realm which is inwardly suited to it, and a way of consciously grasping it, without harming or destroying it.

It is a subject which I busy myself with a good deal – professionally – as colour is one way in, but perhaps more of that another time; synthetic geometry is a way in, though I have only watched and heard it being demonstrated by someone who can do so, it's far too difficult for me and needs a life's work. One comes closer to where science and art, or an artistic way of working at science, are one, where one gets to the living domain. One needs direct experience from inside the thing, not a thinking about it from outside only. [author's italics]

I am trying to get to the end of this letter, as in the next few days I shall not be able to continue. [...]

The weather has been quite respectable for the last two days – before this, continual rain. Love to all three from Gerard.

P. S. Have you read P. de Chardin's book advertised on the back cover of this one 'Le Milieu divin'? That must be most interesting, and perhaps brings the very views that can supplement or complete this book.

*

Considering moon nodes as 'birth situations',[90] Gerard Wagner's third moon node in 1961 at the age of about 56 (the precise time of the third moon node is 55 and almost 10 months) coincides with the development of what could be called the second major phase in his work, and in the long run perhaps the most significant: his research into the subject of metamorphosis, which was especially appreciated by scientists. In this connection we can recall the remark made by Louis Locher-Ernst – 'That is also higher mathematics!' – when shown sketches of Wagner's 'animal metamorphosis' studies. Locher-Ernst was the leader of the Mathematics and Astronomy Section at the Goetheanum, and Wagner had a high regard for him. Wagner also had a special connection and friendship with the farmer Martin Schmidt,[91] who asked the painter whether his colour research could help discover the right soil to foster cosmic and terrestrial impulses in plant growth. Wagner asked himself what colour expressed the forces of quartz and what colour the forces of lime, and thereupon chose carmine for quartz and blue for lime. This is explained in more detail below, where Ernst Schuberth outlined the development of Gerard Wagner's work on the subject of metamorphosis:

> A new field of work opened up in 1956 when a class teacher at the Steiner Waldorf School asked for his help in preparing a main lesson period about plants. Wagner painted his first systematic studies of the way changes in colour lead to transformation of the shape of plants. Quite scientifically, the colouring of each individual element is changed step by step, and the influence this has on the change of shape is then studied. Martin Schmidt, one of the early biodynamic farmers, was able to 'read' these studies and use them for his research into, among other things, the cultivation of seeds. The influences of the warmth, light, chemical and life ethers find expression in the colours. The varying ways in which their forces work together affect the metamorphosis of plant shapes.

THE SCIENTIFIC ASPECT

Purely out of his inner experience of colours, Gerard Wagner was able to take up and work on the questions Martin Schmidt asked him about soil conditions and plant forms. There is a resemblance here to the way a mathematician can grasp the laws of trajectories in the outer world by means of his inner understanding of mathematics. A qualitative 'mathematising' in the realm of colours, experienced inwardly, leads to the forms of living plants in the same way as geometry leads to the forms of crystals. It is not the actual shapes that are described but the archetypal forms and their possible manifestation in the world. In 1957 Wagner also began to study animal forms. The animal series he painted show quite new animal forms – quite amusingly often – that are not externally visible but which arise out of animal soul qualities in the interplay and interreactions of colours.

The forms arising from those pictures are closely related to the individual shapes we see in nature. But during the second half of the 1960s Wagner began to work on studies of the 'archetypal plant' and soon also the 'archetypal animal'. As a tapestry of manifold formative processes, the archetypal plant or the archetypal animal can bring forth various specific forms by emphasising one life process or another. Translated into painting this means modifying the colours used in a way that allows such specialisations to occur.[92]

In his studio in later years Wagner displayed an etching – a portrait of Johann Wolfgang von Goethe: 'My friend', he once said as he looked at it. Gerard Wagner's work with metamorphosis and organic life developed essentially from his research into Rudolf Steiner's paintings, 'Archetypal Plant' and 'Archetypal Animal-Man', which Steiner created by drawing on Goethe's research into plant metamorphosis and animal morphology. The Goetheanistic aspect of Wagner's work was clear to Theodor Willmann who wrote in the monograph of the artist: 'Wagner's works show us clearly how Goetheanism in art can open up the most fruitful paths not only for painting out of colour but also for the living realm of enquiry into nature.'

As to Wagner's far-reaching painterly preoccupation with Steiner's archetypal animal/human being motif, Willmann shows it to be a continuation, now in the realm of the visual arts, of Goethe's discoveries in metamorphosis, and of Rudolf Steiner's spiritual-scientific research into questions of evolution. He says there (continuing from his considerations of the archetypal plant):

Goethe found it a great deal harder to apply this methodology to animal morphology, since here Creation, in developing both the internal and external form of the skeleton, tends far more toward the forms of dead substance, only perfecting these in the spherical curvature of the human head on the one hand, and on the other in the *raising of the whole human limb form to its upright posture*.

Goethe sees in the developing stages of animal forms an evolutionary progress toward this perfection. Yet he does not therefore regard the human being as the highest animal, but as an archetype from which animal life inevitably departs as it leads back to lower developmental stages through prematurity and rigidification. Here Goethe faced the enigma of contrary evolution, which Rudolf Steiner beheld as the law of evolution and counter-evolution as he was embarking on his spiritual enquiries.

To make clear: By connecting with the principle implicit in Rudolf Steiner's sketch 'Archetypal Man' (also known as 'Archetypal Animal'), therefore, Gerard Wagner was able to take up the riddle of this idea of evolution. With his paintings of animal metamorphosis, the whole history of animal painting (from the earliest cave paintings to Franz Marc) attained a new level.[93]

In a letter to his brother Felix, Wagner mentions his scientific-artistic work with agriculturalists, which specially interested him. As he wrote very little about his work during his lifetime, Gerard Wagner's letters to his brother and sister-in-law are valuable for their insights into the painter's thoughts about aspects of his work. In a particularly interesting letter in March 1963, he also looks at the broader picture of his work and task, and assesses his achievement so far:

Dear Felix

It seems a long time since I heard from you (since before Christmas). I have often been wondering how you were getting on through the cold period – imagined you not being able to do much, as far as your trees and shrubs are concerned – perhaps all the more in other ways that one doesn't know of.

Now that the snow is gone, I expect you will be more than just busy. I wonder very much how your trees and shrubs have survived. The fruit trees here, as far as I can see with only layman's eyes, have not suffered – with the smaller shrubs it may be different. It's good to have had the ground so well frozen through. Birds have become pretty rare. We have so many here, normally, but now only occasionally: the blue tits come to the window, yellow hammers – if that's what they are – rather like sparrows, only with a lot of greenish-yellow on them – have been most plentiful, now and then a bull finch, but one sees these seldom. Some kinds of smaller birds seem to have disappeared. For the deer and mountain goats it has been fairly disastrous …

On the whole I like the long winter and snow and the frozen earth, and did not notice the cold too much, although it was more than most years – but it was healthy – after the thaw, one feels one's old ailments coming into their own again, after sleeping for a while …

I wonder whether you see any way of coming over here for your summer holiday this year? … I should like some day to be able to show you a bit more in detail what I have been working at these years, and what gradually gets more distinct contours. Not that I chiefly place value on what one can show outwardly. If there were one or two pupils of whom I knew that they could help others to work along the same lines, then that would be far more worth than any number of my paintings. But to some extent I have made the method of work visible, and hope it may interest someone someday to try it out himself, and come to his own results, which could be far more interesting than my own.

Possibilities are gradually showing themselves of bringing these things to a wider public, just when I realise how necessary it would be for me to be twenty years younger and robuster. Some of the interest I like most comes from agriculturists – practical farmers and scientists in one – they see their problems in mine, and a way of answering from my angle questions which their own work throws up. And this autumn I am to take part in a meeting of young people in Germany – people of the age when they are training for a profession, where a young scientist and botanist and myself together will try to show how, through outer observation of plant forms – (that's his part) and through our experiences of colour (a far longer and more difficult path), one can come to a new way of understanding plant life, and formative forces in nature. (It need not be only in plant life, it could lead into all kinds of other directions, but we are limiting ourselves to this field, which is itself large enough for a lifetime's work.)

This is to be only a small part – one group – of a meeting of a hundred or a hundred and fifty perhaps, which will work in several groups at different subjects, and which will also work together and develop – if possible – a general method of working. One aim being to start from outer (or inner) phenomena, and learn to think exactly about these, and come to an experience of them which includes the whole human being. One might say, find a way from exact science to 'exact art', the latter being what I am seeking. In so far this invitation is very welcome, though rather alarming, when one knows one's own limitations.

But if a few people, as a result, would gain an interest in working at the same thing on their own, then that would be as much as one can hope for. It needs years – and years – of practice, to get anywhere, but it is worthwhile, and has a more than merely personal value.

Talking of these things always makes me think of Bernard Leach, who wrote me once, after I had sent him a few things to see (36 years ago) and told him a bit of what I was doing (which I hardly began to dream of in those days), that 'consciousness was killing for art'. If he understood consciousness as consciousness of the intellect, then that is true, but what I meant then, and know now, is consciousness of a different kind, one without which I don't think art will be possible in the future. But it must be developed, it is not there by itself.

I am reading a book by a girl of about 18 – she can't be much more to judge from language and contents. It is interesting to see what probably quite a lot of people of that age are like inside, before they have yet become themselves, before they have thought a thought of their own. But it could be interesting to get to know them once they have thrown off all fetters and come to be individuals who can think. That will bring forth a very different world from the one we grew up in. To throw away convention is not difficult – we have been in that stage long enough already – to find one's foothold as a human being (not as an animal) without them, is tough work, which we are not too far on with as yet.

I wonder if young people ever read the same books which we used to. Robin Hood for instance? (This one particularly often comes into my mind, as one of the first 'older books' I read.) And do they read Lorna Doone, which mother read to us …?

Wish I had time for books. Many thanks for the little one on Chinese Art – very good little pictures. Love to all three, from Gerard

In the summers or early autumn of the 1960s and 1970s, Gerard Wagner and Elisabeth Koch spent refreshing weeks in the Swiss mountains, in Engadin, Fextal and other places. Wagner enjoyed the mountain air and the revealing sights of nature which he could appreciate with his painter's mind and heart. Time spent in the mountains was the refreshment he needed to 'tank up' for the intensive work in and outside his studio in Dornach. In 1964 he and Elisabeth Koch were in the mountains twice, first in June and then again in September, before he had to prepare for a show of his work as part of a conference of the Natural Science Section at the Goetheanum. Afterwards he gave a week's course to mathematicians.

In the following letter to Felix in September 1964, Gerard Wagner displays his wish to study 'more specialised problems' of plant growth and animal life, in relation to colour and form, and the inner nature of things related to their outer aspects. His statement: 'One has to find a new language oneself' is wonderfully characteristic of his pioneering spirit:

> Dear Felix
> You will think I'm forever gadding about and taking holidays. Up in this kind of surrounding one now and again finds oneself thinking that even the tiniest plant, which is alive and livingly formed and which in each moment of its growth overcomes the weight of its own matter, is more beautiful than all these mountains, crumbling to pieces in their more or less chance shapes. Especially there are such numerous glaciers here, where scarcely a plant grows – only a few very small ones – and then one feels the deadness of all this stone.
>
> All the same, I always like getting up amongst these mountains, and feel better than anywhere in the lower country. What makes them special is the light from morning till evening – especially round about sunset. And to practise thinking, I've no doubt the heights would help one. …
>
> [Letter continues from Dornach]
>
> Days have gone by and those hills seem a long way off, but their effect remains as an extra stamina against cold and the anti-energy effects of Dornach. At once, a lot to do here: a conference of natural scientists here, led by the head of our society (a Dr Poppelbaum, since Albert Steffen died last year); I have a small show to prepare as a contribution to the theme they are working at. Which is – you may wonder at it – the four ethers in connection with the elemental beings, a subject with which I have busied myself with from an artistic angle for a good many years. I don't try to paint ideas which a scientist may have, that would probably lead to a pretty awful dilettantism, but one can come to a metamorphosis of form and colour, while keeping within the purely

artistic sphere, which has a relationship to this subject. If experienced by the onlooker, this can be also a help for him in his own scientific line. After this conference, which I am invited to go to (I'm glad of it) I have a painting course for mathematicians for a week. That is an adventure in pedagogy, as these people are usually very dry and have great difficulty in experiencing anything.

… I am only gradually regaining, or for the first time beginning to gain a slight contact with a commonly known kind of thinking and knowledge about the natural phenomena around us, through reading partly, though this tells me something usually only with any clarity if through my own work I have at least some fairly strong suspicion of the same thing. I realise enough to know that through painting one can come to a lot of truths, but the names are lacking, and the connections with the outer world which we observe. That's why I am especially glad of opportunities of coming into working contact with scientists – all the better if they have sense for art.

I should like to study, in my own way, more and more specialised problems in connection with plant growth, animal life, but I ought probably to take courses in agriculture, botany, chemistry, physics and other subjects too. This life will hardly be long enough for all that. But I'm coming gradually a bit closer to ideas about things, which are after all the common and objective means of communication between humans. Quite often I'm told I ought to publish something, series of plants e.g., and write a text to them. I've tried it even, but with very poor results.

These problems, which usually are concerned with the connections between colour and form – one might better say, the inner being of things with their outer appearances – are not to be put into language. The latter is, unless one is an artist in it – too stiff for something alive. *One has to find a language oneself: series of pictures which enable an exact experience in the person who looks at them and who is willing to take the trouble to really live into them, an experience which then can lead to knowledge in him* [author's italics]. It's a long way round, and most people are not willing or able to make the exertion.

Love to all three, from Gerard

60ᵗʰ Birthday exhibition at the Goetheanum

At the 1966 Easter Exhibition at the Goetheanum, Gerard Wagner showed three paintings in a group exhibition. Subsequently an extensive show of his work took place between 17 July and 7 August and was seen as a celebration of his 60th birthday. The paintings chosen for the exhibition included some of his work on the subject of metamorphosis. Georg Nemes wrote an eloquent review that gives invaluable insights into Wagner's work and artistic individuality:

> *The Art of Painting in relation to Gerard Wagner's Major Exhibition at the Goetheanum in the Summer of 1966*
>
> … Rudolf Steiner revealed within the great span of his world knowledge a foundation for the different arts. He led painting into its own true sphere, that of colour with its inherent attributes. In so far as colour remains fixed on a physical object it conceals its true being. Only when the colour is freed and can float and weave according to its own essential forces, when it can condense and radiate according to inner laws, can it appear in its true reality. Colours can intermingle, sometimes flowing and sparkling in delicate lazures or they can densify into overlapping layers. At other times they can meet and balance each other, forming curves and hollows. In the atmospheric wonders of sunrises and sunsets, in the rainbows and the northern lights, one can glimpse how the magic world of colour appears as if out of a higher world. Colour can only retain this immensely rich life if it lives within the selfless activity of a human ego devoted to colour. It reveals itself only to pure observation. This forms the basis of true artistic technique in painting. Rudolf Steiner recreated the art of painting out of its real origins. Only now in our times is it drawing on its original source. Steiner's inexhaustible impulse in painting which he gave to humanity was apparent in the two cupolas of the First Goetheanum that presented motifs from human and cosmic evolution, as well as in his numerous sketches and lectures. Gerard Wagner has taken all this up in his own way and made it fruitful.
>
> In Goethe's *Theory of Colour*, colour is called forth when streaming light is met and opposed by approaching darkness. It appears out of the illumined darkness and out of the darkened light. Feeling-wise, we connect the great cosmic heights with light and the earth's depths with darkness, and in letting the light from above dive down into the depths, the dark is transformed into glowing colour. This is the mood that pervades so much of Gerard Wagner's life's work. Out of the depths – de

profundis – the Easter message of colour glows upwards. When the dark pole of the spectrum is predominant one sees blackish-brown, reddish-brown, deep blue, violet, deep red, dark green colour tones with their own unique qualities and values. Wagner's colours have a special glow, even his blues and greens despite them belonging to the cold pole of the colour spectrum. The brighter colours appear to blossom at certain points and stand out with a marked intensity. One could say that what shines forth from his pictures is not so much the bright light of the rising sun or the all-pervading light of spring, but rather the meditative quality of the honey-coloured evening light and the rich colours of autumn.

The motifs in his pictures are connected with his need to draw forth colour from dark powers of the depths and relieve them of might and weight. His fundamental theme is the created world with all its manifold layers emerging from the depths of the earth and rising up into the heights. His cosmic dreams, perceived in awakened consciousness, can appear like a kind of Jacob's dream. When Jacob laid his head on the stone in his night's rest after his wanderings, he beheld in dream a mighty ladder with scores of spiritual beings ascending and descending.

In many of Wagner's paintings similar figures flow and surge through these colour spaces, joining each other, hovering and embracing one other. They descend into the gorge of Cain. Gnome-like beings romp through the crevasses and cracks. They form crystals. Symbolic-like figures lie below – a human skeleton in a black-grey coffin. Plants send their roots like feelers downwards. One approaches the different regions of nature in its diverse layers; flowers and trees, the agile world of animals; gentle stags, deer, horses, also the elephant and many others. Human beings appear elevated among the great winged beings who accompany them. These spiritual beings have bodies of colour which extend in wing-like formations. Between the two pinions appears a small head. Even in their smallness, these figures so characteristic of our painter retain a monumental quality through their powerful wings and gestures. Again and again Wagner turns to the layers in the earth's depths where the elemental beings are at work. His spiritual standpoint appears to be the Christ-penetrated Being of the earth, which glows forth from the dark abyss and opens to the whole cosmos.

At the end of his *Theory of Colour* Goethe shares his spiritual insights into the nature of colour. Colours are the 'offspring of the Elohim'. These

Spirits of Form or the Exusiai, as St Paul calls them, are hierarchical beings who, according to Rudolf Steiner's spiritual science, endowed human beings with ego-hood, that individual element which progresses, always true to itself, towards eternity. These beings also had the task of emanating from their very being the flowing world of colours. These colours can meet each other with their own inherent dynamics and create boundaries and contours. Out of the world of surging colours the world of form and shape emerges. On this cosmic borderland Gerard Wagner takes up his position. No matter how interwoven the colours are, Wagner's brush is still able to convey a richness of line and concise outlines or even bold, energetic contours which on occasions appears almost metallic. One example of such abrupt condensing and powerful use of edged surfaces is his 'Baptism of Christ'. This is a work of grandiose monumentality. As is his custom, he has worked repeatedly on this theme, touching upon many different aspects in the many variations he painted … The dark colours become so saturated that an impenetrable, one could almost say, glowing black appears.

When I visited him in his studio, Gerard Wagner explained how he began with a light-coloured background which tones the whole painting surface. Then the moving streams of colour spread out over it gradually and in the course of creative activity these become formed and shaped. The painting is not dominated by great swathes of colour which flood the whole surface; rather, smaller, mobile surfaces meet each other in a lively way. He imbues the surface of the picture with a particular brush technique which creates a unified yet fluctuating interweaving. His highly developed feeling for colour, the austere smoothness and poetic delicacy of the line and the great care taken in the execution of his works, bring something exquisite, something jewel-like amid the richness of all his painterly inventions.

At this point it is not inappropriate to touch briefly upon the biography of the painter. He spent his first six years in Wiesbaden and until the age of 20 lived in England. Then he came to Central Europe, to its heart and centre, the 'Goetheanum', the centre of Rudolf Steiner's work, where he has been working for the past 40 years. It is characteristic of England that a very special connection to form exists there. The aura of its own very individual gothic style is still discernible in these islands with their strong connection to the realm of the elements. In Gerard Wagner this English tendency towards form is integrated into the rigour of the German 'I-impulse', producing his own original artistic individuality. Even his physical body shows a rare delicacy and sensibility right into the slender and sensitive hands. His face reveals goodwill and renunciation; his profile is clearly defined and his nose seems sculpted to embody the shape of the consciousness soul. His noble head is gently curved and crowned with intelligence; he has a distinguished appearance.

His concern with the dark, 'heavy' colour pole and his interest in the structure of colour surfaces leads him to the problem of the mass and weight of coloured surfaces. His themes are devoted more to the dark depths of the earth, where gravity holds sway. He feels attracted to the balance of heaviness and lightness as it expresses itself in colour, and he seeks to develop this and make it accessible as a sphere of its own: a sense of balance in colour within the realm of gravity; a colour-structure problem, important for the aesthetics of wall painting, where painting and architecture connect.

Gerard Wagner's attention is especially focused on the value of form arising from colour. There he meets Goethe's principle of metamorphosis, as Rudolf Steiner used it so fruitfully in the architecture of the Goetheanum, and applies it for his own ends. He studies a colour motif again and again and creates a whole series of variations on the theme. He observes the consequences of changes in form. The motif does not remain fixed but stays in movement. And so he explores, among other motifs, Rudolf Steiner's own painting studies of the 'Archetypal Plant' and the 'Archetypal Animal' through series of transformations.

Goethe developed his epoch-making thoughts on metamorphosis chiefly in the field of botany and then applied it to the bone structures of animal and man. He explored it further in his *Theory of Colour*. This principle of metamorphosis reveals itself in its purest and richest form in the plant realm. Gerard Wagner – lover of the problems of colour and form – devotes himself also to the plant world. With tireless energy he traces the laws inherent in the metamorphosis of colour and form and creates innumerable series of plant studies with a strict discipline of observation. He paints 'meditations', e.g. those concerned with growth and wilting, and he transforms these depending on the colour choice of the toned page, whether it is blue, violet or red. A whole world of delicate plant forms appear before our eyes. Blossoms dissolve and become umbels, the calyxes change into lingulate flowers, broad leaves turn into pinnate ones. These transformations are inexhaustible and

THE SCIENTIFIC ASPECT

are based on the changes of colour and the stages of development of the growing plant.

These impressive pieces of work are done with great love and artistic devotion as well as with an intensity of observation characteristic of scientific experimentation. They are not always metamorphoses in the strictest sense as in Rudolf Steiner's seven stages in the First Goetheanum columns, but are more a matter of gliding transition in lawful variations which lend themselves to infinite elaboration.

Let us now consider the intimate spiritual connection between the world of plants and painting in Wagner's works. Painting is based on the super-sensible capacity of intuition as Steiner describes so vividly in his lecture 'The Being of the Arts'.[94] Intuition means the complete identification of the human I with the object that is to be known. In painting this union of I and object is of a much more imaginative nature. It is the flowing colours on the surface of the picture. The intuition expresses itself through imagination. One finds this too in the plant. Goethe's archetypal plant as a 'logos' form is, in Rudolf Steiner's sense, an intuition. The way it is formed in nature is shown in the leaf and petal, in other words through coloured surfaces. According to Goethe, the plant is purely leaf in its development in both directions – both toward blossoms and roots. Here one can see a distant relationship to the layers of colour in painting ...

Leonardo da Vinci approached the problem of physiognomy with scientific exactitude when portraying the disciples as twelve human characters in his fresco painting 'The Last Supper'. This was the starting point for innumerable famous caricatures by him. Leonardo was exploring how changes in one part of the face transformed the look of the whole face. Many series of metamorphoses of the human face emerged from Leonardo's artistic experimentation in this way. Many were one-sided and exaggerated and yet they followed certain laws and appeared right. Based on a law which he had recognised, Goethe was able to invent 'new' plants, just as Leonardo had invented 'new' faces. Here art touched the realm of exact science. Something that is central to science, namely experimentation, is introduced into artistic activity. Gerard Wagner too broke new ground in this way.

His rich life's work embraces a holistic organism of problems and motifs, as an expression of his creative individuality – as his true 'biography'. At the same time the cosmos is unveiled and captured in the artist's living entelechy. We are given a new view of a world of which we had little inkling.

It is clear that it is not necessary to force art to be new by imposing on it bizarre, intellectual, wilful and questionable procedures. These are easily superseded tomorrow by new and equally forgettable sensations. For true and profound artists the muse has prepared inexhaustible treasures for all times to come. This is the way art can evolve in a really legitimate and original way. The work of Gerard Wagner is a crucial contribution to a new culture of painting.

We offer him our gratitude and deep appreciation and cherish the hope that great tasks will be granted him to fulfil.[95]

THE PAINTING SCHOOL

Apart from his own painting which he considered his chief work, Gerard Wagner's teaching duties grew. By 1967, as he wrote to Felix in November of that year, 'I have five painting courses to give weekly, which includes teaching pupils from the pedagogical seminar here ... Our own "school" – since Michaelmas – is recognised officially as such, and takes a good deal of time.'

The 'Wagner Painting School' evolved from the early 1950s when lessons were given at the Goetheanum, in the North Roof Studio and later also in the Sketches Room. The painting courses offered during conferences were also opportunities to learn from Gerard Wagner or Elisabeth Koch. One person who experienced such courses and began attending conferences just to be able to study painting, was Erwin Thomalla, a professional actor from Germany (see Appendix 9).

In 1964 after attending courses for at least two years, Thomalla, with encouragement from Elisabeth Koch, decided to begin a full-time training and became the first of a group of four pupils who formed the nucleus for what became the Wagner painting school.

He was joined in the same year by Mrs Silbergh, a regular visitor from England, and two years later Susanne Bosse and Marie Keller completed the small but dedicated founding group.

Marie Keller (1910–2012) first met Gerard Wagner when she attended his painting courses in Zurich; and when these stopped in 1962 she joined his Saturday morning course in the Sketches Room at the Goetheanum. She was 56 when she decided she would do the painting training full time, and she describes movingly how she took the courageous step to change her life. This meant leaving her job as interior decorator at Muralto in Zurich and ignoring the advice of those close to her: 'I had two messages from the spiritual world', she said 'first in Dornach I heard a clear inner voice saying "Painting!"– and as I walked into the Goetheanum the next day, I experienced total peace within myself. Returning to Zurich I heard the voice again saying "Go!"'

Looking back at the training with Gerard Wagner, Keller said:

> It was a difficult time but the best seven years of my life. Herr Wagner said very little but every correction was a revelation and a real experience. Sometimes I tried doing two versions of an exercise and asked him

which one was correct but he gave no answer. To begin with I lacked any courage to say more than 'yes' or 'no' to him.

Marie Keller had great respect for her teacher. She said: 'Gerard Wagner suffered a great deal – his life was painting and the true life of anthroposophy. In the early days he earned 5 Francs a day by working at the Goetheanum reception, which was his money for food.' She recalled a participant at the Zurich Painting Course saying to her that Gerard Wagner would not live long and she answered, 'He will certainly outlive you!'

Like Erwin Thomalla, Marie Keller went on to teach in the painting school and continued painting until she was 80. Once, in the 1990s, when Gerard Wagner was telling his pupils about painting as a path of inner development, he gave Frau Keller as an example of someone who modestly and regularly continues with her painting – persevering 'quietly in the background'.

Erwin Thomalla was a gifted artist and a lively, sociable person. As the school grew he became indispensable as a co-worker and colleague of Gerard Wagner and Elisabeth Koch.

In 1967 the small group of students moved with their two teachers to the newly built Atelierhaus on Broisweg. Marie Keller remembered feeling the loss of leaving the Goetheanum and the Sketches Room. The Atelierhaus was built by the initiative and financial support of Margarethe Jung who wanted to support artists in Dornach, many of whom where living in cramped conditions and lacked suitable studios. Initially she had offered the Atelierhaus to the painter Beppe Assenza but after a misunderstanding arose, Gerard Wagner and Elisabeth Koch moved in instead.

The move to the Atelierhaus was announced in the following notice:

> From the beginning of 1967 the painting courses given by Gerard Wagner and Elisabeth Koch, which have hitherto taken place in the Sketches Room at the Goetheanum, will now be offered in the Atelierhaus. This more spacious environment can give the courses a more self-sufficient character and the opportunity for further development.
>
> The wish is to create a training centre for people who are searching for an art-based path of inner training. Through methodical sequences of exercises, this can lead to a deeper understanding of the human being. The attempt will be made to guide students, through their own experience, to the inner laws of colour, leading to an understanding of Rudolf Steiner's 'training sketches' and their connection with nature and

the human being. In this way the 'sketches' can bear fruit for artistic, pedagogical and therapeutic work.

As previously, the courses offer a full-time training as well as lay courses. The curriculum includes eurythmy, study, drawing and handwork. The evening courses for students offered at the Goetheanum will continue to be part of the training.

The 'Gerard Wagner – Elisabeth Koch Painting School' was founded at Michaelmas 1967. Students' work was displayed: pictures of sun, moon and tree motifs painted by Marie Keller, Mrs Silbergh and Erwin Thomalla were shown in the lower studio and the entrance hall. Elisabeth Koch recalled:

> There were many guests and the event aroused much interest and enthusiasm. The methodical structure of the training was considered 'quite new' and was especially praised. Recognition came also from the Dornach quarter: Raske, Brenzel, Greiner, Frau Jung, Ranzenberger, Hausler and others. Anke Usche Clausen from Hannover also expressed her approval.

Part of the exhibition consisted of pupils' work from the different years of the training and demonstrated the sequence of the school's curriculum, which Elisabeth Koch was asked to describe in an article for the art periodical *The Staedtler-Brief*. The first article appeared as a supplement in the summer edition of 1969. This and further articles written by Elisabeth Koch for *The Staedtler-Brief* became the foundation for the later workbook, *The Individuality of Colour*. Further shows of pupils' work were exhibited throughout 1968, at Easter, Summer and Michaelmas, and included examples of handwork and folders made and painted by the students. Elisabeth Koch:

> In the South Atelier we showed five finished artists' smocks from Frau de Cler, Frl. Keller, Herr Thomalla, Frl. Stritter and myself. And on the table were embroidered bookmarks, book covers, mats and so on. This all received acknowledgment and an enthusiastic response.

Gerard Wagner wrote as follows of the handwork activity in the painting school in a letter to his brother in November 1967:

> Our handwork group is also growing, and needs more thorough preparation, as the people not only come with the idea of trying to find out something with us, but with the wish and expectation to learn – also in some cases in order to become handwork teachers. At our last con-

ference of four days, at the school near Stuttgart, where I went over eight years to teach the teachers for a week – always in the summer holidays – we took four of the painting smocks which our Dornach group had made. Each had been designed individually and the work on three of them was technically perfect – we have two professionals at sewing, embroidering and dressmaking – the fourth I had done myself, that is, the 'embroidery' I had done, because I wanted the form to be as exact as possible, a painting garment in blue, violet and light green for Elisabeth, who had done the sewing, and we showed it, although it was only roughly assembled. These garments caused a good deal of interest – the others would have liked to have had them too; one said she would go walking in the street with one on (although they were really only right for the individual for whom they were designed). But it was good that the principle of the thing was accepted, and we gained interest in how this can be worked on in the future; that is, how one can arrive at designs which really suit the person and the purpose.

In the summer of 1969 the painter Beppe Assenza also moved into the Atelierhaus with his students and its official opening was celebrated, this time with a show of the teachers' work: in the lower studio works by Gerard Wagner on the theme of metamorphosis; in the east and attic studios works by Elisabeth Koch, including her series on the festivals of the year, and a series of drawings illustrating her play 'Upsurge of Evil'. Paintings by Beppe Assenza were shown in the west, central and south studios, and Raoul Ratnowski's sculptures were placed in the entrance hall.

Elisabeth Koch wrote the following remarks in the school's journal:

> In his warm opening speech Dr Biesantz wished us well for the future work together, and for mutual understanding. The opening was attended by many prominent people from the Goetheanum including the Executive Council, Emil Schweigler, members of the stage, building-office and so on. Frau Jung said a few words after a former pupil of Assenza's thanked for her generosity.
>
> The exhibition was also well attended during the Goetheanum summer conference: the metamorphosis series found warm appreciation and acknowledgment, as did my 'Upsurge of Evil' series and my work in the attic studio. Dr Friedrich Oberkugler and his wife showed deep understanding for our work and Frau Dr Fiechter requested my four

'Festivals of the Year' paintings for the Clinical-Therapeutic Institute (Ita Wegman Clinic).

The school continued to grow. Erwin Thomalla was attracting pupils with painting courses he was giving at various places in Switzerland as well as with exhibitions in Paris, Berlin and Munich. Marie Keller, after four years of training, was given Gerard Wagner's Saturday morning class, and Elisabeth Koch, as well as her teaching duties at the school, took on Gerard Wagner's painting course at the Teachers' Seminar.

Painting courses in England

Teaching in England began in the summer of 1965 when Gerard Wagner and Elisabeth Koch were invited to give a course at Kings Langley Rudolf Steiner School in Hertfordshire. The initiative came from Mrs Silbergh, and after the course she took the two teachers to the fresh air of the Cornish coast for a well-deserved break. They stayed at Tintagel and visited Gerard Wagner's former haunt of St Ives. Then they had four enjoyable days in London visiting museums, going to concerts and attending the Commonwealth Festival events.

The summer painting courses continued in 1966 and in 1967 at Kings Langley. Both years, Mrs Silbergh organised a holiday in Ireland afterwards for Gerard and Elisabeth. Painting courses also took place at Michael Hall School in Forest Row in 1966 and 1967. In 1966 the course was part of an Anthroposophical Society conference intended to unite the two Societies in England, to heal the divisions after the split back in 1935. The theme was 'The Relation of the Human Being to the Etheric World and to a new Christ-Experience'. A review of the conference praised the painting course which was 'greatly appreciated by the large number of participants who were able to attend it'. In all, Gerard Wagner and Elisabeth Koch taught six times in England between 1965 and 1973. In 1969, Gerard Wagner's paintings were exhibited at Rudolf Steiner House in London during the Easter Festival, and in 1961, for the centenary of Rudolf Steiner's birth, Wagner's paintings of animal metamorphosis shown there created much interest.

*

In the autumn of 1967 Gerard Wagner moved from his two small rooms at Eckinger House, where he'd lived for at least 30 years, to the upstairs flat at Brosiweg 2, previously occupied by the painter Louise van Blommestein.

She was keen for Gerard Wagner to have her studio which was spacious: north-facing windows gave ideal light for painting, and a large west-facing window gave a perfect view of the sunsets over Landskron Hill. For the first time since moving to Dornach in 1926, the painter had his own kitchen and bathroom. In the downstairs flat lived Martha and Hugo Reimann with whom Wagner had a warm connection.

During Gerard Wagner's last two years at Eckinger House, the teacher and artist Hermann Koepke, who lived there too, had many opportunities to meet and observe the painter. He recalled his impressions:

> Gerard Wagner was always friendly and open. I never saw him in a bad mood or depressed. He was never in a hurry but seemed to be in continuous inner activity in connection with his work, never tired or wasting the moment – in process always. Once I met him early in the morning just as he returned from a brisk dawn walk up to the Gempen – his eyes shining.
>
> When meeting him coming down the stairs (he lived on the top floor), the impression was of a spirit 'coming from above', from across the threshold. As he looked at you with his open face and blue eyes, he seemed to drink you in – see far inside you – and at the same time fill you up with warmth and love. I particularly noticed his fine head. He was usually dressed in dark colours, shirt open at the neck – something light, white around the neck.
>
> When he walked, he hardly seems to touch the ground. He was like a being not of this earth – he was already over the threshold. One felt the full and rich way he connected with what he saw and experienced. He observed keenly and was full of awareness for everything and everybody. Usually, around sunset, he would come out into the garden and take in the surroundings. The big larch tree there he planted himself.
>
> He was thin and delicate (one had a feeling of near-transparency). The people in the house would leave their containers or bottles for the milkman, and the amount of money left on the lid told the milkman how much milk was wanted. Gerard Wagner had a small amount, which he carried upstairs as if it was something precious. One had the impression that he was nourished simply by the colours and that small amount of milk. Upstairs he had plants on the window ledge, which he looked at, and looked *through*. He saw more than just the physical.
>
> He painted little pictures which he gave as presents to the older ladies there on their birthdays and other occasions, and he once showed me an

artistic figure carved in wood that was made and painted by the talented sculptress who lived in the house.

Some years later when talking with him about painting animals with children, Gerard Wagner invited me to his studio to study the subject more closely. He always left one quite free, he would never say: 'You should come to see me and learn how to paint animals with children', or anything like that. Instead he said: 'Feel free to sail your boat to my house anytime.'

At the Jakobsberg Rudolf Steiner School in Basel where I taught, some teachers were very much in favour of Wagner's paintings, and others dead against it, claiming it was too spiritual for the children. Gerard Wagner's paintings are from beyond the threshold, and if people don't have a feeling for the 'other side', it's clear that they cannot get on with his paintings.

Another valuable description of the painter comes from the artist Anne Stockton (see Appendix 10) who got to know Gerard Wagner in 1969 after her training in artistic therapy in Boll. She had already seen some of Wagner's paintings in an exhibition that travelled around the United States between 1958 and 1960. Anne Stockton had a long and fruitful friendship with Gerard Wagner as a pupil and as a colleague. When she became the painting teacher at Emerson College in Forest Row, she encouraged her pupils to continue their training at the 'Wagner School' in Dornach; and after she founded the Tobias School of Art in East Grinstead, former pupils of Gerard Wagner's came to teach there.

In her memories of the artist written for the author in 2002, she touched, among other things, on the controversy that surrounded him, and vividly recalled his way of teaching:

> Gerard Wagner was a challenging and controversial figure in Dornach when I arrived there for the first time in about 1969. I had barely heard his name although I had seen a few pictures of his in an exhibition in the USA, and also of Elisabeth Koch, who later became his wife. I appreciated the subtle and brilliant colouring, but the forms seemed strange to me. However they did speak a modern language although perhaps I liked hers more than his. They seemed freer, hers flowed more, his seemed stiffer.
>
> I had been in Art School from the age of 15 to 18 when I saw the first exhibition in New York of the Impressionists and was overwhelmed by

the wonder of it all, by Cézanne, Gauguin and van Gogh! The miracle of painting! But where was that stream of art going? To abstract art, and on, till today one has to ask with ever-greater urgency again: Where is the mainstream of art? What is the relation of anthroposophy and its artists to it? What indeed is art? What does so-called anthroposophical art mean? In Steiner lay a new challenge to be taken up by the serious student.

After my training with Frau Dr Hauschka I wanted to work with the 'sketches' of Rudolf Steiner's, and my friend Martha Havemeyer recommended Gerard Wagner in spite of the question mark hanging over his name. Why was Wagner controversial? Perhaps because he was English, breaking into a then more closed society in Dornach – young and going his own way! He had arrived from England, choosing to follow Rudolf Steiner's insights instead of taking up his scholarship at London's prestigious Royal College of Art. He was drawn immediately to Henni Geck's studio and her teaching based on 'Nine Training Sketches' she had received from Steiner himself.

His independence soon asserted itself with its inherent 'consciousness soul' approach. He pursued his own research, working alone for years. His strongly two-dimensional style, the individualised and unique forms of his trees, animals, human beings and angels, raised many eyebrows. It could be disquieting to encounter his motifs.

How very different from the sometimes near-sentimental tradition of the Waldorf School style of painting many had achieved in trying to respond to Rudolf Steiner's call for a 'universally human style'. When this young painter struck out with his bold and not always harmonious colours and forms, shock waves ensued. Of course there were other painters who had developed individual styles of their own but based, it appeared, on much more conventional forms. Wagner was an uncompromising pioneer in seeking to bring the form out of the colour as Steiner had indicated. His colour was strong and unusual too, and he investigated the dark: there were few light, pale colours in his work, instead, dark colours became light and brilliant by the contrasting darker colours.

There was another matter of much discussion among the artists. Artists can be very passionate about their differences and these were. Some objected that, in seeking such a scientific solution to colour expression – founded on measure, weight, and perhaps number – all artists would end up creating the same picture. Wagner kept his cool but his passion shows itself in the resolute stubbornness with which he followed his own path.

With Herr Wagner there was no spontaneous splashing of colour and no emphasis on strongly one-sided soul moods. He gives each colour its individual say and brings about a balance of the spectrum. This might be considered a more spiritual approach. There is a chorus of all the colours, singing joy! All this I discovered when I decided that this was the Master I sought and I applied to be his pupil, or rather asked him to be my teacher. He led us on a path of mysteries and colour activity, of painting as a path of spiritual training. Over the years he discovered dynamics of colour and secrets of metamorphosis, of the deeds of 'the individuality of the colours', as his very valuable book is called. I spent many visits and months there, and summer courses with him over years, grateful for all his shared discoveries with which he was so generous.

Herr Wagner made a physical impression that changed as one knew him. At first he looked a homely man with thinning white hair, pale blue eyes, his shoulders bowed and making him seem shorter than he was; a modest, small presence which seemed to grow as one entered into longer deeper relation with him. There was something almost gnome-like about him at first, but seeming to grow into a tall distinguished character in his black beret and cape as he walked everywhere about Dornach, attending every possible event at the Goetheanum. His expressions were always changing as he talked, and one became aware of great light in a very gentle face and, as he demonstrated or gestured, of the transparent beauty of his hands.

On our later visits when he showed us his latest paintings, my husband Kurt Falk, who had his own reverence for the art of painting, was deeply interested in the spiritual activity of Gerard Wagner. He plied him with questions, as to whether he painted in sleep, and whether in the etheric or astral realm. His answer: 'Yes, in sleep too, and yes, in etheric realms but in later years, astral realms too, trying to find my way ...' – mysteries upon mysteries.

Gerard Wagner's method of teaching was most interesting. Frau Dr Hauschka's way had always been full of encouragement, beginning with 'Schön! Schön!' (Lovely! Lovely!). She always made positive suggestions about improvementss or change. Wagner's criticism was no-nonsense stuff, but always positive, interesting, and completely appropriate. It was to the point, with the *personal* veiled, but spot-on. When coming to one's side to help one's painting, it was never a critique as such, his mischievous or humorous comments piqued one into new awareness. He had a lovely sly sense of humour which peeked out especially when talking to an English-speaking person. It seemed as if he truly came into his own then. In German he was a more formidable figure.

When we met in the street or at the Goetheanum, his joyful smile greeted me and wrapped me in warmth. I thought in my vanity, 'He does like me'. We all appreciate appreciation. It seemed there were special students too. 'I was loved like his son', said one. Then I set to observing him, especially as he moved about with people. We *all* were like his son. He had no favourite, but he radiated love on all alike. And so we all flowered. He was a sun!

THE PAINTING SCHOOL

Dornach 1970–1989

DEVELOPMENT AND CONSOLIDATION

First Publications

1968 saw the first publication of Gerard Wagner's work, a folder with the title *Plant Metamorphosis* consisting of a series of eight paintings based on Rudolf Steiner's 'Archetypal Plant'. A short review was printed in the book section of a Zurich newspaper on 6.12.1969:

> Eight watercolours entitled 'Plant Metamorphosis' by the Dornach painter Gerard Wagner (introduced by Elisabeth Koch) offer highly original material for practising and enlivening inner perception. In small stages, from page to page, the picture of a plant transforms into another naturally and without artistic self-will. Through colours and forms nature's creative forces can be experienced as the streaming of etheric forces before they manifest in a final shape.[96]

A detailed description of the series of eight pictures was written by Michael Howard, a former pupil. Gerard Wagner responded favourably to Michael Howard's essay, which illustrates the scientific exactitude with which Wagner approached his colour research, placing importance on the order of colours used in a painting:

> The eight paintings clearly show plant forms, but they are unusual because they do not look like any plants we see in nature (see plate 11). They are neither stylised abstractions, nor fanciful imaginations of plant forms. Each painting shows a different plant form, not because they represent different plant types, but because the sequence shows the transformation from a blooming plant in the first painting to a withered plant in the last. The first painting is based on a painting by Steiner called 'Archetypal Plant'; however, Wagner's painting is not a copy of Steiner's. Based on a deep study of Steiner's painting, Wagner came to see a relationship between the order in which the colours are introduced and the form they are given. This discovery is perhaps Wagner's central contribution, and for this reason, we will give special attention to the sequence of colours Wagner used in creating, 'Plant Metamorphosis'.
>
> On the first page, he introduced a warm yellow while holding questions like: Where to place it on the page? How large an area? And how

should it spread on the page: –fading out, fading in or flat and hard edge? He sought to answer these practical questions based on his felt experience of the warm yellow in relation to the vertical white page. Looking at the painting, we can discern that Wagner placed this warm yellow in the upper middle area of the page. On the one hand, his aim was to allow the individual quality of this warm yellow to manifest as fully as possible. At the same time, he tried to harmonize it within the whole page so that it is neither too dominant nor too under-stated.

Wagner begins the second page with the same yellow except that he adds a small amount of violet to it, causing the colour to change to a yellowish, pale brown. Again he asks where, how much and how to place this colour on the page. Although the change in colour is subtle, nevertheless it has a discernibly different quality, so not surprisingly it takes a slightly different form. With each successive page, additional amounts of violet are added to the yellow resulting in corresponding changes in the size and form it takes up on the page. By the final page, the original yellow has so much violet added to it that it becomes a deep brown that can be detected as a small spot of brown in the upper middle area. If we were to see all the paintings together after the application of the first colour, we would see eight vertical white pages as follows: a radiant warm yellow in the upper part of the first painting, with each successive painting showing an increasingly brownish yellow that becomes smaller, less radiant and expansive, so that by the final one we would see only a small 'nut' of brown.

Wagner continues the series by bringing the same cool blue to all eight paintings. However, in responding to where, how much and how to spread this blue, he also again attempts to bring out the quality of the blue while also bringing it into harmony with the previously painted eight steps of yellow as they change by degrees to brown. Whilst the blue colour remains the same in each painting, the form it takes on will be different. In the same way, a red and finally another yellow are brought as third and fourth colours to each painting.

Each colour was applied with the intention of revealing the unique dynamic quality of that colour, while at the same time creating balance, harmony and unity with the existing colours. The only variable in each painting was the first colour – the gradual browning of the warm yellow. The form Wagner gave to each colour, including the first one, was relatively simple. Any inclination to be expressive or fanciful was resisted so that the metamorphosis from a blooming to a withering plant form arose solely in response to the warm yellow fading to brown.[97]

This first publication of Gerard Wagner's work was followed in 1970 by the large-format children's book of the fairytale *Sleeping Beauty*. The striking, non-naturalistic, clear-cut images with their iconic character are very different to most anthroposophically inspired illustrations for children's books. For the overall mood of the story Wagner chose a deep violet blue which fits well with the mysterious night character of the hundred-year sleep. It also contrasts well with the other strongly individual colours. The painter does not shy away from the use of black, here resonant of the evil which in many genuine fairytales plays such a crucial part in the drama of the soul-spiritual events underlying the stories. Following an indication from Rudolf Steiner for the practice of illustrative art,[98] Wagner included different scenes from the story in one painting as was common in the paintings of the Middle Ages.

In 1972, the folder *Animal Metamorphosis* was published by the Philosophisch-Anthroposophischer Verlag, Dornach, in German and English. It was similar to the plant metamorphosis series but more extensive, showing 24 stages of a process of transformation based on Rudolf Steiner's painting of the 'Archetypal Animal – Archetypal Man' motif.

Another folder, *A Glance into Nature's Workshop* was brought out simultaneously in German and English by the same publishers in 1974. Again the subject was metamorphosis, this time showing stages of plant development in 16 paintings with the elemental beings weaving around the plant. It was painted on the background colours of the four ethers: cool blue for chemical ether (spring), yellow and red for light and warmth ether (summer and autumn), and violet for life ether (winter). The series shows a transformation from the germinal shoot to plant growth, blossoming, seed formation, and arrives back at the beginning of the cycle with fresh plant growth.

The English Hall murals

The 1970s were years of intense activity for Gerard Wagner. Whilst some might be thinking about 'slowing down' or retiring at the age of 64, Gerard Wagner was on the brink of two decades of intense work.

In 1971 Rex Raab, who was involved with the continuing architectural and artistic work on the interior of the second Goetheanum, arranged for Gerard Wagner to paint the walls of the English Hall, a lecture theatre. He had first secured the painter a wall painting commission in a private house in Stuttgart about 20 years earlier in 1956/1957, but the English Hall project was the first large-scale wall painting commission that Gerard Wagner undertook. He made some 80 preparatory painting studies and it took six weeks, with the assistance of Elisabeth Koch and Erwin Thomalla, to complete the task. Gerard Wagner's patron Frau Lefringhausen wrote to him enquiring as to whether his idea for a motif had been accepted: 'I wonder how it will go regarding your designs for the new room, and if you will get the commission? How very much I wish it for you, and for us all.'

Felix Wagner, Gerard Wagner's brother, also refers to the project in two letters written around that time:

3.5.1970

Dear Gerard

From your interesting letter it seems as if the years produce a flowering of more and more varied work than ever – rather like Churchill? It will be quite a task, one would think, tackling those vast areas in the new lecture room at the Goetheanum. And possibly three painters won't make it easier than one? I wonder what 'fix' your specialist has for watercolour, and how good the prepared surfaces will be to work on – quite some technical problems. One wonders if this problem ever entered the minds of Michelangelo or Leonardo even, spending years on walls and ceilings, ... They must have been either lucky or clever in finding the lasting colour qualities they did, for us to enjoy now ...

Love from us both and to E.

Felix

10.10.1971

Dear Gerard

You have been so increasingly on my mind lately, chiefly because I see your letter daily in our desk diary, that a start must be made to thank you for your most interesting account of the job in hand at the Goetheanum, which has caused me also to think of you during the past two months standing on planks on trestles while we were standing, not too high probably but perhaps up and down a good deal oftener, on our tripod ladders, bringing down apples. The comparison is possibly far-fetched, since you're creating something directly, following years of study and practice; we're removing directly something that we've only had a small part in creating. It would be interesting to hear how (and why) you deal with your subject(s?) or the thinking behind what one will see on those walls – what an area – and how you achieve it, especially given the peculiar shape of the place (not to mention ceiling, window and light problems in the room). You shall be spared, I think, explaining the result at the end, anyway in a letter. One day, before we're actually dying, we should like to come that way over and see all for ourselves. Meanwhile I do hope you won't find the physical end of it too much – it sounds quite considerable – and that there are enough willing hands around to hump heavy things and prepare surfaces so that you don't have to. Thinking of which, I am able (still am, *Deo Volente* as mother would say) to pick 4 to 5 bushels an hour from 9.30 till 7 pm, and load 350 boxes on to the lorry, after which supper, a bit of reading the paper, and bed – this since August 1ˢᵗ until mid-November. So another crop will have been gathered, in the most wonderful weather, which is just breaking. Prices are up on last year, which they had to be to keep us in growing, but we shan't know till late in the year how much better. … Will write again sooner. Love from us both and our greetings to E. Felix

The basic colour composition of the wall painting of the English Hall was an interplay of red and blue. The receiving quality of blue was painted towards the back of the room whilst various nuances of red surround the speaker's area to help carry the spoken word towards the audience. The back wall has a night mood illumined by a small moon; and on the neighbouring wall a gentle image of the mother and child can be seen. The chief motif on the large wall was of a light-filled being that contrasts strikingly with the large expanse of surging blue surfaces.

Further teaching in England

An invitation to lead a painting group at a conference for members organised by the Anthroposophical Society of Great Britain in 1973 saw Gerard Wagner once more in England, this time at Exeter in Devon. The conference took place between 10 and 16 August and was an important event for Britain, with prominent anthroposophists as the speakers. They included Rudolf Grosse from the Council of the Anthroposophical Society at the Goetheanum, Bernard Lievegoed, M. P. van Deventer, Cecil Harwood and John Davy. Gerard Wagner and Elisabeth Koch taught one of the 30 afternoons groups which were led by artists and scientists such as Lea van der Pals, Olive Whicher, Arne Klingborg, Jorgen Smit, Michael Wilson, Owen Barfield and others. The conference broadened Gerard Wagner's reputation and brought more pupils from England to the painting school in Dornach.

A year later in August 1974, the two painters were asked to give a 10-day painting course at the Sheiling School for Special Needs Children in Ringwood, Hampshire, and afterwards Eve Hardy and her husband, pupils at the Dornach painting school, drove the artist couple to Durham and to Sutherland in Scotland where they stayed for a few weeks. Van James, a former art student from New York who was studying at Emerson College, found his way to the Ringwood Conference through Anne Stockton. It was a life-changing event for him:

> The Ringwood Painting Conference was organised by Eve Hardy, who as a former student of Frau Dr Hauschka, and now a student of Wagner, wanted the latter's work to be brought to England, and to a curative setting. Anne Stockton convinced a small group of the Emerson painting group, of which I was one, to attend the conference with her as our training was based on learning about all the various anthroposophical approaches to the art of colour. We all drove down to Ringwood in Anne's car I believe – a merry band of us.
>
> I had seen the one painting of Wagner's that hung at Emerson and I must say, as an avant-garde art school graduate, I was not impressed. So I didn't expect much from the conference. I think there were about thirty or forty participants and it lasted ten days – a long time for a beginner to paint yellow!
>
> But what struck me was the absolute attention and oneness that Gerard Wagner showed when he came around to place a stroke or two on my picture. In that moment I could see everything that was happening on my page as if by magic. When he went on to help the next person and I was left on my own I could no longer see in the same way, I just struggled.
>
> It was at the conference that I was invited to stop over in Dornach to paint at the 'Wagner School' before going on to start the training at the Hauschka School for Artistic Therapy in Boll which had already been arranged. So I stopped in Dornach on the way, and stayed for four years – I never got to Boll, not even for a visit.
>
> The paintings of Wagner and of the students at his school were not particularly appealing to me. It was the total awareness and connectedness that Wagner had to the colour in the act of painting that convinced

me he was the one I could learn something from. It was the Zen of painting![99]

By the time Van James joined the school in 1974, Gerard Wagner's reputation had grown in the English-speaking world and a good number of English-speaking students – from North America, Canada, Australia, New Zealand and Britain – had found their way to him. Exhibitions of his work had brought pupils, and the earlier courses he and Elisabeth Koch gave in England had left their mark. Erwin Thomalla's painting courses in some of these countries had also helped to spread the word. Thomalla mentioned the growth of the school in his article 'New Standards of Measure in Painting':

> … The number of students grows from year to year with an especially gratifying proportion from overseas so that three of the oldest former pupils of Gerard Wagner have already been active as assisting teachers in the school for several years. As different as the areas of the world from which the students come are, so their aims and wishes differ. There are disenchanted art students who have learned nothing or very little that was satisfactory about colour at conventional art schools. There are teachers who want to study Rudolf Steiner's pedagogical impulse more deeply in their free time, to support painting in Waldorf schools. Or again, there are curative educationalists seeking to learn about painting's healing value. Others study colour in order to produce clothing that accords with and reflects human nature. In all areas the indications and sketches of Rudolf Steiner can be of help.
>
> We can learn to understand a further prompting from Rudolf Steiner, one which is of special importance in painting, in respect of the sketches: the overcoming of weight – the striving to come to a 'floating equilibrium' in a picture This search for balance of all forces at work among the colours according to the relationships of the given space is far more than a mere aesthetic venture. Through our activity we come in the fullest sense to a harmonisation of our own being. Inner and outer correspond. Herein lies the significance of what we do as initial steps toward the development of an art of painting in accord with the deepest aims of humanity in our time.[100]

The Gerard Wagner Foundation in North America

For ten years from the mid-1970s, the school reached its zenith with up to 40 pupils, a number of them who went on to teach or found painting schools themselves and who would play a role in the furthering of Gerard Wagner's work worldwide.

Two pupils, Ted Ormiston and Peter Sagal, returned to the USA in the summer of 1982 with the intention of establishing a painting school, an exhibition gallery and an archive for a collection of paintings by Gerard Wagner, augmented by some from Elisabeth Koch and Erwin Thomalla. The archive included two copies of a collection of photographic slides of the complete collection of Gerard Wagner's paintings taken in 1982 by Peter Sagal. As Peter Sagal recalled: 'This happened at the request of Gerard and Elisabeth, whose intention was to send such collections of slides to other countries in the world, two to the USA, one to Australia, one remaining in Europe and one eventually to go elsewhere, to South Africa perhaps.'

Ted Ormiston with Dr Sasha Stark who accompanied him to the U.S., purchased a house in Philmont, N.Y. that had previously served as a Masonic Lodge. They restored the large, open space on the upper floor which they prepared for exhibitions, and developed a cataloguing plan and methodology for handling artwork loans and exhibits. Ted gathered a group of supporters that included Kurt Leisi and Peter Stebbing to help with the work, and the first modest show of Gerard Wagner's paintings opened in Philmont in early 1983.

It soon became apparent that a clear set of operating principles was needed and that a more formal relationship with the Gerard Wagner Association in Dornach ought to be established. This ultimately led to the formation of the Foundation in Philmont in 1987,[101] with Gerard Wagner himself contributing the funds still needed for the legal completion of the project.

The core intention was to establish a centre that would serve to further the knowledge and understanding of Gerard Wagner's work and Rudolf Steiner's artistic impulse, represented by a variety of works of Steiner's including Albert von Baravalle's model of the first Goetheanum, photographs and artefacts. To keep the collection up to date, it was foreseen that paintings would periodically be exchanged for and sometimes augmented by new ones from Dornach. It was hoped that Wagner would also travel to North America and give a painting course there, but that never happened, and Erwin Thomalla's intention of supporting the painting training with quarterly visits from Dornach did not come about due to his untimely death in September 1983. However, Peter Stebbing gradually developed a full-time painting training under the auspices of the Threefold Educational Foundation at Spring Valley, New York. By 1985 the training had 12 students and in 1987 the 'Threefold Painting School' was recognized by the Section for the Visual Arts at the Goetheanum.

The Gerard Wagner Foundation was eventually extended and expanded by Hans Schumm in Ghent, on the outskirts of Harlemville. Not only did Hans greatly strengthen the basis and expand the operations of the Foundation, but he fulfilled the need for a school of painting founded on the principles of the artistic impulse and work of Gerard Wagner. Through his dedicated work and teaching he has drawn a circle of devoted supporters. Throughout, Peter Sagal, as the other member on the board of the Foundation, has continued to share in the development and implementation of the Foundation's guiding principles. The Gerard Wagner Foundation centred at Windy Hill, Harlemville – the property and land given as a gift from the Anthroposophical Society of North America – is a thriving community today and currently owns 86 works by Gerard Wagner which are exhibited there regularly.[102]

Collections of Wagner paintings grew in other places as well. One began in Australia in 1981 through Kafounrl Kaltenbach, the then General Secretary of the Australian Anthroposophical Society, and soon a number of Gerard Wagner's paintings were hanging in special needs schools and other communities, as well as at the Anthroposophical Society headquarters in Sidney. A small collection in Hawaii came about initially through Virginia Brett, and in Vancouver Katherine Mayne's enthusiasm for the work led her to include her collection of Wagner's paintings in the 'The Albert Steffen Branch' that she led there. In August 1971, she wrote to Gerard Wagner:

> Dear Herr Wagner
> Your picture reached me three days ago and I cannot tell you how delighted I am. It is so beautiful. The colours are radiant and I have just been sitting since then in front of it. The sense of balance you spoke of is truly there and with its quietness – 'active rest' – I like that! – it recalls a few words from *The Philosophy of Spiritual Activity* which I love. I cannot quote them exactly but 'thinking at rest within itself, yet ever in movement'; oh! I love your picture. Thank you, thank you! And I can really feel the therapeutic value of the colours. Now I can really visualise a little bit what the walls in our beloved Goetheanum will have on them. How is the work on them going? I do hope very well.
>
> One thing I wish you had told me is about the mount for my picture. Would you advise a cream colour? And how wide? And a light coloured

wood for the frame? Would you have time to send me that advice in a few words? I shall be very grateful if you will.

My room is becoming like a Wagner picture gallery! Four of them now. Wonderful! I think I shall leave this one to the group. I have not quite decided but I think I should. Two of our members, two very fine young men – one our architect, the other a philosopher – have seen it already and each became completely absorbed in it. And very consciously felt the beauty and living quality of the plant colours.

Again all my thanks and warm greetings from
Katherine Mayne

Being inspired by the paintings they saw hanging in their meeting room, a number of the Albert Steffen Branch members from Vancouver found their way to Gerard Wagner in Dornach, one of whom wrote to the painter after a visit in 1977:

Dear Herr Wagner

My wife Bronwyn and I wish to thank you for your hospitality when we saw you in your studio in April. Your paintings from the dome of the first Goetheanum were very exciting. It is always very hard to create an image of events of the distant past, or future for that matter, as Rudolf Steiner describes them in his lectures. Paintings are therefore very welcome on all those most difficult subjects. But the satisfaction we experience looking at your paintings, of course, went deeper than just complementing knowledge.

We only hope that this won't have been the only opportunity to look at the paintings.

With warm regards, Michael Lange

The handwork impulse

Meanwhile the teaching Gerard Wagner had given in the 1950s in Engelberg for the furthering of the handwork impulse, evolved further through the work of Rolf and Elisabeth Adler,[103] exceptionally gifted artists who spent some time as pupils at the Wagner painting school in Dornach in the late 1960s. In the middle of the 1970s they worked further with Gerard Wagner on the theme of 'colour and clothing', and this included the question of the appropriate clothing for different ages. 'We brought our questions, and Herr Wagner painted his answers', said Elisabeth Adler, 'and he was always open to look together with us at the work we'd done in the meantime. We found that helpful and stimulating.'

As usual, the questions that came Gerard Wagner's way stimulated his interest and led to him undertaking a large amount of work in that field. His strong drive to research led him to paint hundreds of 'experiments' which covered most aspects of Rudolf Steiner's handwork indications. They comprised paintings of dresses and smocks, shoes, gloves and hats, bags for various functions, sewing cases, spectacle cases, tablecloths and mats, pillowcases, bookmarkers, book covers and other household articles. The experience he gained in this way flowed into the work undertaken by Rolf and Elisabeth Adler. In the striking colour combinations of the embroidery they created for clothing, and coverings for household objects, the stamp of the way Wagner used colour is evident. Their impulse was to further the art of embroidery, to 'enhance the artistic creation of cloth and yarn through the painterly use of colour'. Marie Steiner described in her Introduction to a book about handwork by Louise van Blommestein,[104] how embroidery is especially related to the artistic element. The way she here connects soul qualities to the dynamics of colour is reminiscent of Gerard Wagner 's approach to the qualities of colour and their inherent dynamics:

> With embroidery, a path began towards the grasping of the artistic element. A sense for form and colour can be awakened through it. The combining of the nuances of wool, yarn and silk gives the possibility not only of developing insight into colour harmonies, but of taking up the soul aspect of colour into the life of feeling. Through this, one develops sensitivity to what 'activity', 'aggression' or 'loosening' is as colour, and to how these qualities can be applied, as warmth, concentration, support, softening or radiating, as functional additions to the piece of handwork in question.

The painting-sketches Rolf and Elisabeth Adler kept from their work with Gerard Wagner are especially vivid in their spontaneity. And a few sentences written in the corner of the sheets reveal Wagner's insights into the clothing question, especially in regard to the incarnating (or excarnating) human being in the various stages of childhood, youth, adulthood and old age. These paintings were not illustrations of spiritual-scientific facts of human development, of which Wagner was well aware, but rather revelations, insights he gained, from his experiments with colour. On one worksheet Rolf Adler has added a note to the series of illustrations that reads: 'How feeling (orange) descends into the bodily organisation in the different ages of childhood' (See plate 146)

Elisabeth Adler wrote:

> In creating, ever anew, out of the present situation, we tried as much as possible to base our work on our own practice of painting as it was developed by Gerard and Elisabeth Wagner based on indications of Rudolf Steiner, and on the anthroposophical picture of the human being. Embroidery, in connection with clothing and coverings for household items, is, or can become once again, a real art. Our attempts are explorations in this direction.

For the preparation of their handwork courses, Rolf and Elisabeth Adler developed their own list of priorities for the painterly use of colour in handwork:

> 1. Limit yourself to the most essential.
> 2. Be down-to-earth and practical in your feeling perceptions.
> 3. The personal aspect comes to natural expression.

They expressed as follows their view of what was 'most essential':

> To help the human being in the healthy development of body–soul–spirit, spirit–soul–body. The living space, along with its household objects, should be enlivening and genuine in itself and in relation to human beings.
>
> Recognize the source and foundation of the work already existing in anthroposophical knowledge of man and art, and make this conscious.
>
> Create out of the deepest ground of one's own seeking.

Gerard Wagner liked to embroider and he did a little sewing as well. Since childhood he had a keen eye for clothing. When he could afford it he had his jackets and suits made by a tailor in Basel. For these he mostly chose a round neck design inspired by a picture he'd seen of someone in a similar style. He thought it could be an appropriate style for a painter. For everyday wear, Gerard Wagner wore a brown or green-brown corduroy jacket. He had an elegant dark-blue suit made with a stand-up collar – his own design – which he wore to evening events and special occasions. In his studio he always wore a blue painting smock. His outdoor shoes were black and sturdy, and at least in later years, his tread was slow and deliberate. He called it 'my farmer's step'.

Always a keen observer, Wagner would point out clothing, referring to shape and colour, which he felt fitted the human being in an appropriate way.

It could be a shirt with dynamic swirling forms worn by Nelson Mandela, which seemed to reflect something of the life-body of the human being, or a long-sleeved T-shirt of purple and green worn by an electrician working in the house, or a child's outfit he might see when out walking. He commented favourably on the pleasant, bright-coloured garments worn by young children today. For a woman's dress or skirt he pointed out the harmonious effect of the colour lilac (a shade of peach blossom). When asked advice for clothing for an ill child, he suggested yellow on the upper part of the body and a cool red (rose) colour on the lower part. He had nothing good to say about the 'baseball-style cap' with the broad peak, so popular today.

Sometime in the 1990s Gerard Wagner made a visit to the Sonnhalde Home for Special Needs Children in Gempen near Dornach. Angela Zbinden, a student at the painting school who worked at the home, accompanied him and asked for advice for painting therapeutically with the children there. To her surprise, his advice was to begin with clothing. He said: 'Half of the difficulties would fall away if the children wore the right clothes.' In relation to one boy he met there, Wagner drew attention to the disturbance to the child caused by the shirt he was wearing. It had a zigzag pattern of black, yellow, green and violet. He suggested to Angela that she could make the boy a jacket out of peat fibres, and accentuate the neck, arms and centre front. 'He needs "armour"', Wagner said. 'Embroider colours on these three places – the head needs to be carried, the hands aroused for work – the whole human being needs support.'

Gerard Wagner gave his advice in other areas of artistic endeavour as well. Ernst Schuberth recalled his request for Wagner's help in the design of his wedding ring:

> In 1967, when Erika and I decided to marry, I asked Gerard Wagner to elaborate a design for a ring. I wished for a lemniscate form, with a red and a blue stone in each loop, to show the polarity of man and women as well as their union. After some time we received two coloured sketches in which the lemniscates were made up of three forms: on one side more strongly concave and the other convex, and connecting both was a lively independent form. The goldsmith used Gerard Wagner's design to make the rings – mine was larger and flatter, Erika's somewhat smaller and rounder, each with a red ruby and a sapphire. They were clearly different from each other yet belonged unmistakably together.

Exhibitions

In early September 1976 Gerard Wagner was preparing for an exhibition of his work at the Goetheanum Michaelmas Conference. He wrote about it to Ernst Schuberth, at the same time concerned by his perception that Rudolf Steiner's painting impulse was generally being ignored:

> Dear Herr Schuberth
> … I am preparing for the Michaelmas conference show … I have the Terrace Room and Gallery to fill. In the Terrace Room I am thinking of showing work chiefly on the motifs of the large cupola of the First Goetheanum. I have attempted to combine some motifs – 'Eye and Ear' with the neighbouring motifs 'Elohim' and 'Paradise' – or 'Paradise' with 'Egypt' and 'Greece' and so on. Will you be able to see it? You could then perhaps write about painting as a gateway to history – or to the Akashic Chronicles!
>
> When one begins to notice something about it, it seems to one almost unbelievable that in all these years there has been hardly any interest in the sketches of Rudolf Steiner or knowledge of them in our circles. What a meaningful task the painting could have, and what a real anthroposophical life and deed could come out of it. – The sketches could really give one an idea of this.
>
> In a narrower sense, interest in the sketches at the present time would also be important because the tendency to painterly abstraction, which represents an escape from the art of the future and from oneself, asserts itself more and more and does not allow the consciousness of the impulses given by Rudolf Steiner for painting, to become established …
>
> With every good wish for you and your wife and family.
> Heartfelt greetings
> Gerard Wagner

Exhibitions of Gerard Wagner's work were plentiful in the 1970s: in 1970 in Kassel; in 1971 in Berlin at a conference of the Anthroposophical Society; at the Easter Conference at the Goetheanum in 1971, as also at Easter 1972 when the opening address was given by Theodor Willmann; in 1976 at the Aenigma Gallery in Basel, and the above-mentioned exhibition of cupola motifs at Michaelmas at the Goetheanum.

In May 1979 Gerard Wagner was preparing for an exhibition in Paris when he received an encouraging letter from Eckwälden from the artist Marie Krösche:

... Now I wish you all the best for the Paris exhibition. Hopefully it can kindle in people's hearts an acknowledgment of what art can bring, namely a strengthening of the soul and fiery enthusiasm for the spirit, as fruit of the being of anthroposophy.

The exhibition was organised by Sonja Vandroogenbroeck, a pupil of the painting school, and it took place at the Hotel Nikko de Paris which had an adjoining gallery. Arrangements were made to catalogue and transport 80 paintings, and as usual pupils were involved in the event and travelled to Paris to be present at the opening. Sonja enjoyed telling the following anecdote about that occasion:

The party were in the restaurant ordering their meals, which took a little time; then the waiter came to Gerard Wagner and said 'et qu'est ce que j'apporte pour l'initié?' ('And what can I bring the initiate?'). This caused much amusement but also surprise at the waiter's apt intuition!

Sonja also organised exhibitions of Gerard Wagner's work at Basel's Kaserne cultural centre in 1978 and 1979, during which the master painter gave workshops, and examples of students' work were shown.

Preparations for an exhibition at Kensington Town Hall in London, initiated by the painter Gladys Mayer, had been underway for some time in 1978, with many letters and telegrams flying back and forward between London and Dornach. But finally the exhibition was cancelled because of many practical hurdles that could not be resolved at the time. Gladys Mayer though, who had been inspired by Gerard Wagner's latest works of the large cupola motifs in the first Goetheanum (some of the earliest paintings executed with plant-based pigments), refused to relinquish her impulse to show others the paintings, and over the autumn months of 1979 she gave presentations of Wagner's cupola paintings with slides at Rudolf Steiner House, at Temple Lodge, the home of the Christian Community in London, and at Kensington Library. Despite having reached the age of 91 she planned to give more talks in the spring of the following year.

In April 1978 she wrote to her friend Gerard Wagner with her reasons for wanting to show his work in London:

I feel your work is a kind of resurrection of the First Goetheanum paintings, and I think now that people are beginning to awaken to the fact that there is a real spiritual world and that we ignore it at our peril. It seems to me a golden opportunity to put this before a central London public, from where it can radiate widely to the world.

And in May 1978:

> … your Goetheanum Dome pictures showed me, in my conscious etheric picturing, that in some things at least you were painting what I see. Rudolf Steiner told me that I was seeing rightly. I feel confident in my recognition of etheric reality in those paintings of yours. That is why I want to exhibit them in England. Potentially, English people, and beyond them, the Irish, have etheric perception – in contrast to more astral perception on the Continent. So I feel it is your work that should be shown in England more than any I know of the Goetheanum painters. This is quite objective judgment, not just friendship bias. Objectively too, I feel that this work is needed here now.

With this impulse living so strong in her, Gladys Mayer was torn suddenly from earth life in January 1980. John Fletcher wrote to Gerard Wagner:

> For the last few years of her life, she could think of nothing else than an exhibition of your recent paintings in London, and was full of joy when you lent her a set of slides of your paintings which she used at a lecture at Rudolf Steiner House. Her death was in some ways connected with her desire for an exhibition of your work, because she was on her way back from a visit to the Rudolf Steiner Architecture Exhibition in London during the winter, where she had hoped to meet Dr Hagen Biesantz to discuss a possible combined exhibition of your work; but he was not there, and leaving the building and crossing the road, she was knocked down by a motor-cycle and died four hours later without regaining consciousness.

After her death, Gladys Mayer continued to help the painter from the spiritual world. John Fletcher again wrote to Gerard Wagner in November 1981:

> Dear Herr Wagner, Thank you for your very interesting letter. I am so glad that Gladys Mayer's *Colour – A New Approach to Painting* has been of such interest to you and that you are both having such a rewarding experience now in such a remarkable manner. The karmic aspects must be something special.

I am sending you her book, *The Mystery Wisdom of Colour*, which you may already have, as it was first published in 1961 & reprinted 1970 and 1976.

A few years earlier, in an article for the Mercury Arts Group Newsletter, Gladys Mayer had written about Gerard Wagner after visiting him in Dornach:

> … I visited the studio of an old friend whom I had known from the time he first came to Dornach to find his vocation in the Arts. That year was 1926. We both had an academic background, his more adventurous than mine, though mine had been unusual. We both had won distinction in the normal course of studies, but he, much younger than I, had his life centred on painting, and we were both determined to find our way to the basis of colour, following the pioneering steps of Goethe and Steiner.
>
> The Goetheanum had been burned down in 1923, before I arrived in 1924. Rudolf Steiner was alive; but Gerard Wagner arrived only after Rudolf Steiner had died, so there was little of Rudolf Steiner's work to be seen. For me there was the living contact. For Gerard Wagner that too was gone. There were a few faithful artists who had worked with him. There were pastel sketches he had done for the schools, and painted posters for the eurythmy performances – all these from his own hands. There was no teacher – only what we could glean from conversations and from the rather scattered material. And the mighty problem of colour stood before us unmistakably, but the signposts were few.
>
> Gerard Wagner put his life into the paintings; I put my life into AnthropoSophia, and hoped I might find in the painting here what I had failed to find anywhere in modern art. So we found then a natural comradeship of purpose.
>
> Fifty-one years later I went to visit Gerard Wagner in his studio. He was working to recover the vision behind the sketches Rudolf Steiner had given to the artists who had attempted the decoration of the Large Dome of the first Goetheanum, on the themes of the evolution of the earth, from its earliest beginnings through the cultural epochs until the beginning of our time. He showed me the pastel sketches the artists had been given; they also had had Rudolf Steiner to refer to. But these painters had found it difficult enough to re-create his vision – in a new technique and with themes no longer visible and almost unthinkable to human imagination.

Gerard Wagner has worked with these sketches, not copying, but living into their meaning, painting them, two, three, four – many times, until he felt he had reached what was intended.

He showed me picture after picture, so many I could only travel with them into that world he was re-creating – the etheric world of time, of colour, of ancient spiritual experiences, which an earlier people had known, which we all had known in earlier times. I could recognise their meaning to some extent. I had flashes of recollection – forms I had seen, images that come from a supersensible world that seemed preserved only in the Akashic records.

I rejoiced with what I can only call a spiritual joy in this work, which after years of utter devotion, were yielding an entry through the realm of colour, into worlds of the spirit from which thousands of lives to come would be enriched. I felt humbled but exultant that this work of the boy I had known fifty-one years ago had become a light to the future of art. This was how I felt it. This is what it meant to me …[105]

Further publications

1980 saw the publication of the two books written by Elisabeth Koch and Gerard Wagner. One, a workbook, had been in preparation for some years and was to show first steps in the method of painting practised by pupils at the painting school. As previously mentioned, the book grew initially out of articles written for the art periodical *The Staedtler-Brief.*

For the title of the book, Gerard Wagner chose *The Individuality of Colour* – an expression that seems to have had no precedent. A similar expression, though, can be found in the handwriting of Novalis, in his copy of Goethe's *Theory of Colour:* the '*individuality of every colour'.*[106]

The new book was reviewed by the mathematician and pedagogue Georg Glöckler (1933–2019) who gave a concise overall picture of the book's content and made some enlightening comments:

> *Working with Colour*
> The newly published book *The Individuality of Colour* describes a sys-
> tematically structured path of training in colour feeling. The authors
> are leaders of a painting school at the Goetheanum in Dornach. The
> purpose of the book is to show in clear, understandable steps a way of
> working with objective colour experience. The attentive reader will not
> find it easy to follow all the steps right away. The difficulty however lies

not in the way it is described but in the nature of the thing itself. Our usual 'object-consciousness' tends to rely on a more outer colour experience relative to the objects we see. But this does not lead to experience and knowledge of the colour itself. The path of training described here starts purely from colour, for example from a yellow patch on a white surface (in this context white is a colour). In this way it becomes clear that different colours stand in relation to each other and through the soul experience of each person can be felt quite objectively. Questions like: 'How does yellow behave in relation to white? Does it constrict? Does it disperse?' can be answered in similar ways by different people. That is quite remarkable. Is one dealing here with fundamental perceptions, or with axioms in the classical sense?

The method thus developed is in this sense strictly scientific. The results of the observations are nonetheless of a soul nature. From this, it is also understandable that every colour in relation to another has an individual character. The 'tension' between two colours (e.g. red and blue) contains formative, shaping forces, which the painter brings to a state of equilibrium achieved through a training that has been elevated to a practice of soul balance. And through this the form arises. The authors formulate it in this way: 'The way the motif is configured is the motif itself.' An essential question arises here: How is the creative freedom of the painter involved in the process? In the chapter 'Something about Balance', it is emphasised that through the precise way in which 'tensions' between the colours are brought into balance, the artist has to bring his individual creative freedom into play. Seen in this way, it is a meeting between the individual painter and the individuality of the colour. 'The balance question is therefore an I-problem of great significance'.

Underlying the composition of the book are Rudolf Steiner's indications for the development of a new art of painting. And further, the content is based on the sketches for painters given by Rudolf Steiner, the so-called Nature Moods. These motifs relate to sun, tree, moon, animal and plant. Between the painting exercises one can find fundamental principles about 'Fine Art in the Service of Humanity', about the elements earth, water, air and fire, balance, directions of space and about image and lustre colours. It finishes with a chapter about the cosmic colour circle in which the relation of the colours to planets, zodiac sounds and to the categories of Aristotle are described. There is sequential development through the book. It begins with fundamental exercises, develops to training motifs and leads lastly to an artistic understanding of the considerations mentioned here.

The mathematician and pupil of Wagner, Ernst Schuberth, has written a foreword to the book in which he describes vividly those processes taking place when intellectual thinking is held back in an artistic process. To make this clear in a methodical way, Schuberth brings Rudolf Steiner's teaching about the senses into play, and shows how one can find therein a foundation of aesthetics especially for the art of painting which gives it quite new perspectives. A close study of the foreword is recommended, as it is essential for the understanding the book.

The book is for painters, painting teachers but also especially for lay painters. It presents a decade-long path of practice and work which can be pursued by every interested person. For teachers it can be especially helpful to learn why it is pedagogically beneficial to introduce colour perspective before the usual line perspective. But painting therapists can also find a way to deepen their work since the method of practice in this book has a clearly therapeutic character. This book by Elisabeth Koch and Gerard Wagner fulfils a cultural-pedagogical and cultural-therapeutic need. When reading the book, one can feel strongly the responsibility the artist has in the social process of culture.[107]

The book sold out quite quickly and the English translation was just as popular, helping would-be students from further afield and those who were not in a position to join the training in Switzerland. It also served as a reference book for pupils at the painting school.

One 'correspondence pupil' from England wrote to the authors in 1983:

Dear Gerard Wagner / Elisabeth Koch
For several years I have been studying your book *The Individuality of Colour* and have found it a wonderful doorway into the mysteries of colour. I value the way in which one can progress through the book, step by step, in the painting exercises, and how, in working on one exercise, infinite possibilities of variation become evident. For those who, like myself lack the means and the opportunity of training with an artist who has the insight into, and experience of, these new impulses in painting, your book enables development and progress to be made where otherwise it would be full of difficulties.

My only criticism is that – in English publications at least – there isn't more available material developing this painting research. I would like to find out about how to approach the painting of the human being; an approach which would stay faithful to the life and will elements of colour. May I ask you if such work has been developed yet in painting? Is there any published material which would help me to enter this field? If no published material is available, would it be possible for you to give me personally some direction as to how to embark on exercises?

As becomes evident in the progress from Plant to Animal in painting, more developed faculties are needed; I understand too that in the painting of the human being a still greater insight into colour is required.

I look forward to hearing from you and again, thank you for your book *The Individuality of Colour* as a contribution towards the right kind of artistic training.

Yours Faithfully, Alan Thewless

The same year, this correspondent wrote again:

Dear Gerard Wagner

Thank you so much for the care and time you spent in writing to me in reply to my letter. Many of the things you said are very helpful, and indeed I found much that was inspiring. The experimentation you mention with the incarnadine colour is most interesting, and I am looking forward to working with your indications.

For the time being I think that I must deepen my work on the themes of plant and animal, particularly the animal where I have been working on the introduction of fourth and fifth colours into the motif, which seem to work very differently from the fourth and fifth colours in the plant motif. In the animal motif these colours can work on the picture with a powerfully 'animating' quality, whereas, in the plant motif, there seems to be a more fluid relationships of these subsequent colours. The way in which one can enter deeply into the themes through the 'build-up' of colour is profound and most intimate.

I hope that I may be able to develop the faculties to work with some of the indications your letter contained with regards to the painting of the human being.

Thank you also, for drawing my attention to the 13 motif sketches of Rudolf Steiner which I will try to get reproductions of.

Very best wishes, Alan Thewless

The other publication of 1980 was the monograph on Gerard Wagner frequently cited here, *Gerard Wagner – Die Kunst der Farbe* ('Gerard Wagner – The Art of Colour') which, along with a selection of Wagner's paintings, included a short biographical sketch written by him, and longer contributions from Elisabeth Koch and Kurt Theodor Willmann. John Fletcher commented on both books in a letter to the painter in January 1981:

> ... Now I must congratulate you on your two books, *The Individuality of Colour* and your monograph *The Art of Colour*, they are real *treasures* in every way. I only wish I had had *The Individuality of Colour* 25 years ago, it is a treasure house leading into the future – being in English it will bring the *development* of Rudolf Steiner's *new impulse* to the English-speaking world, probably mainly through the Rudolf Steiner schools. Your monograph I find fascinating, despite the text being in German, the coloured reproductions of your paintings from 1948–1979 are especially interesting owing to their chronological order. I was especially pleased to see those of the Large Cupola themes. The cover design is excellent in its colour and form ...

In late 1978, when preparations for the monograph were underway, Wagner wrote to his sister-in-law:

> ... The same publisher who is bringing out the German version of our book (*The Individuality of Colour*) is also bringing out a monograph – so called – of, or on, a painter called Gerard Wagner – the book will be out next early autumn, all going well. About 48 pictures, coloured reproductions, an old friend is writing most of the text, E. and myself are also contributing to the text – for both of us a very difficult task. I've been at it for weeks, or months now, writing, crossing out, writing the same things over and over again, a bit different, and getting it down to as few sentences as possible. I certainly was not born to write in this life.
>
> I am sending you and Mary a sample of what is to appear in the monograph – the picture has been reproduced for a poster for the Paris exhibition – perhaps it can suit as a Christmas card. ...

Earlier in the year, in a reflective letter to his sister-in-law, Gerard Wagner writes about the painting school and getting some of his work in order. The subject of age and how little he feels the years often comes up in his letters to her:

… I suppose I have been too buried over here, and scarcely travel myself. But there is such a continuous stream of visitors to Dornach from all parts of the world – at Christmas, Easter and summer especially, that one feels anything but cut off from the world, even if one does not leave the place. I have been able to get to know a great many people here, some 'significant' ones too – it is interesting to find these people as the truly humble, without airs or pretentions which some less able have sometimes.

In the earlier days in Dornach one felt one knew everybody personally, met them regularly at lectures and performances – there was not a large influx of outside public into the Goetheanum, such as is the case now. The older ones are all gone, mostly died, one's older friends included – and there are so many continually arriving, also new students, that one can go into the Goetheanum when it is full of people – it can seat nearly 1000 at a performance – and scarcely know anybody there. One gets a few new friends, of course, generally through one's work and amongst the pupils.

I come to these reflections through what you say about getting older, and the deaths you mention. Our grandmother was my present age when she died. She always seemed to me tremendously old. Uncles also seemed very old at sixty or less. I wonder sometimes whether these 'old' people also felt in themselves in the same way as I myself do, when I am with children especially – that is, not in any way older than they are. It is surely an illusion to connect a person directly with his age – ages are stages one goes through but the individual himself is neither old nor young, he can take on any age – at any rate, after having experienced them in the natural course of life, he can in retrospect live through different ages, rather like changing ones clothes, which also can let oneself feel different, though one is the same. …

We have a few promising pupils now, who, in their own way, will, one can be sure, carry on the work when we have to give it up. It has taken its time, and had many hindrances to overcome, but it does seem as though a few seeds have been sown which can and will develop further.

We have been trying to get my paintings into a bit of order, putting them into decent passepartouts etc, so that they don't look only like pieces of paper. For many years, all the first years (almost 20 years) I destroyed most of my work – it wasn't worth keeping anyway – and then I used both sides of the paper very often to paint on, which gave our passepartout-maker new problems! Now we have a number of earlier paintings (I take care now not to paint on both sides, but I hadn't the money for paper in those days) in orderly passepartouts, with a painting on both sides.

Work with pupils goes fairly well – we could take far more – and could work better with them if we had larger studios – it is a great handicap having only two not so large rooms. The desire to learn from us is strongly present amongst increasing number of young persons – from England and the USA. We often get asked – but the space ...! and conditions for the English students are difficult, on account of the impossible financial situation. The £ is worth, I believe, less than 4 francs now. Even the dollar is very low, and the Swiss authorities don't allow students to come here unless they say they have money to keep themselves (in this very expensive country) without earning here, which they are officially not allowed to do, except to a very small extent and with special permission.

We are not allowed to forget such problems for a moment – but maybe life would be too easy if one could just 'learn painting' – maybe one needs the other difficulties in order to get sufficient concentration.

It is time I stopped – for your sake at least. Thank you very much for your book at Christmas, for your letters and greetings – also from Mary. Please give her my love and best wishes also, and love and best wishes for yourself – I hope you can keep well in health, Gerard

Rengoldshausen Waldorf School murals

Added to Wagner's own intensive work at the easel, his teaching and the preparation needed for exhibitions, a large wall-painting project at the Rengoldshausen Waldorf School near Überlingen in Germany occupied both Gerard Wagner and Elisabeth Koch for six weeks during the summer of 1981. Fifteen of his pupils painted the classrooms while Wagner and Koch painted the corridors. Wagner enjoyed the large-scale painting and produced some beautiful results. As he did with all such projects, he spent a great deal of time beforehand preparing the motifs which would then appear as if by magic on the walls. He wrote to Dorothy:

> We had a refreshing change during the last summer holidays – together with about fifteen of our pupils, we painted the classrooms and gang-

ways of a large Waldorf School near Lake Constance, on the German side.

For six weeks we were at it. It was a most pleasant work – with plant colours, which are in themselves almost medicine. To be able to work in a big way – life size – over big walls, was a treat. Also Elisabeth was at last able to come to painting again, and it did her a lot of good. The gangways we two did together – the colouring tried to show the mood of the classrooms behind the walls. The classrooms themselves were painted by the pupils in very strong colours, but more or less uni [= one colour painted fairly flat with some transitions but no motif]; the youngest – seven years old, have a strong warm red, the next classes red orange and orange – then it goes to yellow, yellow green and cool green, blue and violet towards the older classrooms.[108]

It was a new venture for us, and from the teacher's view, I think a success. We have been asked to do the same kind of thing for a curative home school quite near to this first place. Maybe that can be done during the next summer holidays. It keeps one young climbing about scaffolding ... and it is not a matter of indifference what kind of coloured surroundings the children have during their schooling time. We (Felix and I) would have been able to learn differently if we had not had rooms like a prison to work and to live in. [See Appendix 11 for more on the painting of classrooms.]

Securing the work: marriage and the Gerard and Elisabeth Wagner Association

As Gerard Wagner approached the age of 80, discussions were underway in his immediate circle as to how best his artistic oeuvre could be taken care of in the event of his death. What form of organisation would provide the best protection and security for his work?

In late December 1981 the works of Gerard Wagner and the Elisabeth Koch Collection were integrated into the Humanus Foundation in Basel. And after 15 further years, a new initiative, strongly supported and carried by Ernst Schuberth, saw the works and assets given over to the newly founded Gerard and Elisabeth Wagner Association so that former pupils and colleagues could take more direct responsibility for Wagner's oeuvre. The Association was founded in November 1997. Its members took up initiatives such as organising exhibitions and conferences, giving lectures and workshops, and publishing the artist's work.

As another measure to secure the work, Gerard Wagner and Elisabeth Koch decided to marry. Towards the end of March 1983, Wagner sent a notice of the wedding to his sister-in-law with whom he corresponded faithfully after the death of his brother Felix in 1975. He also mentioned preparations for the forthcoming Easter exhibition at the Goetheanum:

> Dear Dorothy
> Just in case you don't quite understand the language of the enclosed notice, it says that Elisabeth and I, after 33 years of working together, got married recently. As E. will have the responsibility for my work – paintings etc, when I go, this should make things a good deal easier for her.
>
> We have just been arranging and hanging a show of my pictures, about 90, in the Goetheanum for Easter. It makes quite a good impression – all fairly recent things. Such a show of mine last happened here about 6 or 7 years ago. ...
>
> I will try to get the book I told you of – for Mary – sent off soon. I had hoped to be able to read through most of it, but I just hadn't time. Also to write a letter with it, but I just don't get to either writing or reading except to a tiny extent.
>
> Best wishes to you both – the gardens look wonderful here with the early spring flowers. Elisabeth now – since Christmas – has the flat below me, and looks after the garden – in addition to all the rest she has to do. Love from Gerard – from Elisabeth also!

From this time the painting school community became more connected to the Wagner's home life since pupils helped in the garden, and one lived in the guest room in exchange for helping with housework and cooking. In this way more pupils were able to experience Gerard Wagner in his home environment and share in the warmth and humour at the table. One pupil who cleaned the painter's studio remembered Gerard Wagner's love of all nature's creatures. He would say to her gently: 'Do you think we could leave the spiders undisturbed?'

As in earlier years, many visitors came to see Wagner's work, and had valuable meetings with him and with Elisabeth Wagner. She was always conscious of protecting the master's painting time and welcomed visitors while he painted undisturbed upstairs in his studio. Along with her own creative work she continued to carry the administrative work needed for the running of the painting school and to organise exhibitions and other tasks needed for the furtherance of Gerard Wagner's work. The 1983 Easter exhibition at the Goetheanum mentioned above was followed by shows in Hamburg and in Basel in 1984.

Changes in the painting school

On 28 September 1983 Erwin Thomalla's earthly life ended in the Lukas Klink in Arlesheim, and this tragic event signified the end of an era. The beginning of a new period for the painting school saw Bo Eriksson, still a pupil, taking on the first-year pupils. And after the passing of Beppe Assenza in September 1985, all the Atelierhaus studios were given over to the 'Wagner School'.

It is astounding to think that apart from the large amount of teaching work Gerard Wagner was called to do, and the other tasks which came to him, he managed – using every hour of daylight he could – to produce the enormous volume of work he left to the world. His teaching time was in the afternoons so that he could take full advantage of the daylight for his own work. His preferred period at the easel was eight hours a day and he worked almost exclusively in natural light. As his life on earth was gradually coming to an end he was strongly motivated by the ever-present impulse to continue his own artistic output: 'My real work is done at home,' as he wrote to Dorothy Wagner:

> Through having pupils regularly – we have 25–30 pupils at present who need time and attention given to them; the remaining daylight hours are reserved as strictly as possible for painting, which really demands much more time than I am able to give. Especially now that one's future on earth gets ever shorter, and what one would like to do seems to get ever more, one is continually asking oneself, what is really most important to do. One gets asked to go to this place and that – Hamburg, Lübeck, in North Germany, and elsewhere to give courses or for shows – the contact with people is necessary and pleasant too – but one's real work is done at home.
>
> During this last term our teacher Erwin Thomalla (who helped Elisabeth and myself to run the school for the last twelve years, after being himself a pupil of ours for about seven years) died after a long and very painful illness. He travelled to so many countries in Europe, USA, Australia and New Zealand giving painting courses and quite especially enjoyed this side of the work. Elisabeth and I have the school alone now. One of our eldest pupils, a Swede, who is now in his fifth year with us, helps us, with our help, with the teaching. A very nice person, and able to take initiative and responsibility. Otherwise the school goes well. New

pupils come with new faculties, often more gifted than in former times, though not always as strong in health as one would wish.

… The enclosed card is from a painting (watercolour) by Erwin Thomalla, our teacher, friend and pupil. We are sending these out to friends as a memento. He particularly liked painting plants.

All best wishes to you both – it would be nice if we could meet again – in these uncertain days. Love from Gerard and Elisabeth.

A letter to Gerard Wagner by former pupil Beat Reinhard, which by interesting coincidence he unwittingly wrote on the painter's 78th birthday in 1984, is exceptional for the intuitive way he perceives the painter's work:

Dear Herr Wagner

[…] After the year's study with you, during my eurythmy training in Vienna, I discovered the paintings of Albert Steffen. Those treasures – each a drop of heart's blood – moved me deeply. Then after my training I was in Dornach again where I looked after some older anthroposophists.

I often visited Haus Hansi to take in the enlivening energy of Steffen's colours, but what was new for me during this time was the painting of Rudolf Steiner. Quite different from the watercolours of the poet but I also began to experience the greatness of Rudolf Steiner's paintings. Looking at them, I felt moved with a feeling of well-being. I was filled by quite a different healing force.

Then I got to know different ways of painting in Dornach, which I experienced as genuine endeavours. I think of Herr Jäckli whom I met through the Luckinger family. And it was also in this house that my attention was drawn to you again. I met Torsten Butterweck next door at the Meeting Centre, and he made a great impression on me. Through him, dear Herr Wagner, my eyes were opened once again for what you do. It did me good to hear the young Torsten speaking about you with such conviction. Frau von Bonin spoke very positively and insightfully about your school as well.

Allow me to tell you briefly what I experienced this evening as I looked at a card of one of your paintings that Torsten gave me. As I sat after the turmoil of the day and tried to calm myself, my thoughts began to come together, and I was able to have an inkling about the fundamental concern and aim of your striving in painting. I discovered something free but not arbitrary in your pictures. I felt myself somehow clearer and more collected. I sat there quietly. My thoughts asked for exertion and I obliged. I said to myself: 'The paintings of Gerard Wagner do not speak directly. One needs to be calm and follow the colours and forms as though with the inner eye. It is a fine spiritual weaving into which one enters meditatively.'

Somehow I experienced what you do, dear Herr Wagner, in the following way: it is similar to the exact work of a mathematician. In the same way that a thought logically follows the next, you move within the realm of colour. The mathematician obeys the laws of number, you obey the laws of colour. I experience how you move within the realm of colour laws in a pure way. A kind of chaste 'colour-thinking' expresses itself through you.

The large number and rich variety of your paintings show that spiritual laws do not hinder but are portals to true freedom. None are the same, and yet all are connected inwardly to one another. It is as if they are all woven out of the same spirit.

If one can perhaps experience in the paintings of Albert Steffen something momentary, from the heart, communicating a direct, enlivening message to the onlooker, your striving teaches us something quite different. It is not in the first instance talent or the 'personal' that is evident but it is something achieved through rigorous practice. What belongs to your work seems to be something objective. That is why it is also fitting for other people. Your path has become a path of training for questing human beings.

I consider it very important for this world that, in you, a human being exists, who practises within the pure life of colour, and who leads others into this life of colour. This means through you, as a distinct individual, the pure laws of colour reveal themselves, and in such a way that every well-meaning pupil of the spirit, according to their own capabilities, is able to tread a path within the world of colour.

This seems to me to be a great spiritual deed for our world and for the earth.

Dear Herr Wagner, I felt the urge to tell you this, and I hope I'll always be able to keep an inner connection with you. I also hope very much that I will soon find my way to painting again, which would of course be the surest guarantee of fulfilling my earliest wish.

Affectionate greetings to you and also to your life-companion.

All good wishes,

Beat Reinhard

More wall-painting tasks

1986 was a year for wall painting. During the summer Gerard and Elisabeth Wagner were busy painting murals once more at the Rengoldshausen Waldorf School, this time in the West Building, and earlier in the year they painted a mural at the College of Anthroposophical Pedagogy in Mannheim. During the summer term, in May and June, Wagner, with Bo Eriksson and pupils, painted the corridors and entrance hall at the painting school. The motifs on the first floor of an 'eternally shining sun' and a plant motif were painted by the two teachers, whilst the pupils worked on the ground floor lazuring the walls in a deep rose-red colour.[109]

At the end of the year, restoration work on the wall paintings of the Goetheanum's English Hall was on the agenda. Initially the idea was that the work could be carried out by pupils, of whom Angela Lord was one. She recalled:

> Towards the close of the first day's work however, Gerard Wagner and Elisabeth Wagner-Koch came by to observe our progress. 'Have you a ladder?' asked Gerard Wagner quietly, as he looked up at the central motif. And so began, not merely a restoration, but a full-scale repainting of the walls and two large murals. Outside, snow was falling in the deepening, darkening days of Advent. In the English Hall the space became filled with the ever-deepening richness of the plant colours. Like the elves from the fairy tale of the 'Elves and the Shoemaker', Elisabeth and Gerard Wagner worked throughout Christmas, all through the days and deep into the night.[110]

In January, Wagner wrote to his sister-in-law about the work in the English Hall and the second phase of painting in the Überlingen School:

> Dear Dorothy
>
> I wonder whether you have been getting my letters during the past weeks. I mean, the ones unwritten, and unsent, in which I keep on apologising for not writing. The reason why not is simply – time, or lack of it, added to my normal inability to write a letter anyway. During 'term' time, i.e. while lessons are on, I just cannot get to writing, and the moment we stopped school before Christmas 'holidays', Elisabeth and I were tied to working at wall paintings, which we carried out first 17 years ago and were never quite completed – also through lack of time, the room had to be used for lectures; and now we took the opportunity,

while pupils were mending scratches along the walls – to finish and together refresh the paintings. That got finished these last days.

We have had a good deal of work of this kind during the past year – in Mannheim on a wall in a seminar room, at Easter. Six weeks of our summer vacation were taken up with wall paintings in a big school near Lake Constance in Germany where we had painted classrooms and passages 5 years ago in one half of the school. It is a 'double' school, with twice 12 classes – about a thousand pupils.

This time it was the other half and the teachers asked for 'motifs' (unlike before, when we did colours and forms but without 'motifs'.) That meant 4 to 5 wall paintings about 8 metres long – interesting work, and we were given a free hand to do as we thought best. Pupils from our school helped paint a big hall and classrooms etc.

Other projects keep on being offered. It seems that one is expected to start life again at 80. But this kind of activity keeps one fit – only when it's over, one notices that one would like to be 30 years younger. ...

This reproduction I'm enclosing for you, is from a painting I did in 1942 – during the war. The editor of our *Goetheanum* newspaper (weekly) had it done, as a Christmas gift supplement for the paper – for those who take it. It is not a style, which I now practise, but belongs to the old sort which I can still stand behind. Incidentally, the colours in this reproduction are rather too warm, it was done in a hurry and without correction. ...

In 1986 Gerard Wagner celebrated his 80th birthday and was still very active and showing no sign of slowing down. The previous year Julian Clokie, a nephew from England, visited his uncle in Dornach and noted: 'I remember so well his hospitality and vitality when I met him at Dornach in about 1985 and stayed in the guest accommodation. He almost ran with the enormous coffer I had with me, which I could barely manage to move.'

Gerard Wagner was rarely ill, and a natural, rhythmical lifestyle must have played a role in preserving his vitality. He took daily walks early and at sunset and he travelled comparatively little: mostly to Germany and in the early days (from 1926 to 1939 and 1946 to 1952) took an annual trip to England. He was once in Paris, once in Austria, and the furthest north he travelled was to Finland, to Artjärvi in the summer of 1972, where he gave a painting course; the furthest south he travelled was to Rome. Then too, there was salutary power of painting, which Wagner mentions in his typically understated way in a letter of 1978: 'Standing behind an easel all day is evidently not such an unhealthy form of living. Certainly an active working with colours – especially plant colours – is a very healthy business.'

On his 80th birthday, on 5 April 1986, he received many warm and appreciative birthday greetings, a few of which are cited here:

Dear Herr Gerard Wagner,
We wish to send you warmest congratulations on your 80th birthday. Your deeply colour-imbued being is unforgettable in every encounter, moving as it does from one task to the next without any outer commotion but great dedication, and making Rudolf Steiner's indications for the artist's path visible. With warm wishes, For the Goetheanum Executive Council, Rudolf Grosse

My dear Herr Wagner
Congratulations on your 80th birthday. With best wishes and heartfelt thanks for your great achievements. Yours, Jürgen Schriefer

Dear Herr Wagner
Congratulations on your eightieth birthday for all the very important contributions you have made in all three realms of anthroposophical life: scientifically through your series of Goethean experiments, socially through your untiring teaching activity, and artistically in your artworks where you have developed Rudolf Steiner's indications in a wonderful way out of your own deepest experience. Not only human beings but spirit beings too will accompany your celebration with joy and gratitude. Helen Hoch

Dear Herr Wagner
We feel very connected to you and your beautiful art. Your quiet presence in all the joys and sorrows in Dornach is something exemplary for us younger people: how in such a complex place you are able to shape your life artistically. For this we wish to express our deep gratitude. Ever yours, Sergei and Astrid Prokofieff

Dear Herr Wagner
On this occasion of your 80th birthday I want to take the opportunity to thank you again for everything you taught me. I can now say, after ten years of independent work, that the things I learned form a foundation to which I can return again and again, – a path along which I can progress, albeit with small steps. Peter Schäfer

With these flowers I want to welcome you dear Herr Wagner into the circle of 80-year-olds and to express my admiration for all you have done and achieved in the past decades. Your Elsy Ruschmann

My dearest Herr Wagner
So much warmth and goodwill streams towards us when we turn our thoughts to you on your 80th birthday. For many years we have been able to drink from your deep spring again and again. Last weekend we held an embroidery course (3 days) for women working on the land, which gave them pleasure. Something of what we have received from you was taken up by these young farmers. Their hard work repays you and Frau Wagner. The more I try to connect to colour the more I become aware of the wealth of your achievements, and all that you pour out from this source to others. Whenever I visited you in Dornach, you always had time, an open heart, and listened patiently to my questions. May health and strength for work never desert you. Greetings to you, in faithful constancy. Your Rolf and Elisabeth Adler

And from Theodor Willmann came this poem, with his greetings:

> Behold
> what is to come
> as a shining seed:
>
> The archetype's
> springing fount:
> guard imagination
> in the light
> of the cosmic sun
> in the depths of the soul!
>
> The gates of the spirit
> open our eyes
> to future times!
>
> Prefigure the steps
> of progress's far-off development
> and tread
> the paths
> of discipleship
> in freedom

*Those pupils
who once led the way
to mastery of mankind's
spiritual creativity -*

*may they continually benefit your
artistic activity,
its sacred goal.*

Further exhibitions – Vienna

Gerard Wagner's paintings continued to travel to various places for exhibitions, bringing him further pupils and admirers. In May-June 1982 there was a show in Sydney, Australia; in the autumn of 1982 at the Paracelsus Hospital in Unterlengenhardt; in the summer of 1984 'Motif Sketches' based on Rudolf Steiner's originals were shown at the Goetheanum; and again exhibitions were held there in March 1985 and the summer of 1986; in January-February 1986, through the initiative of Theodor Willmann, there was an exhibition at Fellbach, organised by 'The Society for Culture through Art'; and in October-November 1986 the Goetheanum exhibited a cycle of paintings entitled: 'The Cosmic Mission of Will'. There was also a show at the Christian Community at St Gallen in November-December 1987.

In March 1987, Gerard and Elisabeth Wagner travelled to Vienna for the opening of an exhibition of Gerard Wagner's work organised by a pupil who lived there. As usual with such initiatives, the painting school pupils played a major role in setting up the exhibitions and helping with the transport of the paintings. About 20 pupils travelled to Vienna and were part of the event. Helga Raimund, the initiator of the exhibition wrote:

> The opening of the exhibition was a great success, I remember. We used every corner and wall of the hall to hang the pictures. There was no space left. I also remember transporting the pictures from Switzerland to Vienna. Quite an adventure at the border to Vorarlberg! There were lectures and painting lessons as well, and I remember the discussions with Guenther about Wagner's art and his excitement ... We did a good job for Wagners. Great times!

And Helmut Raimund recalled:

Our culture centre, the 'Stadtinitiative', founded by young people in Vienna, was in the middle of the city. We invited the director of the Albertina Gallery to join us when we were hanging the paintings in the many and high rooms there, and he was so enthusiastic about the work that he held a lecture during the three or four weeks of the exhibition. There were also other lectures about Wagner's work and articles in the newspapers. It was a lively and interesting time.

In his charming and graceful way Wagner painted his 'colour experiments' before the public. If discussion began, if opposition arose, he answered with his paintbrush and let the deeds and sufferings of the colours do the talking. That won over many for an understanding of an art unknown to the Vienna scene up until then.

One should not misjudge Gerard Wagner's childlike openness and ability to wonder. As an esotericist of colour he lived completely in the present, and before the canvas the usual slightly bent and fragile man became erect like a well-strung bow and stamped on the ground during the painting process. When he demonstrated with his brush he made painting teachers despair for he never followed the usual paths – he played with the laws of the colour as they conjured up forms, and in so doing he could always find new, spontaneous solutions.

In April, Gerard Wagner wrote to Dorothy Wagner about the Vienna visit:

Recently we – Elisabeth and I – were in Vienna for ten days – with about twenty of our pupils. We were offered an exhibition of about 100 of my pictures. The rooms had to be got ready, and all helped – it looked very good in the end. Elisabeth opened it, also held a lecture; I – a demonstration with paint brush. We were taken to museums etc in Vienna – a town of the last century, huge palace-like buildings, good style in the old sense, huge spaces and in the centre, at least, one saw no skyscrapers or blockhouses. It was icy cold and deep snow.

E. and I were invited to live in a hotel half an hour outside the town on the edge of Vienna wood – a first-class, big place belonging to the parents of the young girl – a 'half pupil' of ours, who got the exhibition going. It was an interesting trip and also instructive, also humanly very pleasant. The people there – so friendly and warm. It is good for our pupils too to have outings like this – brings them more together humanly.

At the moment we are just beginning our holidays (Easter) i.e. no school – all the more work of one's own – and Elisabeth has a number of lectures with lantern slides to give. Time presses when one comes to the age attributed to me (I say it like that because I imagine a person of 81 years to be someone quite different from what I feel myself to be. If I had no memory or knowledge and were told I was 30 years of age, I could just as well believe it – I just have no feeling for this 81!) Only the thought that I have not much time for doing what I would like, and must do, makes me feel that I must stick to work as hard as possible – also to train the pupils while I can.

Various places begin to offer exhibitions – that means a lot of work for Elisabeth, but pupils are also very ready to help in this matter and they brought the pictures from here to Vienna by car, hung them etc.

One evening at the hotel in Vienna, Gerard Wagner had a fall. Helmut Raimund wrote in this connection of a moving experience he had with the painter:

In the middle of my life I witnessed the transformation of blood into roses. The old man stood beside his bed and smiled. He had wounded his forehead on the bathtub. There were a few drops of blood on his white night shirt. He gazed at me, wide-awake, but a little amused. He knew what I saw. The dematerialization of life.

He was a painter. For over sixty years he had investigated the secret of colours with his brush, he had devoted his life to them and lived in their company. His love for them was full of gentle passion and humour. When he applied carmine, he was guided by the spirit-presence of the colour. It asked him for a particular tone of gold; as contrast, as support, as consolation, and he obliged appropriately. He played and handled the colours with the sincerity of a child and was a scientist at the same time. He noticed their inner graduations, their occult laws and mutual relationships, and let them come to expression on the surface of the paper to tell the story of a sunrise or of the fourfold mystery of bull, lion, eagle, angel, in a human face. He could give his students the sequence of colours which led to the impression of dawn without any will to push it in that direction. 'Just paint this sequence carefully and the colours will create a sunrise themselves.' There was magic realism in his art. He never forced his beloved colours. When teaching, he did not tell his students their occult significance. They had to find that themselves, and first learn to be active in that world of colours.

He had mastered himself. His brush-stroke was firm and confident. But at the same time he stepped back, given over to the thoughts that lived in red, blue, green and purple. The colours themselves had taught him the inner attitude and maturity to make them transparent, for their inherent spirituality to shine through. I never saw such a modest man who helped the powers of creation to come alive in such a gentle and light-hearted manner.

He had not a trace of violence in him so we hesitated at first when his partner informed us late in the evening that the door of his hotel room was locked from the inside and he would not answer her call. We thought to force open the door, but we were afraid of disturbing his peace. We worshipped this man we had invited to Vienna for an exhibition of his life's work. I was alone when he opened the door, and then I saw it. The bloodstains on his snow-white shirt revolved into a cross, surrounded by roses. I heard the name 'Christian Rosenkreuz', unspoken yet vividly and clearly within me. And the man in his eighties smiled; his name was Gerard Wagner. He looked at me as if he wanted to say something.

Whenever I remember this fragile, immaculate man, and great master, in this hotel room in the Vienna Woods, who has mastered painting the symbol of the living Christ with the colour of his blood, I feel ashamed. His gaze still moves me today – the loyalty and purity in it reminds me of an unborn child who has chosen his way on earth; or of a genuine artist devoted in his duty, and selflessly, like flowers or trees, sacrifices himself … [he was] like one of those ancient trees, wounded and gnarled, which after decades of growing and blooming eventually bears fruit. His commitment to the world of colours matured in the purification of his soul and was transformed in the course of his life into a science of the heart. In the middle of my life his smiling countenance showed me the image of the blood transformed and springing forth into living roses. And if I had been awake enough I would have seen into the depths of this holy moment; it was one of sudden insight and understanding between the painter who here 'displayed his wounds', and myself. These delicate roses of blood which I perceived at that moment in a soul realm, yet also with my eyes, were not dissimilar to the roses that sometimes blossomed in his paintings.

After this encounter I had to think about the paintings in medieval hospitals, the contemplation of which granted healing. And I had to consider how experience of the being of colour can build a bridge to the spiritual beings of healing – how nature in the garment of colour smiles on us and brings us nearer to the glory of God.

Since then, I live with the painting that Gerard Wagner gave me after his stay in Vienna. It will ever remind me of the rose-red of earth and the countenance of Christ, which begins to blossom comfortingly in the grieving light of the earth soul.

THE THERAPEUTIC ASPECT

Towards the end of his life, Gerard Wagner's insights into the healing and therapeutic value of colour and painting took on more specific contours. The first time he was brought into direct contact with therapists, or rather with the training of therapists, was in 1975 when Dr Margarethe Hauschka[111] invited him and Elisabeth Koch to give a painting course at her school for artistic therapy in Boll, near Stuttgart.

Frau Dr Hauschka was looking for a successor and wanted to experience Wagner's way of working. It could also have been Wagner's connection to Rudolf Steiner's training sketches and the motifs of the ceiling paintings of the first Goetheanum which encouraged Dr Hauschka to ask him to teach her students: she had a particularly strong connection with the art of the first Goetheanum, and a course on this subject, focusing on the cupola motifs, marked the culmination of the artistic therapy training at her school in Boll. In 1920, aged 24, Margarethe Hauschka (then Margarethe Stavenhagen) had visited Dornach and seen the original Goetheanum with its cupola paintings and the coloured glass windows; and until the end of her life she was deeply thankful to have experienced this 'greatest work of art', as she called it.

In a letter to Gerard Wagner in September 1976, Frau DrHauschka expressed her intention to visit the exhibition of Wagner's large cupola motifs at the Goetheanum and also to visit him 'so as to be able to understand your work better'. We do not know if she ever visited.

The painting course at the School for Artistic Therapy in Boll with Gerard Wagner and Elisabeth Koch took place in the spring of 1975 and lasted two weeks. By the end of the course Frau Dr Hauschka came to the conclusion that Wagner's method and her own were not wholly compatible: 'I would have to begin all over again,' she said. She also thought Wagner's approach was 'more artistic than therapeutic'. Despite the differences in artistic outlook Wagner said the occasion was most fulfilling on a human and personal level. He told warmly of a moment when he and Frau Dr Hauschka arrived at the same time at the door of the dining room and each tried to persuade the other to go in first. Eventually she put her arm in his and said: 'Let's go in together!'

Despite Frau Dr Hauschka's reservations, there was one student in particular who was so moved by the painting course that she went on to develop her therapeutic work based on the method taught by Gerard Wagner, and he remained a guiding influence in her work and life. This was Heilgart Umfrid (see Appendix 12). She made it possible for Wagner to come into contact with therapists and doctors whose work he was able to extend and enhance.

After the training in Boll, Heilgart Umfrid became a pupil at the Wagner painting school in Dornach, and afterwards began practising art therapy at the Paracelsus Hospital in Unterlengenhardt. Recalling her work there, she wrote:

> I was an art therapist for 17 years in Unterlengenhardt. At the Paracelsus Hospital each therapy department was under the care of a doctor, and Dr Hans-Bernhard Andrae [see Appendix 13] was responsible for the painting. He painted a great deal himself, and also engaged in Gerard Wagner's method, so our work together was most fruitful. On the strength of this we decided to organise a further-training course in painting therapy and asked Gerard Wagner to teach and he gladly accepted. Elisabeth Wagner-Koch accompanied him of course. Gerard Wagner came to Unterlengenhardt fifteen times, every summer from 1982 to 1997.

The Unterlengenhardt conferences for art therapists were always special occasions with a festive mood. Of ten days duration, the conferences offered painting, eurythmy to explore the gestures of colour, along with medical lectures and study for which Dr Hans-Bernhard Andrae was responsible. In the evenings Elisabeth Wagner gave lectures focusing on the art of the first Goetheanum and its place within art history, Rudolf Steiner's painting impulse, and Gerard Wagner's work. There were also presentations by art therapists of their work with patients. One evening was always taken up with a concert at the Paracelsus Hospital where Gerard Wagner's paintings were hung. Meals were shared in the dining room where participants were surrounded – from 1987 onwards – by the beautiful and delicate wall paintings carried out with plant-based pigments by Gerard Wagner. And the village of Unterlengenhardt itself, situated high up in the Black Forest with its open and pleasant countryside, made a refreshing change from Dornach. The subject of 'Unterlengenhardt' and the work there, features quite often in Wagner's letters to Dorothy Wagner, and her letters to him: 'I know you both love being there', she wrote. After the first visit Gerard Wagner wrote enthusiastically to her about the possibilities of painting as therapy – 'a living art which can become a living science of healing':

Dear Dorothy

… We were asked last summer to give an exhibition of my paintings in Unterlengenhardt. It lasted for six weeks, during which time Elisabeth and I were invited to be there (I was given a room where I could paint) and at weekends concerts and lectures were given, more or less around the clock. Also, as a chief item, we had a week's work with colour therapists and doctors, which was considered valuable enough for those actively present to wish to make a regular thing of it – at least once a year. We try to help them use colour in a quite fundamental way that is natural to the colour itself, if one can experience it, and so that anyone with an open and unbiased sense can accept it and learn out of his own experience to practise it. A really artistic way of painting will always also be of a healing nature. Colour and painting as a healing process – it is *very* interesting – one could sometimes almost call it exciting when one begins to notice what great possibilities there are in it. Watercolour and plant colours – a 'living art' which can become at the same time a 'living science' – of healing. I won't try to explain something which needs to be *done* to understand it.

The themes of my paintings we showed there – grouped separately in very nice rooms – ranged from trees, plants, animals, religious subjects, motifs given by Rudolf Steiner for a painting school, which I had worked at freely, also including R.St.'s motifs for the cupola of the first Goetheanum, which I busy myself with since almost when I first came here (to Dornach), and also animal and plant metamorphosis – sequences of small paintings of a scientific-artistic nature. About 80 – 90 paintings.

The place is high up, surrounded by fields and woods, next to a big anthroposophical hospital. Considering the distance from any town – it's right in the country – it was surprising to see so many people coming to our show, especially at weekends. Elisabeth was kept very busy leading people around, also lecturing, which she is very good at. (Saves me from needing to speak.)

I must stop. My love to yourself and Mary,

Gerard. Also from Elisabeth.

Dr Hans-Bernhard Andrae wrote a review of the painting therapy courses at Unterlengenhardt:

In the autumn of 1982 an extensive exhibition of Gerard Wagner's paintings took place at the Freie Studienstätte in Unterlengenhardt. At the same time, the Paracelsus Hospital Trust organized a seminar for art therapists, taught by Gerard Wagner and Elisabeth Wagner Koch. The need for such further training in an anthroposophically-founded painting method showed itself to be so essential that since then, each September, a 10-day seminar is led by the two artists and attended by 30 participants from England, Switzerland, Germany, Austria, France, Hawaii and Australia. Many attend the seminar every year and new participants represent the different anthroposophically oriented art schools as well as mainstream academic trainings. The need expressed by all was for up-to-date guidance and stimulus for the practice of art therapy and social therapy. ...

Can all the diverse requirements and expectations of the participants be satisfied in a 10-day seminar? Gerard and Elisabeth Wagner overcame this problem through their untiring energy. In one studio there are 15 easels for those not yet familiar with the painting method; the second studio contains the same number of participants who are already famil-iar with the method and who try to use it in their own workplace. Five hours each day is given to painting.

Circulating from easel to easel, the two master-painters show the method and give indications that are in themselves works of art. Albert Steffen wrote: 'No word is more misunderstood today than method! One confuses it with programme, system, dogma and the like. But it means a "way", a path, and whether or not one treads the path, experiences are gathered.' Only in this sense can the 'method' of Gerard Wagner's find the right understanding. Each of the 30 course participants find, on their own path with colour, the appropriate guidance, but the experiences they gain in the process of painting are their own, though surprisingly they accord closely with those of all the others. Over and above this, they work together on the book *Theosophy* with particular reference to the senses. Daily eurythmy sessions focus on the vowels and consonants and their precise colour figuration – movement, feeling and character of the eurythmy figures – and this enhances the objective experiences participants gain in their practice of painting.[112]

Being an art therapist myself, I participated in the Unterlengenhardt Confer-ences from 1988 to 1997. It was a demanding task to meet the needs of the large groups of participants with different levels of ability and backgrounds. Gerard Wagner did the rounds, on his feet for most of the five hours of teaching time, continually passing from person to person, giving advice and suggestions. As usual, his sense of humour was in full flow and laughter echoed from various corners of the studio. There was a 'beginners' room' as well, led by Elisabeth Wagner, and Gerard Wagner also liked to look in on this throughout the day and give advice. He was not content with the idea that he should concentrate on the 'advanced' students; as a former pupil once said, 'Herr Wagner likes new blood!'

When the participants' paintings were gathered together for a review at various stages of the day, or when an exercise was introduced, Elisabeth would take the lead. When it came to 'community painting' with all participants gathered together to work on one painting, Gerard Wagner took the lead. He also often demonstrated his approach, which was very exciting. One could learn a lot from watching him paint. Sometimes a participant offered their painting for him to improve and he worked further on it in front of the whole group. On one occasion he was given a painting of a plant motif and we all watched as he transformed a naturalistic, pretty flower picture into a magnificent dynamic phenomenon of moving colour. It reminded me of Assja Turgenieff's account of Rudolf Steiner working on the sculpture of the 'Representative of Humanity'. At times, his assistant, the artist Edith Maryon, would prepare the figures for him to work further on. Turgenieff wrote:[113]

> While Dr Steiner was away on his numerous travels to Germany, Miss Maryon prepared the work for him. He had hardly arrived back when he began work once again and it was as if a storm was raging in the atelier. Everything was in movement, all the surfaces and edges of the forms were transformed in a rush of superhuman drama. The eye could no longer rest in the beautiful forms, but had to live with them, pass through them; the forms themselves disappeared to become pure movement, expression and being.

Unlike Edith Maryon though, the painter of the 'pretty flowers' was not particularly happy with the transformation, which meant the painting ended up in my hands and remains a treasured example of what Gerard Wagner wanted to teach us – a dynamic, living style of painting.

> Being able to have Gerard Wagner's teaching non-stop for ten days was unheard of, and a former pupil once remarked that one Unterlengenhardt conference was equal to a whole term of tuition at the painting school. Also the master painter blossomed in the warm and supportive atmosphere created by Heilgart Umfrid and Dr Hans-Bernhard Andrae.

Heilgart Umfrid used to call Gerard Wagner 'The great therapist' and others also experienced him as such. One could learn a lot from his therapeutic insights. Once when we had all painted a blue gesture and a few paintings were gathered and compared, Wagner pointed out one blue picture and said 'Now this blue has so much will, it has boots up to its neck!' The description fitted exactly with the constitution of the person who painted it.

The breathing of the colour was what Wagner mostly referred to as the 'therapeutic aspect', though this differed from what we learnt with Dr Hauschka as pupils of the School for Artistic Therapy in Boll. Gerard Wagner's concept of 'colour breathing' was based on the dynamics of colour relationships, not essentially on a technique, and he often described how the breathing process arises through the polarity of colour contraction and expansion, tension and slackening, which he called 'soul-massage and therapy'.

Heilgart Umfrid's *leitmotif* for her own work, which she particularly experienced through Gerard Wagner therapeutic approach, was the statement Rudolf Steiner gave during a lecture to the workmen of the first Goetheanum: 'We must be able to understand health and illness in relation to the theory of the colour.'[114]

The Paracelsus Hospital murals

The dining-room wall painting at the Paracelsus Hospital came about through the initiative of M. Gehrke, a co-worker there, who suggested to Gerard Wagner that he paint a 'fresco' in the hospital. When asked where he would like to paint he said in the Chapel of Rest; but as the room was rather dark and not conducive to long hours of painting, Dr Andrae suggested the dining room, which Wagner was happy to accept.

The wall painting executed in plant pigments brought an ethereal and magical atmosphere to the room. Whist eating, one was surrounded by a beautiful panorama of images of nature – of plant, animal, human being and the elemental beings, not forgetting the Madonna motif as Persephone, the soul of nature. The daily experience of the healing effect of plant colours in such a large format gave an inspiring focus for work at the hospital.

Dr Hans-Bernhard Andrae took a special interest in the mural and followed its development:

In 1987, during the month of August, Gerard Wagner and Elisabeth Wagner-Koch painted the walls of the Paracelsus Hospital dining room with plant-based pigments. A great number of paintings done as preparation for this great work were also on display. In them one could see various starting points for the coming task, which was the creation of a wall painting 'with a joyful, uplifting mood'.

For us to see the development from these preliminary works to the actual 80 square metres of wall surface was like experiencing a mighty step into a new dimension. The patients and co-workers of the hospital were able to follow every step of the process as meals continued in the dining room while the work was in progress. Only then, or when daylight faded, did the painters rest their brushes.

To begin with, the four walls, each about the same size and adjoining each other at an open angle, were painted in a background colour: the first wall in blue, the second yellow, the third warm red and the fourth a cool red. Through the overlapping of the colours, green and orange arose as background colours as well. Then followed a sequence of colours, painted flowingly through all the coloured surfaces, and in each one the colours configured themselves differently. It was astounding to see how the colours – painted out of a feeling for balance –responded in such different ways to the different colour backgrounds. …

The wall in a blue background colour, displayed a hovering, shining yellow being drawing the plants of spring from the depths of earth. The wall in a yellow background conjured, beside the blossoming of summer, a delicate Madonna motif surrounded by purple-red beings: a process of soul-unfolding observed by a human figure, as an I-form standing on the earth. Above the figure stood an enormous angel indicating the direction. This was followed by the wall in a warm-red background, its mighty flood of colour and form softened by another Madonna form appearing out of wonderful gold-green hues of colour. And finally, the grandeur of a Madonna motif appears in a radiant golden aura, summoning a mood of Christmas: developing, forming, creating the sheath for a spiritual seed.

The human figure was included here too, now seated, and gazing upon the central motif as one who can lead into deed what he has perceived. In this way out of the music of the colours the four seasons of the year emerge for the viewer as intimate motifs of soul and spiritual development.

The painting was executed in plant-based pigments on walls prepared with a natural primer. The experiences already gained with plant colours reveal themselves here too: the colours keep their radiance in every form of lighting and please the observer even in artificial light.

On 13 September 1987, the festive opening of the mural took place in the presence of the artist couple, Gerard and Elisabeth Wagner, together with a great number of friends including Theodor Willmann who held the celebratory lecture on the theme 'The Meal as Archetypal Image of Community'. Through his deep connection with Gerard Wagner's painting, he was able to open our eyes for this work of art in a very beautiful and meaningful way. In the daily rhythm of the hospital's community life, it will play such an important role. In the streaming layers of its colours, as we can now clearly see, the elements of earth, water, air and fire weave together to embody the processes of nature. And the nurturing, preserving powers of motherhood, living in these imaginative pictures of the cosmic-earthly yearly rhythm, awaken in the observer a sense of the archetypal unity of body, soul and spirit in earthly incarnation.[115]

Gerard Wagner was 76 when he started collaborating with Heilgart Umfrid and Dr Andrae; and in those last 17 years of his life he deepened his research into therapeutic processes in colour and incorporated it more strongly into his teaching. The 'therapeutic question', as he called it, was what brought me to Dornach in 1993 to learn from him. Anne Stockton wrote in her essay 'Memories of Gerard Wagner':

> After a time, I realised that embedded in the work and teaching of Gerard Wagner was a deep understanding and insight into human nature, and his training did have a strong element of healing as well as self-knowledge hidden in it. Later in his work with Caroline Chanter, a trained therapist who became his pupil and afterwards teacher in his school, one had the feeling he was enlarging his knowledge of therapy from her, as the long wished-for fulfilment of a more conscious work of healing.

Dornach 1990–1999

THE FINAL PERIOD –
NEW IMPULSES FOR PAINTING

The Foundation Stone Hall murals

In 1990, Christian Hitsch, the leader of the Section for Fine Arts at the Goetheanum, asked Gerard Wagner to paint the walls of the Goetheanum Foundation Stone Hall. He was helped as usual by Elisabeth Wagner and a pupil or two. Wagner painted some of the 'motif sketches' relating to the human being. He chose 'The Three-Fold Human Being'; 'The Human-Being in the Spirit'; 'The Spirit in the Human Being'; 'The Human-Being in Relation to the Planets'; 'The Fourfold Human-Being as Eagle, Lion, Bull, and Angel'. 'The Three-Fold Human Being' sketch is, according to Gerard Wagner, the most important of Rudolf Steiner's sketches. He often drew attention to it and pointed out the colours of the four ethers in it and their relation to the human being's threefold organism.

Angela Lord, a pupil who had helped with previous wall painting projects wrote from Tobias School of Art with her good wishes for the work:

> I send you both my very warmest wishes and hope that you are both in good health and strength. I hope that the painting in the Foundation Stone Hall is not too strenuous – I would love to be there, to see the work in progress. It is now, in retrospect, that I begin to appreciate ever more deeply, the opportunity of having worked with you both at Rengoldshausen, and in the English Hall. As well as learning from the colours, I learned so much from your steady mood of concentration, which provided a strong atmosphere into which one could 'place one's being as an instrument for the colours'. This quiet inner wakefulness is proving to be one (of the many!) qualities of soul which continue to grow as a deepening relationship to colour also grows. It is a quality, in this hectic modern world, which gives the beginnings of a quiet, firm steadiness of soul, which I notice more and more, as a direct result of the painting process. I begin to perceive now, something of the reality of the 'training path' for the painter, and the transformations which this path can bring about. The perceptions of both the outer sense-world, with its myriads of astounding forms and colours, and my own inner

perceptions of the thought-world, become almost daily, intensified and clearer. One learns to 'see' with one's whole organism, in the same way, perhaps, as ancient man could hear with the whole sense organism. ...

In December 1990, Ted Ormiston, a former pupil of the painting school, wrote 'Herr Wagner completed all the murals in the Foundation Stone Hall this summer and appears to be as young as ever.'

Teaching in the painting school continued through the 1990s even though Gerard and Elisabeth Wagner were considering stopping and handing over to younger persons. He wrote to Dorothy Wagner:

> Elisabeth and I, we are gradually giving over our teaching work though we still take pupils on two or three days a week. It is hard to find people who would carry on our work in the school in the same way as we have done hitherto. Young people usually have more wish to be 'artists' than to learn or to teach painting. It's harder than one could ever have imagined, but worthwhile. And one is always learning new things – never more than now, when one must think of rounding off and stopping.

In July 1992, a few hours before a planned journey to Kiel to paint five walls in the Chapel of Rest in the Christian Community Church there, Wagner had a collapse. The Chapel of Rest wall painting project was close to his heart and he had been preparing for it for many months. He settled on a motif showing the soul and spirit of the deceased person rising from the earth through the elemental world in the company of a Christ-like angel. It was never carried out but a series of exceptional paintings remain.

In early 1993 the almost 87-year-old painter contracted pneumonia and was forced to take to his bed for some time. The illness, however, brought new creative powers with it. By March, Wagner was back at the easel and even if initially he had to paint sitting down he was soon back on his feet. As his forces returned, he began a new era of artistic work. The paintings became ever more vibrant, light-filled and dynamic. In July 1993, an exhibition showing new works opened at Haus Ganna in Dornach. Eve Ratnowsky wrote a review in which she mentions the change she perceived in Wagner's work:

> It was clear from the outset while we were setting up the exhibition, that all we had hitherto understood and loved about Gerard Wagner's art had begun to shift into a new dimension. Our aim was to bring paintings

created soon after Easter 1993 into juxtaposition with others from the post-war years.

We move in an entirely different sphere when we seek to experience the interval between the early works and the most recent. Everything is new, for the painter as well as the observer. The blue, the yellow-green, the violet – it is all new. Everything expresses itself directly in the here and now. Here too, dramas are played out between powers of light and darkness, but they are dramas filled with the depth of joyousness! All is movement in these most recent paintings – condensing and expanding movement. Here and there the flooding colours settle into shapes and motifs. We find the Madonna with the Child, figures pay homage, angel beings, an upright human figure supporting a rainbow, forms the shape of cross with his stance; the deep blue background draws us on, now lifting us to the spreading yellow-green of a mysterious, all-knowing pinioned being.

Whereas in their colours and motifs the earlier, darker pictures call up death experiences and resurrection forces, these new ones take us much closer to the realm of birth. Our will is addressed. There is no distance between picture and observer. We are called on to immerse ourselves, to join the battle, share the creativity, and let ourselves be swept along. We cannot draw away from the impelling upward force.

Gerard Wagner's world of colour accompanies us into the night. This painter who stands day by day before his easel tells us that he too goes on working in the night, though not at painting a picture but at plumbing the depths of living and moving colour.[116]

Meanwhile, in August 1993, Wagner wrote to his sister-in-law about his new lease of life:

Here we have work in over-plenty. Elisabeth and I had intended to go up to Kiel, North Germany, to paint the walls of a Christian Community Church where the body of the deceased person is laid during the three or four days before cremation. I had been working on the 'designs' for five small walls – for nearly nine months. Two days before we intended travelling – I had a fall, and we had to put off going. The next opportunity will probably be next spring.

After this interlude I somehow managed to get pneumonia (I'm never ill otherwise). Elisabeth, with the doctor's help, pulled me through. I was probably less conscious of what was happening than Elisabeth was.

Now I feel I have been given a new lease of life, and this affair has given me quite a new impulse for painting. And the next few years here will bring quite new and not easy tasks. I would like to have thirty years of good health in front of me!

The enclosed card's original was in a show of newer and older paintings which I had here in Dornach recently. We also had a show in Frankfurt (on the Oder, not Frankfurt am Main), now Poland, for two months. We will have a show in November in Baden-Baden with newer paintings, in a public gallery which was offered us.

In an article in *Das Goetheanum*, Ernst Schuberth described some of the subjects Gerard Wagner tackled in his paintings in the last years of his life:

After that illness a new creative period began. Throughout his life he had followed events in the world by reading daily newspapers, and by talking with others. He was deeply moved by the political changes of the early 1990s, but also by the increasing danger human beings were posing to themselves. What happens in the inner being of someone who has taken drugs? How does the semi-reality of the television screen affect us? Where is the meaning in the destiny of a child with physical or learning disabilities? How is a quarrel or murder seen spiritually? Some of these new pictures are shatteringly up to date in the way they wrestle for understanding and search for healing, balancing forces. Wagner was able to delve into such questions whenever he found ways of depicting them as a matter of colour.[117]

Renovation of the Great Hall of the Goetheanum

During the years 1996–1998 the Great Hall of the Goetheanum was renovated. The artist, architect and sculptor Christian Hitsch, leader of the Section for Fine Arts, was responsible for the remodelling and designing of the space, which included painting of the ceiling. Preparation began some years earlier and a group of painters met to consider an appropriate theme. After a great deal of discussion, as well as various samples painted by members of the group, it was decided to recreate the motifs of the large cupola from the first Goetheanum, and work began with help from Rudolf Steiner's original sketches.

Although Gerard Wagner's advanced age meant he did not actually paint on the ceiling of the Great Hall, he was involved in the preparation work. The painters met regularly and the meetings led to fruitful and sometimes challenging interactions between the three artists and their respective schools of painting. Christian Hitsch, Walter Roggenkamp and Gerard Wagner took turns, each drawing on their own specific artistic approach, to lead the group's study of one of the cupola motifs. Wagner's approach was not easily taken up by those who had not trained with him, and with this in mind a member of the group wrote to him in anticipation of the next workshop telling him of the difficulties some experienced with his approach. He wished Wagner much success in his preparations, and asked him to 'try his best to find a way that the others would be able to receive'. Gerard Wagner answered this rather audacious letter from his former pupil with understanding, and with his usual humility:

Dear Graham,

Many thanks for your letter of Feb. 15. Ever since it came I have been meaning to write. Ever since it came I have been confronting myself with the situation which my 'yes' to your request involves.

I see no reason for 'personal' difficulties. Where lies the difficulty? Each person has had his individual approach in artistic training – his inner experience has been found, awakened by the way he has gone. Outwardly one can communicate one's ways of working – one's inner experiences one cannot, unless one's path has been at least to some extent the same ...

Concretely: the 'A' (ah) motif ('The Round of Seven') is chosen! The colours for this sketch of Dr Steiner's are the same as his first training sketch, 'Sunrise': red, yellow, violet; violet, red, yellow; violet, yellow, red – on a background colour or on white?

Dr Steiner's writes beside his pencil sketches for the eurythmy figures: *first* movement, *then* feeling, *then* character. Extremely important. Why?

Following this by experimenting, one discovers that the form of the speech sound, the figure, is dependent on this very *sequence* of colours. Very important from a purely painterly point of view for the painter who is searching for *form out of colour*. And it is here in this area, perhaps chiefly, where understanding, or to begin with 'not being able to understand' lies. Yet it is precisely in the experience of this phenomenon: in the time element, how form arises *out of* colour, through the order of the colours, through a sequence, that if different people could acquire these experiences they would have a common foundation for artistic work. One finds the indications of how to come to this colour experience, or to practise in this direction, from Dr Steiner. Do we have enough people who want to go this way? An individual thing! Dr Steiner and the colour, and *oneself,* they are the teachers. The problem of working together and of artistic understanding lies chiefly here.

So it would be an aim for me to present the path from yellow-blue, sun- and moonrise and sun- and moon-set, to growing and fading – plant life, to animal forms, and further to the cupola motifs of Rudolf Steiner. A quite certain way to the last still evades me. I search for it constantly. But also if I could present it through painting, e.g. the 'A' (ah) motif, the *how* of the experience is not conveyed only by looking at the finished picture. Words don't help here – only long practising. Whoever would be prepared to give the time to a schooling path, as I try myself – to join in – I would always be willing and ready to help them. It does not happen 'short and swift' of course.

In how far it would be wished that I help the group as is stands at present, I must try to find out before the painting conference begins. Not everyone would be willing when they notice how the work would be approached. They must then be free to go to another group before the conference lists are planned.

So in the meantime this is how the situation looks for me – uncertain. But I hope to speak to a few members of the group soon.

Please excuse the bad writing. I am *very* unused to writing a letter.

All the best and warm greetings, Gerard Wagner

Before the executive council's final decision to reproduce the 'large cupola' motifs of the first Goetheanum, the painters worked on various ideas and came up with some interesting alternatives. When Wagner was asked what motif he would choose to paint on the ceiling, he said: 'Study *Occult Science* – the stages of earth evolution, of warmth – light – water – earth. That is colour – the different stages of earth development.' He suggested an exercise using the following sequence of colours: red (warmth), yellow (air), blue (water), earth (violet), which accords with this evolution.

During this period he also executed some beautiful ceiling paintings based on a composition that accentuated centre and periphery. These gave the impression of looking into a flower that opened up into a heavenly sphere of angelic beings. Regarding an actually circular picture format Wagner said: 'The round format, with its inner and outer aspect, centre and periphery, relates much more to a reality than the rectangular format we usually paint on.'

When painting the models of the Goetheanum ceiling, Wagner felt it more appropriate to be looking down at the ceiling or up at it instead of painting it face on. He placed his own models horizontally on a stool and looked down into them as he was painting.

From two visits in September 1995 I have the following diary entries:

> I visited G.W. – Thomas came too. He was working on a 'ceiling'. As we entered he said with joy: 'I've painted a ceiling!' There was a very serene and special mood in the room and I felt gruff interrupting him. He said he took white to begin with, then cool red, yellow, blue and violet. He talked about groups of colours: yellow and blue creating green, and incarnadine made up of black, red and white together, and then taking them apart. He talked about the first lecture in *Das Wesen der Farben*:[118] green, then rose, white and black, 'all the colours in fact'. And rose as enhancement of all the colours. Does that mean they are all contained within it? He said white was the most important colour.

As we have seen, the cupola motifs of the first Goetheanum had long been of special interest to Gerard Wagner, and this project of the Goetheanum ceiling painting called forth a new phase of intense work for him. Many striking paintings were done, which opened up new dimensions of research and produced extraordinary sequences of metamorphosis of some of the motifs. A sequence that particularly stands out is that of the 'Ear and Eye' motif which undergoes a metamorphosis through a series of five paintings. Wagner also explored the question of the changed form of the ceiling from the first Goetheanum building to the second – from dome to trapezium – and how this change would have influenced the way the rainbow-coloured background should be painted. Interesting examples can be found amongst the models of the ceiling now in the Wagner archives in Dornach. Gerard Wagner's own research, which began at least 40 years earlier, led him to the conclusion that the various motifs of the large cupola were all transformations of *one* fundamental motif that changed its configuration according to the background colour it was painted on. When he was asked what the original motif was, he answered: 'It began with Saturn ...'

*

In the summer of 1995 Witali Kovalenko, a Russian anthroposophist from Moscow, came to Dornach to make a film about Gerard Wagner. Andreas Weibele helped with the technical side of things, and an assistant or two were on hand to help with translating. During filming one could not help feeling sympathy for the 89-year-old as he sat under hot lamps being interviewed or when he gave a long, strenuous painting demonstration. The film is valuable despite its technical shortcomings. Elisabeth Wagner is seen giving a presentation of Wagner's work, and one sees Wagner in his studio painting a large cupola motif.

During the interview he spoke of the painting process:

> One needs simply years of practising – I needed a few decades to begin with. It is difficult to explain; one can experience it if one practises, and one can begin to experience it when one sees how it comes about. But the process must be seen – one cannot explain it. It must go through the eye *and* the feeling, and with the feeling one can perhaps enter into it. Then speaking stops and one comes into seeing, into 'experienced seeing', and one learns through it. Yes, then it's mute, one can only show without words what one thinks, through the doing itself – create series of pictures, simple colour problems, show how one proceeds.

In another scene in the film, with the workbook *The Individuality of Colour* on the table before him, Gerard Wagner answers questions about the exercises in the book and the painting method he has developed:

> ... It is the colour's own life that we try to discover, how form arises through colour. Not that one takes a form from nature but rather one notices when experiencing colour that nature is in the colours themselves, and that they are really creative forces: yellow that becomes red; blue that becomes indigo and violet – together they belong to a totality. Following Rudolf Steiner one would say: the colours have created the whole of nature: mineral, plant, animal, human being – and if one could work out of these forces, a new art of painting could come about. This is in the long run what we want to search for. We can, of course, only achieve the very first step.

And when asked about the special emphasis on objectivity in this method of painting:

> There is really a strong scientific element in painting simply through the exactness, but exactness of colour qualities. It is a goal that one strives for, not that one can achieve it.
>
> Yes, clear feelings, and quite impersonal, in a way it is not to be found in human beings, but what one could really wish for in human beings. That is what makes it so beautiful.

Throughout the 1990s, Gerard Wagner continued to teach at the painting school, usually twice a week in the afternoons from 2 pm to 6 pm. There were no such things as tea breaks when he was teaching. What also took up more teaching time in those last years were the afternoons and weekends when he gave his time to individual pupils or to small groups of graduate pupils. These sessions could be called 'master classes'. They took place chiefly in Gerard Wagner's own studio where his latest works could be seen, and the painting on the easel showing work in progress was usually the first topic of conversation.

These classes took the form of community painting, meaning that the group worked on one picture together. How should we begin? was always the first question. Who wants to take the brush and which colour should we choose? The attempt was made to follow brushstroke by brushstroke as the colour came onto the sheet, and to bring to consciousness to what was happening between the colours and to oneself. As one pupil painted the others looked on.

The brush was passed around to whoever wanted to continue either with the same colour or with a new colour. The choice of colour would be discussed, with Wagner giving suggestions as to the most appropriate and lawful colour to use. The most interesting moments were of course when he himself took the brush, and disappointment could ensue when he passed the brush on fairly soon to one of the pupils.

Attention was drawn to the interplay between the colours, to their reaction to one another, rather than to their 'rightness' or 'aesthetic' value. We were encouraged to *look*! What did that brushstroke of red cause? How do the other colours react to it? What colour is being called for now, and why? Usually a communal session like this went on for two hours without a break until the process found its lawful conclusion and had been rounded off to a balanced organism. There wasn't time enough to pay much attention to the finesse in the laying on of the colour but the sketches that arose are alive in their immediacy, and their unpolished spontaneity impresses everyone who sees them. One came away from those sessions with a feeling of freedom yet grounded in the basic laws of the colours. It gave a sure footing for one's own practice.

There were often visitors in Gerard Wagner's studio. Amongst them were former pupils who brought tales of their latest initiatives and of their home countries, and there were strangers who had heard about Wagner's work, and just dropped in. I remember one such visitor from the US who was given a paint brush almost immediately on arrival, and we watched as Herr Wagner drew responses from her with a continual stream of questions; such as: was she satisfied? If not, why not? What did the picture need? And so on. He never let up, asking her questions continually and a little brusquely, and I wondered if she was really enjoying the procedure. But some years later I met her accidently at the Goetheanum and she told me she never forgot that session with Gerard Wagner, and how he brought her totally 'to herself' in that one session of painting.

A couple from Athens came with the hope of buying a few paintings. I recorded in my diary:

> The Greek couple from Athens came to visit and they had a very pleasant conversation with G. W. He talked about how form comes out of the colour, and gave this example: ' How would you feel if you came into rooms of different colours – your gesture would change depending on the colour of the room, wouldn't it?' And similarly, if you heard sounds, say A, E, I, O, or U? You wouldn't make the same gesture for those different sounds.'

Gerard Wagner was keen to bring to his pupils' attention the need to develop their ability to *experience* different colour sensations. He used various examples. One visitor was given a demonstration: Wagner began tapping on different objects with a spoon – on a glass, a cup, a plate etc., thus showing the different qualities of sound coming from each object. Another time he spoke of a wine taster who has to compare the sensations of taste of the different wines so as to access their qualities. To learn about colour, pupils were encouraged to find similar ways of 'tuning in' to colour, or 'tasting' colour.

90th birthday

On 5 April 1996, Gerard Wagner celebrated his 90th birthday with a small gathering at home and a large pile of cards and letters from former pupils and friends. Pupils filed into the living room singing and carrying flowers; and when the revered teacher was asked what his birthday wish was, he said: 'My wish is to have no wishes.' The following examples are typical of the many good wishes he was sent:

> Dear Herr Wagner
> My heartfelt good wishes for your 90th birthday. I would like to say that I not only appreciate you very much as a painter and teacher but just as much as a human being. As a human being you are just as important to me. Much love and I wish you all the best for the Easter days.
> Kurt Leisi

Dear Gerard Wagner

My best congratulations on your 90th birthday.

I will never forget you and your pictures.

   With love from J. Halvor Jensen (Danish student 1986–1990)

Dear Herr Wagner

I wish you all the very best for your 90th birthday. I sincerely hope that you have many healthy years before you in which to paint. Through your pictures and your research you give humanity a healing remedy that is necessary at this time. We are grateful to you for that. I would like to help your work become better known.

I hope many people will take up your indications.

   Erik Rau

Most honoured, dear Herr Wagner

In the Goetheanum I read the accounts by Christian Hitsch and S. O. Prokofieff written in honour of your 90th birthday. They warmed my heart. In thought I join all the others and shake your hand most warmly. I think back with gratitude to my first meeting with you. Fresh from the GDR and somewhat of an outsider, I felt it significant that the first familiar faces I met in Dornach were those of you and the person always at your side – Frau Elisabeth Wagner. After that I was often able to be your guest and experience in that little studio the concentrated attentiveness, the sensing, the listening, during the act of painting of the 'initiate of the being of colour'. Your paintings are gifts in visible form from the other side of reality. In conversation at the table you were mostly a quiet, attentive listener with your aura of light-filled, warm-hearted benevolence perceptible. Obviously your dialogue with the being of colour – the painting – is for you therapy as well as a source of spiritual-bodily rejuvenation. In your way an example to us all. On reflection I experience each meeting I had with you as an offering of destiny. May the strength be granted to enable you to continue your work on the physical plane, to remain faithful to the earth.

   In gratitude

   Yours, Rudolf Bodenlos

Dear Herr Wagner

I marvel at the active nature of your deeds, your consistent creative energy and your loving interest in the creative work of others. I had the pleasure so often to meet you on the way to the Goetheanum. With heartfelt greetings, Bertha Wolf [extract]

Most honoured, dear Herr Wagner
Although I was only able to take part in painting courses with you at the Goetheanum for one year, 1965/66, (yellow-blue-red and blue-yellow-red), I feel myself always as a thankful pupil. (I am a eurythmy therapist and curative educationalist). 'It is our breathing-exercise', you said to me, as I told you about a patient who felt very well when she looked at this colour-study and said that she became quite 'free'... had heart-circulation problems. [Name unknown]

Dear revered Herr Wagner
For your 90th birthday we would like to send you our most heartfelt congratulations. Through the coloured walls of the school's east block and the motifs of the west block, we feel connected to you daily, even if this is not always conscious. Walls form our life-spaces, protect us and at the same time form a barrier to the outer world. What we experience daily in an enlivening way together with numerous children, youth and adults, is a view into a world of colour beings, the significance of which we cannot yet fully comprehend. Yet, on this special anniversary we would like to thank you deeply from the bottom of our hearts for the wall painting you did in our school (Rengoldshausen Waldorf School).
    With gratitude, in the name of our college of teachers,
    Elisabeth Wilde

Excerps from a letter from Gerard Wagner's former pupil, the art therapist Heilgart Umfrid:

Dear Herr Wagner
When thinking of the coming birthday of my highly esteemed teacher of many years, one looks back at one's own life: when was it that I first met this respected teacher? One of the various courses taught at the school was a fourteen-day course with Gerard Wagner and Elisabeth Wagner-Koch. The theme was colour. In the morning and afternoon painting lessons you both led us in such a friendly and loving way into the being of colour that it was possible, through striving for balance, to get to know the different colour qualities, and to learn what it means to 'paint out of colour'. For me personally this colour experience was a revelation! And I knew after this course that I must continue on this

path to reach real colour experience. I also came to the clear realisation that looking for balance is an archetypally therapeutic activity: 'Balance creates progress.'

At Michaelmas, a year and a half later, I came to Dornach, to the painting school, and during the first week I had the good fortune to see an exhibition at the Goetheanum of Gerard Wagner's cupola paintings. The impression that I had come to a mystery centre was so powerful that it compelled me to spend hours in the exhibition room. One day I met you there and you explained to me: 'Rudolf Steiner would not have come to the configuration of the dome motifs without the coloured backgrounds on which they were painted.' And a further statement from yourself at a later date: 'It (painting out of colour) comes about through a purely artistic search for balance, accompanied by the question of how Rudolf Steiner came to these forms.'

Now I could understand the words, 'Form is the work of colour'; this mysterious activity that accompanies our striving and leads to the conviction –through your masterful way of teaching – that a particular order of colours is the key to the configuring of motifs, and that this question of the background colour plays such an essential part.

When the exhibition was over, there was a conference during which the original sketches of Rudolf Steiner's were displayed in the Sketches Room. I was completely surprised by *how* Gerard Wagner's pictures, which I had seen in the exhibition, rose up before my inner eye as I looked at the original sketches.

After this I witnessed your 'cupola paintings' here in Unterlengenhardt, as part of an extensive exhibition of your work in the summer of 1982. And once again, it affected me deeply!

Every suggestion by you, every conversation with you is precious, and the greatest gift for your approaching anniversary would be to hope that all that has been achieved will come to fulfilment in the coming years. I am convinced that it will!

All good wishes and for your continuing good health!

In gratitude

Heilgart Umfrid

Words of appreciation came also from Christian Hitsch on behalf of the executive council at the Goetheanum:

Anyone who feels drawn to painting inspired by anthroposophy will sooner or later meet the work of Gerard Wagner. No one who has the good fortune of knowing him personally can help feeling great admiration for his unique life and work, whose abundance and wealth could hardly be surpassed. 70 years of his life and more have been devoted to the world of colour with an intensity that one could hardly imagine if one did not see it for oneself.

Visiting Gerard Wagner in his painting sanctuary one is always touched by how his whole being and intent is painting. His exceedingly delicate, refined figure seems transparent. His shining eyes and delicate face, surrounded by smooth white hair, smiles lovingly. When he shows his latest works, his youthfulness of soul causes one to forget his advanced age. He wants to know what the beholder experiences in looking at his works, and soon he tells how these wondrous watercolours arose. It sounds as if it had been so simple and natural – and this is how they do seem to arise under the hand of the master: If you begin with this colour, then add the second and third colours, while exercising all the painter's senses, these pictures arise. Each colour is fully experienced and has its place. An organism of constantly changing colours develops, whose forms arise out of the colours themselves.

Gerard Wagner's method is strict, arising wholly out of colour. 'Colour alone is the teacher,' says the creator of these works. Gerard Wagner has discovered and developed the living law of colour sequence in a fully conscious way. Yet however strictly and consistently he follows this, he executes his works with equal lightness and playfulness so that a beginner in the method can hardly believe it has arisen through lawful necessity. This cannot be immediately perceived in Wagner's 'finished' paintings with their enormous wealth of motifs. One experiences it only when one follows the inner structure of the painting as it developed. Unfolding before the eye, each stroke of the brush reinforces the impression that, yes, it cannot be otherwise. One experiences how law overcomes itself as it were and sheds every compulsion: the pictures shine free, always forming a whole. One can feel: here you can breathe, here you are welcome; here you can live and you are raised up with heart and soul to a higher world!

Just as all true art only speaks through itself, so a closer knowledge of Gerard Wagner's works also lets us feel that his work is unthinkable without anthroposophy; it just couldn't exist otherwise! The being of anthroposophy can emerge in the most varied forms. In addition to its scientific nature it can appear in purely artistic form. It works in the soul, cultivating artistic forces in those who can absorb it. What is then released has an individual character. It is possible to feel this in something like the following way: 'If you want to know a certain aspect of our creative activity,' say the colour beings, 'then look to our servant Gerard Wagner. We entrust ourselves gladly to him, his soul has become a portal through which we can speak to human beings. In nature we are bound. In the soul we can find ourselves free. Ever new aspects of our being are revealed through the soul of our master. In the shades cast by colours we speak of the higher worlds to which we belong.' One could also put it like this: whoever wishes to develop a sense for how nature lives and weaves in colour according to artistic laws would be well advised to study Gerard Wagner's works!

Thus his paintings have their own specific language. They are unmistakable. True objectivity in art is at the same time wholly individual. The laws are overcome by the force of the creative soul, which feels them and gives them life. True freedom does not contradict the laws. Within them the artist discovers and creates new ones. New ways of creating are born! Gerard Wagner continually stresses two things: active devotion to Rudolf Steiner's artistic work, and the being of colour, which he ceaselessly seeks to fathom in an anthroposophical way. Spiritual science is a path which can teach us to look at colours in such a way that they reveal their nature. One can only do this by becoming a painter. Colour creates new organs in the soul of the painter, through which it can speak. Thus the painter Gerard Wagner is also always a researcher. And his research is filled with deep devotion and reverence. It is as if colours stream towards Gerard Wagner because he loves them. Whoever experiences him at work will feel that his whole being becomes the breathing soul of colour. Colour streams through him effortlessly. The painting, the painter himself, becomes a painting. An unborn essence hovers around what is arising; the final result is an image of it. Thus it is a joy to look upon the fruits of Gerard Wagner's feeling eye and hand in his preoccupation with the work of Rudolf Steiner. He is a true witness to the fruitfulness of the ideas of anthroposophy! One can sense that the quantity and quality of his works, his teaching, his research, are one of the great accomplishments of the century.

May these words stand, in all humility and with admiration, for our unspeakable gratitude in meeting him, and in honour of his 90th birthday – which he will undoubtedly spend painting.[119]

A few months later, in the summer of 1996, Ernst Schuberth opened a special exhibition of Gerard Wagner's work at the Goetheanum. Many friends and pupils gathered to celebrate the fruits of a lifetime's work. Walter Steffen wrote the following review:

Death, the Initiate, the Child
In April this year Gerard Wagner reached the age of 90, and in honour of this occasion the Section for Visual Arts at the Goetheanum will be hosting an exhibition of his paintings from 29 June to 11 August. Elisabeth Wagner-Koch has arranged the works in the staircase, mezzanine, gallery and Terrace Room. Selected sequences of paintings from the mid 1950s, 1970s and 1990s are shown in groups, with the main emphasis on works painted in the last two years.

As I make my way among the many groups of paintings carefully and spaciously presented at various locations in the building, I am soon absorbed and lifted up into an all-embracing world of moving colour. The works communicate balance and harmony to the observer. Although unobtrusive and reserved in one way, there is nevertheless such an abundance and variety that I can do no harm by beginning with one aspect only. In many of Gerard Wagner's paintings, always in new and surprising transformations, we see the figure of Ahriman and experience the forces in his environment and the way he influences his earthly realm. Darkness thickens and congeals into Ahriman's actual form, or it is only the tenebrous wings of his helpers or a skeleton in the earth's crust that are visible. In other pictures the crust of the earth holds a sepulchre in readiness.

Again and again to put such matters forward, to remain completely true to the task of sharing through art in the labour of bringing light and finally redemption to the forces of darkness, this in itself would be a lifetime's achievement. There is something religious about the steady repetition of such a motif, yet at the same time the works are also purely artistic in the ever new and surprising transformations which they offer. A painter will surely not be quick to muster the courage and persistence needed for the task of constantly putting the characteristics and forces of the 'Lord of darkness' in their proper place and bringing them out into the light.

Rudolf Steiner had the figure of Faust painted (and later painted it himself) in the small cupola of the First Goetheanum. Actually his concern was not so much for this specific individual as for the need to show in that place a representative of initiation in the age of the consciousness soul. Death was depicted beneath this representative, a skeleton as the basic chord of modern initiation. But this would have been untenable artistically, as well as being uncreative, if a third element had not also been introduced. In the painting in the cupola, this third element took the form of something like the figure of a child hovering nearby. This expressed the purity and modesty of the new spirit experience which ensures that a wide-awake I-consciousness, specifically owing its existence to the forces of death, is present in every kind of encounter with the spirit. Precisely this kind of threefold patterning was what seemed to me to show in Gerard Wagner's paintings. I have already mentioned the death element, the skeleton. Then comes the figure of the initiate, or of one who is about to be initiated, frequently with a lemniscate inscribed upon the heart. Above and beyond these two elements a third is conjured, something that comes and goes, rises and falls, resounds and is hushed in the dance of colours. All this combines to give me a sense of that child being revealed in the pictures. That child's magic breath of the future shimmers, sounds and sparkles, pouring itself into the coloured space of the picture and reaching far into the depths of the darkest corners.

In a lecture of 25 January 1920,[120] Rudolf Steiner spoke briefly about the threefold patterning of 'death, the initiate and the child' as being one of the most important Imaginations of present and future times, and then apologised for being so brief about something so essential. Gerard Wagner has worked at this archetypal image all his life. It seems to live most urgently within him. Artistically speaking I can almost sense how an archetypal image or process of this kind imbues his painter's eye, his whole painterly human being, and is always present when he is working artistically. (Other artistic Imaginations newly given to humanity by Rudolf Steiner can no doubt also be found in Gerard Wagner's world of colour.)

It is so very easy to paint a picture to death by working at it for too long. Then the skeleton wins. Gerard Wagner works at his paintings for a long while; he dares to do so. But because he paints in the light and with the winged power of that child, a child that is to be found in modern initiation science, his paintings do not die an ordinary death but reach into inexhaustible depths.

The intellect is interested in sequences. It asks how a colour changes step by step if you keep adding the same amount of another colour to it. This leads to the colour scales we all know, painted in ever the same rectangular shape. Gerard Wagner also asks himself what happens if a red or a peach-blossom colour is changed by adding black to it. But with his pictures he shows us something else. Look, he says, the more the red changes, the more it becomes a blue-red, or a black-red, or a black-violet, the more will the form it creates also have to change. Within the overall context of the moment every colour creates its own form. If the painter fails to notice this and robs the colour of its formative effect and formative world, he steals from it the best fruits of its labours.

With this in mind it is interesting to examine one of the pictures in the Terrace Room, the second on the long wall counting from the door. There is something most unexpected and creative about the sequence of figures. Start with the middle one in red and peach-blossom and follow the eight steps. You find eight forms, each one different in its movement and its shape, growing increasingly shadowy, like a ladder of colours running from peach-blossom-red right through to the black-violet, the indigo-violet of the cross. The power of the child transforms this depiction of death, this sequence, into something like a musical scale, a heavenly ladder that can lead artistically into the depths and midst and heights of spirit realms.

And one can also sense how Wagner's *oeuvre* as a whole, going from painting to painting, represents a steady march from stage to stage. His pictures always pose questions which are answered by those that follow, while sowing new seeds to be answered by others still to come. Yet every work can also stand entirely alone.

To embed is the opposite of to exhibit. Gerard Wagner's art is wholly embedded in Rudolf Steiner's artistic impulse and thus also in the work of others. In this case I sense the collaboration of a special influence, the influence of plant pigments and thus also of their creators. Without the life's work of someone like Georg Meier, from which the manufacture of today's pigments has emerged, I would not be having the experience of colour here bestowed on me. I can also sense many other connecting threads within the overall organism of art as an impulse of anthroposophy. The work of Gerard Wagner, as an especially pure manifestation of it, occupies a place at its very heart.[121]

The Hermitage exhibition, St Petersburg

What must surely count as the most significant exhibition of Gerard Wagner's work was at the Hermitage Museum, St Petersburg which took place between 28 October and 25 December 1997. The 90 paintings were chosen to represent three major phases of Wagner's work. Elisabeth Wagner, who put together an extensive catalogue, described the three areas as:

1. The early work with its iconic character, which demonstrates a connection to Russian art.
2. The scientific work leading to 'metamorphosis' – a new motif in painting.
3. The late work with its central theme of the human being.

A congress on the artistic and scientific aspects of colour entitled 'The Artist and the Philosophy of Colour in Art' accompanied the exhibition; and a number of the speakers came from anthroposophical circles. Amongst them were Sergei O. Prokofieff speaking on 'The Seven Liberal Arts and the New Path of Initiation'; Ernst Schuberth on 'Gerard Wagner – Life and Work'; Heinz Georg Häusler on 'The Goetheanistic Approach to Art as an Impulse for the Future'; John Ermel on 'Rudolf Steiner's Architectural Ideas in the Context of Modern European Architecture'; Elisabeth Wagner on 'The New Impulse in Painting'; Christian Hitsch on 'Goethe's Theory of Metamorphosis'; Peter Stebbing on 'Goethe's Theory of Colour'; Daniel Moreau on 'Modern Art – Goethe or Beuys'; and Iwao Takahashi on 'Light in Art in Eastern Asia'. Ernst Schuberth recalled how the exhibition came about:

> The impulse for the Hermitage exhibition was a folder of small paintings by Gerard Wagner which I took with me on a visit to the newly founded Waldorf School on Kristowski Island. A school parent, who happened also to be a publisher, saw the paintings and took them to the vice-director of the Hermitage, who was at once eager to exhibit them. The curator Viktor Pavloff then visited Gerard Wagner in his studio in Dornach and was impressed with what he saw. After intense discussions and negotiations between the Hermitage and Elisabeth

Wagner, the show took place at the Menchikov Palace – a wing of the Hermitage Museum.

Elisabeth Wagner accompanied the work to St Petersburg and was present, with Ernst and Erika Schuberth and some former pupils from Russia, at the opening of the exhibition. Christian Merz, a former pupil from Switzerland was present as well and because of his familiarity with the Russian language, he was able to give valuable assistance to the practical side of the project. The comments in the visitors' book demonstrated that the exhibition made a strong impression and visitors were deeply moved by the paintings.

This showing of Gerard Wagner's work at one of the most prominent art centres in the world, was a fitting finale and culmination to six decades of exhibitions during his lifetime, beginning so simply in 1939/1940 in the joinery workshop at the Goetheanum. Interestingly enough, the most appreciative response to that very first show came from a Russian – Marie Savitch (1882–1975), a eurythmist who had originally studied painting in St Petersburg.[122] Gerard Wagner had a strong connection with Russian people and in turn was loved and appreciated by them. To see the way in which some visitors to Dornach from Russia held the painter's hand in theirs was something quite moving. 'I *am* a Russian', Wagner once said about himself. According to Rudolf Steiner the next epoch in the development of humanity will evolve out of a Slavic impulse led by the Russian people.[123]

Bernd Lutz, a former pupil of Wagner's, draws attention to this future aspect in his 2019 essay 'Sources of Artistic Imagination – Gerard Wagner's Love for Novalis' 2019.[124] There he writes:

> … What Rudolf Steiner characterised here as a future goal (in art), has been brought into the present and developed to a high mastery by Gerard Wagner. And we who have known him personally and experienced his modesty, his childlike and open interest for everything, the compassion and kindness in his eyes, have witnessed a future form of humanity.

(The sixth post-Atlantean cultural epoch Lutz refers to here, which will follow our present 5th cultural epoch, is represented artistically by Rudolf Steiner in his painting of the 'Slav motif' in the small cupola of the first Goetheanum.)

The St Petersburg exhibition did not however mark the end of Gerard Wagner's work: for the next year-and-a-half he taught two afternoons a week at the painting school and continued to work daily at the easel.

In 1998, the now 92-year-old painter had a number of collapses. Doctors could find no cause but it was clear that Wagner himself knew the reason. These moments of losing consciousness could happen when he was painting at the easel, and this in itself pointed to the state of consciousness he spoke of when painting. 'In painting,' he said, 'one is in a higher state of consciousness.' The divide between earth consciousness and supersensible consciousness was becoming less defined for Gerard Wagner. And this also expressed itself in the changing configuration of his organism.

Over the Christmas period of 1998, Gerard Wagner was in the Ita Wegman Clinic for a few weeks during which time he gave a few painting lessons from his bed. Back home his routine carried on as usual. Visiting the artist's studio in March 1999, painter Andrea Hitsch gives a charming glimpse of a typical day at his home. She wrote:

> A sunny afternoon in March was drawing to a close. Heinrich trampled next to me, his left hand in mine. Our goal was Brosiweg. A little steep road led upwards, we opened the gate and rang the bell – a little hand broom hung on the front door.
>
> Soon a face muffled against the cold, with large glasses, peered out from the partly opened door. Heinrich took a step backwards! 'Oh, it's you, come in, I'm battling with flu and that's why my head must be kept very, very warm.'
>
> Frau Wagner led us first to her archive in the cellar. Heinrich noticed the smell of apples. On a tidy shelf were numerous folders: Frau Wagner was archiving her husband's work, thousands and thousands of paintings. From one folder emerged page after page of photographs of the master's early work: intense and vivid paintings of flowers, animals, Mary, angels.
>
> 'Are we going now, Mama?'
>
> Now the way led up steps, and then further upwards again. Frau Wagner rang the long, pleasant-sounding chimes in the entrance and we stepped into Herr Wagner's painting studio. The 92-year-old master stood there surrounded by pictures which all seemed alive. A delicate smile from a slightly inclined head welcomed us into the ring of paintings.
>
> He was painting with a pupil at the easel. Frau Wagner put this or that picture before us, for Heinrich wanted to see an angel. There were also many birds singing a marvellous chorus in the dark red and blue scent of blossoms.

What we beheld in the paintings were no longer objects. His paintbrush obeyed him as he lifted a splendour of colours far above the sense perceptible world. He moved in the realm of the elements. Painting had become prayer for him and one could but be pious in the presence of the master in the blue smock.[125]

A few months later, in May, Gerard Wagner was able to have the pleasure of his niece Mary Ingham's company for a few days. On 26 July after a more critical collapse, an ambulance was called and he was taken to the Ita Wegman Clinic. On arrival, the senior physician was swiftly by his side and said simply and emphatically: 'Total exhaustion!' And Wagner replied: 'Yes – many changes ...' (He meant changes in his organism.)

After the solar eclipse on 11 August he regained a little strength but remained in the clinic, bedridden for the last two-and-a-half months of his life, during which time the doctors noted his unusually regular and unchangingly rhythmical heartbeat.

In the late afternoon of 13 October 1999, in the company of Elisabeth Wagner and Caroline Chanter, Gerard Wagner gently and consciously exhaled for the last time, purposefully releasing his soul and spirit from his physical body. The cremation took place in Basel on 18 October.

Theodor Willmann sent a poem written for his colleague:

> *To our beloved, revered friend in the spirit, Gerard Wagner*
> Who passes here – step after step
> emerging from the hut of his mastery,
> taking the path of the morning sun
> toward Mont Salvat? ...
>
> Sure of the dawn? ...
> Sure of inward meaning?
> Of new day's beginning?
> Ascending the forested slope? ...
>
> This is the first beginning:
> his new work
> at the shrine of resurrection:
> The god's new Word of creation![126]

And Torsten Steen, a former pupil, composed these words of gratitude:

The paradox

The death of Gerard Wagner confronts us with a paradox: that of a person profoundly alive, resting with every fibre of his being in the breath of the cosmos, receiving from it everything – and especially so in his very last days although the physical body was fading like the leaves outside; still he let the world sound through him, like a mighty orchestra. In contrast we young ones: wooden, hampered, stammering, half-dead despite our bodies being fit and active.

The Rose Cross

Wagner taught us the true nature of dying while still alive: letting go of the illusion of everything we regard as vital, self-preserving. To surrender yourself to colour means to open your heart and no longer cling to anything. Yet what else is this but dying? To relinquish yourself into the abyss of nothing, trusting so much, with such inner wakefulness, that you can endure it until the cosmos of colour reconfigures the self. Which of us pupils succeeded in enduring this and really pursuing this path? Putting it more simply we could also say: Without the black needle's eye of the cross, whence would spring the roses that blossom outward from it, and configure the true self?

The mystery

To see Wagner die means to understand Wagner. It means to experience a profoundly awake, active human being who does not root his spiritual existence in the dungeon of the intellectual ego. That died a long time again, as he taught us. A teaching without words for those who have heart and eyes.

What it was that painted

We observe how he painted. Everything happened 'from without'. Colour was the instigation, while the unspeakable, the 'whole' shaped it. No human being can paint like this. Time and again we were astonished at this teacher-painter, who found the courage, as he painted, to become what there are no words for. Even the word 'nothing' can be misunderstood.

The true picture

At the very end Wagner painted a picture that in fact he had been painting for a very long time, for ever really. I only saw it at the end. He was painting very consciously, as he always did. But now he could do it directly, without a brush. His shaping spirit reached deep and revealed the body's transience. The body followed inevitably and necessarily, as the brushstroke follows the body. Now a painting has been completed. The hand of the artist begins anew.

Thanks
What does one feel, lifted far beyond oneself, toward such a teacher? He shows us what is essential. We experienced true, spirit-born being. This was more than we could have expected – a gift. For this there can be only wordless gratitude.[127]

An obituary from the Goetheanum leadership was written by Sergei O. Prokofieff:

On 13 October 1999, Gerard Wagner crossed the threshold into the spiritual world, a moment when one of the most significant anthroposophical artists returned to his spiritual home.

As an academically trained painter he met the work of Rudolf Steiner in 1925 and devoted his whole life to the artistic impulse in anthroposophy. The most notable quality in his creative soul was the selflessness with which he approached the world of colour as a revelation of spiritual reality.

Gerard Wagner consciously put the arena of his soul at the disposal of those spiritual beings who live behind the colours and who seek to reveal themselves through them. Because of this he has become one of the greatest Goetheanistic painters of the twentieth century. Just as Goethe allowed natural phenomena to speak through his soul and was able to hear their secrets, Gerard Wagner lived in a similar way with the world of colour. The way of observing nature phenomenologically as Goethe did (see Wagner's sequences of metamorphoses) was raised to the level of highly artistic works. In this way he united art and science in his creative activity and produced a new synthesis of the two. In so doing he stood at the threshold of the spiritual world, which became a reality in colour in his pictures.

In the process of painting this contact with the higher worlds gave his art a religious element. This quality can best be characterised in Rudolf Steiner's words from the beginning of his book *Knowledge of the Higher Worlds*: reverence, devotion, wonder. This was the prevailing mood in Gerard Wagner's studio when he was painting. In his life's work one can experience the great Rosicrucian synthesis of science, art and religion, which gives an intimation of something to be achieved in humanity's distant future. One could even say: This is how art will look one day in the future.

The departure of this artist from the world was something quite special. Before he passed over, he spent several weeks in the Ita Wegman Clinic surrounded by people devoted to his care, tended also by his life companion and co-worker Elisabeth Wagner-Koch. During one visit he appeared at first to be far away from his body. Lying there very still, breathing gently and with closed eyes, he appeared as if immersed in intensive creative work.

When he was told 'Sergei has come', he slowly opened his eyes and was immediately present, looking at the visitor with unspeakable gentleness and goodness. Then he said clearly and deliberately, 'Good-bye'. At that point he closed his eyes and one had once again the impression that he was continuing the work he had interrupted. What kind of activity could this have been? An answer came: Just as in his life as an artist the body served him as a selfless sense organ so that higher spiritual laws could imprint themselves in the colours and forms of earthly matter, so now the artist was gazing with growing wonder and devotion at the great divine work of art – the human body. No longer did he gaze through it into the outer world but he approached it from the periphery, perceiving the indescribable beauty of colours and forms in all the life processes. Out of the realm of the head there appeared a kind of stream of light which gradually spread out and was received by the darkness pervading the limbs. From this conversation of the polarities arose the rainbow, pulsating rhythmically, and uniting man and the cosmos in its coloured breathing. In such a way the deeds and suffering of the light are manifest in the human heart.

Rudolf Steiner calls this process: 'The wonderful mystery which lives between lung and heart'; a mystery in which the human being can experience, how 'in pulse and the rhythm of the blood ... the God-given cosmic pictures powerfully manifest'.[128]

For many weeks the soul of the artist experienced the indescribable beauty of these cosmic pictures and could recognise in them the life of the cosmos before leaving this body and moving from his own work to the creators behind it.

One can gain an intimation of the jubilation of the spiritual world when his soul was received into this realm. This soul while on earth was devoted with such selflessness and purity to those beings who manifest here in forms and colours. He helped them to speak and appear in our world. They received new colour names through him. Now he is among them, received with the same admiration and wonder as he accorded them here on earth. A great artist, creating through the language of colours, has returned to his eternal home.

All those who met Gerard Wagner, friends, colleagues and students alike will remember his goodness and his delicate frame which radiated a peaceful light. In his studio, pointing at the last almost completed picture when earthly words seemed to fail, he would merely whisper: 'This is how it would like to become.' Not he but the spirit that filled his picture now wished to speak. Through his works the spirit can continue to speak beyond the death of the master.[129]

And Christian Hitsch wrote on behalf of the Goetheanum Visual Art Section:

Whoever was able to regularly visit the great painter Gerard Wagner during his final days on earth could experience the events around him in a kind of imaginative parable. His extremely delicate, almost translucent body, was bathed in and interwoven with a space pervaded by colour which seemed to be linked in a living way with all the wealth of colour in the world. In this aura, the three women who were caring for him seemed like three soul-forces lovingly embedded in it, completely dedicated to the master's life. The increasing splendour of the autumn colours, the changing colours of the plants as the seeds matured, as well as the streaming back to the cosmos of their life forces, all this seemed equally to belong naturally to the surroundings of the master. What was happening through him and with him was reflected in the colour phenomena of nature. Becoming free of physical substance in a final glowing in colours, in this way the soul of the master lived on in all the resplendent colours around him. The luminous quality of colour-rich autumn: the fruits and seeds ripened by the light, bowing to the sun as the evening of the year approached – the earthly and heavenly forces in balance. Thus his death took place in the sunset of autumn, in the sign of the Scales (13 October 1999) while the beginning of his life (5 April 1906) occurred at the spring equinox in the sign of the Ram, which itself is a figure of the forces of sunrise.

Between the moods of sunrise and sunset his life as a painter unfolded. These are moments of balance in the course of the day and of the year when the colour-filled being of the earth's aura manifests in its most beautiful way. These are the images which Rudolf Steiner has given as key motifs for the schooling of a new kind of painting, and which Wagner used constantly, painting as a researcher, and researching as a painter. Researching how 'to paint out of colour', how to find form out of the creative forces in colour, is the central theme of his life. There seemed little else in the miracle of this life besides his own painting and his teaching of painting. In fact it was hardly possible to speak with him about anything else: more precisely, he spoke little, he preferred to speak with the paintbrush, by doing. That was the language of Gerard Wagner's – an active language of colour.

He stood buoyant and upright – in balance (he had no inclination for sitting!). His feet placed well and firmly on the earth, connecting with below, his head as if united with the heavenly sphere, and between these he breathed in colour as he painted. His paintbrush moved in its own incomparable way over the surface of the picture, in which he seemed measured into a small cosmos. In this way he experimented with the colours and the feelings they aroused. The paintbrush glided with curiosity over the surface, sensing, questioning, feeling the lightness and heaviness of the colours, their brightness and darkness, their warmth and cold ...

And so he discovered for himself and for a new art of painting the very important law of colour sequences: a first colour in conversation with the next builds up to a colour-soul relationship which presses for a specific configuration. In this way motifs of a completely new kind could unfold, created by the colours themselves. Rudolf Steiner's challenge, that all activity and form in a picture should develop from a feeling for the colour, became a reality in Gerard Wagner's artistic work – individualised by him in a unique way so that it became objective. One could also say: through him and his work, this indication of Rudolf Steiner's could be grasped, because it is directly observable. The diligence and the discipline imbuing his research as an artist have such an unbelievably convincing quality, such truth, that Rudolf Steiner's indications speak to us directly through them. Gerard Wagner belongs to that special group of people who have made Rudolf Steiner's indications into the central theme of their lives and so live as genuine representatives of anthroposophy. For him painting is a path of schooling. Painting: colour released from the object, suspended freely in space! Yet he did not stop there. Spiritual beings incline from the other side of the colours. The colours themselves are creator beings. As such they fill the newly gained picture space with imaginations.

What began at the beginning of the century as a decisive new impulse in painting, namely, the detaching of colour from the object, has here become deed. However, Gerard Wagner does not dwell in a vague, abstract colour realm; he overcomes abstract painting and painting becomes new – embodying the essence of colour. His work, extending through most of the 20th century, will ray out into the future and reveal itself more and more as a light-filled example of the new and true spirit of our times.

His entire being bowed before the mystery of colour in a loving, joyful yet serious way, full of devotion and dignity. His life and work itself became a living metaphor of the creative power of colour![130]

GERARD WAGNER AS TEACHER

Life itself is rather like colours, sounds and energy. The Romantic
studies life, just as the painter, musician and mechanist
study colour, sound and energy. A careful study of life makes
a Romantic, just as a careful study of colour, form, sound
and energy, make a painter, musician and mechanist.

NOVALIS[131]

Gerard Wagner was loath to theorise. His words were concrete and based on his own experience. Pupils of his so often heard him say, 'To answer that question, we need a sheet of paper and paint'. Then the work could begin.

Wagner had his own code of etiquette when teaching. To begin with he usually asked the pupil most courteously what colour he or she was painting. This question made a connection immediately between pupil and teacher, and the interaction could develop from there. If he felt it would be helpful to demonstrate something (Wagner was known to say comparatively little but show a lot), he would ask if he could 'make a stroke on the painting', doing so in such a charming and friendly way that no one, as far as I know, ever said 'no'.

One overall aspect of Gerard Wagner's teaching was his humanity. The individual meeting between teacher and pupil seemed to go beyond instructions about how to work on one's painting. His reaction to the painting was not always pleasant for the pupil but it was genuine, and one felt that his advice and guidance contained something relevant to one's own present soul situation. Yet he did not need to know more about the student than became apparent through their direct encounter before the easel, with both teacher and pupil engaged in solving a colour problem as it worked itself out on the paper.

Ernst Schuberth recalled his experiences as a pupil in the 1960s:

> When teaching, Gerard Wagner went around to each student and, standing before their painting, he would 'drink it in', become one with it. He tested his own feeling for healthy balance against the picture so as to be able to restore the lost balance in the pupil's work. Standing in his firm black shoes he would often sway from left to right and right to left, or sometimes stamp strongly on the ground to find the right support. As a doctor might visit his patients and identify himself with the patient's illness so as to find the right way forward, Gerard Wagner

'incarnated' himself into the pupil's picture in order to discover the necessary balance. Once found, he would make the appropriate supportive brushstroke – sometimes to the dismay of the pupil who saw his painting entirely 'disfigured'. If the necessary correction proved too great, he would sometimes simply walk past pupil and painting. The path of training demanded the overcoming of a subjective feeling of wellbeing in favour of the objective reality of the painting. Whoever found this unacceptable was free to go their own way.

In the later years (late 1980s and 1990s), when I was a pupil, he carried with him a brown leather briefcase that had obviously seen a few decades of wear and tear; and once he was in the studio he would take out a few brushes and a white cloth. As he made his rounds of the pupils, some already painting, some waiting, he used the white cloth to show 'colour measuring' on the page. The white cloth helped to answer questions like: 'Can the green carry the brown? Is the red enough to balance the violet?' Out came the white cloth and he would hold it up to the painting to cover a part of it, showing the pupil the amount of extra weight that still needed rebalancing. And he would use the handles of his paintbrushes, which were generally black or brown, to show the effect of the dark colour on the other colours by holding up the brush against certain places in the picture.

Colours were alive in Gerard Wagner. He felt life's experiences and occurrences as colour experiences. He often related everyday occurrences to colour so as to help make colour experiences more vivid for pupils. His references were down to earth and easy to understand. When describing a living tension between colours, for example, Wagner often used the comparison of flying a kite, and suggested that the pupils should practise kite flying; or he compared it to putting up an umbrella on a windy day and feeling the pull of the wind, or the tension felt when pulling a cat's tail!

The vital dynamic of concentration and expansion within the activity of the colours was an important subject for Gerard Wagner, and he had various ways of conveying this to pupils in imagery. He once likened it to an Englishman with his love of telling jokes. When, for example, he painted a strong red into the green, which made a concentration of dark colour, he showed how this caused the other colours to 'expand', to 'shoot up', as he said, 'to the top of the page'. He explained: an Englishman with his consciousness soul feels so trapped in his physical body that he has to make a joke, and this causes him to 'shoot up' out of it and escape.

He made pupils aware of the feeling connection with the colour experiences one has continually in daily life but are not noticed or brought to consciousness: 'How does the colour of something make one feel,' he would ask, 'the colour of a leaf, a flower, the sky? Does one open or close inside?' He described what reveals itself through the colour yellow in the following way: 'Try to bring the feeling you have to consciousness, say, when you meet someone on the street and they walk straight past you or smile at you. What you feel in the second case is "yellow".'

Sometimes Wagner used a simple way of getting pupils to look at their paintings objectively. One pupil was having trouble seeing what was too prominent in his picture, and Gerard Wagner suggested a way of recognising it. He said: 'Imagine you are looking out of the window into nature – now put your picture there. What would attract your attention the most? And after noticing it, ask yourself how that makes you feel.' This method was a help for pupils in learning to judge their painting in relation to what we normally see in everyday life, and whether something appears ugly or beautiful and so on. It brought one down to earth.

As a pupil of Gerard Wagner, you noticed his awareness of human affairs and his grasp of reality when he spoke of colour situations and problems. His knowledge of mechanics, the dynamics of force and motion, emerged especially when he described the action of colour. His references to literature revealed that he was widely read. And the nursery rhymes, children's stories and adventure stories of his youth were still alive in him. Since one aspect of colour law is the principle of opposition, of colours 'battling' with one another, he had many stories of battles, of choosing the right weapons at the right time, and of gladiators entering arenas. The Bible story of 'Daniel in the Lion's Den' was a favourite.

Other comparisons he used were innocent and charming: 'The blue was getting so weak it needed a doctor', or 'Violet is like an agreeable old lady, wise and neutral about things.' On one occasion, when a pupil set violet next to the brown (violet having little opposition or contrast to the brown), he said it was like 'grandmother coming to visit, or someone else's grandmother, and one knows that nothing is going to happen for the next hour or so'. When bringing yellow to a particular colour situation he once said with a twinkle in his eye: 'Yellow is a weak colour in such strong company but when it is used effectively in the right place, it can work strongly – like a mouse which is small but can be so powerfully effective as to make a woman jump up on her chair!'

He once said that introducing red, for example, too early in a particular painting, was like 'giving a lamb chop to a baby'; and in relation to another inappropriate choice of colour he said this was like 'a child entering an adult's world'. About the introduction of a pleasant shining colour into a painting dominated by dark colours, he said: 'You wouldn't give a bunch of flowers to a coalman!' To green he once said, 'Green is a living colour but mute, without movement, like a little boy at school who doesn't say anything.' When black was suggested in an inappropriate situation, he said: 'Black would be like putting a chimney-sweep into paradise.'

The different stages of childhood were very much alive in him; it was as if his memories of his own childhood continually rose up in him. This too he related to colour and painting. Of one of the 'Nature Mood Sketches' – 'the shining moon' – he said: 'It has a rocking motion like a child on a swing, when one was still united with everything.' Another painting he compared to a ten-year-old child – still in the full 'joy of life'. In one painting he pointed out two different worlds and said: '... like boys at public school playing the fool one minute and attending chapel the next'.

Memories of former pupils

A selection of reminiscences by former pupils who attended the painting school in the middle to later years, between 1976 and 1997, give a varied picture of Gerard Wagner as both teacher and person:

> *Gail McManus, US 1976–1984*
> When I first met Herr Wagner I was in the downstairs studio of the Goetheanum Painting School in Dornach. It was my first day as a student in the school and I had little idea what to expect. The door opened and a hush fell over my fellow students, one of respectful delight in the presence of the gentle, unassuming man who entered. He greeted the students with his conscious handshake and direct, appreciative gaze. Then his attention turned to me. After a brief explanation of the manner in which I should do so, he told me to paint yellow. With hopeful concentration, for the next two hours I painted yellow onto my large sheet of white paper. When I returned home for a midday meal I noticed myself hiccupping continuously. Returning for the afternoon session at the painting school, Herr Wagner gazed quietly for some moments at my attempt to capture something of the nature of yellow. He said, 'Well, it is as if your yellow has hiccups.'

Each summer I would arrive in Dornach after lengthy hours of travelling from New York. That same day I would eagerly visit Herr Wagner and his wife, Elizabeth Wagner-Koch. At the ring of his doorbell, he would descend from his studio and welcome me warmly with 'Grüß Gott!' Upstairs, we would chat about my work over the past school year and about the painting school. The spontaneity and gladness with which he welcomed me always set the tone for my studies with him each summer. As I came to know him better, I perceived that he greeted each student who came to his door with equally appreciative interest.

A wonderful treat awaited me when I was invited to Herr Wagner's studio to see his paintings. Sometimes I brought friends. Herr Wagner would place paintings on easels and on the floor, stooping to change them with agility beyond his age, and with quiet, humble grace. I was reminded of 'the washing of the feet'.

Of course there was that affirmative tap of his foot as Herr Wagner advised a student to boldly place a colour into his or her painting. The tap seemed to say 'No nonsense! Be brave and do what must be done!' When I was attempting to learn to paint animals, Herr Wagner demonstrated for me the direction I needed to take by painting in front of me four little painting sketches of creatures. He showed me how, by varying the colour 'mood' of the background colour, as well as the colour of the ground on which the animal stood, the form of the animal changed accordingly although the colour of the animal's body remained the same. Together we experienced an animal emerge in each sketch. Some looked quite humorous; and as the animals took shape, Herr Wagner chuckled occasionally at their appearance.

Herr Wagner seemed never to judge the outcome of a student's painting work. He would stand in deep concentration before each painting, as if to become purely a vessel, to listen to the needs of the colour conversation on the easel and to offer advice without imposing his will on others. Students were deeply grateful for the respect he gave them and it opened the way for us to look at ourselves and our work truthfully.

Ans Groene, Holland, 1979–1984
In Allgäu, in the mountains, stands a lime tree which Herr Wagner grew from seed on his balcony. He gave me the sapling during the Easter holidays of 1982 and I took it with me on the train. When I got home it was snowing; and now the sapling is a majestic tree.

As I lived near his house, I often went shopping for him, mostly for milk and cheese. He loved Roquefort. As he was busy painting in the mornings he would leave his shopping list on the front steps of his house. I still have some of those amusing shopping lists. One is of a fortified castle of cheese being eaten by a mouse. If no list was on the step I rang the doorbell and Herr Wagner appeared in his blue painter's smock with a paintbrush in his hand. In his studio I noticed only finished pictures on the easel. He did not like to show unfinished paintings, although he liked to paint before students.

When we painted the walls of the Rudolf Steiner School in Überlingen I can remember Herr Wagner high up on the scaffolding exclaiming how horrible he found it that people could watch him painting. A friend of mine visited us there and asked me whether Herr Wagner had children. 'Oh,' I answered, 'Herr Wagner has many children, and I am one of them.' And since then this feeling has never left me.

little wisdom
"Strong Rock."

Bernd Lutz, Germany, 1983–1990
It was the end of term and all students had shown their work and said what they had learnt during the term. Afterwards, as we were all getting ready to leave for the holidays, I went to Herr Wagner to say goodbye. I told him I had the feeling (I was in the third year of training), that I

knew absolutely nothing. His eyes started to shine and he said that that was very good, I did not need to know anything in order to paint – as a painter one cannot be stupid enough.

Interest

At the end of my third year I spent three months high up in the Swiss Mountains on an Alp with a large herd of cows. I had vivid experiences of nature there, especially when the cows were being driven to pasture. Afterwards I was eager to share all this with friends but no one seemed particularly interested. However, when the new term at the school began I unexpectedly found an eager listener. Herr Wagner wanted to know all about the cows, how they behaved, and what other animals were there and so on.

Building a hut

Herr Wagner liked to begin every term with the yellow-blue-red exercise. Once he related it to the task of the esoteric pupil as described in the book *Knowledge of Higher Worlds*, in the chapter 'The Transformation of Dream Life'. Rudolf Steiner says there that a pupil who wants to be active in the spiritual world with clear judgement in his perceptions, needs to 'build a hut'; 'He must seek out some place, thoroughly investigate it, and spiritually take possession of it. In this place he must establish his spiritual home, and relate everything else to it.' For Herr Wagner the yellow-blue-red exercise was the hut to which one could always return when losing the ground under one's feet and the ability to judge one's work.

The plant motif

The plant was the theme of the term. We painted various blossom colours first, and then tried to experience how the green behaves as it grows up towards the red, yellow, or blue blossoms. Painting the blossoms first was unusual and Herr Wagner commented: 'The plant does not actually grow in the sequence of time as we know it. The blossoms which appear last actually come first; the green growing up from the earth is determined by the still invisible blossom. In nature the plant is subjected to certain conditions. When I let plants arise out of the colour they can be more truly their essential reality than in nature.'

Stuck
I stood helpless before my picture and had no idea what colour I should use. As Herr Wagner at last came to me, I asked him if he would use blue. His answer: 'Not if my name were Bernd Lutz.'

Dissatisfaction
As I expressed my dissatisfaction about the qualities of my paintings, he said: 'Your dissatisfaction is your most important commodity.'

Matching colours
With my new green pullover and matching red scarf I met Herr Wagner in the corridor of the school. He looked attentively at the colours and said: 'That suits well – I mean to the colours of the face.'

A court jester
At an end of term presentation a pupil and myself gave a cabaret-like performance. Herr Wagner was delightfully amused and said: 'We really need here at the school something that kings and their courts had in past times – a court jester.'

A different point of view
A painter from a quite different school of art was invited by a few pupils to give a lecture at the Wagner school. From the start I found myself inwardly rejecting what he said. I saw though that Herr Wagner listened very attentively and then, in questions, touched on points which could further elaborate the ideas expressed by the lecturer. I was deeply impressed.

Full of myself
It was in my fifth year when I noticed for the first time how form can arise out of a colour experience. Full of myself, I brought my work to the school. Herr Wagner looked at it, nodded his head and said: 'Take it off the board and stretch a new paper.' At first I fell into a hole, but then noticed how his reaction had given an enormous incentive for further work. I met him a bit later in the corridor and he said: 'You can perceive a lot.'

Vienna
On the occasion of an exhibition of Herr Wagner's work in Vienna, he, Frau Wagner and a number of pupils drove there to help set it up and attend the opening. One day was also set aside for visiting the Vienna

Art Museums with their rich treasures. I decided, though, to take time to commune quietly with Herr Wagner's paintings. As I walked into the exhibition I noticed two others had had the same idea: Herr and Frau Wagner were there deeply engrossed in his paintings. On the journey we spoke about a painting of Raphael's that was being restored there. For Herr Wagner the strong contemporary desire to preserve art works of the past for eternity was questionable. He said something like this: 'Every period really demands its own art. The artist creates essentially for his contemporaries.'

Back to oneself.
When Herr Wagner heard about an accident that had happened to a pupil who was not paying attention in the street, he said 'Yes, one must be careful when painting, one always goes somewhat out of oneself, but every sentence of Rudolf Steiner brings one back to oneself.'

Ingrid Marl, Germany, 1986–1990
Gerard Wagner had an unforgettable way of correcting paintings. He stood with his black heavy boots next to me and looked in a very concentrated way at the painting without saying a word. Suddenly he stamped on the floor loudly and I knew exactly what he wanted to say: 'Where is the ground? Bring some weight to the bottom of the picture!' It was very rare for Herr Wagner to give any praise when he corrected a painting. If praise did come he usually said: 'That's not at all bad', and the pupil went home feeling deeply satisfied.

When we were painting and the door opened, and Herr Wagner quietly entered, the atmosphere in the studio changed immediately. A great peace descended as we waited expectantly for our interactions with the master.

At one point I was bewildered with a red-green exercise. Herr Wagner approached and asked: 'May I do something to your picture?' (He always asked before he painted on a pupil's picture). Then he added: 'But I will completely ruin it! Give me black.' And he placed a few definite brush strokes between red and green. Immediately peace came to a chaotic situation. Herr Wagner looked at me and said: 'Thus one can rescue a hopeless situation simply with a little black!' Yes, and I can say that I learnt from Herr Wagner to know black and to paint it, which had previously been impossible. Herr Wagner showed me that when I painted black, light appeared somewhere else, in another place. This experience affected me deeply and I will never forget it.

As I lived in the Wagner household I got to know his English sense of humour during mealtimes. Once Frau Wagner said something which caused him to say to her: 'How do you know that?' 'Well Gerry, I am clairvoyant,' she said. He continued eating for a bit and then said, 'But not very much.'

Concerning small everyday things Herr Wagner was very correct. He never forgot anything. He was very interested in world events. It was impressive how he kept up an interest in his former students' work. He asked questions and listened well.

Unforgettable for me was the 1988 painting conference in Unterlenge-hardt. Our theme was the 'Threefold Human Being' motif by Rudolf Steiner. At about this time I was having a crisis in the painting school and thought I could not go on with the training. Herr Wagner came to me and saw straight away that something had changed in the meantime. He said: 'You've made a big inner step!' I felt recognised, and confident that I was on the right path. From that moment on I became a pupil of Herr Wagner's. At the end of the training in the summer of 1990, when I showed my work, I said to Herr Wagner: 'For me the training was at the same time a school of life.' He smiled and said: 'Yes, that is so.'

From his sick bed at the Ita Wegman Clinic in 1999, he looked intently and with almost childlike pleasure at pictures on the theme of the zodiac and the consonants I was working on. On a Sunday in September, a group of us who were attending the art therapy conference in Dornach came to say goodbye. A painful and difficult moment. As Walter Kap-fhammer announced in a clear strong voice that we were all there he briefly opened his eyes.

Since his death I have felt his presence keenly when I work with students and patients; and when I gave courses in Georgia he was close. How thankful I am to feel the support and strength that his presence gives me.

Marianna Caluori, US, 1993–1995
On first meeting Herr Wagner, I was impressed by the duality of his being; the knowledge and wisdom he held and gave so effortlessly, balanced by a rich sense of humour. There was an unmistakable twinkle in

his eye, and this humour was ready to leap forth at the most surprising times!

Picture a painting class in session. Silence permeates each studio, the only sounds coming from the paints being mixed in their pots. The students are hardly breathing, they are so seriously intent on their exercise. Suddenly, without warning, a rich, resonant voice, full of drama, sounds forth: 'Cannons to the left of them, cannons to the right ...' Herr Wagner is reciting 'The Charge of the Light Brigade' as he stands before someone's painting. Peals of laughter from the students; a welcome sense of relaxation can be felt.

Once, I went to his studio to see his recent work. His voice was full of awe as he showed me his yellow and blue exercise. Frau Wagner said to him: 'You've done that exercise hundreds of times', but for him it was like doing it for the first time. The magic, the mystery of the colour-world lived in him always, and his approach as a 'spiritual-scientific researcher' kept his child-like freshness fully alive.

Sometimes I was lucky enough to meet Herr Wagner walking to the painting school. You were aware that you had probably never walked so slowly in your life, yet that was the beauty of it. Every moment was precious for his insights about nature, filled with love and wisdom, were given with such reverence. You felt that anthroposophy was really living in him. You never felt a hint of arrogance in Gerard Wagner, only awe, wonder and reverence.

On two occasions I was present for Herr Wagner's birthday. I was very excited when I learned that his favourite flower was the pansy. This had been my favourite in childhood. I made sure I found pansy plants to take him on his birthday, and told him of my shared love for them. He took me to his desk: there were eight or nine tiny empty medicine bottles. Each held a single pansy flower, all facing towards him as he sat at his desk. He smiled, turned to me with widening eyes and said: 'If pansies were animals, they would be lions!'

When I turn my thoughts to Gerard Wagner, I am at once filled with two feelings: reverence and delight.

Christa Dönges, Switzerland, 1992–1997
Appearance
Herr Wagner's appearance was something special. He appeared taller than he was. His figure was slim, almost slight. He walked with a strong,

considered step, somewhat bent over, leaning a little forwards. It was a special experience to hear Mr Wagner speak: his melodic voice and his wonderfully soft rolling 'r'.

Painting lesson

The very first painting lesson I had with Herr Wagner deeply impressed me. It happened during my second year of training for which I was grateful, since before then I would not have been able to appreciate what he gave. I was standing at my easel and trying to paint an exercise. The page was divided into small surfaces and I remember that I did not have the necessary feeling for the colour to be able to paint the colours in harmony with one another on the coloured backgrounds. I was bewildered and was waiting longingly, albeit with some trepidation, for Herr Wagner's suggestions. At last he came and, after looking at the chaos on my paper, asked if he could paint on my picture. He took the brush and painted strong, large surfaces of colour. Immediately, although there were only two colours on the paper, they began to shine. I also learnt to separate the picture into two parts, an upper and a lower part, which gave some orientation for the feelings.

Herr Wagner spoke very little about the paintings, in fact he said almost nothing. He *showed* what he wanted to say with the paint on the paper. That always made the strongest impression and one could follow it and understand it. A few of his brush-strokes changed the painting immediately in the most impressive manner. Then he might say a few words to make the correction clearer. Sometimes he used a blank sheet of paper (or his arm) to cover part of the painting to see how it stood in balance between above and below. Usually it was too heavy below.

At an end of term presentation, one student's paintings were predominantly in brown and black tones. He observed the work thoroughly before getting up and placing a vase containing a single red rose against the painting. We could observe how the red created a 'shout of joy' amongst the dark colours and brought them into balance.

At the painting school Herr Wagner joined in most of the events, sometimes enjoying long lectures asleep! We often had meetings in which our social problems with one another came up. Once Herr Wagner was there and heard us discussing and arguing. Suddenly he banged his hand down on his briefcase that was resting on his knee and said that we were wasting precious time. We should paint, and the colours would reveal the social problems that we were trying to solve. We were rather perplexed as we had never experienced Herr Wagner so emphatic and did not understand what he meant. Then he said we should imagine a picture with all the colours in harmonious relation to each other, and then suddenly black appears! Black would make all the other colours weak and would upset the balance. What this really means I am learning now gradually to understand. Look for balance and paint in relation to this balance.

At home
At home Herr Wagner was always very open and communicative and happily showed his latest paintings. There was usually a group of pictures to see. Once, as we were looking together, he said something which I will never forget. He said how important it was, after one has done or read something, to let it resound before starting on the next thing. Only later it came to me how necessary this is for deepening understanding. There were many things which Herr Wagner gave me for my life, and the more I try to connect with them the more valuable they prove to be.

Painting as a path of inner transformation

It was clear to Gerard Wagner that what Rudolf Steiner gave as a path of painting could be at the same time a path of inner transformation during which a person undergoes a process of soul and spiritual development. In his monograph *The Art of Colour*, Gerard Wagner describes the path as one of becoming 'truly human':

> But even if one should never reach the goal of finding form out of colour – of lifting the 'Veil of Isis' – *the process, the practice itself is a path towards becoming truly human,* and whoever notices this cannot help but continue on the path.

In correspondence between Ernst Schuberth and the author, both of us pupils of Gerard Wagner, Schuberth has given valuable insights into aspects of the painting training as a path of inner development. Amongst other things he describes hindrances and challenges that a pupil must endure when attempting to enter into the true life of colour, and the courage needed to engage with a new mode of intuitive experience whilst leaving the security of everyday thinking behind (see Appendix 15).

WAS GERARD WAGNER
A PUPIL OF RUDOLF STEINER?

There is Goethe's colour theory, yes,
but Rudolf Steiner revealed a new colour theory to us.

GERARD WAGNER

Sometimes people ask whether Rudolf Steiner was Gerard Wagner's teacher. The answer is 'yes', even though the young painter came to Dornach over a year after Rudolf Steiner's death. Wagner investigated and made use of every indication he could find by Rudolf Steiner about colour, painting and art, not only in the latter's lectures and books, but in what he gave for eurythmy, for the stage and in other contexts.

The three lectures known as the 'colour lectures' were given to painters in Dornach in May 1921.[132] Rudolf Steiner clearly thought painters lacked an objective foundation that could sustain their practice, and the lectures form the basis of a far-reaching theory of colour, which includes practical suggestions for painting.

In the first lecture, before introducing a quite new system of colours, Rudolf Steiner goes straight to the need for the artist to *experience* colour if it is to be understood. And this can happen best, he says, through experimentation. He then gives a comparison of three different two-colour relationships: the first is the colour green (a 'green meadow') with red-coloured shapes in it; the second example, green with peach-blossom shapes; and the third, green with blue shapes. And he asks, 'How does the quality of the green change in each example?'

Rudolf Steiner offers these comparisons in a lively, imaginative way, and says the two respective colours together create a complex of feelings. To experience these 'feeling-complexes', he says, it is not enough simply to look at the colour, one must look at the colour with the soul's eye. In other words, lift the colour experience 'up into one's life of feeling'. Gerard Wagner made this comparative method his own, developing it to a high art in his painting research; and naturally it also formed an essential part of his teaching method. He would often refer to a path of painting as a 'feeling training'. 'Our task as painters', he explained, is to develop a feeling for colour which leads to the all-important question of how form arises out of colour ... an interest in the colour itself needs to be developed, not the outcome in terms of forms or end results. When experimenting, one needs to notice sympathy and antipathy between the colours just as one experiences sympathy and antipathy between people, for instance. Notice what feelings come up when changes in colour occur. Leave everything aside but the colour – paint together –watch the phenomena – make the experiences and feelings conscious ... All the feelings we have are in the colours. One can't experience the colours without exertion; it's an effort to bring our feelings to consciousness. We should work towards being able to experience what we see, and to observe what we experience.

After stressing the need to develop an experiential capacity, Rudolf Steiner goes on to develop new aspects of colour. He introduces two groups of colours: image colours and lustre colours. The first group of colours, consisting essentially of black, green, peach-blossom and white, Steiner connects with the four kingdoms of nature, mineral, plant, animal and human being, whose totality also composes the fourfold human being of physical body, etheric body, astral body and I:

> By taking the kingdoms of nature in this way, I am able to ascend stage by stage from the lifeless to the living, then to the realm of ensouled beings, and finally to beings of spirit. In a similar way I can go from black to green, to peach-blossom and to white. Just as I can ascend from the lifeless through the living to beings of soul and spirit, so the world around me appears in its images as I go from black to green, to peach-blossom, and to white. [...] The world is there before me with its minerals, plants, animals and its spiritual kingdom – in so far as man is taken as the spiritual. As I ascend through these realities, nature reveals their images to me. They are reflections cast by nature. The coloured world is not reality, even in nature itself it is only image. The image of the lifeless is black; of the living, green. The image of the soul is peach-blossom; and of the spirit, white. By these means we are led to the objective nature of colour.[133]

Following this, the three lustre colours – yellow as the lustre of the spirit, blue as the lustre of the soul and red as the lustre of life – are brought into connection with thinking, feeling and will, the threefold human being. These three colours are active and have an inner quality of will impetus. Comparing them to the solar system, Rudolf Steiner says the lustre colours have characteristics of the planets, movement for example, whereas the image colours, like the zodiac, are motionless and have a pictorial quality like the various configurations of stars. The lustre colours have an *inner* drive which wants to be fulfilled – yellow must shine outwards, blue inwards, red is the balance between the two:

> We have seen that yellow, by its very nature, wants to grow paler and paler towards the edges, that it wants to radiate. Blue wants to dam itself up and red to be uniform, a still redness. Or rather we should say that it wants neither to radiate nor to be dammed up but to be effective everywhere; it wants to hold the balance between radiating and being dammed up, between flowing out and damming up. …
>
> We have seen how differently yellow and blue are constituted. Red, yellow and blue are quite different from black, green and peach-blossom. In contrast to the colours that have an image quality, red, yellow and blue have quite another character, and if you recall what I have said about them you will be prepared for the term that I am now going to use to characterise the difference. I have called black, white, green and peach-blossom picture or image colours. I will call yellow, red and blue 'lustres'– lustre colours.
>
> Here lies the essential nature of, and principal differences within, the world of colour:
>
> Black, white, green and peach-blossom have an image character – they are pictures of something. Yellow, blue and red have a lustre-character – something shines from them. … Here we have a definite colour-cosmos. We see the world as interweaving colour; we must go to the colours themselves in order to understand the laws that govern them.[134]

In this way Rudolf Steiner gave a clear colour cosmos to those who seek to discover it; along with the two types of colour, image and lustre, the painter is given a technique of painting, a practical basis out of which to work. In the interplay between the two colour groups, lustre colours, says Steiner, are to be transformed into image colours and image colours into lustre colours. In Gerard Wagner's later work this transfer of image into lustre colours and vice versa is raised to a high level and is visible in the quality of light he invokes within his colours.

Not wanting to explain things intellectually, Wagner would encourage his pupils to try to experience the difference between the two groups of colours:

'The names don't help', he would say, 'one needs *experiences*. The lustre colours are easier to experience whereas the image colours are related to thought and to an enhanced inwardness.'

The following remarks by Gerard Wagner about the image colours are taken from notes the author made after painting classes, between 1993 and 1999. Even without their context they could be valuable and interesting especially for fellow painters. Violet, being in the same family as the cool red colours, is included as an image colour. Peach-blossom is also referred to as rose, cool red or carmine. (The five peach-blossom colours in Rudolf Steiner's twelvefold colour circle span from violet through magenta to deep rose.[135])

GREEN
Green has no enhancement and no astrality.
Green is a gentle, harmonious, self-strengthening colour.
Green is a lovely colour. Here Wagner quoted: 'Faith is the substance of things hoped for, the evidence of things unseen.' King James Bible, Hebrews 11:1.
Green are the living thoughts of Faust, Brown is the pedantry of Wagner (the character in *Faust*).

PEACH-BLOSSOM/ROSE/COOL RED
Peach-blossom doesn't want anything for itself – it's neutral.
Peach-blossom is outside feelings. It would be a good colour to have in court rooms.
Peach-blossom is invisible.
Peach-blossom is the etheric body.
Peach-blossom can make peace with all and everything. It's also a soul colour. If one is at the end of one's tether and needs help, imagine peach blossom.
Peach-blossom is the most important colour.

VIOLET
Violet is an old colour.
Violet is neither light nor dark.
Violet is an I-colour. It's beyond space and time.
Through violet we contact the living world.
Violet is the colour of memory; through one's memory one can come to oneself.
Violet is the most living colour – it's life ether.
Everything will be violet one day.

WHITE

White is the highest colour, below it are the peach-blossom colours, all are I-colours.

White is all the virtues.

The I, the ego, is in the white – it's a 'nothingness' in a way.

With white one puts oneself in the picture.

White is the human being.

BLACK

Black gives the human being an I-consciousness.

Black and brown are related to our intellectual thinking and sense perception of the outer world.

Black and brown are outside the colours; violet and rose are outside the temperaments.

Black puts us right into ourselves, into our bones.

Black is always alone.

Black annihilates our feeling of self –on a feeling level; in white we experience ourselves again.

Painting in watercolour

The question has sometimes arisen as to why Gerard Wagner painted exclusively in the medium of watercolour and did not experiment with other mediums. When the painter Henni Geck asked Rudolf Steiner for suggestions for a new art of painting, his instructions were to paint in the medium of watercolour the training sketches he had initially carried out in pastel. He used pastel simply for its directness and availability. The sketches he did for the artists who were painting the large and small cupolas of the first Goetheanum, were also executed in pastel. Steiner was very clear however that the new impulse in painting depended on the fluid medium of watercolour; he describes the importance of this in the lecture of 9 June 1923, 'Spirit and Non-Spirit in Painting'. He describes painting the Virgin Mary out of colour:

> … You feel it in an artistic way the moment you create with red and with blue and with light, experiencing as you do so that the relationship of the light to the colours and to the darkness is a world in itself. So that all you actually have is colour, and colour tells one so much, so that out of the colours themselves and the play of light and dark the Virgin Mary is created.

To do this you would have to know how to live with colour, of course, colour must be something you live with. Colour must mean for you something that has become emancipated from matter and weight. For heavy matter puts up resistance to colour when you want to use it for art. It is therefore contrary to painting altogether to paint with palette colours. These always show a certain heaviness when one has them on the canvas. One cannot live with palette colours either. One can only live with liquid colours. And in the life a person shares with colour when he has it in liquid form, in the unique relationship he has with it when he puts liquid colour on to the paper, colour comes to life and the world comes to life through colour.

A real art of painting arises when one grasps the nature of appearance, of revelation for what one is forming on the paper. A world will grow out of it by itself. For if you understand colour you understand a world ingredient. Kant once said: 'Give me matter and I will make you a world out of it.' Well, you could have given him a great deal of matter but I can assure you he would not have made a world out of it, for a world cannot be created out of matter. You would more readily create a world with the mobile tools of colour. You could create a world out of those, because every colour has its own direct personal relationship to one of the world's particular spiritual elements.[136]

Watercolour as a medium is generally appreciated for its qualities of freshness and light. The technique of thin veils or glazes allows for a transparency of colour which heightens luminosity. The English painters of the 18th and 19th centuries, especially William Turner and John Constable, are known for watercolour paintings which so naturally conveyed the elemental turbulence of sea and sky and the potent action of light. In her *Fundamentals of Artistic Therapy*, Dr Margarethe Hauschka elaborates further on the qualities of watercolour.

Spiritual Science teaches us that in world evolution colour was created through the interaction of light and darkness. In Rudolf Steiner's descriptions of the evolution of the world it is during the time of the Old Moon, the planetary condition before that of the earth, in which colour, or the colour-ether, arises, when angel beings weave light and darkness into each other. Old Saturn was still dark and brought forth warmth; in the time of Old Sun, light came into being and, as a further stage of condensation, air. On Old Moon, light and darkness were woven into colour and, as the shadow of colour, water came into being. Colour and water stand therefore in a world-historical relationship.[137]

When teaching, Gerard Wagner often drew pupils' attention to the importance of watercolour as a medium. He said among other things:

Dr Steiner chose this technique for a special reason – it is transparent.

Dr Steiner knew what he was doing when he gave this watercolour painting. One comes into a region one does not normally enter, which is invisible.

We are now on the earth in the physical world, but we have made the journey from Saturn, to Sun, to Moon and to Earth. We see the physical things around us but not what is behind them: we don't see the growing plant, the etheric world, for instance. In our normal state of consciousness we cannot get behind the physical, for this we need a new state of consciousness. One needs watercolour to develop this consciousness, not oil, watercolour is transparent.

The use of plant colours was also essential for the development of Gerard Wagner's work. He began using plant-based pigments in the early 1970s. They were made by Günter Meier (1921–2003) who produced and researched plant colours at the Goetheanum Plant Colour Laboratory for many years. Plant colours were used by Rudolf Steiner for painting the two cupolas in the first Goetheanum, and it is clear that his intention was to connect the use of plant-based pigments with the new impulse in painting. The first documented reference by Rudolf Steiner to the use of plant colours was in August 1911 in Munich. The first plant-colour laboratory was established at the Goetheanum in 1914.[138]

The two-dimensional picture plane

Another indication given by Rudolf Steiner for the new art of painting is an emphasis on the two-dimensional surface, the two-dimensional picture plane. In comparing the experience of two and three dimensions Gerard Wagner makes it clear why two dimensions are more appropriate for painting. In the Introduction to his 'Animal Metamorphosis' portfolio, he wrote:

If we try to look at nature, not as though it had spatial depth, but as though everything were next to each other on the same plane, then we can experience how such a concentration on the two-dimensional can cause our normal everyday consciousness, which tells us 'this is a stone, this is a tree', gradually to recede; and on the other hand we begin to experience with increasing intensity the inner quality of the colours, gestures, substances etc. which we perceive. We feel more as though we were part of the things themselves, rather than looking at them from outside.

Children live in such a relationship to their surroundings up to a certain age. But this feeling of being one with the world around fades away when they learn to grasp things three-dimensionally and to comprehend them intellectually.[139]

The two-dimensional world is therefore conducive to experiencing the *inner qualities* of colour. Rather than actual motion forwards and backwards in space as in the physical world of three dimensions, in the two dimensional world of colour one can have a *feeling experience* of moving forwards and backwards. An example from everyday life could make this 'forwards' and 'backwards' in feeling clearer: if we feel warm towards somebody our feelings move *towards* them. This gesture, a positive one, can be experienced as a warm colour. On the other hand if we feel repelled by somebody or something we move away from them inwardly, the colour in this case would be on the cold side. The two-dimensional world is a soul world, a world of feeling. Living in two dimensions increases the perception of colour whilst line perspective creates spatial depth and belongs to the usual three-dimensional consciousness we have in everyday life.

To the well-known polarity of the actions of red and blue in colour perspective – red coming forward and blue going back, Wagner adds other colours: 'Red and yellow come forward, blue goes back and green is in between. Violet and rose don't fit with colour perspective in this way – they are in a different world, on a different level.'

In his lecture 'From Space Perspective to Colour Perspective' (2 June 1923[140]), Rudolf Steiner reiterates the feeling nature of the two dimensions:

Whenever we raise ourselves above the three dimensions of the physical world into the etheric world, everything is two-dimensional. We can only understand the etheric world if we think of it as two-dimensional. … Everything of a feeling nature in us has no relation to three-dimensional space, only the will has that, whereas feeling is always two-dimensional. Therefore we find that everything of a feeling nature in us can be reproduced in the two-dimensional medium of painting, if we rightly understand these two dimensions.

And in regard to our feeling nature, Rudolf Steiner describes how painting arises in the interplay of the astral body (feeling body) and etheric body. He gives a foundation for the various arts in relation to the interaction of the members of the fourfold being of man: physical body, etheric body, astral body and the I (the higher member descends into the lower: when sculpting, for instance, the laws of the etheric descend into the physical body, and when painting the astral body descends more deeply into the etheric body):

> If we do the same in connection with the astral body, as it were pushing what is in us of an astral nature a step lower down into the etheric body, we are pushing down what lives inwardly in man. Now nothing arises that could truly have a spatial nature, for the astral body, when it moves down into the etheric body, is not entering a spatial element: the etheric body is rhythmic and harmonious, not spatial. Therefore what arises can only be a picture, indeed a real picture, in fact the art of painting. Painting is the form of art which contains the laws of our astral body, just as sculpture contains the laws of our etheric body and architecture those of our physical body.[141]

Gerard Wagner referred in the following way to this relation of the astral body to the etheric in painting and its connection with finding 'form out of colour':

> The different colours are the astral element – the feelings – and they influence the etheric formative forces in various ways, leading to form. The yellow will do it in a different way to red or blue. This is form out of colour.

He never tired of reminding his pupils of Rudolf Steiner's challenge to painters to find 'form out of the colour – to take the first step into the living world'.

Wagner understood this new task of finding 'form out of colour' to be intrinsically connected with the development of consciousness that enables experience of the etheric world. Interestingly enough, art history shows that the beginning of the present fifth post-Atlantean epoch coincided with the achievement of artists and architects during the Renaissance in grasping three-dimensional line-perspective. A new direction in art, the impulse of painters at the end of the 19th century, was to depart again from the three-dimensional world and enter into colour itself.

In the lecture 'The Creative World of Colour',[142] Rudolf Steiner approached the need to include the elemental world, the world of etheric formative forces, in art:

Art must endeavour to penetrate again into elemental life. Art has spent long enough merely observing and studying nature, and trying to solve nature's riddles by reproducing in another form what can be seen by penetrating into nature. Yet what lives in the elements is still something dead to modern art. ... Art will arise anew when the human being learns how to enter into elemental life with his innermost soul. People may argue that this ought not to be done, but this is only prompted by laziness. Human beings will either live their way with full humanity into the forces of the elements and accept the soul and spirit creations around them, or art will become more and more the product of individual hermits; in which case we might come across things of considerable interest with regard to the psychology of individuals, but art would never give us the achievements that only art can give. We are speaking very much of the future times when we say things like this. But what must happen is that we go to meet the future with eyes that have acquired insight through spiritual science; otherwise we shall only be able to see a dead and dying future ahead of us. ... Bridges must be built between what are still abstract ideas of spiritual science and what flows from our hands, our chisel or our brush.

Wagner was clear that Rudolf Steiner, in his own artistic work, had given examples of a new art. In the Introduction to the 'Animal Metamorphosis' portfolio, he wrote:[143]

How does form arise out of colour? This is how, at the beginning of our century, Rudolf Steiner formulated the question which is decisive for painters today and the next future.[144] He showed the painter how to gain a deeper and objective feeling for colour and through this, to come to an experience of the world of formative forces. In his sketches and paintings he gave examples of how colour leads to form. For this reason, these works can be regarded as the beginning of a new art of painting which is in accordance with the development of modern consciousness. To create form out of colour means entering through colour into the world of formative forces.

In the training sketches for painters, a new way of painting can be discovered. As pupils we did not copy the sketches, but Wagner presented them to us in such a way that the creative principles within the sketches could be revealed through colour exercises based on them, and the creative elements, through practice, could become tools for individual work. The fact that the work is not easy and demands years of practise means naturally that progress is 'slow'. But in a fast world the value of slowness is finding its place. And on the subject of perfection, Rudolf Steiner said in relation to the new art of the Goetheanum building:

> The important thing is not the perfection we achieve in what we must will to happen, but that a start is made on what must come to life here, however imperfect it has to be. For everything new that comes into the world is imperfect compared with the old that has stood the test of time. The old has reached its highest level, whereas the new is still in its infancy. That is self-evident.[145]

The 'training sketches' executed by Rudolf Steiner, in which he gave examples of how form comes out of colour, were the source of Wagner's own learning initially, under the tutelage of Henni Geck. They comprise 'Nine Nature Moods' consisting of sun, moon, and tree motifs, and continue with the more complex themes of the 'motif sketches' which Steiner often did in relation to subjects he was lecturing about at the time. The four watercolours which conclude his painting work were included by Gerard Wagner as learning material in the painting training, as were the motifs given by Rudolf Steiner to the teachers of adolescents at the Goetheanum's 'Friedwart School'. These were also motifs of nature and included two motifs of the human being.[146]

The training sketches for painters carried out by Rudolf Steiner were as follows:

9 Nature-mood sketches May/June 1922
1. Sunrise 1
2. Sunset 1
3. Shining Moon
4. Summer Trees
5. Fruiting and Blossoming Trees
6. Moonrise
7. Moonset
8. Sunrise 2
9. Sunset 2

Friedwart sketches 1923–1924
1. Sunrise
2. Sunset
3. Trees in Sunny Air

4. Trees in Storm
5. Sunlit Tree by a Waterfall
6. Head Motif
7. Mother and Child

Motif Sketches 1922 – 1924
1. Group Souls – The Human Being
2. Light and Darkness (Lucifer and Ahriman)
3. The Seer between Marianus and Gabrilein
4. Distance and Space Arise
5. The Threefold Human Being
6. The Human Being in the Spirit
7. The Spirit in the Human Being
8. St John Imagination
9. Druid Stone
10. The Human Being in Relation to the Planets
11. Elemental Beings
12. Adam Kadmon in Early Lemuria
13. Three Kings Motif
14. Colour sketch for The Moonrider / The Moonrider (watercolour)

Watercolours
15. New life, Mother and Child
16. Easter, Three Crosses
17. Archetypal Plant
18. Archetypal Animal – Archetypal Human Being

Balance – approaching composition through the art of 'measuring-in'

> *Everything that man makes, is a man –*
> *or (quod idem est), is an element of man –*
> *a human being (science, works of art etc.).*
> NOVALIS[147]

The ancient Greek sculpture known as the 'Charioteer of Delphi' or Heniokhos, the Rein Holder, from the sanctuary of Apollo in Delphi, was an image Gerard Wagner liked to bring into connection with painting. The sculpture is thought to be of the charioteer not in action during the chariot race, but afterwards, when, having won the race, he completes the lap of honour around the arena. The figure stands upright, his garment in vertical folds as in a Greek column, in a gesture of inner balance and calm self-confidence.

Gerard Wagner had a photograph of the Charioteer in his studio and often drew pupils' attention to it, in connection with an anecdote he liked to tell about Rudolf Steiner's first suggestions for the new art of eurythmy. According to Lory Maier-Smits, the first eurythmist, Rudolf Steiner said to her: 'Stand upright and try to experience yourself as a column – from the balls of your feet up to the head, and learn to feel this upright gesture as I.' 'He was not satisfied with what I did,' she said, and he repeated, 'the weight rests on the balls of the feet, not the heels!'[148]

Speaking of this gesture, and similarly emphasising the balls of the feet, Gerard Wagner would say: 'The feeling that comes from this gesture of uprightness is our instrument for painting.'

In *The Individuality of Colour,* Elisabeth Wagner-Koch elucidates aspects of the upright human form in relation to painting:

> We learn to recognize the living order implanted in the human form as the *measure* by which we shape the picture. 'Form' is to be understood here in Goethe's sense, as the spiritual standard of the human being that underlies the form of the physical body.
>
> This measure is something objective. It is common to all human beings. It provides the basis for forming judgments that possess validity for everyone, since the individual element in every single human soul can freely unfold within it.
>
> Let us look at this human 'Gestalt':
>
> Through the body, human beings are incorporated into space. The directions: above-below, forwards-backwards, right-left, determine the relationship to our surroundings.
>
> Through our limbs we are adapted to earthly gravity (below). Our head is formed as a likeness of the spheres (above). In arms and hands we experience most strongly the qualitative difference of left and right. The human being strides forward from the invisible into the visible.
>
> Yet we should not be in the position of determining these directions without having a feeling for the *middle*. Human beings orient them-selves at every moment of their waking consciousness through this middle – even if remaining quite unconscious of it. It alone guarantees our existence as beings poised in balance. Every moment of falling out of balance results in an alteration of consciousness. Thus human beings in

their unique interplay of forces are ruled and ordered by this sovereign power of the middle or centre.[149]

Through one's feeling of the centre and the directions of left-right, up-down and so on, one learns to judge balance in the painting. The balance, or lack of it, can be felt within oneself in relation to what is happening between the colours on the page in the following way:

Whatever we paint, whatever the motif, be it the simplest colour relation: the measure is always 'the human being'. ...

We ourselves feel drawn into heaviness if the lower picture area is overburdened. We raise ourselves up when, reaching into the upper picture area, we experience ourselves in our head. If the lower region is too weak, we lose the ground under our feet; if it is too light above, our consciousness threatens to ebb. If we bring too much above, however, a new feeling of confinement threatens at once.

Head and feet in their polar tension never make a satisfying whole. We feel how we would ourselves be torn apart if we were not to find the middle. From it, the living, moving rhythm proceeds without which a living balance cannot last. If we do not have the middle, this 'hold', we shift helplessly from above to below, from right to left ...

The striving for healthy wakefulness and uprightness permits us to find a hold in the threefold organism of the picture. ...[150]

The Waldorf teacher Wilhelm Boos (see Appendix 14) had a particular interest in this activity of 'measuring oneself' into the picture. In relation to the 'Charioteer' he applied this 'self-measuring-in' not only to paintings but also on other works of art – sculptures and architecture, and also to landscape. For him, the 'measuring-in' activity became an important aspect of his pedagogical work. He described in detail the soul process involved in this in an article in the periodical *Stil*. For the purpose of this book it will suffice to include the following part of Wilhelm Boos' article to help clarify the connection with the Charioteer to the process of 'measuring-in':

One takes into this soul process one's own bodily structure as a oneness, and tries to experience it at a feeling level. This process is normally unconscious and must be developed so as to become a foundation for measuring oneself in. For that purpose the image of the Charioteer, which represents the whole bodily structure of the human being, can provide a mirror in which one can measure the feeling of the oneness of one's own build.[151]

Wilhelm Boos also points to the spiritual scientific foundation of the process and significance of 'self-measuring-in' by referring to the first chapter of *Theosophy*, 'The Nature of Man',[152] in which Rudolf Steiner describes the connection between the structure of the human body and the human I. Towards the end of the last section, 'Body, Soul and Spirit', he writes: 'The body builds itself up out of the world of physical matter in such wise that its construction is adapted to the requirements of the thinking ego.' Without this foundation, the act of 'self-measuring-in' cannot be fully appreciated.

The painter and author Andrea Hitsch had written enthusiastically to Gerard Wagner about working with the 'Charioteer of Delphi' during a conference in Vienna:

> 2 October 1980
> Dear Herr Wagner
> I think of you so often, and thank you for constantly drawing our attention to the 'Charioteer'.
>
> Last weekend during an architecture seminar, which took place in the Rudolf Steiner School in Vienna, 70 participants practised 'self-measuring-in' on a very large shaded drawing of a temple – and came to a single judgement! What an experience!
>
> My dear husband, who jointly leads the seminar, led us sensitively into the new experience. He has often spoken with Herr Boos, and practised with him.
>
> The initial awakening of each of us to this bodily experience was just wonderful. The endless gaze of the roof gable into the world, the wide support of the pedestal, the uprightness of the columns – thus the temple reveals itself through the awakening of bodily experience from head to foot. It came to us that the morning verse can be an image of the temple:
>
> *I look into the world (roof gable)*
> *Wherein there lie the stones (pedestal)*
> *Where living grow the plants (column)*
> *Where feeling live the beasts (capital)*
> *And within man ensouled (inner space)*
> *A dwelling to spirit gives ...*

Thus the human being builds up his own body.

Often I thought of you and wished you could be here together with your help and indications which wake up the questions within us.

Time and again, we were able to feel what a great objective key we have through the bodily form of the human being. It lies hidden within us as an 'open secret'. It asks to be discovered and activated. This Charioteer would like to become ever more strongly 'Charioteer' – herein lies the freedom of the human being.

Please accept this modest greeting, which is simply to say that I often think of you, and would like to thank you. With heartfelt greetings, Andrea Hitsch

Painting as tightrope walking

In attempting to paint out of colour according to Gerard Wagner's method, one tries to place each brushstroke of colour on the paper with an awareness of a feeling of balance. An appropriate image for such an activity was given by Rudolf Steiner to the painter Anna May (1864–1954), who passed it on to her niece Dr Margarethe Hauschka, who then passed it on to her pupils. He said this: 'The activity of painting is like tightrope-walking.' On the tightrope every minuscule movement has consequences for staying in balance and remaining on the rope, and this acute feeling for balance can be used and developed when painting. 'The Representative of Humanity', the wooden statue carved by Rudolf Steiner and his colleagues, is an archetypal image of balance. The central figure, an image of the Christ, holds the balance between the two opposing forces of Lucifer and Ahriman. Characteristic aspects of this polarity can be found in the human being at different levels. At the physical level as: old – young; hardening – softening; sclerosis – inflammation; nerves – blood. At a soul level as: pedantry – fantasy; criticism – enthusiasm; reason – imagination. And at a spiritual level as waking up and falling sleep.[153]

Polarity belongs also to colour. In Goethe's colour circle, for instance, yellow and violet are polarities, as are orange and blue, and green and red. Gerard Wagner taught that the chief polarities to be reconciled with one another in the act of painting are the warm and cool colours, light and darkness, expansion and contraction, and the polarity of living and lifeless colours. These groups of two opposing qualities reveal a significant connection with the two opposing forces of Lucifer and Ahriman: warm colours and living colours, together with light and buoyancy, are the luciferic aspect, while the cold, lifeless colours together with weight and darkness, are the ahrimanic aspect. In the painting by Rudolf Steiner of the Representative of Humanity, the middle figure in warm yellow, holds the balance between Lucifer in a warm colour soaring above in the light, and Ahriman, painted in black, below in the earth. As mentioned above, polarities in the human being can be found at the physiological level as well as at the soul-spiritual level. Such polarities are held in balance through the forces of the human centre, the human I.

Gerard Wagner emphasised the role of the human centre, the heart, in the act of painting. He said:

> The heart, the I, is our instrument for painting.
>
> One paints out of a feeling of balance – from the most human feelings.
>
> A picture should create a harmonious totality: no colour should be egotistical, just there for itself. All the colours in a painting strive towards the human I.

And asked what makes a picture artistic, he said:

> A good picture should not have a trace of sensation in it.
>
> A picture must be brought to a stage that allows someone to look at it in stillness; the picture should not be allowed to rob a person of his freedom. This requires us to paint as much as possible in broad surfaces yet with exactness.

(Sensation would belong to the luciferic side whilst anything that coerces the observer would belong to the ahrimanic side.)

Rudolf Steiner approaches the character of the human centre in a lecture about poetry and drama. Describing the polarity of dramatic and epic he says that the epic is connected with the upper gods, the dramatic with the lower gods while the centre, the inherently human quality, is the lyrical element:

> One might say: here we have the fields of earthly existence; out of the clouds descends the divine Muse of epic art; out of earthly depths there rise, like vapour and smoke, the Dionysian, chthonic divine-spiritual powers, working their way upward through men's will. We have to penetrate earth regions to see how the dramatic element rises like a volcano, and the epic element sinks down from above, like a blessing of rain. And it is here upon this same plane as ourselves that the cosmic element is enticed and made gay, joyous, full of laughter, through nymphs and fire

spirits; right here that the messengers of the upper gods cooperate with the lower; right here in the middle region that man becomes lyrical. Now man does not feel the dramatic element rising up from below, nor the epic element sinking down from above; he experiences the lyrical element living on the same plane as himself: a delicate, sensitive, spiritual element, which does not rain down upon forests nor erupt like volcanoes, splitting trees, but, rather, rustles in the leaves, expressing joy through blossom, wafts gently in the wind. In whatever allows us to divine the spiritual in matter upon our own plane, enticing hearts, pleasantly stimulating breath, merging our souls with outer nature, as a symbol of the soul-spiritual world – in all this there lives and weaves a lyrical element which looks up with a happy countenance, to the gods of the underworld. The lyrical can tense into the dramatic-lyrical or quieten itself down into the epic-lyrical. For the hallmark of the lyrical, whatever its form, is this: man experiences what lives and weaves in the far reaches of the earth with his middle nature, his feeling nature.[154]

What Rudolf Steiner seems to be indicating here is the intrinsic character of the new impulse in art which he called a 'universally human style'.[155] In a conversation with the artist Assja Turgenieff, Rudolf Steiner reiterates the 'middle path' as characteristic of a new tendency in art when describing the Goetheanun building in Dornach:[156]

> The Impressionists have already had their say in art. In colouring, in plein-air, open-air colour, they have achieved something new, but it was not enough: they excluded man himself, and so their trend in art could not develop, but had to come to nothing. Expressionists build on themselves alone; they do away with the world, and because of this they finally become completely unimaginative – completely abstract. They end by being able to draw nothing but lines and geometrical figures. These people have already occasional glimpses into the spiritual, but they are only fleeting glimpses, only moments. There is nothing artistic in a moment. The anthroposophical style will lie precisely between these two tendencies.[157]

Looking at the different periods of Gerard Wagner's work, one can observe the lyrical element in its various forms. In the early work, the lyrical element tensing into the dramatic-lyrical, and in the later work its quietening into the epic-lyrical. The paintings of his late period could therefore be called an enhanced lyricism in which the dramatic-lyrical and the epic-lyrical are united.

Gerard Wagner understood the chief tasks of the painter proposed by Rudolf Steiner as follows:

> To find form out of colour.

> To take a first step into the living world.

> To investigate beauty and ugliness: to include ugliness; to make the ugly beautiful.

> To paint into the light.

Of the first three tasks Wagner said (among other things):

> To paint out of colour means to paint free of mental images.
> Painting as a process is a kind of conscious sleeping. All conceptual activity goes to sleep. Only feeling and will remain, together with a consciousness that perceives it all. Conscious feeling streams into an activity of will instead of mental images.

> Working with contraction and expansion, with blossoming and withering in colour brings one into the living world.

> One can paint an evil happening but it must be painted so that the picture works on a person in a healthy way.

Although he spoke of it, Gerard Wagner did not elaborate further on the fourth task. His reserve was a sign that this was only to be achieved through a higher level of 'painting'. Johannes Thomasius, the painter in Rudolf Steiner's Mystery Plays, speaks as follows in *The Soul's Probation* of the mystery of 'painting into the light':[158]

> *I learnt to live with light*
> *and to observe in colour*
> *the deed of light –*
> *just as the pupils of true mysticism*
> *see in the realm of life beyond form, beyond colour,*
> *the deed of spirit and the being of soul.*
> *Trusting this spiritual light, I learned to join*
> *my feeling with the flowing sea of light,*
> *my life with glowing streams of colour.*
> *Growing to feel the spirit powers' work*
> *in the light's weaving, free of matter,*
> *in colours' life, where spirit fullness is.*

COLOUR AS A LANGUAGE

Gerard Wagner had an interesting relation to language and his very own way of expressing himself. He could say a great deal without speaking, and he did not talk for the sake of it – out of politeness or to cover up a silence as most of us do. His words were appropriate and genuine. He lived so deeply in colour that his real language was a painterly language. As Margrit Engler wrote: 'Daily I am able to experience the joy of being surrounded by this beautiful living world of pictures ... May the outside world find ever more interest and love for your great language – painting.'

The subject of language was essential to him. He would often refer to colour as a language. He would say during painting classes:

> The language of colour was once an archetypal language understood by everyone. Its alphabet is the colours, there are not many. Imagine going into a yellow or blue room, for example, one *becomes* that colour – the whole organism is involved. As in eurythmy: the gesture 'A' opens, 'E' closes and 'I' is self-assertion. Try to bring these 'sounds' to consciousness. The colours make up the whole person.

In the Introduction to the portfolio, *A Glance into Nature's Workshop*, he wrote:

> Colour is itself a language which needs no further explanation. Experiencing it can lead us into the objective world of human feelings, as also to the forces working in nature. As a key to the inner being of man and nature, colour offers a field of investigation where future scientists and artists can meet.[159]

In the published portfolios depicting metamorphosis, Wagner did include a short text explaining how he had gone about it. He wanted to make it possible for those who were interested in following the process, to participate, to follow how the form arose out of colour. These sequences of metamorphosis have in the meantime become well known and the accompanying texts are taken for granted. However, a few lines of a letter of 1975 from the English artist and editor John Fletcher to Gerard Wagner shows us just how new this approach really was:

I was very interested in what you say about showing the public the 'process' leading to a composition, through colour to the gesture or form, in a *series* of paintings – perhaps like your beautiful series in the portfolio *A Glance into Nature's Workshop*, a series of 16 which I showed at Rudolf Steiner House last term.

Wagner also used words when talking about his artistic-scientific work. Before his other paintings he was mostly silent. He let the paintings do the speaking and explanations were avoided. When pressed he would often turn to humour. Once when a somewhat irritated observer said she did not know what a certain figure in one of his paintings was supposed to be holding in its hand, Wagner said with a smile that he didn't know either.

Throughout the years he rarely explained or analysed the deeper aspects of his painting activity; instead he would answer questions by drawing attention to the source, to Rudolf Steiner and the challenge he gave painters to 'find form out of colour'. On one occasion he did try to explain to a group of artists how he worked. Rex Raab mentions this event, which probably took place in the 1960s, in his essay 'Impressions of Gerard Wagner':

> Gerard Wagner's approach to art was not free of problems for other people. There was for instance, an occasion in the Dornach glass engraving studio, in which artists of the most varied descriptions were gathered. Gerard spoke of the way in which he experienced the creative process in painting. It is possible, he said, to live in the whole nature and character of the colours, so that they produce their own activity within the soul, so to speak, whereby the act of painting assumes an inevitable or objective quality. The expression he used on that occasion was 'Es malt in mir' ('It paints in me'). This called forth an incensed protest from the poet Paul Buhler, from Stuttgart, who for some time had edited the weekly *Das Goetheanum*. 'No artist,' he asserted, 'should assume to set himself up as an absolute exponent of an art in that way. Art is the effort of the individual, aiming towards a goal he cannot say he ever reaches.'

After this rejection at the glass engraving studio, there is no further reference in Wagner's biography of an attempt to do the same thing again, at least not in the same way. Wilhelm Boos, though, was very interested in Wagner's way of working. He visited Wagner in his studio on a number of occasions right into the 1990s. He brought his own paintings and examples of the children's work and the two shared their current activities and concerns. In 1969 Wagner wrote a letter to Wilhelm Boos (probably the longest letter he ever wrote), and described how he approached the activity of painting:[160]

27.11. 1969

Dear Herr Boos!

I often think of your article you sent me to read some time ago. Unfortunately I don't have it all exactly enough in my memory. I had hoped it would be published. The need for a method of schooling a capacity for objective judgment seems to me a matter of urgency.

Measured against the standard of the human being, all areas are related and belong together as one judgment. In my own area of colour: if one had developed enough colour feeling, I believe one would come to an experience of the complete human being and to judgment by experience, but in teaching, as the pupils are just beginning to learn colour-feeling, one needs help in other ways so as to link to capacities somewhat more awake than a feeling for colour.

Your exercises on the paragraph from *Theosophy* for instance, and those exercises you did with us in Ottersberg with forms of animals related to the places in one's organism where they can be experienced, are examples of the kind of help needed. In the closest circles, and with colleagues, there is often reserve about developing the possibility of testing the objectivity or one-sidedness of one's own subjective judgment which one once had. Artists, especially, do not want to go in this direction. As the practice of art is at the same time a process of discernment, of judgment, they are avoiding a vital opportunity to progress.

Apart from the general need to have help alongside the actual painting, also for our pupils, there lives in me at this moment a strong wish for clear formulation of such exercises that can help give certainty in artistic judgment. Presuming the Philosophisch-Anthoposophischer Verlag agrees again, I would like to bring out a series of pictures, this time based on Rudolf Steiner's painting 'Archetypal Man' (sometimes called Archetypal Animal): the watercolour of the floating, swimming being as human being, animal and plant in one; and through consolidation lead this towards individual animals on the same principle as my plant series. As this motif is somewhat more difficult for most people to live into than the plant, I'd like to try in a foreword, for those who want to engage with these things seriously, to help with the question: How do I come to a valid judgment about it, come to an answer? This is necessary as a safeguard against criticism from within our own circles (of arbitrariness, dilettantism, presumption etc); and because I intend these experiments, to be elementary steps showing a path leading from colour into life, which can eventually be accepted as a path everyone can pursue, as scientifically provable, whereby one considers the whole, overall process involved both in painting and judging a picture.

The 'alpha' is to measure oneself into the white (or coloured) surface while the 'omega' is the experience of the finished painting that gives one an experience of the awakened I-consciousness of the full threefold human being.

The fact that only little consciousness is present in the first step is shown by the second step, when one measures, say, black into the white surface. The qualitative experience of the black unites with an inner experience comparable to 'black', and allows one to place the black – on a horizontal format – below. In so doing one becomes conscious of the lightness of the white, perhaps now for the first time, and its quite different quality. This 'becoming conscious of white' begins with the first brushstroke of black, as it is applied to the bottom of the paper. Following step-by-step the feeling of becoming awake, caused by the addition of black, one reaches the point where one says to oneself: I can tolerate only so much, if I bring more black it will oppress me, stifle me, meaning my consciousness will be diminished again (if I take it too far it will rigidify me and make me ill). So I can say: so much black can be held in balance by so much remaining white, and I can pursue this state of balance and notice: so much lifelessness to so much life; so much weight to so much counter-weight; so much closedness to so much openness, and so on. My consciousness is a stage more awake when it experiences the balanced relationship between black and white than it was when it experienced the white surface only. But it is far away from a state of complete human consciousness, which is immediately apparent when one begins to introduce a third colour, e.g. green. One experiences right away, when beginning to measure in the green to the black and white, that its place is determined by it being lighter than black and denser than white, that the 'spreading out', in relation to black, is caused by it being less concentrated, so the green surface will be larger than the black one. Again the lighter value of the green causes an upward direction away from the black. One experiences 'enlivening' through the green, and black getting lighter through the green. The remaining white changes in quality, and appears pushed back and empty. One

COLOUR AS A LANGUAGE

experiences also the green as more *active* than black. In particular one feels more alive in oneself through the green, and in one's consciousness a good bit more satisfied than before.

Nonetheless, if one were to ask oneself how it feels in the world which has so far arisen, one must affirm: if nothing more would come to enhance one's consciousness, if I were able to experience only what the three present colours give me, I would be in a very dull, lifeless condition compared to my awakened I-consciousness; and one becomes conscious of this once more as one begins to measure the fourth colour, red, into the first three. A much stronger living quality than was possible through the green arises, a liveliness and energy which is experienced much more inwardly, which connects to a quite different member of the human being, which is lighter still, which is much more capable of overcoming the deadness of the black, which is much more concentrated (and therefore smaller amounts are enough than were needed for green); which enlivens the green (that otherwise, as we now notice, left us feeling thoroughly phlegmatic or at least in a vegetative state), and makes us feel awake, cheerful, with heightened sensibility – and one could say a thousand things more. I will forego further description of this example.[161]

If one considers the colours at hand as they appear one after the other in relation to time, then the order in which they appear is determined by the motif; space, quantity, quality – the unfolding will be determined by the deeds and sufferings of their successive qualities. The colours affect each other through 'enlivening', 'deadening', 'alleviating', 'oppressing', 'expanding', 'cramping'; their place is determined by the way they give direction and shape gesture, through their behaviour and inner mutual relationship.

The colours connect with the different members of the human being: black, green, red with dead, living, ensouled; and they work through soul experience as far as the bodily realm, life realm, soul realm, giving an inwardly richer consciousness. It is precisely this experience of becoming ever richer in consciousness that still allows one to choose this or that colour, until one can say that the experience of the colours in the picture gives one the full experience of one's own being. Then the goal is reached. This is arrived at by holding up to the colour this consciousness of the whole human being as the goal from the very beginning; by placing the experience of full I-consciousness next to the experience of incompleteness that the first colour, or the first with the second, or the first three together give one.

To begin with one has nothing outwardly; out of I-consciousness one gives oneself an area of *space* – then it is a practical thinking exercise leading through all twelve categories (Aristotle, see the cycle *Human and Cosmic Thought*[162]) or twelve worldviews, until the experience – for colours *are* only in so far as they are *experienced* – has built up the whole human being for oneself. These colours are – as experience – in the astral body. But they connect with all members of the human being: black with the physical body (bones), green with the life body, red with the life of the soul, warm red differently from cool red, blue with feeling soul and so on. (I don't want to imply something very general with this, as to be exact one must go very much into detail; every statement here could be countered by several opposing ones.) You connect physical body, life body, soul, spirit, with the colours. When you state that 'one should experience oneself as I to the very limits of one's skin' (surely the outer form of the human being is the organ for I-perception?), can one not say there is a bridge of tension there, a tension in consciousness spanning between I-consciousness and the experience of the greater I (the image of the whole cosmos, or the I, embodied in the skin-enveloped form), encompassing also etheric body and astral body? Is it not so, when measuring into a given space, that one first of all places the etheric body and astral body into this space, and then, after this beginning, that, using the organ 'astral body' (I'm not concerned right now to find a precise and technically correct name for soul members) one hearkens to the needs which this beginning within the totality – that has now positioned itself within space – calls forth and physically fulfils. Thus, in accordance with the laws of the astral and etheric, the feelings brought into the etheric body (which can take hold of objective colour feeling), and the colours physically visible but illumined by the 'astral body', are rendered outwardly visible.

In the process of painting it is mostly enough to be ask oneself what one is experiencing. If this is uncertain or does not say anything further, one can help oneself by putting the questions one by one to the astral body as to whether, in relation to this or that colour, it is satisfied – in relation to time, space, quantity, quality, action, suffering, behaviour, place, relation, substance, being or appearance. The I-consciousness in thinking can put the question, while the I in the astral body, that this astral makes visible as far as the etheric body and with help from the physical body (and physical colour), gives the answer. The abstract image of the point in the circle, or I-consciousness, becomes I-experience, in that the first advances through astral body and etheric body towards a totality. The content of the cosmos comes into this 'excursion' in as far as the subjective can be kept out of the colour experience. The etheric body can take hold of an objective colour feeling.

It seems to me that at a time when we should be gradually including the etheric in art and knowledge, a real need arises to first consider our sensory-moral experience of colour, perception in general, because subjective experience cannot grasp the etheric, and also to consider the experience one must have of the relation between weight and counter-weight. The plant overcomes weight every instant of its life. Only through the experience of balance between weight and counter-weight can one enter the element of plant life – or one should perhaps say that when one enters it one experiences there a balance of weight and counter-weight. Likewise in painting one comes only really into the realm of the living (taking hold of the etheric) as far as in every moment, through the experience of the region above (from the astral), one brings weight and counterweight into balance. (In the given example one must experience white's counter-weight and the weight of black together, the white just as tangibly as the black.)

Now – I cannot readily present such thoughts or processes in a foreword. I also do not want to interpret what is shown but rather describe exercises which can help the onlooker to feel his way in, and leave the rest up to him. I could imagine, as a possibility, a fitting exercise from your text could be quoted, if you would allow it, and I could perhaps simply show the connection between the process and the relevant pictures ...

Recently I have painted the same series for the third time, 24 paintings each time, which offers much more than a series of eight. I am thinking of making a series of possibly 12 or 14 pictures out of the 24, which allows the whole development to be more fully experienced, to lengthen the steps between the pictures, even if it makes the 'science', which is clearer in smaller steps, somewhat more difficult. ...

I am writing this in the meantime without knowing whether it will be possible to realise this idea, so that you can perhaps already consider whether you could write something in the foreword, and so you also know why I must think so especially, and often, about your article. G.W.

In Boos's answer to Gerard Wagner, written 19 May 1970, he writes: 'Your letters open up an important perspective for me. You describe the process of painting as a human developmental process.' This phrase echoes Wagner's statement regarding the direction of a future art: 'To make the human being once more the foundation for a new art.'

Wilhelm Boos had a further question about the origin of 'colour-measuring', which Gerard Wagner answered in a shorter letter:

28.1.1970

Dear Herr Boos

In the lecture 'Measure, Number and Weight', given by Rudolf Steiner in Dornach on 29.6.1923, one can find his brief indication about the measuring of colour. He says here among other things: '... qualitatively one measures with the red, with the stronger shining colour, the weaker shining yellow.' The word intensification (red the intensification of yellow) is not used here, but still it seems to me this formulation could include an experience of intensification and more, light and dark, for example, and other things.

Dr Steiner speaks of an experience in the I and astral body during this activity of measuring. The 'measuring-in', I would say, occurs when, with this consciousness, one approaches a given, physically delimited space or surface which one takes up qualitatively in one's consciousness and then, from I and astral body, newly replenishes, shares and so on, with other qualities.

There is no doubt a relation here with the soul aspect of which Dr Steiner speaks at the beginning of that chapter in *Theosophy*, whereby recognition of truth is not dependent on our personal sense organisation. Immersion in perceptible space during the measuring-in process, the qualitative grasp and qualitative shaping within this space through the measuring that the I and astral body undertake, is closely related to a process of cognition.

Other than the passage mentioned here I know of no other which deals directly with measuring. Nor about 'measuring-in', although I believe I have come across words of Rudolf Steiner's which seem to be spoken out of a knowledge of this 'measuring-in', but I do not know

COLOUR AS A LANGUAGE

exactly where. As far as I know he did not use the phrase measuring-in (Einmessen). But it is a good one.

GW

In the lecture referred to above, Rudolf Steiner says the following:

Anyone who attains consciousness in his ego and astral body outside the physical and etheric bodies eventually realises that these free-floating colours and sounds also have something of a similar nature, yet it is different. Free-floating colours have the urge to vanish into the far reaches of the world; they have anti-gravity. Earthly things press towards the earth's centre (downward arrows); these (upward arrows), press outwards to be released into world spaces. And there is certainly something similar to measurement here. You discover it if you have, let us say, a small, reddish cloud hemmed in by a larger yellow formation. Although you do not use a measuring stick, you measure the weaker-looking yellow one qualitatively by means of the red one. And just as the measuring stick says, 'That is five metres' – here the red one tells you: 'If I were to spread out, I should go into the yellow five times. I must expand, I must get larger, then I shall become yellow'. This is how the measurements take place here.

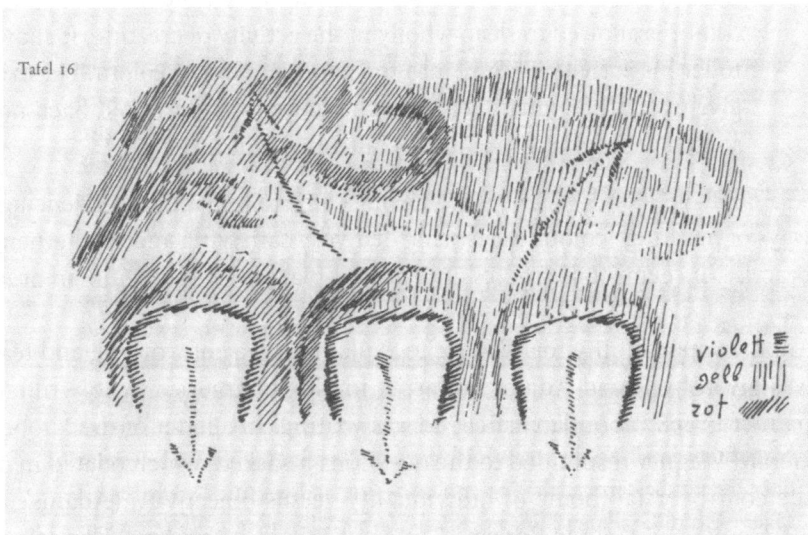

Tafel 16

violett
gelb
rot

[...] And when one begins to be conscious of what it is like to be out there with one's ego and astral body, one comes to the point of ascertaining something like measure, number and weight, but now it is of an opposite nature. And when eventually one's seeing and hearing out there ceases to be a confusion of red and yellow and of different sounds, one begins to perceive the spiritual beings who realise themselves in these free-floating sense impressions. Then we enter the positive spiritual world, the life and activity of spiritual beings. Just as we enter the life and being of earthly objects here on earth by checking them with scales, measuring stick and our calculations, we likewise enter into an understanding of spiritual beings by acquiring a purely qualitative anti-gravity, that is, a desire to expand into the world spaces and to measure colour by means of colour. Spiritual beings of this kind permeate everything that is outside us in the kingdoms of nature'.[163]

Rudolf Steiner's comments on colour measuring were researched and developed by Gerard Wagner and thus integrated into his working method as a whole. He refers to this measuring activity in a few modest and precise words in his monograph:

A special help in eliminating arbitrary subjectivity is an exercise given by Rudolf Steiner which indicates 'qualitative measuring'. Measuring colour qualities is so important because it helps the painter to develop wakefulness and direction, while at the same time his experiencing of colour is allowed to sleep wholly in the activity of creating. It allows him to let his activity 'dream' into the experiencing of colour. He strives to give over all his own feeling to the doing – and to hold back nothing, so that feeling becomes pure, controlled will activity.[164]

As a pupil of Gerard Wagner's and having come to him after experiencing other ways of painting, 'colour measuring' felt very satisfying and strengthening to practise. It seems to be rooted in a deeper place within the human organism.

Another opportunity for Wagner to explain his way of working and teaching was given by David Adams, an artist in North America, who wrote to the painter in 1987 about an article he was writing. In a letter of 10 October 1987, Gerard Wagner responded to the questions he asked, which related in part to the controversial theme of individuality versus objectivity, (Adams's article, 'Six Decades of Colour Research', was published in the American *Journal for Anthroposophy*, Summer 1988).

Dear David Adams

Many thanks for your letter. I'm most grateful for your trouble and interest. Your questions certainly are hard to answer – and you must please excuse shortness – I cannot ever write for long and must avoid doing it as far as possible.

If you work with Dr Steiner's paintings and sketches, with the question of how he came to these motifs, if, as his teaching says, he followed what the colour wanted to do, then you find you need first to *learn to experience* colours, singly, then 2 or 3 together, see how they react etc. It may take years before you begin to feel any kind of necessity ... here a long story. You can find part of the answer in our *Individuality of Colour* and in the monograph on G.W.

Yellow, blue, red – is a different motif from yellow, red, blue, or blue, red, yellow etc.; each leads to different forms. One needs to practise a good deal to gain experience here – 'musical' experience. One can take a colour sequence, once found, and paint it on all possible different ground colours – i.e. one colours the page yellow, orange, red, violet, blue, green, and paints the same colour sequence on each, measuring the colours – always looking for balance of the whole, and one will notice how, through the different ground colours, a motif goes through a metamorphosis. – Colour mathematics. Practice of this kind can lead to finding how plants, growth, animals, human beings can be found 'out of the colour' – how results also can be checked through repeated experiments, i.e. how motifs in general arise.

The direction in which one experiments, the end motifs to which they lead, will naturally be individual and depends on one's choice of colours, on one's inborn tendencies to certain subjects, or simply when a certain subject matter is wished for and one goes in search of it. But in spite of individual colour choice, the results could well be harmonious together even if done by quite different persons, provided they strive for objectivity of the whole and work in the same way. The 'same way' includes asking the same questions re: balance of warm-cold, light-dark, light-heavy etc.

Direction is individual; the way colour is put on, measured, balanced etc. should be objective – if enough balance is exercised. But we are all at the first beginnings of a method which perhaps will become generally used and developed after a few lifetimes. Metamorphosis – series of a motif changing in small stages, is a way of learning about colour and form, also a way of self-control.

Objectivity is an aim, it's too early to speak of it being realised.

Maybe in a general way you can get an idea from these few very poor indications, but one must *see* the process to understand from inside. Words are hardly much use …

Best wishes and many thanks

Gerard Wagner

A painting as a work of art

In the following rare 'notes' from 1998 Gerard Wagner stresses the importance of Rudolf Steiner's own painterly works and their relevance for a new impulse in painting:[165]

A painting, if it is at the same time a work of art, will convey a complete human experience purely through the medium of colour and form. The whole human being = the threefold human being (Rudolf Steiner's motif sketch). The wholeness of our being lives in the experience of the colour circle, in its polarity and intensification: yellow to warm red, blue to cool red, and in incarnadine – black, white, red. In the balancing of the polarities: in and out breathing, concentrating – expanding, tightening – loosening, warming – cooling, enlivening – deadening, and so on.

The various colours, even singly, lead into the different regions of nature, the human being, and the cosmos. E. g. yellow, red, blue, cool red to the four ethers: light, warmth, chemical and life ether. Brown and black lead into regions lying far outside the purely human. Incarnadine (black, white, red) = the incarnated I in the physical body.

The painter schools himself through the experience of his own colour wholeness. He wants to convey this complete colour experience through the picture. If he takes up a colour on a white or coloured paper, this colour is a single part taken from the inner colour totality of the painter, or of nature. He experiences the need to complement this one colour with a second one – an intensification or a polarity, and then again through a third, fourth etc. colour, until an experience of what has appeared outwardly, together with the inwardly experienced colour totality of his own being, has arisen.

How the path – the process – develops from the single colour through to the harmonious totality, how it forms itself to motif, depends largely on the choice of the first colour, or on the relation of the first two colours to one another. The aim lies always in the attainment of the harmonious totality. – The choice of the first colour determines the way one reaches the goal. If one takes brown or black as first colour, one has deadness as a beginning, and what follows will need to accommodate this within the human 'wholeness'. This can happen in different ways.

There are 'artists' whose art consists of allowing themselves to be tied up with a rope by someone else and then freeing themselves from it. The painter places himself through the choice of the first colour (s) in an unfree situation, and searches for the way to experience his freedom again in the recreation of harmonious totality.

Rudolf Steiner: The painter lives between astral and etheric bodies during the activity of painting. (Lectures 2 & 3: *Art as Seen in the Light of Mystery Wisdom.*[166])

One sees in the sketches of Dr Steiner how the astral colour forms the etheric body. With physical eyes one sees the imprint of a pure, super-sensible reality. Hence the value of these 'sketches' and the importance of a schooling path based on them.

It is to be understood that what Rudolf Steiner called for, he carried out himself. Looking at his pictures, one sees the revelation of the astral in the etheric. Objective and in full consciousness, brought into visibility through the human being.

This is the 'how' of the process! The 'what' one sees with eyes. How does one understand what one sees?

The (long) path of the painter would be to school an objective colour feeling which, at the same time, is the entry to the objective etheric world of formative forces; to follow the process of creating as the picture unfolds, and to bring it to one's consciousness.

The way to grasp the 'what' – to let colour and form work on oneself, leads to the experience of inherent spiritual reality. Herein lies the value of these visually perceivable images, pictures indeed, but more than mere images. ('Pictures which can act as beings'.)

To tell of this 'what' is anthroposophy – the teachings of anthroposophy. Or to tread the path of experiencing thought forms in their genuine spiritual reality. Just as the taking in of anthroposophy in thought form can be the first step towards one's own 'seeing'; allowing these pictures to work on oneself, the taking in of these images can be a first step towards experiencing their reality. Astral body and etheric body vibrate within a spiritual reality when perceiving visually. That is the value and task of these pictures. Then, as help for understanding from the 'earthly' side come communications from the spiritual researcher – mystery wisdom. From the same source as mystery wisdom, the pictures also come – two languages for the same thing. Both are there to help us toward the source, through thought, through experience of the picture – ultimately to their reality. The experienced picture stands between earthly and spiritual reality.

EPILOGUE

The physician Walter Kapfhammer, who knew the painter and his work well, illumines a further and future aspect of Gerard Wagner's achievement; and as such his words stand as a fitting end to this biography:[167]

> Rudolf Steiner gave painters the future task of coming to the configuration of their paintings out of a feeling for colour; and not, in the usual way, from an idea or concept. This enigmatic ideal, to find 'form out of colour', still remains a task for the artist today.
>
> I have the impression that Gerard Wagner is one of the few painters, as far as I know, who have made this 'painter-ideal' his life's work. He approached the challenge with deep earnestness and a strong resolve, and has trodden vital steps along the path.
>
> Painting in a manner that allows the form to arise from a feeling for the colour is only possible when our ordinary feelings ('I like it' or 'I don't like it') have undergone purification. It is a process that can unfold on this artistic path of training given by Rudolf Steiner. In this regard Gerard Wagner formulated the phrase: '*Feeling can become a research instrument.*' If the transformation of feelings referred to here can be achieved, the sphere of feeling in the human being can even become a power of knowledge, an organ of perception.
>
> At the Christmas Foundation Meeting, Rudolf Steiner gave, among other things, what is known as the Foundation Stone Meditation. In a sense the whole of anthroposophy is encompassed in this meditation, which, in an intimate and profound way, reveals the mystery of the threefold human being. The second verse, the middle of the first three, can enlighten one as to where within us the process is located which leads to the transformation of the feelings into an instrument of research: in one's heart-centre, or more exactly as expressed by Rudolf Steiner, in the 'beat of heart and lungs', for this is the constitutional centre of the rhythmic process in human beings, where continual rebalancing occurs in the tension of opposites – between our upper and lower systems:

O human soul,
you live within the beat of heart and lung
which leads you through the rhythms of time
into your own soul nature's feeling:
practise spirit awareness
in soul composure
where surging deeds of worlds' evolving
unite
your own I with
the I of worlds;
and you will feel truly
within the human working of the soul.

For the will of Christ holds sway to all horizons,
bestowing grace on souls in rhythms of worlds
Spirits of light!
May there be kindled from the East
the fire that through the West takes form,
that says:
In Christ death becomes life.
The elemental spirits hear it
in East, West, North and South:
may human beings hear it.

With this in mind, the great Michaelic task of the future, given by Rudolf Steiner in the first of his Michael Letters,[168] shows itself in a special light. He writes there:

'Michael frees the thoughts from the region of the head; he opens a free way for them to the heart.' And further, as a Michaelic mission of the time: 'Hearts should have thoughts!'

'I have the feeling
I have only done the
first half of my work.'

Gerard Wagner, 1999.

APPENDIX 1

Gerard Wagner's maternal grandfather and grandmother, and the connection with Caspar Hauser

MATERNAL GRANDFATHER: HERMANN LANGE

Gerard Wagner's maternal grandfather, Hermann Ludwig Lange, was born in Plauen on 10 May 1837, the third of seven children. His father, Ernst Friedrich Lange, is referred to as 'a citizen of some standing in Plauen and the head of one of its oldest established families'. The flyleaves of the old Lutheran family Bible show an unbroken record of direct succession for over two hundred years. It is not known if the Wagner and Lange families knew each other personally but certainly the Langes, being one of Plauen's oldest established families, with their large house in the centre of town by the historic Town Hall, were well-known there. Hermann Lange's son Ernest Lang gives an idea of life in Plauen when his father was growing up:

> As the custom formerly was, the old family house was a combined dwelling house and business premises. From the fragmentary chronicles connected with it, and from quaint and devout entries in the old family Bible, one is able to visualise a line of honest burgesses living earnest, peaceful and industrious lives and acquiring through their trade or profession, if not wealth, the advantages of certain modest amenities of existence along with a considerable degree of culture. In this atmosphere of self-respect and the solid virtues, Hermann Lange in his turn grew up and, furthermore, developed a taste for engineering in the mechanical workshops of his father ... After finishing his school career with every distinction at 17 years of age, young Lange was entered as an apprentice at the engineering works of Mr. F. A. Egells in Berlin where he remained from April 1855 to July 1858. Here his industry and trustworthiness speedily gained him favour and, young as he was, he was frequently employed in delivering and erecting machinery. [...]
>
> His apprenticeship at an end, the choice of a suitable technical school fell upon Karlsruhe where Professor Redtenbacher's fame as an exponent of the theory of machine and locomotive construction was attracting students from all parts of Europe. ... It must not however, be imagined

that Mr Lange was too absorbed in his studies to enjoy the social amenities of student life. This was far from being the case as his interests were both very human and many-sided and he had the capacity for both giving and receiving friendship. He became attached to the Saxonia Corps and took part in its activities ... At Karlsruhe also, Mr. Lange first met the lady who was later to become his wife, Stephanie Elizabeth Mayerhöffer the second daughter of Stephan Mayerhöffer, a Counsellor in the Ministry of Finance of the Grand Duke Friedrich of Baden.

Mr. Lange's mind was bent upon taking up locomotive work and he had not long to wait for the desired opportunity. His career had been followed with friendly interest by many at home, and it was through a mutual friend of the Lange and Beyer families that Mr. Lange's aspirations came to the knowledge of Mr. Beyer, who thereupon wrote and offered him work at Gorton Foundry, the work place of the firm Beyer-Peacock in Manchester. This meant a break in the Plauen tradition, but his father, looking into the future, foresaw an era of new industries in which his sons could best carve out new careers for themselves. ... It thus came to pass that [in January 1861] Mr. Lange bid good-bye to his home, and the scenes of his youth, and set forth with high hopes towards the land which was destined to become the one of his adoption.

Described 'as a powerfully-built young Saxon of four-and- twenty desirous of acquiring English experience' Hermann Lange speedily made his mark as a draughtsman of unusual ability, and four years later in 1865 became Chief Draughtsman of the firm. And 'at the end of this eventful year Mr. Lange fulfilled the romance of his student days by leading Miss Mayerhöffer to the altar.'[169]

MATERNAL GRANDMOTHER: STEPHANIE MAYERHÖFFER

Hermann Lange's future wife followed him to England in 1862 and before they married she spent two years studying at a well-known ladies seminary at Southwell in Nottinghamshire.

Stephanie Elizabeth Mayerhöffer was born in Karlsruhe, in Baden-Württemberg, southwest Germany, on 1 February 1839. The second of five children, her father Stephan Mayerhöffer (1800–1867) came from the Odenwald, an area rich in myth and legend coloured by its association with the Nibelung saga, and its hero Siegfried.

As a boy of twelve, Stephan Mayerhöffer remembered 'the passage of hungry and ragged French troops on their way back to France from Moscow in the fateful year of 1812'. On coming of age, he broke with the family tradition of teaching at the Catholic School at Siegelsbach, and after training as a clerk entered Baden's civil service. The Lange Family chronicle identifies his first place of employment at Bruchsal, where:

> he was attached to the service of the widowed Stephanie, dowager Grand Duchess of Baden, the former Stephanie de Beauharnais, adopted daughter of Napoleon I, and a romantic figure of those times.[170] From this appointment he was transferred to Karlsruhe where his daughter Stephanie Elizabeth was born.

Stephan Mayerhöffer's connection to the House of Baden lasted for almost 50 years. He was employed throughout the reign of three Grand Dukes, Ludwig Leopold, and finally Friedrich.

Stephan Mayerhöffer had a special regard for Stephanie Beauharnais, the mother of Casper Hauser. He named his daughter after her. Andrew Lang, Gerard Wagner's cousin, whose knowledge of the family and memory of events, people and dates was said to be 'encylopedic', recalled:

> The family tree of the House of Baden is of personal interest to me. From earliest youth I was told that my grandmother Stephanie was named after Stephanie Beauharnais. Indeed, I used to believe that the latter Stephanie was my grandmother's godmother; and it is only recently, when re-reading my father's biography of his father, and finding no reference to this godmother relationship, that I have come to entertain doubts about this.[171]

Stephanie Mayerhöffer's early memories centred around dramatic events in Karlsruhe during the revolutionary period of 1848–49, when Grand Duke Leopold had to leave Baden and Prussian troops were called in to quell the rebellion. One of the Grand Duke's Ministers was hidden in her father's house, and the maid with whom she took her daily walks used to drag her along, when out of sight of the house, along the byways to where Hecker and Struve, the revolutionary leaders, were haranguing the mob. Frightened and unwilling though she was, the nine-year-old, nevertheless imbibed a certain 'freedom of ideas that was to remain with her through life'.

Stephanie Mayerhöffer was known for her brightness of intellect and became her father's companion 'in the mental pursuits of his leisure hours'. Later in life, in England, she associated herself with the feminist movement and became involved in the establishment of the Women's College in Brunswick Street, Manchester.[172]

APPENDIX 2

Milestones in the anthroposophical movement related to the early life of Gerard Wagner

RUDOLF STEINER'S LECTURES IN WIESBADEN

The first two lectures of 29 January and 1 February 1908 were given shortly before the death of Max Wagner. The lecture titles were: 'The Being of Man in the Light of Spiritual Science' and 'The Secret of Death and the Riddle of Life'. In 1909 two lectures were given on 24 and 25 January, about two months before Gerard Wagner's third birthday, with the title 'How and Where does one find the Spirit'. In 1910 two lectures were given on 14 February, almost exactly two years after Max Wagner's death: 'The Being of the Plant and the Relation of the Human Being to the Plant World' and 'The Reception of Christ in the West'. In 1911 two lectures were given on 7 January almost six months before the Wagner family left Wiesbaden for England: 'The Effects of Moral Attributes on Karma' and 'Human Soul and Animal Soul, Human Spirit and Animal Spirit'.

The lecture titles are all quite striking when seen in their relation to Gerard Wagner's later work. The lecture 'The Being of the Plant and the Relation of the Human Being to the Plant World' stands out particularly when one thinks of Wagner's extensive colour and painterly research into the world of plants.

See Hans Schmidt, *Der Vortragswerk Rudolf Steiners,* Philosophisch-Anthroposophischer Verlag, 1978.

THE MALSCH BUILDING – SEED FOR A NEW IMPULSE IN ART

In Guenter Wachsmuth's *The Life and Work of Rudolf Steiner*. p.73/75. Philosophic Anthroposophic Press, 1955, the author cites 1906, the year of Gerard Wagner's birth, as the year Rudolf Steiner gave the first impulses for new forms of art:

> At this time the first impulses were given in Munich for the artistic development of the movement, and this city later on became the centre for this activity. Dr Steiner had already spoken there on 10 November 1905, on 'Art and Artists', and now, in conformity with the spirit of the city, he chose for his lectures on 17 and 18 January 1906 the themes

'Sculptural Art' and 'The Art of Sound'. What was here initiated achieved its large-scale realisation ... through the inauguration of the Mystery Dramas, which had the effect of infusing new life into all the arts.

What began at the Munich Conference as the inclusion of art evolved later into a new style of art that grew out of the same seed as the thought world of anthroposophy. Rudolf Steiner writes of two streams within the Anthroposophical movement, and compares what took place in Munich to what had hitherto developed in Berlin:

> The situation at Munich was different. From the very beginning an artistic element was active in the anthroposophical work there. One could assimilate a worldview such as anthroposophy in a completely different way than one could through rationalism and intellectualism. The artistic *image* is more spiritual than a rationalistic concept. It is alive and, unlike intellectualism, does not kill the spirit in the soul. Those in Munich who set the tone and built the membership and public audiences there were likewise the ones in whom this artistic feeling worked. [...]
>
> Because of the way the work of anthroposophy had proceeded in Munich, the 1907 Theosophical Congress arranged by the German Section took place there. The congresses, which were held previously in London, Amsterdam, and Paris had included arrangements for addressing problems related to theosophy in lectures and discussions. These were based on the same pattern as the usual scholarly conference. Many of the arrangements were modified in Munich. We (the organisers) provided a large concert hall to serve the Congress, along with interior decoration, whose colour and form would artistically reflect the prevailing mood of the subject under discussion. The artistic environment would become one with the spiritual activity there. In relation to this, I placed a great value on allowing artistic feeling to speak, and avoiding abstract, inartistic symbolism.[173]

On the night of Gerard Wagner's third birthday, 5 April 1909, under the light of the pre-Easter full moon, Rudolf Steiner laid the foundation stone of the building in Malsch, a village near Karlsruhe. Steiner called this building 'the first Rosicrucian temple to stand upon the earth'. The idea of the building grew out of the 1907 Theosophical Society Congress at Munich (see quote above), where Rudolf Steiner included, for the first time, various forms of art in the decoration of the Conference Hall. The walls were draped in deep red and works of art were displayed. These included columns and capitals relating to the seven planets which inspired a young man, Karl Stockmeyer, to ask Rudolf Steiner about a possible building in which the columns could play a part. Their collaboration resulted in the construction by Karl Stockmeyer of the small building at Malsch – a 'model building' – which was the forerunner of the subsequent Goetheanum at Dornach. As the Munich Congress is considered to be a defining moment in the development of artistic impulses arising out of anthroposophy, the small building at Malsch takes on special significance.

Rudolf Steiner's address at the laying of the foundation stone at Malsch was recorded from memory by Hilde Stockmeyer. The following excerpt is therefore an approximation of Rudolf Steiner's words:

> Digging under the ruins of many ancient houses, one can find human skeletons. There is a reason for them to be there. In earlier times, one knew that a new building must develop an inner life. This meant, originally, that spiritual life must flow through every building if it is to bring blessing. A decadent time understood this outwardly and established the practice of embedding a living slave under the building. What should really be buried with the foundation stone are the feelings and thinking and wishes of blessing of those who built the building and of those who wish to use it.
>
> Thus, we want to lower the foundation stone of this temple into the womb of our Mother Earth, in the face of the rays of the full moon shining upon us amidst the plant world that sprouts around the building. And as the moon reflects the bright sunlight, so we want to reflect the light of spiritual-divine being. We want to turn trustingly to our great Mother Earth, who bears and protects us lovingly, and we want to entrust to her the deeds of the building ... (then followed a reading of the content of the deeds).
>
> At the same time, all of us assembled here want to plant our wishes and blessings with this document and remind ourselves again and again of this moment and of that which has flamed through our souls and hearts. Then will our attitude and way of thinking work on, supporting and protecting this temple building, the existence of the Malsch Lodge. We want to call down upon the stone and the Malsch Lodge the blessing of the masters of wisdom and harmony of feelings and the blessing of all high and highest beings, the spiritual hierarchies, who are connected with earth evolution.
>
> We implore that they let their power stream into this foundation stone and allow it to work on within it so that all that is thought, felt,

willed, and done over this stone may be in harmony with them and be ensouled by their spirit.

Let the light of the Spirits of the East
Shine upon this building;
May the Spirits of the West let it ray back;
May the Spirits of the North strengthen it
And the Spirits of the South warm it through,
So that the Spirits of the East, West, North and South
Stream through this building.

Our Mother Earth suffered pain as she solidified. It is our mission to spiritualize Earth again, to redeem it by reworking it through the power of our hands into a spirit-filled work of art. May this stone be a first foundation stone for the redemption and transformation of our earth planet, and may the power of this stone multiply a thousandfold.

As we rested in the bosom of God, cared for lovingly by divine forces, there wove in us the all-pervading and enveloping Father Spirit. But we were still not conscious or independent. Therefore, we descended into matter, to learn to develop consciousness of self here. There came the evil; there came death. Yet Christ also worked in matter and helped us to overcome death. When we die thus in Christ, we live. We will overcome death and spiritualize matter and make it divine through our strong power. Thus will awaken within us the power of the Hallowing One, the Holy Spirit.

Thus resounds at this place as truth-wrought Word:

Ex Deo nascimur,
In Christo morimur,
Per Spiritum sanctum reviviscimus.

Out of God we are born,
In Christ we die,
Through the Spirit we are reborn.[174]

APPENDIX 3

Rex Raab, 1914–2004

By Christian Hitsch. Abbreviated version of an obituary published in *Das Goetheanum*, 2004.

Born on 7 April 1914 in London, Rex Raab began his architectural studies as soon as he left school, subsequently practising with various firms including H. S. Goodhart-Rendel. Here he also met Walter Gropius and Sir Raymond Unwin (1863–1940), pioneer of the garden city movement. In 1937 he qualified with the Royal Institute of Architects and also became a member of it.

Following the period of his life described above, when he encountered the Goetheanum building and anthroposophy, he studied these with the greatest imaginable keenness and intensity. As a pupil of Oswald Dubach (whose biography he later wrote), he came into contact with people who, only a few years earlier, had played a major part in creating the mighty concrete building according to plans by Rudolf Steiner – artists who had themselves known Rudolf Steiner, and were still inspired by the brilliance and energy of those times, as well as sorrow at the loss of the first Goetheanum: Assja Turgenieff, Hilde Boos-Hamburger, Carl Kemper, Margarita Voloshin and many, many more. He came to know and love them. The breadth and depth of his mind, and his artistic sensibility, preserved these impressions vividly within him. These seeds fell on fertile ground, growing and growing and eventually making him not only a creative artist of universal scope but also an exemplary teacher. In both speech and writing, down to the smallest details, he was able to convey things vividly by virtue of an outstanding memory founded on faithful and attentive observation.

Between 1941 and 1945 he served as an ambulanceman in the army, and until 1948 in post-war army service in Austria, gaining experience of life and the world. He came to know and love Central Europe, especially the German-speaking countries. Thus from 1951 he worked for two years as a Waldorf teacher, and then, in 1954, started his own architecture company. Now began his career as an architectural artist: the design and planning of several Waldorf schools, curative homes, seminaries, kindergartens, churches, houses, and interior design, both at home and abroad. The list of his major works includes the New Church in Berlin, in collaboration with Helmuth Lauer; the Engelberg Waldorf School; Ekkarthof curative home in Lengwil-Oberhofen (Switzerland); Dortmund Educational and Social Centre, and the church of The Christian Community in Heidenheim. A highpoint of his career were the extensions at the Goetheanum (especially the interior of the west wing and the foyer at terrace level, the English Hall, in collaboration with Gerard Wagner, landscape design around the Goetheanum, redesign of the Red Window, and the transformer station opposite the boiler house).

Those familiar with his approach and his works will discern how universal his architectural concerns were. He liked to call architecture the 'mother of all the arts', and was convinced that no building could truly house the human being and human culture without colour and an all-pervading sculptural element. Himself deeply schooled in the arts (architecture, sculpture, painting, music, speech, poetry and eurythmy), he put his whole humanity into his work. His special inclination for everything practical, necessary and purposeful drew on a lofty idealism, and was always all the more realistic precisely because of that.

For him there was no such thing as a mere exterior that could not be raised into a higher, human element. His imagination was always precise and objective. He often succeeded in conjuring, with the simplest means, a satisfying, purposeful and human-scale overall effect. One might also say that the spirit of anthroposophy was at work in him: individualizing, characterful in form and expression, humane in purpose and influence. He always represented anthroposophy freely and courageously, from the very centre of his being, tirelessly pointing to its germinal power, its innovative and revolutionary qualities. This soundness of soul and enthusiasm enabled him to inspire and support a whole new generation of architects, but also made him an arbiter and conscience of Rudolf Steiner's artistic impulse.

When I took up my job at the Arts section in the Goetheanum, Rex Raab supported me with advice and in practical ways. One piece of advice was this: invite all artists, and answer all letters! Underlying this was the wisdom that an art, to become culturally effective, must be sustained by a real spiritual and human community founded on true fraternity.

As fate decreed, around a hundred letters between Rudolf Steiner and Edith Maryon were rediscovered at the beginning of the 90s. Rex Raab began to write the biography of Edith Maryon who, coming from England like himself, had felt strongly drawn to Rudolf Steiner and his work. In both of them, England visited Central Europe! Rex Raab gave a vivid and exact account of her life and work, and her friendship with Steiner. This book enabled many members to understand Edith Maryon's importance for the art of the Goetheanum, and her exemplary work as an artist in free service to anthroposophy.

Shortly before his 90th birthday, as Rex Raab crossed the threshold, the countenance of his youthful soul shone out, as did a sense of his freedom and joy in sharing his wealth with all friends beyond the threshold. He was a truly cosmopolitan soul!

APPENDIX 4

Gladys Mayer, 1889–1980, by John Fletcher

Gladys Mayer devoted the greater part of her life (60 years) to Rudolf Steiner's anthroposophy; for most of this time she was dedicated to promoting the new impulse in painting, especially through colour.

She was an artist trained in the traditional manner. She trained in the Fine Arts for six years at the Liverpool School of Art and spent a year in Spain, Egypt, Greece, Italy and France, studying the art galleries and museums. In 1915 she had read a book in the British Museum Library, *The Way of Initiation*, by Rudolf Steiner – the only one, among many books of an occult nature that made a lasting impression on her. After seven years, she was to meet this book again on the book table at Stratford-on-Avon, during a Conference on 'Drama and Education' in 1922, during Rudolf Steiner's first visit to England after the Great War. Later she became disillusioned with the modern trends in art and started studying political economy, writing and lecturing in 1918 to support newly established women's rights. In 1922 she attended Rudolf Steiner's course of lectures in Vienna on the relationship between East and West.

A decisive turning point came in her life during a visit to Dornach in 1923. She was given personal instruction by Rudolf Steiner and she had to make the decision which way her life would now go – within the Anthroposophical Society or outside it. She decided her future life would be with the Anthroposophical Society. She returned to England, settled her affairs and then went back to Dornach and asked Rudolf Steiner how she could help in the work. He did not give her a direct answer but asked her if she wanted to help in painting. She was doubtful because the Dornach approach was so different from her own. Rudolf Steiner said 'Work very hard, then perhaps you can help.' She began to do so. There were few to advise but she was getting advice from Rudolf Steiner at night (as spiritual experience).

In 1953 Gladys Mayer founded the Mercury Arts Group, and Baron Arild Rosenkrantz became an honorary member. Over the years, apart from exhibitions, the Group and Gladys Mayer produced a series of folders – text booklets describing fundamental exercises in creating out of colour through rhythmical metamorphosis of seven images, with sketched illustrations, which reached, beyond England, as far as Africa, New Zealand and America. The method she learnt can be seen in much of her work from the 1950s through to the 70's. In 1961 many of the folders were incorporated in an illustrated text book – *The Mystery Wisdom of Colour*, with a revised edition in 1970, and a reprint in 1976.

List of Publications:
Sleeping and Waking in the Life of Art (1930)
Behind the Veils of Death and Sleep
Colour and the Human Soul (1961)
Colour, Healing and the Human Soul
The Mystery Wisdom of Colour (1961)
Gifts of the Seasons (1971)
How Art Speaks (1972)
Universal Science For Our Coming Age (1980)

APPENDIX 5

Elisabeth Wagner-Koch, born 1923

Elisabeth Koch was born on 29 June 1923, 30 miles south-west of Hannover on the Wickershausen Estate. Her father was a farmer. She was the youngest of four children, an active child who loved nature and climbing trees with her two brothers. When she was four-and-a-half the farmhouse burnt down. She often recalls an event that happened the day before the fire: she saw a manikin, a 'fire-manikin', as she called it, under the rose bush, which seemed to her to cast a huge, dark shadow over the house.

After the fire the family moved to Bodenengern near Rannenberg in Auetal where their country life continued. Elisabeth's wish as a young girl was to become a trapeze artist; extremely agile, she could not only do handstands and somersaults easily, but was able to do movements that other children could not.

After two years at Bodenengern, the mother, Maria Koch, moved with her children to Hannover, to her parents' home, where they lived in two small rooms. While the accommodation was tight, the culture surrounding the young Elisabeth was extensive and her grandmother's house was beautifully furnished. Her two brothers went to boarding school and her parents, Ernst and Maria Koch, separated. The move to Hannover from the countryside of Bodenengern was felt by Elisabeth as a deep loss. She recalled how her school essays all began with the words: 'When we were still at Bodenengern ...'

Shortly before her 15th birthday, Elisabeth was involved in a traffic accident which left her with serious injuries from which she was not expected to recover. In fact a report in the local newspaper (she was riding a bicycle when a lorry ran into her and over her) referred to the event as a 'fatal accident'. It took a year for her to recover, during which time she had private tuition and learnt to read and write again. In her own words the accident 'slowed her down'. She became quieter and more studious and she read a great deal. At the Lyceum state secondary school she met a group of girls who had just come from the newly closed Hannover Waldorf School, Gertrud Maassen and Renate Soltau among them. They would remain life-long friends and all three became deeply connected to anthroposophy and were active within the movement.

Two years into her sculpture training with August Waterbeck, Elisabeth began a Red Cross nurse-assistant training and worked in a lazaret nursing the war-wounded. Through this work and the experiences she had as a result of her accident, her knowledge of physiology and medicine grew. Apart from her interest in and gifts for the arts (poetry as well as the visual arts), Elisabeth Wagner-Koch's intellectual and practical knowledge, enriched by her intensive study of Rudolf Steiner's works, extends into many areas of life. (For further reading: Ernst Schuberth, *Elisabeth Wagner-Koch – eine biographische Skizze,* 2020 (Elisabeth Wagner-Koch – a biographical sketch). See also: Franz Lohri, Elisabeth Wagner – *Katalog zur Ausstellung im Goetheanum 2020* (Catalogue of an extensive exhibition of her work at the Goetheanum), 2020, Verlag am Goetheanum.)

APPENDIX 6

Theodor Willmann, 1902–2003

Theodor Willmann was the youngest person to be inaugurated into the priesthood of the Christian Community, the ceremony being carried out by Steiner himself. When illness interrupted his young life Rudolf Steiner advised bed-rest for a year, and he gave the patient the following meditative verse (saying emphatically: 'Practise that!'): 'Life loves lessons – lessons love life.' This mantram accompanied Willmann through his long life and became his life-motif. He turned to agriculture and became an inspiring figure within the biodynamic movement and the Anthroposophical Society. His life was not without personal tragedy: the death of his beloved elder daughter Sieghilde, the fatal accident of his second wife, and the illness and death of his third wife Ingeborg (Kempf).

Always innately an artist, he created remarkable sculptures in clay and stone, and also reliefs in copper. His intimate knowledge of Rudolf Steiner's art history lectures and his especially strong connection to the northern stream of art history gave an inspiring dynamic to his lectures on Albrecht Dürer and Mathias Grünewald in the Wagner painting school. Theodor Willmann was one of the few who quickly saw the significance of Gerard Wagner's work.

Gerard Wagner's meeting with Theodor Willmann was significant for him and his work. Willmann had been shown round the first Goetheanum by Rudolf Steiner, witnessing the cupola painting created by Rudolf Steiner himself. See Theodor Willmann, 'Der Baugedanke des Goetheanum' ('The Conception of the Goetheanum Building', translated in this volume) in *Gerard Wagner – Die Kunst der Farbe*, op. cit.

DANIEL MOREAU RECALLS (News for Members 37/2003): Kurt Theodor Willmann was an avid traveller, traversing both land and knowledge widely. He was conversant on any topic and delighted if one wanted to accompany him. Indeed he often walked up and down the garden, fully engaged in conversation; and then on 10 May he walked ahead of us, fully conscious, crossing the threshold into the 'New Garden'. His tall, wiry figure is an ever-present image to those left behind. His steps seemed to be in harmony with God and earth and could wrest syllables and melodies from her. He was an individual who had ears for the landscape and able to express its message in epic words, lifting the chrysalis and the butterfly into other spheres as if they were myths.

Yes, with his profound insights into all areas of culture, this well-travelled man surprised most people; no fellow raconteur went away from these spirited conversations without inspiration for his particular field. A Goethean spirit stood before one pondering, contemplatively, observing. Art and culture lived in his presence.

This great soul wanted to transmute the phenomena of nature into art: speech, poetry, fine copper engraving, chords on the piano. Inconsequential babbling was not tolerated. Trivial matters should never hinder conversation as it sought to deepen. Quietness of deliberation and meditation were his striving.

Theodor Willmann, a Goetheanist of the spirit, was of the opinion that there should be a strict separation between the esoteric and the exoteric. The destructive pleasures of flightiness should not encroach upon the world of silence, of the visible invisible, of the audible inexpressible. His striving for discernment, for presence of mind at the threshold, was indomitable and unshakeable.

He demanded a lot from his listeners, not just to remain fully present in the rarefied air of the threshold, but to have the stamina to accompany him in spiritual community throughout the journey of lengthy lectures.

This life journey was a long one, a century long, full of creativity and rich in friendships. There are many friends in the spirit who share these thoughts and look back with gratitude upon his journey, hoping to walk anew with this great spirit at the high threshold of inexhaustible life.

> *You walk above in light*
> *On soft ground*
> *Blessed spirits!*
> *Glittering breezes of Gods*
> *Touch you gently,*
> *Like the fingers*
> *Of the artist who strokes*
> *Sacred strings …*

HÖLDERLIN

APPENDIX 7

Frida Lefringhausen, 1901–1996

An abbreviated version of a biographical note written by Hans Börnsen on the occasion of her 80th birthday, summer 1981 in *50 years at Haus Arild*.

Born in Mettmann in the Rhineland, Frida Lefringhausen grew up in the countryside, where she had a happy childhood and then experienced the devastating shocks of the First World War. Afterwards, with great love for the little ones, she began her first professional job as a kindergarten teacher. There followed training and work in nursing and years of intensive activity in the various fields of child and family guidance. She had deep insight into the most difficult social conditions of city life. After a few years spent in Switzerland, where she worked as a nursery school and sports teacher, she worked in Hamburg in various state children's homes and in adolescent counselling.

During the Second World War she developed the work of the children's home Haus Arild, in Hamburg's Bergedorf district, and after the war, under her guidance, anthroposophical curative educational work began in Bliestorf. Frida Lefringhausen has been a wellspring of continuing impulses for the development of the Bliestorf Social Therapeutic Community for adults with learning difficulties, for the associated biodynamic farm with 15 supported individuals and also for a Waldorf kindergarten serving the local village. In the same way, the creation of a basic training in curative education at Haus Arild under the auspices of the Rudolf Steiner Seminar in Eckwaelden, with 20 seminarists, is thanks to her initiative.

Frida Lefringhausen started the Turmalin Foundation for the support and development of anthroposophical initiatives in curative education, agriculture and art. She is the leader of the Bliestorf anthroposophical branch and a central figure in the Religion teachers' conferences held at Haus Arild, which are imbued with an unusual inwardness and intensity.

The children love to be close to her, especially the co-workers' little ones, who are not yet of school age. She gathers them around her regularly for special occasions.

APPENDIX 8

Ernst Schuberth, born 1939

Abbreviated from Albert Schmelzer's essay in celebration of Ernst Schuberth's 70th birthday.

Ernst Schuberth was born in 1939 in Danzig (now Gdansk) as the third of five children. The parents came from evangelical pastor families with broad spiritual interests. After the First World War there was no money for the father's aspirations to study law, so he became a customs official for the Danzig city-state.

The child showed an early and perhaps unusual aptitude for independence. In particular, hints from a brother four years older than himself triggered 'research activities'. So for example, as soon as the opportunity arose for him to 'escape' (from supervision), he tried to detect oncoming trains by laying his ear to the railway lines. He also investigated other practical matters at a very young age.

In January 1945 the family, without the father, were able to leave Danzig on a train for wounded soldiers. They found a place to stay, near to the mother's parents, in Wildberg, in the Neuruppin district, and were then overrun by the Russians. There ensued hard times of famine, illness (typhus) and death in the family. The paternal grandmother, who had fled with them, took a particular interest in the child Ernst, who remained surprisingly healthy.

The next stop was Hannover (after two and a half years on the Lüneburg Heath) where the father was able to work as a customs official again. The nine-year-old Ernst went into Class 4 of the Waldorf school, thus beginning his time as a Waldorf pupil. At the end of Class 8 Ernst, fed up with school, wanted to become a carpenter, which the father did not allow. But a love of woodwork stayed with him.

In the summer term of 1959, after school-leaving exams, he began a teacher-training degree in mathematics and physics in Bonn. From now on his time was clearly divided: seven months of the year he studied his chosen subjects diligently, but for the other five months he was in Dornach occupied with anthroposophy.

During these 'Dornach years', he pursued and deepened various impulses that would occupy him for the rest of his life: mathematics and geometry, colour, anthroposophical social sciences and biodynamic agriculture. In 1959 Ernst Schuberth heard a lecture on projective geometry given by Louis Locher-Ernst. He listened, fascinated by the thought of how consciousness can lift itself to infinity in clear thought processes – this is what he had been waiting for! Tragically the ensuing collaboration was cut short when Louis Locher-Ernst had a climbing accident. Ernst Schuberth was given the opportunity of publishing the literary estate of this revered teacher and editing new editions of his work.

Of course Ernst did not miss the chance of deepening his understanding of Waldorf education before his time in Dornach came to an end. After his first degree in 1964, he worked at the Georg Unger Institute for Mathematics and Physics. Here he got to know several friends who had made significant contributions in the fields of mathematics and physics such as Peter Gschwind. In 1965/66 he completed the Dornach teachers' seminar, under the guidance of Georg Hartmann, occupying himself very intensively with Rudolf Steiner's lectures The Study of Man.

In the midst of all this were significant personal and professional developments. On New Year's Day 1967 Ernst and Erika Seidel were married. At that time Erika had already been four years at the Rudolf Steiner School in Munich, working as class teacher and English teacher. Ernst followed her and in 1968/69 took on her class as class 6 which he carried through until class 8. At the same time he taught physics in class 13 and gave the non-denominational religion lessons.

In the meantime, his dissertation 'The Modernisation of Maths Teaching' (completed in 1969) was much read and discussed in the academic world. Professor Horst Karaschewski encouraged Ernst Schuberth to apply for a professorship at Bielefeld University. In the summer of 1974 he became full professor for mathematics and maths teaching. At the end of 1977 he was approached by Dr Benediktus Hardorp and asked if he would found a Waldorf Seminar in Mannheim. Thus the work of the Education Centre in Mannheim began.

With the political changes in 1989, Ernst Schuberth's work took on a new international dimension. It finally became possible to promote Waldorf education in previously East Bloc countries. In 1990, at the request of the Rumanian government, he founded a Waldorf teacher training in Bucharest. He gave public courses on Waldorf education in St Petersburg and supported Angelika

Kohli in the founding of the St Petersburg Rudolf Steiner School. At the same time came the call from Astrid Schmitt-Stegmann asking him to take part in the summer courses for class teachers in Sacramento, California. In this way a period of regular collaboration began in California which soon included further education courses for upper school teachers. This activity went hand-in-hand with his work in the East, most recently also courses in Taiwan.

Ernst Schuberth's extraordinary energy and focus are apparent from the fact that, alongside his various courses, lecturing and organisational work, he has also produced a wealth of publications.

APPENDIX 9

Erwin Thomalla, 1925–1983

Based on his autobiographical notes and a conversation with Jennifer Müller

Erwin Thomalla was born on 8 December 1925 in the village of Michelsdorf in upper Silesia, south-east Germany, today Michailowicz, Poland. Erwin was the older of two brothers. When the father left the family to seek his fortune in America the child was barely 18 months old. The two boys were then brought up by their mother and grandmother. The father returned when Erwin was almost 11.

At the age of 14 he encountered the theatre and decided then that it would be his life. At 18 he was called up and after nine months active service he spent over three years as prisoner of war – first in the USA and then in England.

Returning to West Germany he pursued his wish to be an actor. Working alongside well-known actors he discovered 'the highs and lows' of theatrical life. Through a friend he came into contact with anthroposophy. Whilst performing in Switzerland he paid a visit to the Goetheanum in Dornach and was moved by the eurythmy in the Ariel Scene of Goethe's *Faust*, but also by a painting he saw which he later discovered was by his future teacher Gerard Wagner. His attempts to join the Goetheanum stage group did not bear fruit but he discovered the painting classes of Gerard Wagner and Elisabeth Koch.

His work as a teacher in the 'Wagner School' took him to Germany, France, England, USA, Australia and New Zealand where he also exhibited his well-loved paintings. A collection of his work is preserved at the Wagner Archives in Dornach.

APPENDIX 10

Anne Stockton Falk, 1910–2012

Abbreviated from an obituary by Manning Goodwin

Anne Stockton was born in 1910 in New York City, where she attended a Montessori nursery and then the Brearley School. At age thirteen she and her family opted for an artistic training, first with a year in Florence and then eventually by attendance at the Art Students' League. Painting was to be her life and she was deeply impressed by the first show of Cézanne, Gauguin, and Van Gogh at the Modern Museum. But the whirl of debutante balls and a rich social life in the circles of her Mother's Repertory Theatre work and her Father's French Line law work swept her off her feet, as did her marriage at nineteen to Sage Goodwin.

The latter's architectural work took the young couple to Santa Fe, where Anne participated with her oil painting in the exhibitions and artist colony of the town. They moved back to Connecticut as a family with two boys, but Anne suffered post-natal depression with the second child, and then her younger brother died, as did a beloved grandfather, and then at the end of the thirties her Father.

Anne and the extended family were in turmoil, but Anne's mother had made contact with anthroposophy. This became a solace as well as a consuming interest for Anne. Her marriage did not survive, but she returned to New York to participate vigorously in anthroposophical activities and the first anthroposophical summer conference at Threefold Farm in Spring Valley, N. Y.

Later she was a member of the Council and Executive Committee of the USA Anthroposophical Society. She travelled and she took every opportunity to meet and learn from each painter and art teacher inspired by anthroposophy: from Richard Kroth and Pat Erickson through to the varied artistic approaches of the painters and art trainings within European anthroposophy.

In 1966, Anne attended the Hauschka School of Painting and Therapy in Bad Boll for two years to obtain a diploma, perhaps the first in her life. With her training there and working as art therapist briefly at Arlesheim, Anne considered that she had found her life mission. But her first step in 1968 was a stint as painting teacher and college faculty colleague for eleven years at

Emerson College in England. She pitched herself into the work with gusto. Ever popular with students and highly appreciated by colleagues, she might have considered this the zenith of her career. But she capped it in 1972 with marriage to Kurt Falk, art historian, agronomist, painter and author-to-be of a book *The Unknown Hieronymus Bosch*.

In 1979, Kurt and Anne had the opportunity to start their own initiative the *Tobias School of Art, Painting and Therapy*, of which she was principal. In her teaching she formulated a curriculum for her students which sought to arrive at a free style of painting that united the varied methods and indications she herself had received, but allowed each student to explore their own creativity and solutions. The eulogies she received from students during her life and after her death gave voice to their appreciation of their training, the inspiration for a full and rich life which they perceived as Anne's gift to them. She resigned as director of Tobias at the age of eighty and determinedly and happily continued to work. She spent five years working on a series of fifty-two Soul Calendar paintings, published as a book with verse translations by her son, Rufus Goodwin. She continued attending painting conferences, usually accompanied by a clutch of students, and travelled to teach workshops or visit people, often in tandem with a younger fellow teacher.

Anne convened a group of painters to research the question 'How to paint an altar picture in our time (and depict Christ).' She helped prepare the Guggenheim Exhibition in New York entitled *Rudolf Steiner: Architect and Artist*. She convened study groups in her house on anthroposophy, literature, conversation, and art. Though hospitalised with pneumonia aged 87, she celebrated her birthday with a party in Paris. Aged 93, Anne joined the Christian Community, and on her 100th birthday was pleased to receive a birthday telegram from the Queen. In her last year she stayed in bed, in the end unable to communicate but at peace, and taking pleasure in the wind whistling amongst the apple trees outside her window.

APPENDIX 10

APPENDIX 11

Excerpts from Rex Raab, 'A motif in Rudolf Steiner's education which is largely ignored or even opposed', in: *Art Section Newsletter,* spring 1998, issue 10.

At the beginning of this year an experience came my way which filled me with joy. It clearly confirmed once again that Rudolf Steiner's expectations were rooted in life itself. A former student of a Steiner (Waldorf) school was telling me about her time in the lower grades. She could not know how valuable to me her testimony was to be. She said: 'The murals in the classrooms made us feel we were in paradise! To begin with, it was pictures in Class One, drawn from fairytales, which were to us the most beautiful. As soon as we moved on to Class Two, however, we found the murals of St Francis to be the loveliest. In Class Three, with its plant motifs, and Class Four with its animal motifs on the walls – eagles near the sun, lions, stags in the moonlight – it was these which in turn became the most beautiful for us. The artistic treatment of the classrooms gave our soul a special nourishment year by year that will last, I do believe, for the rest of our lives.'

What could be more natural, therefore, than that every dedicated teacher would want to see that every schoolchild should come under the beneficial influence of such favourable elements in their daily environment? Yet in practice this is still very far from being the case. And that is the urgent matter that I would like to bring to the attention of all teachers in Steiner (Waldorf) schools.

To begin with, a summary of what Rudolf Steiner outlined three-quarters of a century ago. These crucial passages in his argument are to be found in the transcripts of the faculty meetings in Stuttgart, 1919–1924:

1. May 1919: In a lecture on adult education four months prior to the opening of the first Waldorf school. It includes a moving passage commencing: 'Oh what a crying shame, that our children are put into school rooms which are truly barbaric surroundings for their young souls!' As an antidote or creative answer to the problem, Steiner points to the art of painting. That would be an appropriate way for the artist to approach the task of training him or herself himself both in technique and in making a truly social contribution.

2. November 22, 1920: 'It has struck me … that the walls should not simply confront us as walls, but that they should have something of the pictorial

element about them, but it would have to be done very carefully ... Where are the painters who could do something like this? It would have to be prompted by the class teachers in question. And then it would have to be carried out in a really artistic way. There should be nothing inartistic.'

4. January 1923 (after a further year-and-a-quarter): 'Take it then as the establishing of an ideal: The artistic treatment of our schoolrooms should arise out of pedagogy itself. What we find in the classrooms would then, perhaps, be best extended into the adjacent areas.

There follows a detailed description of the pictorial treatment of the school-rooms from the first to the twelfth grade, which should be sufficiently well known, although it is always worth re-reading the exact formulations and the approach implicit in these indications. What 'came' to Rudolf Steiner did not come overnight but represents the mature results of years of scientific and psychological research which is, accordingly, to be taken seriously. For some time now I have had the conviction that school interiors treated as Steiner outlines – although it would have to be a complete realization – would be the most powerful remedy against the detrimental effects of television.

APPENDIX 12

Heilgart Umfrid, 1928–2012

From the memorial address.

Heilgart Umfrid was born to a pastor's family on 23 April 1928 in Kaisersbach, Welzheimer Wald, as the third child of four sisters. She was a cheerful, sensitive girl with a love of music, and from an early age displayed great strength of will. At the age of nine, Heilgart heard J. S. Bach's St Matthew Passion with her mother and sisters. She was so moved by it that she urged her mother to let her go again. This was impossible for financial reasons, but at last her mother suggested that she phone the organist and ask him if she might sit with him in the organ loft during the concert. She called him, agreed it with him, and walked alone all the way from Dachswald to Stuttgart's abbey church. Thus – at just nine years old – she immersed herself again in the music and the story of the Passion.

After her schooling (attending the two last classes of the reopened Uhlandshöhe Waldorf School after the war ended) she wanted to study music. But her father's early death, and the difficult war and post-war years, meant insufficient money for these studies, and so she had to relinquish this desire. But she remained deeply connected to music throughout her life. She sang in various choirs and played the piano, and later the harpsichord.

At the age of 20 she started to train as a bookbinder, at the same time studying at the book design academy and completing her master craftsman's exam in 1955. She founded her own workshop, as training workshop, with 5–6 staff. Among much other work, Wuerttemberg's national library commissioned her to bind the facsimile of the Stuttgart Psaltery, with commentary (two volumes, in an edition of 600 copies). In other words, 1200 vellum-bound books! In 1964 she was appointed to teach bookbinding at the state academy for the pictorial arts. She devoted 26 of her 84 years to this craft, which she practised lovingly with care, precision and a sense of beauty. She became a master in the art of bookbinding.

In 1974, with much resolve, she embarked upon a new path, giving up both a well-regarded job and financial security to train in artistic therapy. She attended the art therapy school in Boll run by Frau Dr M. Hauschka and subsequently trained in painting with Gerard Wagner at the Goetheanum painting school. In Gerard Wagner she found a teacher able to instruct her in Rudolf Steiner's colour sketches.

In 1979 she took over painting therapy at the Paracelsus Clinic in Unterlengenhardt and introduced painting with plant colours. In 1982, together with Gerard and Elisabeth Wagner and Dr H. B. Andrae, she initiated and oversaw the annual further training week for art therapists in Unterlengenhardt. Last year she was present to witness the 30th anniversary of its existence.

After 17 years of working at the Paracelsus Clinic, in 1994 she founded her own studio for art therapy at Haus Morgenstern in Unterlengenhardt. She continued to train students who wished to complete their studies in painting therapy at the Goetheanum with the diploma in this field.

People from many continents came to Heilgart Umfrid to be introduced to this new form of therapy by her. They now work worldwide. The training centre for artistic therapy founded by her and Hans-Bernhard Andrae was closely connected with the Medical Section in Dornach.

In Heilgart Umfrid one saw a person who, with her focused strength of will and loving care, embodied what it truly means to be a therapist.

APPENDIX 13

Dr Hans-Bernhard Andrae, 1928–2005

From an obituary by Siegrun Andrae.

Hans-Bernhard Andrae, born in Berlin on 13 February 1928, was the fourth and youngest child of the family, and very much a late arrival. His childhood was shaped by his father, who was an archaeologist and the excavator of Babylon, Assur and other sites. A buildings historian, he was also commissioned to set up the Middle-Eastern department at Berlin's Pergamon Museum. This cultural wealth played a large and vivid part in the life of the family, and became a deep and absorbing interest for the child from his earliest infancy. His open-minded mother surrounded her young child with the wonderful protection of a blossoming, flourishing garden, and so a love of nature was planted in his heart from the beginning. His parents were active in founding The Christian Community in Berlin, and in setting up the Rudolf Steiner School there. Thus anthroposophy formed the firm foundations of family life.

At the age of seven, Hans-Bernhard started to attend the Rudolf Steiner School. Under the guidance of his beloved teacher Anni Heuser, he was happy and untroubled there until the Nazi regime shut the school down, abruptly ending this period in his life. A trial period at a state secondary school led to his decision, at the age of 14, to begin an agricultural apprenticeship instead, at the Hessel estate's biodynamically run farm in Thuringia. Here Martin Schmidt and his wife gave many young people an opportunity to experience anthroposophy in daily life. Besides the hard work of farming, there was much cultural study and activity. But then the community had to flee before the Russian invasion, trekking across closing borders and, by the utmost efforts of all, initially settling in Hambach and Rittershain.

After seven years in all of working on the land, Hans-Bernhard Andrae took his farm-assistant exams in Stuttgart/Ludwigsburg in 1949, following which he attended the Stuttgart Waldorf School's proseminar course, where he met several figures who became important to him – chiefly Carl Kemper and also, among others, Eric Schwebsch and Herbert Hahn.

From the beginning of 1950 to the end of 1952 there followed three years at the Ita Wegman Clinic in Arlesheim. He worked here first as a gardener but was later given a position by Erich Kirchner as trainee in the clinic's administration department. During this period Hans-Bernhard made the decision to study medicine. He later wrote:

'These three years at Arlesheim not only encouraged me to pursue the profession of physician but also, based on insights and experiences I gained in the organization and running of the clinic, gave me the courage in 1970 to collaborate with Volker Bergengrün in transforming the Paracelsus House sanatorium in Unterlengenhardt – which had stood empty for three years – into a clinic for internal medicine and expand it into a financially sustainable operation. I owe the success of this development work, despite all the obstacles of that time, above all to the impulses I was fortunate to receive during the three years I worked at the Clinical-Therapeutic Institute – the present Ita Wegman Clinic – from Erich Kirchner as well as from the other colleagues of Frau Dr Wegman who were still working there at the time.'

After the period in Dornach, having attended a one-year course of evening classes in Berlin, he passed the Abitur (school-leaving exams) as an external candidate and then studied medicine at Berlin University from 1954 to 1959, with a subsequent period as assistant physician until 1963. During all these years of training he also studied anthroposophic medicine under Herbert Sieweke, with bi-annual participation at conferences of the physicians working group at the Goetheanum.

After these 14 'journeyman years', during which, in 1962, he started a family – with the arrival of children in 1963 and 64 – he set up his own anthroposophically-oriented general practice in 1963 in the Nikolas-See district of Berlin, which he ran for seven years.

Among much else, he was especially concerned at the clinic with eurythmy therapy and art therapy, above all with painting using plant colours. Since he had a special relationship to the world of colours he was able to work artistically with plant-based paints, and immerse himself fully in this work with patients. He was able to make suggestions and offer stimulus of great importance for both patients and therapist. Thus, in collaboration with the painting therapist, he developed very worthwhile and innovative approaches in therapeutic painting.

In 1993, at the age of 65, he retired from the Paracelsus Clinic and, until about 1998, was able to pursue the tasks that he had set himself. Thus, as long as he was still able, much music-making continued at home. He played the flute, and, at his request, we were much preoccupied with Bach's 'Art of Fugue', playing all 18 fugues alongside many other pieces. Then his previously inexhaustible strength started to leave him rapidly. All the skills and abilities he had acquired took their leave one by one. He could no longer take hold of his body, to the point where he became an invalid, and soon all his bodily functions succumbed. Yet the spark of his I maintained itself in his body, and so on 26 August 2005 he was able to step consciously into the world of spirit. The period of confinement to his sick-bed lasted seven years, during which he was wrapped in the warmth of the household around him.

APPENDIX 14

Wilhelm Boos, 1914–2008

An address given by Manfred Seeger at the School of Spiritual Science memorial meeting in 2008.

I had the good fortune to work with Herr Boos for almost ten years, from his 82nd year onwards. I had asked him whether he could give me feedback about the quality of my Waldorf teaching. He agreed to do this. The pupils will remember how he came into the class on the same day every week, sat down on a chair near the teacher's desk, drew out a small white card and carefully wrote down the date.

Herr Boos followed each lesson attentively, sometimes writing on his card. Sporadically he would hit the table suddenly with the flat of his hand, making the children jump. In time we got used to it as a sign of his enthusiasm when a part of the lesson went especially well.

Occasionally he asked if he could be involved in the lesson. At these times he had conversations with the class, leading the children's attention to things that he considered were important, and to their interconnectedness.

I enjoyed having him in the class. One day I asked him by what criteria he judged my teaching. The answer was: 'It's quite simple. Body, soul and spirit. In the morning the children carry their bodies into the classroom. Then the teacher begins to develop sympathy in the children for the material. I call that soul, and that works quite well. Yes, and what is spirit? When the children have connected to the subject in this way, spirit is when the teacher, through intelligent and imaginative task-setting, awakens the children's own activity of discovery and takes these results seriously. This is an area we are not so good at. But it is extremely important!'

The observations he made on the little card served him as memory prompts for regular debriefing. It soon became known that Herr Boos was a very helpful mentor, and many class teachers approached him. He soon came to be the one most aware of the standards of teaching in the school.

During in-service training days, both the new and the more experienced teachers felt motivated to strive for the ideals of Waldorf Education. Herr Boos became a central person in this area because he had an overview of the educational standard of the school from a Waldorf perspective, due to his regular presence in the classes.

He described what he felt was especially successful, and connected it to key statements by Rudolf Steiner. Herr Boos had a strong impulse to awaken an interest in the practical value of anthroposophy in those present. He was a scientist and tried to penetrate scientific thinking with soul. He often spoke of how Rudolf Steiner said to his pupils: 'Place what I have said before your soul' – that is to say: *experience* it. A characteristic sentence expressing Herr Boos's striving was: 'Sensitive awareness in your feelings is the basis for a secure relationship to the child's inner life.' He found that the right sensitivity of feeling arose in him when he meditated on thoughts from *Theosophy* or *Study of Man*.

We worked so many times with the theme of the temperaments: observing what is weak or strong, turning your attention more to external things or to inner conditions, observing the difference if your attention passes over an object or dwells upon it. His methods in plant observation led to amazingly consistent results. The correct (true) thoughts were always woken up by the right feelings. 'Waking up' was one of his favourite phrases.

In latter years he took over the painting lesson in my class. In the afternoon you could find him in the classroom mixing the colours. He adjusted the colours one to another as a musician tunes his instrument or a cook seasons his dishes. There it was again, sensitive awareness trained by the texts of spiritual science. The children worked on the same painting for up to 6 or 8 hours, with concentration and commitment. These pictures did not of course look like the other water-colour pictures of the Lower School. This led to criticism and questions.

With Herr Boos what stood out was his discernment. He differentiated between Waldorf convention (which has established itself in the course of years and by tradition become accepted) and lessons where the body soul and spirit of the children is activated in the above-mentioned way. I asked the children: What do we remember when we think of Herr Boos? One pupil said: 'I found he was quite wise.' Yes, I can only confirm this. It was a new kind of wisdom which he had won for himself by dint of hard work in life, and by studying the principles of spiritual science.

APPENDIX 15

Painting as a Path of Inner Transformation

Excerps from letters writtten by Ernst Schuberth, 2019. Translated by Matthew Barton.

Re-reading the Christmas Foundation cycle (GA 233), I came upon the passage where Rudolf Steiner gives an account of the Hybernian mysteries. In lecture 4 he describes the despair suffered by the pupils of these mysteries. This reminded me very much of the experiences we painting pupils underwent with our teacher Gerard Wagner, despite all his kind and loving guidance. You will surely have experienced this too: not being able to achieve what was necessary. Outer conditions are easier today than back then, but inner ones are certainly not. This also shows us the truth of this path. It is a mystery schooling.

It seems to me that it will be important to engage with this question: What makes Gerard Wagner's school of painting instruction an esoteric path? What are its stages and degrees? How do we encounter the adversary powers and the Guardian upon this path? In what sense is it a Christian path?

Here our words falter and stumble. With every task that Rudolf Steiner gave us – whether in medicine, the arts, agriculture or education – he pointed at the same time to a mystery path. To what degree do these paths of schooling lead us to deepened insight into the human being and the world? Think for a moment of how differently we learned to observe the world of plants through our study of painting, or what a pupil reveals of himself when he paints.

Is this the result of a spiritual schooling?

I will try here to record a few of my own experiences.

The first step for me was to ask how I can detach colour from things or concepts of things so as to arrive at pure colour experience. We always see colours attached to things: they are affixed to them. But surely we must come to colour experience without seeing or picturing things …? A first step …

So the first step is to separate our colour perceptions and sensations from ideas about things and thus achieve pure colour perceptions. This signifies a battle with our daily thinking, which seeks to dampen every sense perception into a concept or idea. We really only know such a condition when something frightens us because we cannot immediately recognise what the thing is we are seeing. It is an exceptional state that we cannot endure for long. When painting this may not be alarming, but the temptation always exists to couple a form with an idea ...

Describing such temptations sounds very abstract and inconsequential. But underlying this are real battles that can lead us into deep despair. The second step, really, is to experience pure colours as active. They bear within them a will impulse. The yellow finds a red, which initially attracts and then repulses it. In each colour live impulses of movement, as we can study in eurythmy. Their will element comes to expression especially in the relationship of two colours to one another. Can the painter allow the will impulses of colours to come to life and activity within him, without compelling them into relationships alien to them through his own egoistic, shaping intent?

In a third step, besides the movement dynamic which the colours develop in their interplay with each other, we also come to know the rich inner life of the gradually awakening colour world: one colour warms another or is exhaled by it. A third colour dies away or grows rigid through a fourth. Lack or 'thirst' can arise if a colour proves to be too weak in its context. The whole wealth of life processes can be rediscovered in the ocean of colours. Health and sickness can be found within a colour composition.

Rudolf Steiner describes this life emerging into sensory perception in aesthetic creativity and enjoyment most beautifully in his lectures on *Cosmic and Human History*, in the first volume entitled *The Riddle of Man. The spiritual background to human history*, and especially in the lecture of 15 August 1916:

> What does this mean? It means that the human being will inwardly modify his zodiac with its twelve sensory realms. He will modify it in such a way that life processes now unfold more than sense processes within this zodiac with its twelve sensory realms; or rather, that processes now unfold which, while initiating the sensory process, reconfigure it within the sense realm into a life process – and thus raise the sense process out of the dead quality it possesses today, commuting it into life. In this way a person will see but in his vision something will at the same time come to life; he will hear, and at the same time something will live in his hearing that otherwise only lives in the stomach or on the tongue. The sense processes will be brought into motion. Their life will be stimulated.

He then goes on to say this:

Then the life processes must also be changed. And this occurs by virtue of them becoming more ensouled than they are ordinarily in earthly life. The three life processes – respiration, warmth, nutrition – will in a sense be integrated and ensouled, will appear in more soulful form. In ordinary breathing we inhale air's coarse materiality, in ordinary warmth circulation we absorb heat and so on. But now a kind of symbiosis takes place; in other words, the life processes then form a unity when they are ensouled. They are no longer separate as they are presently in the organism but they form a kind of connection with each other. Within the human being, respiration, warmth and nutrition create an intimate community: not material nutrition but something that is a nutritional process; the process unfolds but we do not need to eat to instigate it, and it does not occur alone as it does when we eat, but in interplay with the other processes. In the same way the four other life processes are united. Secretion, conservation, growth, reproduction are unified and in turn form a more ensouled process, a life process that is more soul-imbued. And then the two parts or aspects can themselves reunite, so that, for instance, not all life processes work together at once but interact in such a way that they subdivide into the three and four, the three aspects working with the four …

This gives rise – in a way that resembles but is not identical with how things are at present on earth – to soul powers that have the character of thinking, feeling and will. But these are different now: not thinking, feeling and will as on the earth but somewhat different. They are more like life processes, less like the distinct and separate life processes presently on the earth.

Then he says, very briefly summarising:

Real human aesthetic conduct involves enlivening the sense organs in a certain way, and ensouling the life processes.

For a painter like Gerard Wagner, engendering an aesthetic constitution as Rudolf Steiner describes it requires steps governed by the I, rather than either the creation of visionary or intoxicated states, or intellectual abstraction. First comes a conscious engagement with a thinking that seeks to form concepts of things. This power of thinking, which daily life facilitates, has to be restrained by the will; and this, along with thinking itself, is one of the most arduous exertions.

We know that in states of intoxication, sense perceptions can become more vivid, and that artists who cultivate this can thereby gain stimulus for their aesthetic creativity. But this path dulls the power of the I. By contrast, an engagement, with picturing thinking as described, strengthens the true power of the I without lapsing into abstractions – the latter created precisely by our judging and conceptualising thinking. Those who try to pursue this path will know the bitter and harsh experiences they meet at this threshold. Like the mathematician who must wrestle with temptations and bitter disappointments in his search for truth, so also the artist who seeks to follow this modern path.

What I have written so far is really only what a painter needs to do to prepare his constitution, and not yet painting itself. ... When a master like Gerard Wagner paints, the transition into an artistic constitution has long been practised, and can more easily be adhered to. The most important question then becomes this: What do I wish to paint? This concerns the *motif* in the broadest sense. Even when someone asked Gerard Wagner to paint a particular motif, he did not start from a pictorial idea, which some call *Imagination*. This must be preceded by a non-pictorial *Intuition*, which, in terms of the Philosophy of Freedom, we can also call *moral Intuition*.

I want to try to describe two examples of this. The first comes from soul experience. I can inwardly experience my thinking as dead, as described in Act 1 of *Faust*. Similarly, *The Chymical Wedding of Christian Rosenkreutz* or *Hamlet*, describe such inner death experiences. Helplessly we face the soul-devoid rigidity of our thinking, that can only grasp sense perceptions, create mental pictures or logically connect thoughts.

If we seek a colour experience that corresponds to this pictureless inner experience, at one extreme we can find black, which Rudolf Steiner also describes as the *spiritual image of the lifeless*. Yet knowledge alone of this characterisation cannot help us give expression to this inner experience, but only pure colour experience. Just as knowing the theorem of Pythagoras is different from understanding and demonstrating it, so mere knowledge of the characteristics of black is different from our own authentic experience.

As Gerard Wagner described this to me, there is a whole series of paintings in which, in terms both of placing and quantity, he began with a relatively arbitrary black, and then tried to *redress* this action of black with living and ensouled colours. It is worth dwelling on this *redress*. If the black were simply to be erased, the strong formative impulse emanating from it would be lacking; the picture would inwardly collapse like a flower that one tears from the ground. Its strong power remains active in everything that subsequently develops. It is accentuated as an important part of a new sphere of life.

Just to be clear, I will add that it is not a matter of painting pretty flowers around the black to gladden the heart. An inner path is involved through which I overcome within myself the death forces I experience in black through the colours themselves, allowing them to arise. Perhaps it is true to say that no painting of Gerard Wagner's lacks – in some form of metamorphosis – this balance between life and death, weight and lightness.

Now the second example:
The plant motif
In every blossoming (annual) plant, we find the polarity of seed and flower. The germinating seed is the gift, now implanted in earth, of the previous growth cycle. A dark, moist humus full of mineral substances encloses it. It offers itself up to new life. Light and warmth first draw forth the root network, and then the seedling strives upward toward the light- and warmth-imbued air. But it can only flourish if it continues to be sustained by the darkness and moistness below. In the truest sense of the word, the life process of plant development remains 'earthed'. How many times in our life have we been privileged to watch how the most diverse plants germinate, blossom and ripen! Each spring has given us this gift: an experience of the wealth of unfolding life.

If we meditate upon growth and flowering, a feeling-thought arises in the soul, one no longer bound up with a single, observed plant, but containing the process of growth and blossoming itself. This is not some abstraction from all the single instances we have witnessed, but rather the very essence that in all single instances makes the life processes what they are. If we did not gain a living grasp of this essential and integral quality, the visible transformation before us would be only an outward process, like something mechanical.

As a geometer one feels oneself vividly reminded of the formation of a pure geometrical concept. Back in childhood, already, a semiconscious or unconscious experience of the circle developed in us from the many circles we saw. We may have experienced this already with the 'morning circle' in kindergarten, or as a wreath of flowers; perhaps we drew circles, or walked them, or engaged actively with them in some other way.

But what a huge step it is to become aware of the pure concept of the circle! Now we can relate it to other concepts, that of the straight line, of the curve, of the angle etc. We are no longer dependent on seeing a saucer or lampshade – which on closer observation, turn out not to be perfect circles anyway. Only the pure concept of the circle, released from all materiality – we can call it 'sense-free' – gives us access to the realm of geometry, which consists not only of spiritually perceived forms but the discovery of their *interrelationships*.

This process comes very close to the release of colours from the ideas of things by means of which we first grasped our surroundings. This release leads us to the 'pure' colours, and really only through these can we find our way to artistic engagement with them. In their essential or intrinsic qualities encompassed in Intuition, we enter a distinct world of boundless unfolding.

Every person who tries to pursue this path will know that at this threshold powers await us that can weaken and unsettle us. Is this not merely a process of abstraction? Surely, we have simply perceived from our many individual observations common traits which we accentuate, while ignoring other traits. Are 'pure concepts' and 'pure colours' in fact merely pale abstractions from the 'real', tangible world?

This seeming explanation, which conceals our real experience from us, overlooks the fact that already when we consider a 'common trait' – which, in the strict sense, can never exist in actual experience – the comparison thus invoked must always be grasped intuitively.

The transition, the threshold identified here, requires *courage* of us. Courage for our thinking as it releases itself from ideas and enters the world of pure conceptual relationships.

Another danger is to seek to regard what we grasp in thinking only as a pure, Platonic world of ideas which no longer has any existential relationship with the experiential world. But the fact that we possess, in this ideal realm, a power that enables us to creatively engage and intervene in the perceived world as, say, an engineer or artist, goes beyond this idealism of 'pure ideas'. Strength and love for creative action preserves us from an illusory abstraction.

Now let us return to the growth process. If we have raised ourselves in the manner described to the pure, picture-free idea of growth, we can try as artists to connect this experience again with our experience of the world of colours. Having developed a selfless sense and feeling for colours, we can discover how growth and flowering, experienced in their purity, can come to life again in sensory appearance. All dark, broken colours – from black through to the many tones of brown – give us a descending weight in the space of the painting, while all shining, 'pure' colours raise us upward. Thus if a painter seeks to depict a plant motif as colour process rather than as a likeness of something outwardly perceived, he should not think of the image of a particular plant. The contrast of weight and lightness within which plant growth lives, is alive also in the colour relationships between the groups of colour described.

To put this in more tangible terms, let us describe here a possible colour sequence: we start with black, heavy in colour (though it is not *physically* heavier than any other colour!) which bears downward on the white paper. Painted in the right measure, it gives us 'ground under our feet'. If we then choose a radiant yellow, it will rise sun-like above the black and at the same time conjure a first resolution of the tension created in the interplay between black and white. If we now add a green, this enlivens the dead black, at the same time striving towards the yellow and granting it a first relationship to the darkness. A red can strengthen the light, breaking the green in the right measure and to some degree rendering it more earthly, at the same bearing warmth into the painting. Light blue gives breadth and space …

No doubt many will say in response to this little sketch: But we know all this from outward observation. Surely what I think I am depicting in terms of a pure colour process is in fact merely nature's early imprint upon me? Here, again, courage is required to trust our own inner powers of observation, similar to what we need when passing into pure thinking. …

But observation of germination, growth and blossoming does not fully encompass the life cycle of the plant. Fading and dying belong to it too. How do we find this as colour process? Assuredly there are many ways to do so. One possibility is, as already briefly suggested, to increasingly penetrate a green with red.

Here we find something like a process of lignification, of wood formation. The green slowly dies away to olive green and brown. If no wood forms, the plant remains gradually turn to humus. The wood-forming process stops short of the death process.

Let us summarise briefly: Just as an ascent to pure concepts makes knowledge possible, so developing pure perception and enlivening it in our feelings makes possible an art that at the same time becomes insight. We can gain a very great deal above and beyond ordinary science if we cultivate artistic perception and insight! In relation to natural processes, we can put it like this:

Nature processes are colour processes, and colour processes are nature processes. Once this is acknowledged we can understand Rudolf Steiner's account, drawn from anthroposophical spiritual science, of how, at a certain stage of evolution, the higher hierarchies originally gave rise to everything as beings of colour.

NOTES AND REFERENCES

1   David Wood, *Novalis. Notes for a Romantic Encyclopaedia*. State University of New York Press 2007, p. 12.

2   *Gerard Wagner – Die Kunst der Farbe*, Verlag Freies Geistesleben 1980.

3   Rudolf Steiner, 'Where and How Do We Find the Spirit? CW 57. Lecture of 6.5.1909.

4   Antique Collectors' Club, 1994.

5   Caroline Chanter, *His beloved St Ives*. Iris Books, 2012.

6   Part of the 'Foundation Stone Meditation' spoken by Rudolf Steiner on Christmas morning 1923.

7   From a biography of Hermann Lange by Ernest Lang, published in the Beyer-Peacock Quarterly Review, 1928.

8   Rudolf Steiner, *Our Connection to the Elemental World*, CW 158. Lecture 14.11.1914. p. 53/54. Rudolf Steiner Press 2016.

9   Wolfgang Schuchhardt and Herbert Rieche (eds.), *Mittel Europa. Landschaften – Völker – Kulturen*. Urachhaus, 1978.

10   Hermann Leippert, *Städtebilder und Landschaften aus aller Welt. No. 9*, München, A. Bruckmanns Verlag. Late 1880s.

11   Op. cit., see note 7.

12   *Wiesbaden Official Guide, 1903*.

13   *Gleitlager für die Welt. Glyco-Metall-Werke*. Wiesbaden-Schierstein, 1972.

14   Now 15 Uhlandstrasse.

15   From the poem 'O may I join the Choir Invisible', sometimes called simply 'The Choir Invisible' (1867) by George Eliot.

16   From the prose poem 'The Spanish Gypsy' (1868) by George Eliot.

17   From 'The Ladder of St Augustine' by Henry Wadsworth Longfellow, 1807–1882.

18   George Frederic Watts. British painter and sculptor, 23 February 1817 1 July 1904. He was associated with the Symbolist movement and painted many allegorical works of Hope, Love, Death, Destiny etc. These were intended to form part of an epic symbolic cycle called 'The House of Life', in which the emotions and aspirations of life would all be represented in a universal symbolic language. He conceived his vision of a building covered with murals representing the spiritual and social evolution of humanity. In 1843–1847 he visited Italy and was inspired by the Sistine Chapel and Giotto's Scrovegni Chapel. He also took a short trip back to Italy in 1853 and visited Venice, where 'Titian became even more of an inspiration'.

     Watts wrote: 'I paint ideas, not things. My intention is less to paint works that are pleasing to the eye than to suggest great thoughts, which will speak to the imagination and the heart and will arouse all that is noblest and best in man.' (*George Frederic Watts –The Complete Works*, https://www.georgefredericwatts.org.)

     Some of Watts' paintings were on display at the 'Munich Congress' of 1907. In

Rosicrucianism Renewed, CW 284, SteinerBooks 2007, Mathilde Scholl writes that amongst the various works of art exhibited at the Congress were reproductions of paintings by G. F. Watts. ('The Congress in Munich', Mathilde Scholl, p. 136.)

A further interesting fact came to light through the architect Rex Raab. In a letter to the author of 9 January 2002 he wrote: 'As regards the possibility of two painter-lives following fairly rapidly (with only one life in between) I can contribute something of interest. Margarita Woloschin, whom I had the great pleasure of knowing quite well, told me that Steiner had told her that Titian reappeared in the 19th century as the English painter and sculptor, G. F. Watts. Think: Titian, the Venetian colourist, and then G. F. Watts, with his "Hope", with its hopeless mood! Yet this is so revealing for us in England. It confirms that strong bond of the Venetians and not only Watts, but then Turner, Ruskin, Rossetti and others.'

19   Fr. L. C. Frhr. v. Médem, *Wiesbaden,* 1880.

20   Rudolf Steiner, *Architektur, Plastik und Malerei des ersten Goetheanum.* GA 288. Lecture of 25.1.1920. Rudolf Steiner Verlag, 2016, p.73.

21   Rudolf Steiner, *Colour* CW 291. Lecture 9.6.1923: 'Spirit and Non-Spirit in Painting'. Rudolf Steiner Press, London 2012, p. 160.

22   Rudolf Steiner, GA 206. *Menschenwerden, Weltenseele und Weltengeist.* Lecture of 12.8.1921. Rudolf Steiner Verlag 2019, p. 118.

23   *"… nicht nur ein gebogenes Stück Blech!" Ein Lesebuch zur Firmengeschichte.* Published by Federal-Mogul-Wiesbaden GmbH &Co.KG. Verlag für regionale Kultur und Geschichte, 2005.

After Max Wagner's death the company continued to develop and in 1917 Glyco was the largest specialist factory in Germany for assembled plain bearings; in 1937 it became the largest friction bearing supplier in Germany; in 1974 the largest friction bearing supplier in Europe. In 1990 Federal-Mogul Corporation USA acquired the company, now called Federal-Mogul Wiesbaden. It remains on the same site where Max Wagner began it. A history of the firm records: 'Max Wagner left behind an undertaking that withstood all ups and downs. It did not make the owners wealthy but in specialist circles it made a name for itself.'

24   Excerpts from Max Wagner's letters and helpful information was kindly supplied by Herr Ekkehard Kurz, Verein ehemaliger Mitarbeiter und Mitarbeiterinnen der Firma Federal-Mogul/Glyco e.V.

25   Rudolf Steiner, CW 291, lecture of 26.7.1914: 'The Creative World of Colour' in *Colour* by Rudolf Steiner, p.76. Rudolf Steiner Press, London 2012.

26   Rudolf Steiner, GA 168. *Die Verbindung zwischen Lebenden und Toten,* lecture of 16.2.1916. 'Das Leben zwischen Tod und neuer Geburt'. p. 18. 1968 edition.

Similarly, Rudolf Steiner described how the quality of an intense colour experience is related to Imaginations experienced in a higher state of consciousness:

The red colour appears to one also in the spiritual world but it is not anything material – behind the red is a spiritual soul being – behind the red is the same as that which you feel within your soul. In the world of Imaginations in the spiritual world, colours are experiences – the red, the blue are experiences. One can call these experiences red or blue but they are quite different from the sense impressions of the physical world; they are much more inward and we are much more inwardly connected with them. When seeing the red of the rose you are outside it; in the red colour of the spiritual world you feel yourself within it. When perceiving the colour red in the spiritual world, 'will' develops, a strong effective will of a spiritual being. And this 'will' radiates and that which radiates is red. But you feel yourself inside the will, and this feeling of being within it, this experience one calls 'red'. The physical colour is like the frozen spiritual experience, like a condensed spiritual experience.

In GA 159/160, 1980. *Das Geheimnis des Todes,* lecture of 17.6.1915. 'Erfahrungen des Menschen nach dem Durchgang durch die Todespforte', p. 322.

27   *Gerard Wagner – Die Kunst der Farbe,* op. cit.

28   Ibid.

29   From Witali Kovalenko's film *Die Malstunde* ('The Painting Lesson'), Dornach 1995.

30   Eleanor C. Merry, *My Meeting with Rudolf Steiner. A Testimony to the Spiritual Guidance of Destiny.* Typescript kindly provided by Thomas Meyer.

31   Rudolf Steiner, *Our Connection with the Elemental World.* Lecture 15, November 1914. CW 158, Rudolf Steiner Press 2016, p. 80.

32   Girolama Savonarola, Dominican friar and preacher 1452–1498. Gerard Wagner had an art card portrait of Savonarola which he showed to the author. The figure of Savonarola clearly had much importance for him through his deep interest in the chief Renaissance painters, particularly Raphael and the sequence of his incarnations as given by Rudolf Steiner in his last address on 28 September 1924 (CW 238). Rudolf Steiner wrote about Savonarola on a number of occasions, comparing him with the gentle and obliging painter Raphael. In CW 62 (*The Mission of Raphael in the Light of Spiritual Science,* lecture 4, 30.1.1913) he described how the:

… stormy words of Savonarola reverberate in us if we give ourselves over to them; words with which he captivated all of Florence, so that people not only hung on every word, but worshipped him as though a higher spirit stood before them in that ascetic body. As a kind of religious reformer Savonarola had transformed the city of Florence. His preachings pervaded not only religious ideas, but the entire city-state. Florence stood wholly under the influence of Savonarola, as though a divine republic of some sort were to be founded. And we then see Savonarola fall prey to the powers he had spoken out against, morally and religiously. The moving scene arises of Savonarola being led with his companions to the martyr's pyre. From the gallows he turned to look down upon the people gathered there, who had for so long been enthralled by him, having once hung on his every word. This was in May of the year 1498. Having now forsaken him, they viewed him as a heretic. However, in a few among them, including artists, the words of Savonarola still echoed on.

And in CW 292 (*Art History as a Reflection of Inner Spiritual Impulses,* lecture of 1.11.1916, Steiner Books, 2016, p. 43), he writes:

… To this list, we also have to add Michelangelo's experience of the change that happened in Florence with the appearance of Savonarola, which triggered a protest in church life against something entirely characteristic of Christianity at that time. The freedom enjoyed by the arts that came about with Leonardo, and many others like him, could only develop by elevating Christian ideas that had come about through the Mystery of Golgotha, above their moral aspect: the ideas of the Trinity, the Last Supper, the connection of the earthly and the supersensible, and so on. When lifted out of the moral sphere, these conceptions had taken on an imaginative character, a free imaginative character, which resulted in their works of art being more worldly, more earthly, but with the inclusion of the holy figures. It had been rendered objective, distinct from the moral aspect. So it was that Christian ideas, separated from their moral conception, drifted over into the purely artistic realm. It was an entirely natural transition; but involved the casting off of the moral aspect. Savonarola is the great protester against this stripping away of the moral aspect. Savonarola introduced the protest of morality against the moral-free (I do not say *immoral*, but *moral-free*) art.

33   Austin Wormleighton, *Morning Tide. John Anthony Park and the Painters of Light. St Ives 1900–1950.* Stockbridge Books, 1998.

34   Quoted in David Tovey, *Creating a Splash*, Wilson Books, 2009.

35   *Gerard Wagner – Die Kunst der Farbe* ('Gerard Wagner – The Art of Colour'), op. cit.

36   David Tovey, *St Ives (1860–1930) The Artists and the Community – A Social History*, Wilson Books 2009. For further accounts of the St Ives Art Colony, see: Marion Whybrow, *St Ives, 1883–1993, Portrait of an Art Colony*, Antique Collectors' Club, 1994; Austin Wormleighton, *A Painter Laureate – Lamorna Birch and his Circle.* Sansom & Company, Bristol, 1995; David Tovey, *Sea Change. Fine and Decorative Art in St Ives 1914–1930.* Wilson Books, 2010.

37   Florian Roder, *Der Mondknoten im Lebenslauf.* Verlag Freies Geistesleben, 2007.

38   Rudolf Steiner, quoted in Crispian Villeneuve, *Rudolf Steiner in Britain.* Vol II. Temple Lodge 2004, p. 1112.

39   Crispian Villeneuve, *Rudolf Steiner in Britain*, Vol II. Temple Lodge, 2004. p. 939.

40   Marie Steiner, 'Rudolf Steiners Lehrtätigkeit in England' in *Das Goetheanum*, 2.1.1927. Translated by Johanna Collis, 2017.

41   See note 35, op. cit., p. 962.

42   Ibid. p. 714.

43   Ibid. p. 1062, as reported by Marie Savitch.

44   Extract from *The Concise Dictionary of National Biography*, Oxford University Press 1992: Sir William Rothenstein (1872–1945) Painter, and Principal of Royal College of Art; educ. at Bradford Grammar School; studied at Slade School and Académie Julian, Paris; executed remarkable series of portrait drawings and lithographs; professor of civic art, Sheffield 1917–26; principal, Royal College of Art, 1920–35; trustee, Tate Gallery, 1927–33; member, Royal Fine Art Commission, 1931–38; liberal-minded protagonist of the artist in society; published memoirs in 3 volumes; knighted 1931.

45   *Gerard Wagner – Die Kunst der Farbe* ('Gerard Wagner – The Art of Colour'), op. cit.

46   The subjects for the tapestries were chosen by Pope Leo X, the Medici Pope. He selected themes connected with the history of the early church, specifically episodes in the life of St Peter and St Paul. The motifs of these monumental works of art (the smallest painting measures 3×4 m.) are: *The Miraculous Draught of Fishes, Christ's*

Charge to Peter, The Healing of the Lame Man by St Peter and John, The Death of Ananias, The Blinding of Elymas, The Sacrifice at Lystra, St Paul Preaching at Athens. The cartoons of three subjects – *The Conversion of St Paul, St Paul in Prison* and *The Stoning of St Stephen* – have not been preserved. See: Graham Reynolds, 'Raphael Cartoons', Victoria and Albert Museum, London 1974.

47 Albert Steffen (1884–1963), poet, painter, dramatist, essayist, novelist. Member of the executive council of the Anthroposophical Society at the Goetheanum and from 1925 its chairman.

48 Rex Raab, 'Hookway Cowles – Brush Strokes by a Grateful Friend', obituary for the Anthroposophical Society in GB newsletter, November 1987.

49 Bernard Crompton-Smith, 'The "English Week" at Dornach. August 1926' in *Das Goetheanum,* August 1926.

50 *Gerard Wagner – Die Kunst der Farbe* ('Gerard Wagner – The Art of Colour'), op. cit.

51 Article published in *Anthroposophy*, 1923.

52 Erika von Baravalle, 'Die Baugestalt des zweiten Goetheanums als Michaelbotschaft', in *Was in der Anthroposophische Gesellschaft vorgeht* (anthroposophical newsletter), 7.7.2006.

53 Albert von Baravalle, 'Das Baumotiv des 2. Goetheanum', in: *Das Goetheanum* 1952, no. 12.

54 Henni Geck (1884–1951), German painter who had an academic art training in Berlin, Düsseldorf and Munich. In 1914 she moved to Dornach to help with the artistic work on the first Goetheanum building. See: Peter Stebbing (editor and translator), *Conversations about Painting with Rudolf Steiner,* SteinerBooks, 2008.

55 Walter Roggenkamp, 'Henni Geck. Malerisches gestalten aus Bildkeimen', in *Die Drei* July/August 1989.

56 *Gerard Wagner – Die Kunst der Farbe* ('Gerard Wagner – The Art of Colour'), op. cit.

57 Ibid.

58 Gerard Wagner described the tragedy that led to the closure of the painting school, as far as he could remember it, to Ernst Schuberth in an interview on 29 September 1979:
The Mystery Plays were being rehearsed inside the building and the stage sets made. Frl. Geck was always there during the rehearsals as she painted the programmes for the artistic performances, and she saw the scenery for the Sun Temple Scene of the first Mystery Play painted by Scott Pyle and Mrs Pyle. It was a kind of replica of the first Goetheanum stage with the columns and architrave made of board, a painted copy of the group statue and above it the cupola painting. Frl. Geck then wrote a very critical letter to Marie Steiner, which she got her students to sign. This all took place shortly before the 1929 General Meeting of the Anthroposophical Society which then consisted almost entirely of this event. The painters complained bitterly about Henni Geck and there was, anyway, a rather bad feeling towards her because of her reluctance to show others, who asked to see them, the sketches and watercolours that Rudolf Steiner had done for her. She always maintained that she needed the sketches for her work and had no time. It happened then that during the General Meeting, or

soon after it, Dubach, Kemper, Pozzo and Roman Boos came into the studio and took all the sketches away from her. One pupil was present in the studio, Herr Becher, the oldest pupil at the school, a very nice person and a friend of mine. He told me afterwards what had happened. One of those men stayed close by Frl. Geck the whole time as they thought she could destroy the pictures rather than have them taken from her. That was the end of the school, of course, and for a long time Frl. Geck did not set foot in the Goetheanum. That was the tragic event.

59 In *What is happening in the Anthroposophical Society. News for Members*, 21 April 1929: 'Resolution of the General Meeting of 6 April 1929 regarding the motion of 5 April. The General Meeting asks Frau Dr Steiner, in her role as Executor of Dr Steiner's artistic legacy, to see also that the sketches carried out by Dr Steiner, which are currently administered by Fraülein Geck, be made available in an appropriate manner for artistic strivings within the Anthroposophical Society.'

60 *Gerard Wagner – Die Kunst der Farbe* ('Gerard Wagner – The Art of Colour'), op. cit.

61 Ilja Duwan, born 10.12.1898 in Kiev; studied acting and painting; fled to the West during the Russian Revolution; in Berlin he met Marie Steiner. He came to Dornach a few weeks after Rudolf Steiner's death and decided to commit his life to anthroposophy and to the work of Marie Steiner. For seven years, from 1928 to 1934, he played the role of Johannes Thomasius in the Mystery Dramas. From 1940 he and his wife Ida Duwan (Nater) built up their own initiative in Bern. Ilja Duwan died 14/15 March 1976. See: Walter Rudolf Hausammann, *Ilja Duwan, Wichtige Lebensabschnitte und Motive aus seinem künstlerischen Schaffen*. Private publication by the Pflegestätte für musische Künste, Bern 1988. Edwin Froböse, also a pupil of Marie Steiner's, wrote of Ilja Duvan: 'Through Duwan a new element entered our group. For him movement was the natural expression of his strong dramatic talent. Through gesture he sought the way into language, and after uncompromising labour, and in a relatively short space of time, he found his way into the spirit of the German language.' In Edwin Froböse (1900 -1997), *Mein Weg zur Goetheanum-Bühne*, Stuttgart 1979.

62 Ernst Schuberth and Gerard Wagner in conversation, 29.9.1979.

63 See: *Marie Steiner-von Sivers. Ihr Weg zur Erneuerung der Bühnenkunst.* Rudolf Steiner-Nachlassverwaltung, 1973.

Premières included Rudolf Steiner's Four Mystery Plays:

1928 *The Portal of Initiation*

1928 *The Soul's Probation*

1929 *The Guardian of the Threshold*

1930 *The Soul's Awakening*

1931 *Pandora* by Johann Wolfgang von Goethe

1931 *Echnaton, the Godforsaken One* by A. Dubach-Donath

1933 *The Fall of the Antichrist* by Albert Steffen

1933 *Hiram and Solomon* by Albert Steffen

1935 *The Death Experience of Manes* by Albert Steffen

1935 *The Abduction of Persephone, Prelude to The Sacred Drama of Eleusis* by Edouard Schuré

1937 *Adonis*, an Autumn Festival by Albert Steffen

1937 *Faust 1* by Johan Wolfgang von Goethe, unshortened

1938 *Faust 1 & 2* by Goethe, unshortened, first complete performance Summer 1938

1939 *The Sacred Drama of Eleusis* by Edouard Schuré

1940 *Pestalozzi* by Albert Steffen

1941 *Danton und Robespierre* by Robert Hamerling

1942 *Journey to another Land* by Albert Steffen

1943 *The Bride of Messina* by Friedrich Schiller

1944 *The Maid of Orleans* by Friedrich Schiller

1945 *Mary Stuart* by Friedrich Schiller

1948 *Iphigenia* by Goethe

64 Ernst Schuberth and Gerard Wagner in conversation, 29.9.1979.

65 Ernst Uehli, *Das Albert Steffen Buch*, Verlag Birkhäuser, Basel 1944. Uehli (1875–1959), was a prominent anthroposophist, art historian, teacher, and colleague of Rudolf Steiner.

66 Albert Steffen, *Begegnungen mit Rudolf Steiner*, Verlag für Schöne Wissenschaften, Dornach 1975; 'Aus Rudolf Steiners letztem Lebensjahr', p. 354.

67 Novalis, *Die Lehrlinge zu Sais*. Gedichte und Fragmente, Reclam 1969.

68 Rudolf Steiner, *Vergangenheits- und Zukunftsimpulse im sozialen Geschehen*. Lecture of 6 April 1919, GA 190. Rudolf Steiner Verlag 1980, p. 140.

69 Gerard Wagner, *Die Kunst der Farbe* ('The Art of Colour'), op. cit.

70 Typescript 2001.

71 This was the General Meeting of the Anthroposophical Society during which Dr Ita Wegman and Elisabeth Vreede were expelled from the Anthroposophical Society.

72 Gennady Bondarev, 'The Icon and the New Impulse in Painting. Gerard Wagner – Painter and Anthroposophist – Early Work'. Article in *Stil*, 1996/97. Translated (2000) from German by Johanna Collis with a few amendments by Simon Blaxland de Lange after comparing the English version with the original Russian.

73 *What is happening in the Anthroposophical Society. News for Members*, 10 August 1941.

74 Ibid. 1 Feb. 1942.

75 Ibid. 14 May 1944.

76 The Tuesday evenings could refer to Gerard Wagner's continual study of Rudolf Steiner's artistic impulses. An announcement in *Das Goetheanum* in 1941 advertises 'Sculpture classes in the joinery workshop on Tuesday evenings'. In 1929 a sculpture course had likewise taken place on Tuesday evenings, accompanied by Steiner lectures and slides 'relating to the sculptural problems of the First Goetheanum and the new sculpture and architecture arising out of anthroposophy'.

77 Martha Reimann-Zürcher, 1898–1978, who wrote the poem below, published in an anthology of her work *Stufengang*, 1937.

Oh if only we might learn anew
to understand the language of the dead –
we would not flit so haphazardly
and whirr and err.

Their gaze delves deep and gravely searches,
they smile a yes – they murmur a no
to all our thoughts and striving.

If in wakefulness you first
offer up your aims to their gaze, you can learn
to weigh things up in their light.

Whether what you intend will have
good, or fleeting or even evil outcomes,
their gaze will not prohibit you from acting; but

their knowledge-dispensing light
will make you free
to ponder on what your will is striving for.

78   Rex Raab, 'Impressions of Gerard Wagner', 2002. (The wall painting referred to is known as the 'Allgeyer' picture, and was painted in a private house in Stuttgart in 1956/57).

79   Florian Roder, *Die Mondknoten im Lebenslauf,* op. cit.

80   Arild Rosenkranz, *A New Impulse in Art* ('Recollections of an Unusual Artist' by Gladys Mayer), New Knowledge Books 1967.

81   Arild Rosenkranz, *A New Impulse in Art,* op. cit.

82   Eleanor C. Merry, *Life Story – An Autobiographical Experience of Destiny,* Mercury Arts Publication, 1987.

83   Gladys Mayer, 'The Initiate and the Teacher', *The Golden Blade* 1959.

84   August Waterbeck, German sculptor: born 1875 in Amelsbüren, Münster. From 1893–1896 he trained as woodcarver in a workshop for ecclesiastical art in Wiedenbrück. From 1897–1902 he studied with Edmund von Hellmer in Vienna. From 1903, worked as freelance sculptor in Hannover. Died 1947 in Hannover. (Wikipedia)

85   Theodor Willmann, 'Schlaf und Tod' ('Sleep and Death') in *Gerard Wagner – Die Kunst der Farbe* ('The Art of Colour'), op. cit.

86   Rudolf Steiner, *Study of Man.* CW 293. Lecture 9 of 30.8.1919, Rudolf Steiner Press 1966.

87   In *50 Jahre Haus Arild*, Haus Arild 1999.

88   Conversation between Ernst Schuberth and Gerard Wagner, 16.10.1979.

89   *Gerard Wagner – Die Kunst der Farbe.* ('Gerard Wagner – The Art of Colour'), op. cit.

90   Florian Roder, *Die Mondknoten im Lebenslauf,* op. cit.

91   Martin Schmidt (1892 –1964) was a farmer active within the biodyamic movement, in which he played a significant role. He was present at the Agriculture Course given by Rudolf Steiner in 1924. His specialist area of plant research focused on the cultivation of rye.

92   Ernst Schuberth, 'Gerard Wagner – Ein Leben im Dienst der Farbe' in *Das Goetheaanum* 19.12.1999, no. 51/52. Translated by Johanna Collis.

93   In: *Gerard Wagner, Die Kunst der Farbe* ('The Art of Colour'), op. cit. 'Lehre der "göttlichen" Natura' ('Teachings of the "goddess" Natura')

94   Lecture of 28.10.1909.CW 271.

95   Georg Nemes (architect) 1900–1978.

96   In *Tagesanzeiger Zürich*, Saturday 6 December 1969: 'Das Neue Buch – Blick auf an-
     throposophische Literatur aus dem Philosophisch-Anthroposophischen Verlag am
     Goetheanum.'

97   'Plant Metamorphosis' in the essay 'Gerard Wagner's Contribution to the Art of Paint-
     ing' by Michael Howard, November 1976 and reworked May 2019.

98   Rudolf Steiner, *Wesen und Bedeutung der illustrativen Kunst* ('Illustrative Art – its Es-
     sence and Meaning'), two Lectures held in Dornach on 3.12.1917 and 15.1.1918. Sektion
     für Redende und Musische Künste am Goetheanum, 1940.

99   Van James, painter, author, art teacher and lecturer, General Secretary of the Anthro-
     posophical Society in Hawaii.

100 *Unpublished article, 1970s.*

101 The first annual meeting to form the Foundation took place on 28 November 1986.
     Additional board members – Peter Stebbing, Gail McManus, Geraldine Winter, Alex-
     ander Winter and Hans Schumm –were welcomed, and the articles formulated by Ted
     Ormiston and Peter Sagal were read out. 1 July 1987 was the official documented date
     of the founding of the Gerard Wagner Foundation Inc. as a not-for-profit corporation.
     After the death of Ted Ormiston on 9 March 1998, Peter Sagal and Hans Schumm be-
     came the chief co-workers and directors of the Foundation.

102 From documentation provided by Peter Sagal and Hans Schumm.

103 Rolf-Magnus Adler, 1922–1995; Elisabeth Adler (née Maaßen), 1925–2014. In 1960
     Rolf and Elisabeth Adler left the Engelberg School and turned to private curative edu-
     cation work. Their interest in handwork developed further with the help of Ilse Molly,
     with whom they worked in Freiburg making children's smocks; and from her they
     learnt basic dressmaking patterns. They were invited to join a 'clothing group' in Un-
     terlengenhardt which included the physicians Dr Renzenbrink and DrBühler, textile
     producers Assmus, Hess and Cloos, and other teachers and artists.
         Regular sessions at Lauffenmühle curative home gave the Adlers an opportunity
     to work with people with special needs and with young people. Contact with the kin-
     dergarten movement, through E. Kraft (at Uhlandshöhe) and Freya Jaffke (in Reutlin-
     gen), led them to the annual international kindergarten conference in Hannover, in
     which they took a leading part for 20 years, up to 1996. They also gave courses for
     teachers and parents. In Freya Jaffke's workbook for the kindergarten movement on
     sewing, embroidery and dressmaking for children and adults (*Handarbeit. Nähen,
     Sticken, Schneidern für Erwachsene und Kinder,* Verlag Freies Geistesleben, 1996), the
     work of Rolf and Elisabeth Adler is well represented.

104 See *Artistic Handwork Based on Instructions and Designs by Rudolf Steiner* by Louise
     van Blommestein, Philosophisch-Anthroposophischer Verlag am Goetheanum, Dor-
     nach 1934. Translated by Matthew Barton 2019.

105 From Gladys Mayer, 'The Rhythm of Seven' in *Mercury Arts Group Newsletter* no. 62,
     Whitsun 1977.

106 Florian Roder, 'Novalis – Die Verwandling des Menschen', in *Mystischer Gebrauch der Farbe*, Urachhaus 2000.

107 Georg Glöckler, in *Die Drei. Zeitschrift für Wissenschaft, Kunst und soziales Leben* 1980/1981. The book appeared in German as *Die Individualität der Farbe*, Freies Geistesleben, 1980; and in English as *The Individuality of Colour*, Rudolf Steiner Press, 1980.

108 For Rudolf Steiner's suggestions for the appropriate colours for the different classes 1–12, see Andreas Mäckler, *Anthroposophie und Malerei* ('Anthroposophy and Painting'), Dumont 1990, p. 84.

109 Maria-Clara Eriksson, 'Wandmalerei im 'Atelierhaus in Dornach' in *Das Goetheanum* · 1986.

110 In *Was in der Anthroposophische Gesellschaft vorgeht* (anthroposophical newsletter), March-April, 1987.

111 Dr Margarethe Hauschka, 1896–1980. A survey of her life by Irmgard Marbach was published in *Heilende Malerei. Dokumentation zum 100. Geburtstag der Maltherapeutin Dr Margarethe Hauschka*, M. Hauschka Schule, Boll über Göppingen, 1996.

112 Extract from Dr Hans-Bernhard Andrae, 'Gerard Wagner in Unterlengenhardt. Painting and Teaching. The Path to an Artistic Therapy', typescript 1988.

113 Assja Turgenieff, *Erinnerungen an Rudolf Steiner und die Arbeit am ersten Goetheanum*. Verlag Freies Geistesleben, 1972, p. 97.

114 Rudolf Steiner, *Colour*, CW 291, Rudolf Steiner 2012, p. 140: 'The two Fundamental Laws of Colour Theory in Sunrise and Sunset and the Blue Sky. Health and Illness in relation to the Theory of Colour'. Lecture of 21.2.1923.

115 Extract from Dr Hans-Bernhard Andrae, 'Gerard Wagner in Unterlengenhardt. Painting and Teaching. The Path to an Artistic Therapy', op. cit. In 2004, the wall paintings were destroyed during renovation works at the hospital. Heilgart Umfrid who had accompanied every moment of their creation, and documented the whole process*, was deeply affected. She recalled: 'In 1993 Dr Andrae and I were both pensioned off from the hospital. Our further-training courses continued but we had to witness the destruction of the dining-room wall painting because of renovation work. That was a shock, and incomprehensible for many people.' *Heilgart Umfrid's documentation is available to order from the Rudolf Steiner painting school, Atelierhaus, Brosiweg 41, CH–4143 Dornach, Switzerland.

116 From Eve Ratnowsky, 'Ausstellung im Haus Ganna', *Goetheanum Wochenschrift*, July 1993. Translated by Johanna Collis.

117 Ernst Schuberth, 'Gerard Wagner – A Life in the Service of Colour', excerpt from an article published in *Das Goetheanum* no. 51/52, 19.12.1999, translated by Johanna Collis.

118 Published in English as *Colour*, op. cit.

119 Christian Hitsch (for the Executive Council and Section Leaders at the Goetheanum), 'For Gerard Wagner in Honour of his 90th Birthday on 5 April 1996', published in *Das Goetheanum*, April 1996.

120 In: Rudolf Steiner, *Architektur, Plastik und Malerei des Ersten Goetheanum*, Dornach 1972.

121 Walter Steffen, 'Impressions of the Gerard Wagner Jubilee Exhibition in the Goetheanum' in: *Das Goetheanum*, July 1996, translated by Johanna Collis.

122 See Peter Stebbing, 'About the Painter Gerard Wagner' in: Elisabeth Wagner-Koch / Gerard Wagner, *The Individuality of Colour*, Rudolf Steiner Press 2009.

123 Rudolf Steiner, *The Challenge of the Times*, CW 186. Lecture of 8.12.1918: 'The Innate Capacities of the Nations of the World.' US Rudolf Steiner online Archive.

124 In the Gerard and Elisabeth Wagner Association newsletter, 2019.

125 Andrea Hitsch, 'Der Meister in der Blauen Kittel', translated by Caroline Chanter.

126 Published in: *Was in der Anthroposophische Gesellschaft vorgeht* (anthroposophical newsletter), no. 51/52, 19 December 1999.

127 Torsten Steen, 'A spirit-born painter. A pupil's expression of thanks' in: *Was in der Anthroposophische Gesellschaft vorgeht* (anthroposophical newsletter), no. 51/52, 19 December 1999. Translated by Matthew Barton.

128 Rudolf Steiner, CW 260, lecture of 25 December 1923.

129 Sergei O. Prokofieff, 'This is how it would like to become' in: *Was in der Anthroposophische Gesellschaft vorgeht* (anthroposophical newsletter), 19 December 1999. Translated by Christopher Cooper and Caroline Chanter.

130 Christian Hitsch, 'Leben mit den Farben-Schöpferwesen. Gedenken an Gerard Wagner. Eine persönlich-überpersönliche Erinnerung' in: *Was in der Anthroposophischen Gesellschaft vorgeht* (anthroposophical newsletter) no. 51/52, 19. December 1999. Translated by Christopher Cooper.

131 David Wood, *Notes for a Romantic Encyclopaedia*. State University of New York Press 2007, p. 180.

132 Lectures given 6–8 May 1921, published in *Colour*, CW 291, op. cit. Albert Steffen attended the three lectures given in Dornach in May 1921, and wrote a résumé of each one. In a lecture of 2 June 1923, Steiner said of Steffen's résumés: '... I should first like to recommend that you look again at what I once said here about the world of colour, which Albert Steffen has rendered so well that it reads better than the original. It can be read in the periodical *Das Goetheanum*.'

   Albert Steffen's résumés are to be found in his book *Geist Erwachen im Farben Erleben*, Verlag für Schöne Wissenschaften, Dornach 1968. An English translation by Caroline Chanter is available from the Rudolf Steiner Painting School, Dornach.

133 Rudolf Steiner, lectures of 6–8 May 1921 in *Colour*. CW 291, p. 26, op. cit.

134 Ibid. p. 35.

135 See Elisabeth Wagner-Koch and Gerard Wagner, *The Individuality of Colour*, Rudolf Steiner Press, 2009.

136 Rudolf Steiner, *Colour*. CW 291, op. cit., lecture of 9 June 1923, Dornach: 'Spirit and Non-Spirit in Painting', p. 163.

137 Dr Margarethe Hauschka, *Fundamentals of Artistic Therapy*, Rudolf Steiner Press. 1985. Chapter 4: 'Indications for Therapeutic Treatment'.

138 Rudolf Steiner, *Farbenerkenntnis*, GA 291a. Rudolf Steiner Verlag 1990, p. 403.

139 Gerard Wagner, *Animal Metamorphosis*. Philosophisch-Anthroposophischer Verlag, Dornach, 1972.

140 Rudolf Steiner, *Colour,* CW 291. p. 150, op. cit.

141 Rudolf Steiner, *Art as Seen in the Light of Mystery Wisdom,* CW 275, lecture of 29.12.1914: 'Impulses of Transformation for Man's Artistic Evolution'. Rudolf Steiner Press 1984, p. 36.

142 Rudolf Steiner, *Colour,* CW 291, op. cit., lecture of 26 July 1914, 'The Creative World of Colour', p. 73.

143 Gerard Wagner, *Animal Metamorphosis,* op. cit.

144 The 'next future' refers to the remaining years of the present fifth post-Atlantean epoch that began in 1413 and will end in 3573. Each post-Atlantean cultural epoch lasts 2160 years.

145 Rudolf Steiner, *Art as Seen in the Light of Mystery Wisdom,* CW 275, op. cit., lecture of 28.12.1914: 'Technology and Art', p. 29.

146 See *Rudolf Steiner – Das Malerische Werk,* Rudolf Steiner Verlag 2007, GA 13 – 16/52 – 56.

147 David Wood, *Novalis. Notes for a Romantic Encyclopaedia,* op. cit., p. 42.

148 Lory Maier-Smits, 'Erste Lebenskeime der Eurythmie' in: *Erinnerungen an Rudolf Steiner,* Verlag Freies Geistesleben 2001.

149 Elisabeth Wagner-Koch, Gerard Wagner, *The Individuality of Colour,* op. cit., p. 67.

150 Ibid. p. 68.

151 Wilhelm Boos, 'Das Sich-Einmessen. Eine grundlegende Methode zur Werk-Erfahrung.' *Stil,* Easter 2008/2009.

152 Rudolf Steiner, *Theosophy,* CW 9, Rudolf Steiner Press 1970, p. 41.

153 See Rudolf Steiner, *From Limestone to Lucifer,* CW 349, lecture of 7 May 1923. Rudolf Steiner Press, 1999, p. 193.

154 Rudolf Steiner, *The Arts and their Mission,* CW 276, lecture 2 June 1923. Anthroposophic Press. 1964, p. 41.

155 A term relating to a new art style thought to have come from Rudolf Steiner, which has long been used in anthroposophical art circles.

156 Rudolf Steiner, *Architecture as Peacework. The First Goetheanum, Dornach 1914,* CW 287, lecture of 18.10.1914. SteinerBooks 2017.

157 Assja Turgenieff, *The Goetheanum Windows.* Rudolf Steiner Publishing Co. 1938.

158 Rudolf Steiner, *The Four Mystery Plays,* CW 14: *The Soul's Probation,* Scene 3, p. 160. Rudolf Steiner Press 1982.

159 Gerard Wagner, *A Glance into Nature's Workshop. An artistic and scientific study.* Philosophisch-Anthroposophischer Verlag 1974.

160 This and the following letter translated from the German by Caroline Chanter.

161 The process is not brought to a conclusion and so the 'last step', the achievement of full consciousness of the 'whole human being', is not yet described. Further colours would be needed for that. However the first few steps Wagner describes can give an idea of the whole procedure, and of how exactly he follows the painting process consciously.

162 Rudolf Steiner extended the original ten categories of Aristotle to twelve categories. See *Human and Cosmic Thought,* CW 151. In the workbook *The Individuality of Colour,* the twelve categories are described further in relation to the painting process.

163 Rudolf Steiner, *Colour*, CW 291, op. cit. The lecture 'Measure, Weight and Number' of 29.7.1923, p. 178. This lecture was given as lecture 3 of the cycle *Initiation Science* (CW 228) which addresses the science of spiritual knowledge.

164 *Gerard Wagner – Die Kunst der Farbe*, op. cit.

165 Translated by Caroline Chanter.

166 Rudolf Steiner, *Art as Seen in the Light of Mystery Wisdom*, op. cit.

167 Letter from Walter Kapfhammer to the author on 14.3.2019. Translated by Caroline Chanter.

168 Rudolf Steiner, *The Michael Mystery*, Anthroposophical Publishing Company 1956, p. 11.

169 From a biography of Hermann Lange by Ernest Lang, published in the Beyer-Peacock Quarterly Review, 1928.

170 Stephanie Napoleon, Grand Duchess of Baden, 28 August 1789, Versailles – 29 January 1860 Nizza.

171 My enquiries at the Karlsruhe Landesarchiv, and research by an independent expert, have found no record of Stephan Mayerhöfer at Bruchsal. Further research is still needed to discover if his first workplace was indeed Mannheim, where Stephanie Beauharnais lived. There could have been confusion in the family over Bruchsal which was the home of Stephanie Beauharnais's mother-in-law, Grand Duchess Amelie. Research has also shown that Stephanie Beauharnais was not one of the officially recorded godparents of Stephanie Lange. In any event, it is very interesting that a thread connects Gerard Wagner to Caspar Hauser through his great-grandfather Stephan Mayerhoffer. The events surrounding Caspar Hauser's destiny at that time must have been known about and talked about amongst the employees of the House of Baden and in connecting family circles.

172 Op. cit., see note 7.

173 Rudolf Steiner, *Rosicrucianism Renewed*, CW 284. SteinerBooks 2007, p. 25.

174 Rudolf Steiner, address on the occasion of the laying of the Foundation Stone for the Rosicrucian Temple of the 'Francis of Assisi' Lodge at Malsch, 5/6 April 1909. In *Rosicrucianism Renewed*, CW 284. SteinerBooks 2007, p. 144.

BIBLIOGRAPHY

Rudolf Steiner: *Nature's Open Secret. Introduction to Goethe's Scientific Writings*, CW 1, 2000, Anthroposophic Press

Rudolf Steiner: *Artistic Sensitivity as Spiritual Approach to Knowing Life and the World*, CW 161, Rudolf Steiner Press

Rudolf Steiner: *Connection between the Living and the Dead*, CW 168, 2017, Rudolf Steiner Press

Rudolf Steiner: *Spirit as Sculptor of the Human Organism*, CW 218, Rudolf Steiner Press

Rudolf Steiner: *Kunst und Kunsterkenntnis*, GA 271, Rudolf Steiner Verlag

Rudolf Steiner: *Art as seen in the Light of Mystery Wisdom*, CW 275, Rudolf Steiner Press

Rudolf Steiner: *The Arts and their Mission*, CW 276, Rudolf Steiner Press

Rudolf Steiner: *Rosicrucianism Renewed, The Theosophical Congress of Whitsun 1907*, CW 284, 2007, SteinerBooks

Rudolf Steiner: *Architecture as Peacework. The First Goetheanum*, Dornach, 1914, CW 287, 2017, SteinerBooks

Rudolf Steiner (Ed. Christian Thal-Jantzen): *Architecture as a Synthesis of the Arts*, CW 286, 1999, Rudolf Steiner Press

Rudolf Steiner: *Architecture, Sculpture, and Painting of the First Goetheanum*, CW 288, 2017, SteinerBooks

Rudolf Steiner: *Colour*, CW 291, Rudolf Steiner Press

Rudolf Steiner: *Farbenerkenntnis*, GA 291a, Rudolf Steiner Verlag

Rudolf Steiner: *Art History as a Reflection of Inner Spiritual Impulses*, CW 292, 2016, SteinerBooks

Rudolf Steiner: *Wandtafelzeichnungen zum Vortragswerk* XVIII, GA K 58/18, Rudolf Steiner Verlag

Rudolf Steiner: *Das Malerische Werk*, GA K 13–16/52–56, 2007, Rudolf Steiner Verlag

*

Andrei Belyi, Assya Turgenieff, Margarita Voloschin: *Reminiscences of Rudolf Steiner*, 1987, Adonis Press

Caroline Chanter: *His Beloved St Ives. The Painter Gerard Wagner at the Cornish Art Colony 1924–1925*, 2012, Iris Books (out of print)

Fant/ Klingborg/ Wilkes: *Rudolf Steiner's Sculpture*, 1975, Rudolf Steiner Press

John Fletcher: *Art Inspired by Rudolf Steiner*, 1987, Mercury Arts Publication

Dr Margarethe Hauschka: *Fundamentals of Artistic Therapy. The Nature and Task of Painting Therapy*, Vol. 2, 1985, Rudolf Steiner Press

Dr Margarethe Hauschka-Stavenhagen: *Fundamentals of Artistic Therapy based on Spiritual Science*, Vol. 1, 2005, Mercury Press

Michael Howard: *Art as Spiritual Activity. Rudolf Steiner's Contribution to the Visual Arts*, 1998, Anthroposophic Press

Van James: *Spirit and Art. Pictures of the Transformation of Consciousness*, 2001, Anthroposophic Press,

Van James: *Drawing with Hand, Head and Heart. A Natural Approach to Learning the Art of Drawing*, 2011, SteinerBooks

Van James: *Painting with Hand, Head and Heart. A Natural Approach to Learning the Art of Painting*, 2020, self publishing

Elisabeth Koch/K. Theodor Willmann/Gerard Wagner: *Gerard Wagner. Die Kunst der Farbe*, 1980, Verlag Freies Geistesleben
(Gerard Wagner. The Art of Colour, monograph. English translation by Katherine Rudolph: exploringtheword.com.au)

Angela Lord: *Art, Aesthetics and Colour. Aristotle – Thomas Aquinas – Rudolf Steiner*, 2018, Temple Lodge

Franz Lohri/Ernst Schuberth: *Elisabeth Wagner. Ausstellungs-Katalog, 2020*, Verlag am Goetheanum

Gladys Mayer: Colours. *A New Approach to Painting*, 1988, Rudolf Steiner Press

Gladys Mayer: *The Mystery Wisdom of Colour*, 1988, Rudolf Steiner Press

Eleanor C. Merry: *Life Story an Autobiographical experience of Destiny*, 1987, Mercury Arts Publication

Sergei O. Prokofieff: *Eternal Individuality. Towards a Karmic Biography of Novalis, 1992*, Temple Lodge

Sergei O. Prokofieff: *Relating to Rudolf Steiner and The Mystery of the Laying of the Foundation Stone*, 2008, Temple Lodge

Sergei O. Prokofieff: *Rudolf Steiner's Sculptural Group. A Revelation of the Spiritual Purpose of Humanity and the Earth*, 2013, Temple Lodge

Wilhelm Rath: *The Imagery of the Goetheanum Windows. An interpretation in verse form.* Translated by William Mann, 1976, Rudolf Steiner Press

Rex Raab: *Edith Maryon, Bildhauerin und Mitarbeiterin Rudolf Steiners*, 1993, Verlag am Goetheanum

Florian Roder: *Novalis. Die Verwandlung des Menschen, Leben und Werk Friedrich von Hardenbergs*, 2000, Urachhaus

Florian Roder: *Die Mondknoten im Lebenslauf*, 2007, Verlag Freies Geistesleben

Arild Rosenkranz: *A New Impulse in Art*, 1967, New Knowledge Books

Peter Selg: *Edith Maryon. Rudolf Steiner und die Dornacher Christus-Plastik*, 2006, Verlag am Goetheanum

Peter Selg: *The Figure of Christ. Rudolf Steiner and the spiritual intention behind the Goetheanum's Central Work of Art*, 2009, Temple Lodge

Peter Selg: *Rudolf Steiner. Life and Work, 1861–1925*, 2015–2019, SteinerBooks

Peter Selg: *Rudolf Steiners Atelier. Die letzte Lebenszeit/The Final Years* (Bilingual publication: German & English), 2019, Verlag des Ita Wegman Instituts

Martina Maria Sam: *Rudolf Steiner. Kindheit und Jugend*, 2018, Verlag am Goetheanum

Albert Steffen: *Geist-Erwachen im Farben-Erleben*, 1968, Verlag für Schöne Wissenschaften, Dornach

Peter Stebbing: *Conversations about Painting with Rudolf Steiner. Recollections of Five Pioneers of the New Art Impulse*, 2008, SteinerBooks

Peter Stebbing: *The Goetheanum Cupola Motifs of Rudolf Steiner. Paintings by Gerard Wagner*, 2011, Rudolf Steiner Press

Assya Turgeniev: *Rudolf Steiner and work on the first Goetheanum*, 2003, Temple Lodge

Assia Turgeniev: *The Goetheanum Windows with personal reminiscences of Rudolf Steiner's explanations on the theory and practice of glass engraving*, 1938, Rudolf Steiner Publishing Co. and Anthroposophic Press

Gerard Wagner: *Pflanzenmetamorphose* (Plant Metamophosis). Folder with a series of 8 prints, 1968, Philosophisch-Anthroposophischer Verlag (out of print)

Gerard Wagner: *Animal Metamorphosis*. Folder with a metamorphic series of 25 prints, 1972, Philosophisch-Anthroposophischer Verlag

Gerard Wagner: *A Glance into Nature's Workshop*. Folder with a metamorphic series of 16 pictures, 1974, Philosophisch-Anthroposophischer Verlag (out of print)

Elisabeth Wagner-Koch/Gerard Wagner: *The Individuality of Colour*, 2009, Rudolf Steiner Press (out of print)

ILLUSTRATIONS (PLATES)

3 *View of Plauen, 1850*

LINEAGE AND PARENTAGE

Plauen
Altmarkt m. Rathaus u. König Albert-Denkmal

26681

4 *Plauen, Market Place and Old Town Hall, 1908*

LINEAGE AND PARENTAGE

Johann Casper Neupert
Carpenter

Johann Friedrich Wagner
Bleacher
— Johanne Christiane Neupert

Heinrich Ludwig Gross
Weaver
— Christiane Sophie Vogel

Johann August Wagner
Tanner
9.3.1790–24.8.1842
— Sophia Magdalena

Heinrich ‹Ernst› Wagner
Weaver
6.11.1827–29.9.1896
— Christiane ‹Luise› Gross
24.3.1827–9.11.1903

Max Wagner
28.3.1860–18.2.1908

Johann Ernst Lang
1698

Joseph Mayerhöffer
Schoolteacher
— Franziska

Ernst Friedrich Lange
27.2.1809–1865
— Emilie Louise Türmnel

Johann Stephan Mayerhöffer
1800–22.11.1867
— Elizabeth Dick

Ludwig ‹Hermann› Lange
10.5.1837–14.1.1892
— Stephanie Elizabeth Mayerhöffer
1.2.1839–6.1917

Julia Lange
2.8.1868–27.2.1952

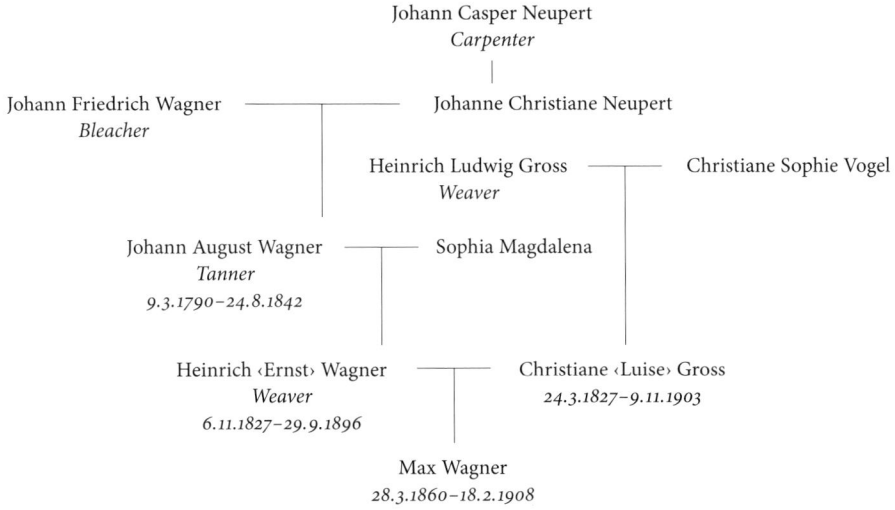

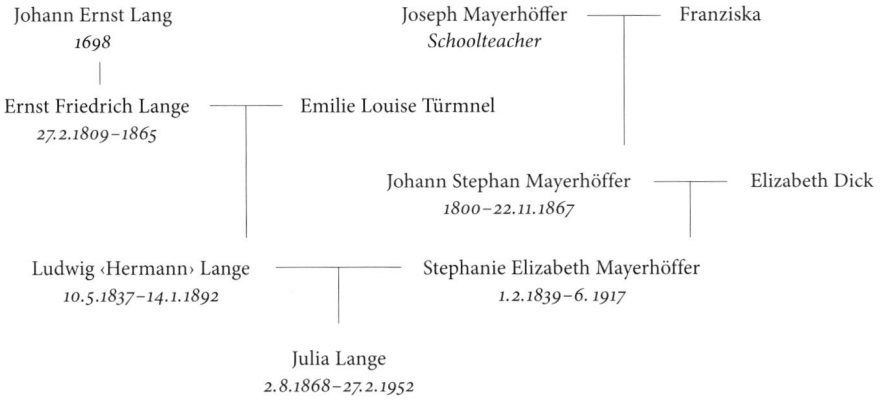

5 *Wagner and Lange Family Trees*

LINEAGE AND PARENTAGE

6 Heinrich Ernst Wagner (1827–1896), ca. 1883

LINEAGE AND PARENTAGE

7 *Plauen School Photograph, ca. 1870, Max Wagner 4th from right, sitting*

LINEAGE AND PARENTAGE

8 *Stephanie Beauharnais, Grand Duchess of Baden,*
   by James R. Swinton, London 1852

LINEAGE AND PARENTAGE

9 *Stephanie Mayerhöffer, Karlsruhe 1860*
9a *Hermann Lange, Karlsruhe 1860*

LINEAGE AND PARENTAGE

10 Hermann Lange, Manchester 1890

LINEAGE AND PARENTAGE

11 *Stephanie Lange, Manchester 1890*

LINEAGE AND PARENTAGE

M. GUTTENBERG PHOTO.   MANCHESTER

12 Julia Lange, ca. 1879/80

LINEAGE AND PARENTAGE

13 Julia Lange and Siblings: Rose, Julia, Ernest, Gertrude and Emily, 1881

LINEAGE AND PARENTAGE

14 Julie Lange, Manchester 1889, aged 21

LINEAGE AND PARENTAGE

15 *Max Wagner, Melbourne (Australia) 1889, aged 29*

LINEAGE AND PARENTAGE

16 Julie and Max Wagner, Hampstead 1895

LINEAGE AND PARENTAGE

17 *Wiesbaden, ca. 1908, by Hans Lack*

LINEAGE AND PARENTAGE

18 Hot Springs, Wiesbaden 1905

LINEAGE AND PARENTAGE

19 *Kurhaus with Flower Garden, Wiesbaden 1905*

LINEAGE AND PARENTAGE

20 *Uhlandstrasse 9, Wiesbaden 1899*

LINEAGE AND PARENTAGE

21 Max, Julie and Roland Wagner, 1899

LINEAGE AND PARENTAGE

22 *Julie, Roland and Max Wagner in the Black Forest, 1903*

LINEAGE AND PARENTAGE

23 Christmas 1903, Roland Wagner

LINEAGE AND PARENTAGE

24 Max Wagner, Wiesbaden 1904

LINEAGE AND PARENTAGE

25 Max Wagner, 'From Max to Julie', Wiesbaden 1904

LINEAGE AND PARENTAGE

KAISERLICHES PATENTAMT.

PATENTSCHRIFT

— № 133883 —

KLASSE **47*b*.**

AUSGEGEBEN DEN 6. OKTOBER 1902.

MAX WAGNER in WIESBADEN.

Lagerschale oder Platte aus einer Verbindung von widerstandsfähigem Metall und Weichmetall.

Patentirt im Deutschen Reiche vom 25. September 1901 ab.

Die Erfindung betrifft Lagerschalen, welche aus Weißmetall oder anderen Metallen oder Legirungen hergestellt sind, die an sich keine genügende Festigkeit besitzen, um der Dehnung, Verbiegung oder Abscheerung Widerstand zu leisten, welche durch Beanspruchungen durch die gegen sie liegenden Arbeitsflächen verursacht werden.

Die Erhöhung der Widerstandsfähigkeit der Legirung wird dadurch erreicht, daß man ein aus härteren Stoffen — Stahl oder Eisen — gezogenes, gegossenes oder zusammengefügtes Geripppe mit der Legirung umgießt oder in sonst eine feste Verbindung bringt.

Zum besseren Halt für das umgegossene Lagermetall ist das Gerippe mit Durchlochungen, Vorsprüngen oder Vertiefungen versehen, als Geflecht oder Gitter ausgebildet, derart, daß es sich der äußeren Form des nach dem Vergießen des Lagermetalles oder Legirung gebildeten Körpers anpaßt, von der Legirung jedoch umflossen ist.

Als besondere Ausführungsform soll das im Lagermetall liegende Gerippe dazu dienen, bei Troglagern die zur Zeit aus Gußeisen oder Bronze hergestellten Schalenkörper, in welche das Lagermetall eingebettet ist, fortfallen zu lassen.

Vermöge der dem Lagermetall durch Umgießen eines aus Eisen oder Stahl oder andere feste Metalle bestehenden Gerippes mit demselben verliehenen Widerstandsfähigkeit können die Lagerschalenkörper unter gänzlichem Fortfall der früheren gußeisernen oder bronzenen Untertheile ausschließlich aus der Lagermetalllegirung hergestellt werden.

Fig. 1 und 1a stellen die bisher übliche Anordnung in zwei Schnitten,

Fig. 2 bis 8a stellen Ausführungsformen der Erfindung dar.

Die Vereinigung von harten und weichen Metallen zu einer Lagerschale ist schon in verschiedenen Formen bekannt (z. B. durch die amerikanischen Patentschriften 497210 und 629395). In diesen Fällen aber handelt es sich um die Herstellung einer aus beiden Metallen bestehenden Gleitfläche und nicht um ein Skelett, welches, an keiner Stelle der Gleitfläche hervortretend, dem Weichmetall von innen den genügenden Halt giebt, um durch die Vereinigung der beiden Stücke eine vollständige Lagerschale herzustellen, welche außer dem Weichmetall kein Gußmetall zu enthalten braucht.

Während in Fig. 1 und 1a das Lagermetall nur als Futter Verwendung findet, der aus Gußeisen oder Bronze hergestellte Schalenkörper jedoch die Ausschließung von Formveränderungen bezweckt, wird nach der neuen Erfindung der Schalenkörper ganz aus der Lagermetalllegirung, welche zur Erhöhung ihrer Widerstandsfähigkeit gegen Dehnung, Verbiegung und Abscheerung ein aus Eisen oder Stahl gebildetes Gerippe in sich aufnimmt, hergestellt.

Es wird hier auch eine vereinfachte Bearbeitung beim Einpassen der Schalen in den Lagerkörper erreicht, die Auswechselbarkeit

(2. Auflage, ausgegeben am 19. Dezember 1907.)

26 Max Wagner's patent, 1901

LINEAGE AND PARENTAGE

27 *Prospectus from the early days of the company*

LINEAGE AND PARENTAGE

28 *Julie, Felix and Roland Wagner, 1904*

LINEAGE AND PARENTAGE

29 *Roland, Julie, Max and Felix Wagner, Badenweiler 1905*

LINEAGE AND PARENTAGE

30 'Hope', by George Frederic Watts, 1886

LINEAGE AND PARENTAGE

31 Julie Wagner with Gerard Wagner, Münster am Stein July 1906

EARLY CHILDHOOD

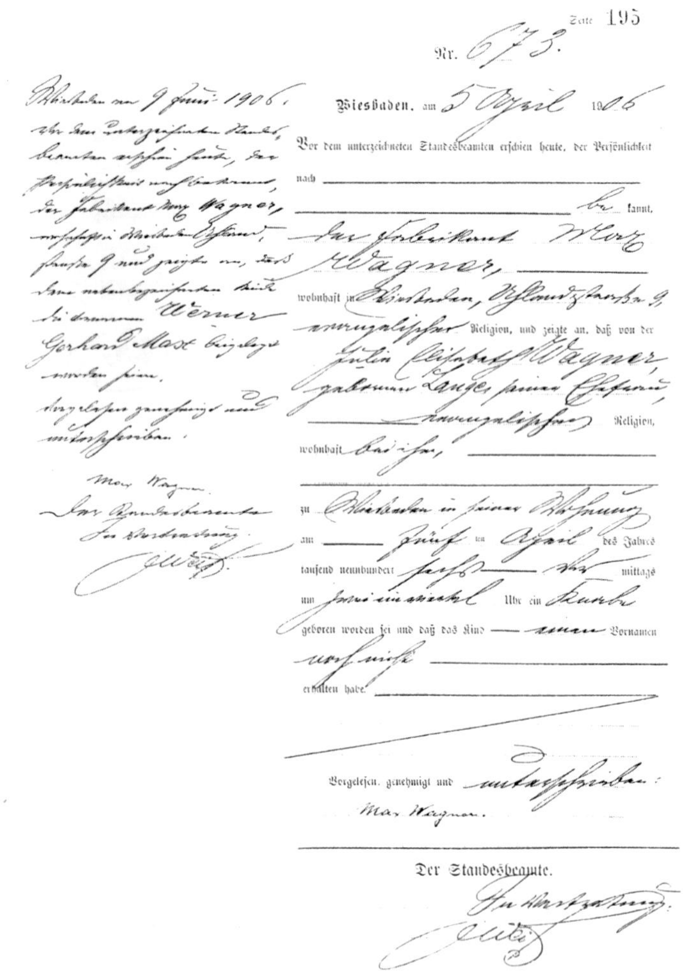

Nr. 673.

Wiesbaden, am 5 April 1906

[Handwritten German birth certificate record, largely illegible]

Der Standesbeamte.

32 *Gerard Wagner's Birth Certificate, 5 April 1906*

EARLY CHILDHOOD

33 Felix, Roland and Gerard Wagner, 1906

EARLY CHILDHOOD

34 Roland, Max, Felix, Julie and Gerard Wagner, 1906

EARLY CHILDHOOD

35 *Felix, Gerard and Max Wagner, Kleine Frankfurter Straße, Wiesbaden 1907*

EARLY CHILDHOOD

36 Felix, Max and Gerard Wagner, Kleine Frankfurter Straße, Wiesbaden 1907

EARLY CHILDHOOD

37 Gerard Wagner, 1907

EARLY CHILDHOOD

38 Gerard and Julie Wagner, 1908

EARLY CHILDHOOD

39 Julie Wagner in mourning with her three sons, 1908

40 *Gerard and Felix Wagner, Black Forest 1908*

EARLY CHILDHOOD

41 Nerotal, Wiesbaden 1898

EARLY CHILDHOOD

42 *The Russian Church of St Elisabeth, Neroberg*

EARLY CHILDHOOD

43 *'The view from our window', Neroberg Strasse 15, 1909*

44 The sitting room, Neroberg 15

45 *The study, Neroberg 15*

EARLY CHILDHOOD

46 Gerard and Felix Wagner, Neroberg 15, 1909

EARLY CHILDHOOD

47 Gerard Wagner, 1909

EARLY CHILDHOOD

48 *Felix, Roland and Gerard Wagner, Neroberg 15, 1909*

EARLY CHILDHOOD

49 *Gerard and Felix Wagner with Miss Collette, 1910*

EARLY CHILDHOOD

50 Gerard and Felix Wagner, November 1910

EARLY CHILDHOOD

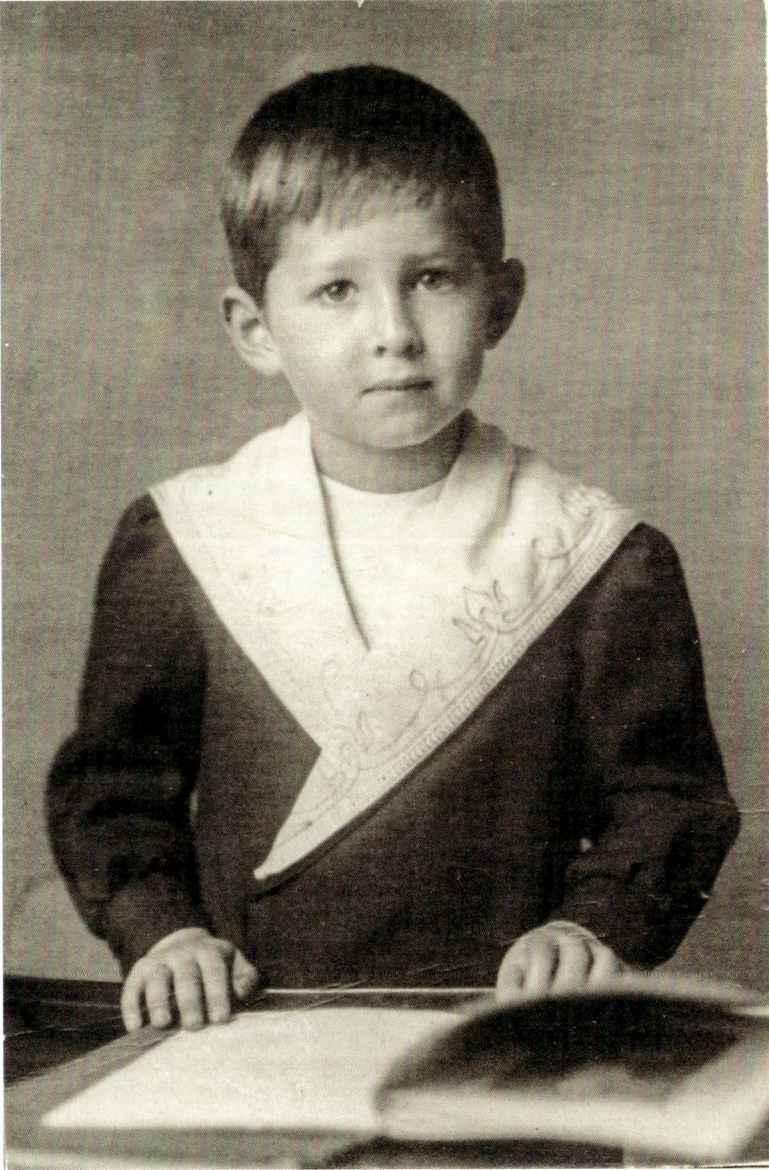

51 Gerard Wagner, November 1910, four years old

EARLY CHILDHOOD

52 Gerard, Felix and Roland Wagner before the move to England, Idstein June 1912

Bowdon

53 Map of Cheshire, 1842

BOYHOOD

THE FIRS. BOWDON.

54 *Westholme, Bowdon 2007*
55 *The Firs, Bowdon*

BOYHOOD

56 *Gerard Wagner, Westholme June 1913*
56a *Felix Wagner, Westholme June 1913*

57 Julie Wagner, October 1913

BOYHOOD

58 Gerard and Felix Wagner, Michaelmas 1913

BOYHOOD

*59 School in Bowdon, Gerard Wagner first from right, sitting;
Felix Wagner fifth from right, standing, 1914/15*

IN LIGHTER MOOD

BY Wagner Barker & Co.

A WONDERFUL CONTRIVANCE.

A servant-maid from the country who had never been used to cooking by the help of a gas-stove took a situation in London. Her mistress, when showing her the use of the stove she lit the burners to show her new new maid how it worked. Then she went leaving the maid to her own domain. A fortnight later she asked Mary how she liked the stove.

Mary beamed enthusyastically.

"Oh! ma'am" she said "its a wonderfull stove, you lit it for me when I came and it has not gone out from that time to this."

i' faith 'tis a cold (k)night

RESOURCEFUL.

an army officer's wife, who was giving a small luncheon party at her home in Madras not long ago, remembered, to her horror, that she had forgotten to order any cheese, and that cheese unhappily, formed the staple diet of the vegitarian guest of honour. Towards the close of the meal, she was about to appologise for the omission when to her surprise, the native servant entered, bearing the required dish. She was amazed at this forethought and after the guests had departed, she asked him how he had managed to procure the cheese at such short notice.

"Oh, Mem Sahib." he replied with a smile "me emptia all de mouse traps!"

60 *'In Lighter Mood', by Gerard Wagner, 1913/14*

BOYHOOD

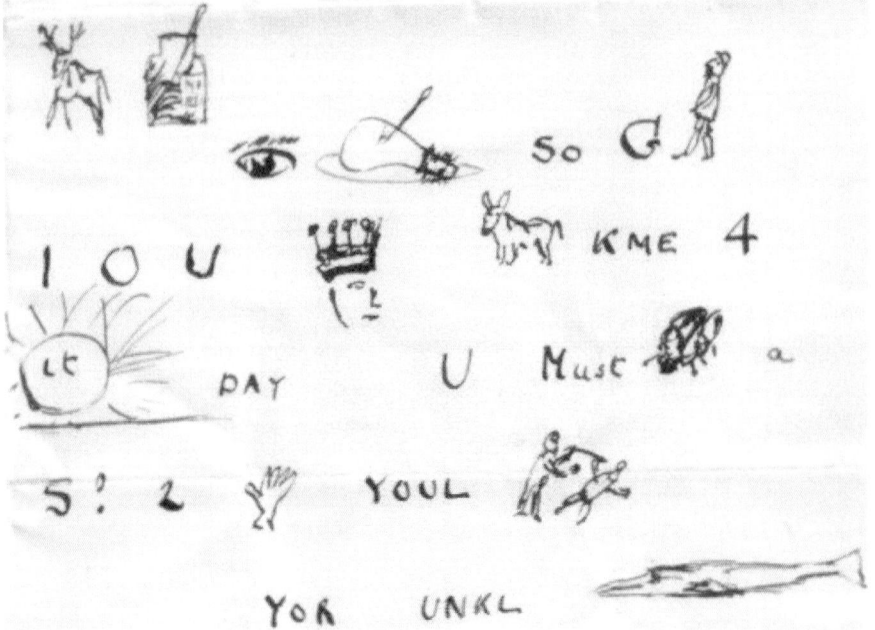

61 *'Pickles', Gerard Wagner, March 1916*
Dear (deer) Honey, I (eye) am (ham) so glad (G + lad) I owe you (I O U)
half-a-crown – Ask (ass + k) me for (4) it on Sun-day – You (U) must
be (bee) a … – Your uncle Pike (The last line still needs deciphering!)

*62 Gerard Wagner aged nine with cousin
Philip Sugden, August/September 1915*

BOYHOOD

63 Gerard and Felix Wagner with Ernest Lang's family, 22 April 1917

64 *Felix Wagner, Sheila Fleming and Gerard Wagner, August 1917*

65 4 Belfield Road, Didsbury, Manchester 2010

66 Julie Wagner, Belfield Road 1918

67 Gerard Wagner, Belfield Road 1918

BOYHOOD

Mr BEEVOR'S HOUSE ALDENHAM SCHOOL.

68 *Aldenham School, Hertfordshire 1970*
68a *Beevor's House, Aldenham School 1910*

YOUTH

69 *Gerard Wagner, Aldenham School, Easter Term 1918*

YOUTH

70 *'Daffodils', by Gerard Wagner, March 1918*

YOUTH

71 'Julie Wagner', by Gerard Wagner, August 1919

YOUTH

72 Gerard and Felix Wagner, Belfield Road 1919/20

YOUTH

*73 Summer Holiday in Grenoble (France) 1921, Gerard Wagner
first right sitting; Felix Wagner first right standing*

74 'Mater Misericordiae', by Fra Marie Bernard, Abbaye Grande Trappe, Orne

YOUTH

75 *Beevor's House 1922, Gerard Wagner, back row,*
third from right, Aldenham School

YOUTH

76 *Beevor's House 1922, Gerard Wagner back row, first left*

77 'Annecy in the Moonlight', by Gerard Wagner, summer 1921

YOUTH

78 Julie and Gerard Wagner, Penrhyn Bay summer 1922

79 Felix Wagner, Belfield Road 1923
79a 'Roland with his Chestnut Tree', Roland Wagner, Idstein ca. 1917

YOUTH

80 'That I might drink and leave the world unseen',
Ode to a Nightingale by John Keats, by Gerard Wagner, July 1923

YOUTH

81 St Ives, by Thomas Paster

APPRENTICESHIP AT ST. IVES

82 John Anthony Park, St Ives 1925, photograph by Gerard Wagner

83 *'Fringe of the Tide' (St Ives), by John Anthony Park, 1932*

APPRENTICESHIP AT ST. IVES

84 'St Ives Morning', by John Anthony Park

APPRENTICESHIP AT ST. IVES

85 *'Back Road St Ives', by John Anthony Park*

APPRENTICESHIP AT ST. IVES

86 Porthmeor Sea Wall and Studios, St Ives 1936

APPRENTICESHIP AT ST. IVES

*87 Gerard Wagner's Loft Studio, Porthmeor Sea Wall,
1924–1925, photograph by Gerard Wagner*

APPRENTICESHIP AT ST. IVES

88 Gerard Wagner, St Tropez Spring 1925

APPRENTICESHIP AT ST. IVES

89 Gerard Wagner and John Park, St Tropez Spring 1925

90 Martigues (South of France), by Gerard Wagner, 1925

91 Grimaud (South of France), by Gerard Wagner, 1925

92 '*Gurnard's Head*', by Terrick Williams

TINTAGEL CASTLE.
(Drawn by Percy Dixon. Engraved by T. Kieu.)

93 *Tintagel Castle, Cornwall 1892*

APPRENTICESHIP AT ST. IVES

94 *Map of England/Wales*

APPRENTICESHIP AT ST. IVES

95 *Trafalgar Square, London, 1920s*
96 *Victoria & Albert Museum, Kensington, London, 2008*

STUDENT AT THE ROYAL COLLEGE OF ART

97 *Victoria & Albert Museum showing the entrance to the Royal College of Art, 2008*

STUDENT AT THE ROYAL COLLEGE OF ART

98 Kensington Gardens/Hyde Park, oil sketch by Gerard Wagner, 1925

STUDENT AT THE ROYAL COLLEGE OF ART

99 In Kensington Gardens, London, oil sketch by Gerard Wagner, 1925

STUDENT AT THE ROYAL COLLEGE OF ART

100 'Autumn', Hyde Park, London, by Gerard Wagner, 1925

STUDENT AT THE ROYAL COLLEGE OF ART

101 'Dornachbrugg', pen & ink drawing by Anton Winterlin, 1860

DORNACH 1926–1949

*102 Looking towards Reinach from the Dornach Hill,
photograph by Otto Rietmann, 16.5.1914*

DORNACH 1926–1949

103 *Close up of plate 102 showing the area where Gerard Wagner lived in Reinach (Group of houses in middle distance)*

DORNACH 1926-1949

104 Rudolf Steiner with his model of the first Goetheanum,
photograph by Otto Rietmann, 16.6.1914

DORNACH 1926–1949

105 *The first Goetheanum, photograph by Otto Rietmann, May 1921*

DORNACH 1926–1949

*106 The High Studio with the plasticine model
of the sculpture 'The Representative of Humanity', 1916*

DORNACH 1926–1949

107 Model of the head of 'The Representative of Humanity'
by Rudolf Steiner, 1915, photograph by John Wilkes

DORNACH 1926 – 1949

108 *Rudolf Steiner in his studio working on the sculpture*
'The Representative of Humanity', photograph by Otto Rietmann, 6.1.1919

DORNACH 1926–1949

109 *'The Representative of Humanity'*

DORNACH 1926–1949

110 *The second Goetheanum under construction,*
photograph by Otto Rietmann, 13.7.1926

DORNACH 1926–1949

111 The second Goetheanum,
photograph by Pieter van der Ree, 15.3.2012

DORNACH 1926–1949

112 *Portrait of Gladys Mayer by Lena Maas, 1924/25*

DORNACH 1926–1949

113 *Rudolf Steiner lecturing during the East-West conference
in Vienna 1922, drawing by Gladys Mayer*

DORNACH 1926–1949

114 'Gerry and Inge at Haus Wessel', Easter 1927

DORNACH 1926–1949

115 *Gerard Wagner with Aunt Lily and family at Figino, 27.3.1928*

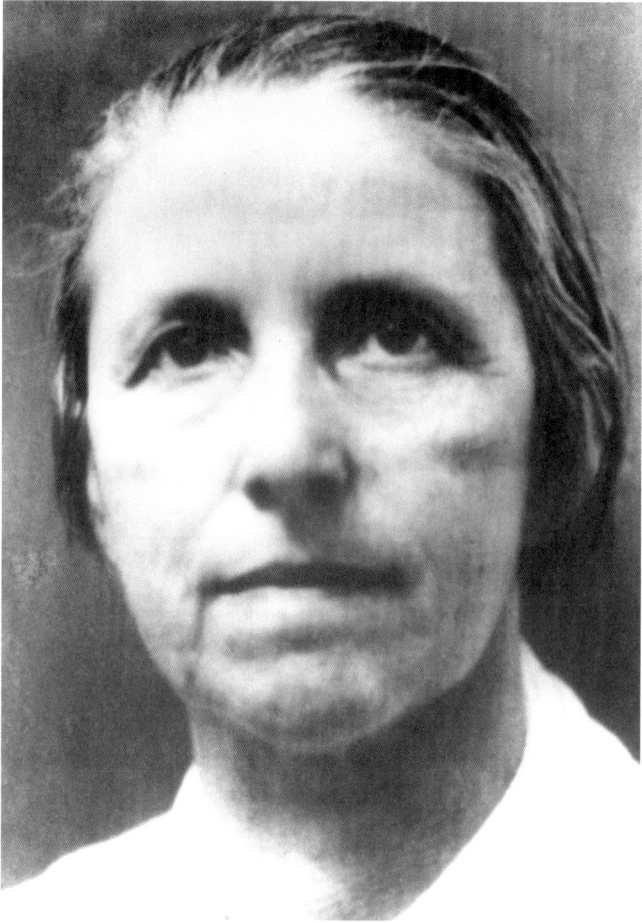

116 Henni Geck, 1884–1951, ca. 1932

DORNACH 1926–1949

117   *The Training Sketch 'Moonrise' by Henni Geck*
117a   *The Training Sketch 'Moonset' by Henni Geck*

DORNACH 1926–1949

118 *The High Studio where Henni Geck's school was situated, 2005*

119 *The Egyptian Temple Scene from 'The Soul's Awakening', Mystery Drama by Rudolf Steiner, performed by the Goetheanum stage goup, 1930*

DORNACH 1926–1949

120 'The Casting of the Brazen Sea', Scene from Hiram and Solomon,
a drama by Albert Steffen performed by the Goetheanum Stage, 1933

DORNACH 1926–1949

Rietmann-Haak

121 *Albert Steffen, 1925, photograph by Rietmann-Haak. A photograph in Gerard Wagner's possession: cut out of a leaflet announcing a new book publication*

122 Drawing by Gerard Wagner, 1930s/40s

123 *Drawing by Gerard Wagner, 1930s/40s*

124 Drawing by Gerard Wagner, 1930s/40s

125 *Drawing by Gerard Wagner, 1930s/40s*

126 *Andrew Lang, Gerard Wagner, Julie Wagner, Dorothy Wagner,*
Felix Wagner and Susie Lang, Bowdon 24.7.1933

DORNACH 1926–1949

127 *Felix and Dorothy Wagner, summer 1933*

DORNACH 1926–1949

128 Gerard Wagner, 1939

DORNACH 1926–1949

129 Gerard Wagner, 28.6.1943

DORNACH 1926–1949

130 *Gerard Wagner, Cathleen O'Donnel and (Ethel Bowen-Wedgwood?),*
in front of the 'Eckinger Schreinerei', late 1930s/40s

A — B. 90 cms.
B — c. 80 —
Tiefe   20 —.

Es wäre sehr praktisch
vielleicht, wenn das oberste
Brett, unter der Vase, sich
abheben liesse.

131 Sketch by Gerard Wagner of his studio at the 'Eckinger House',
Blumenweg 3, 1930s/1940s

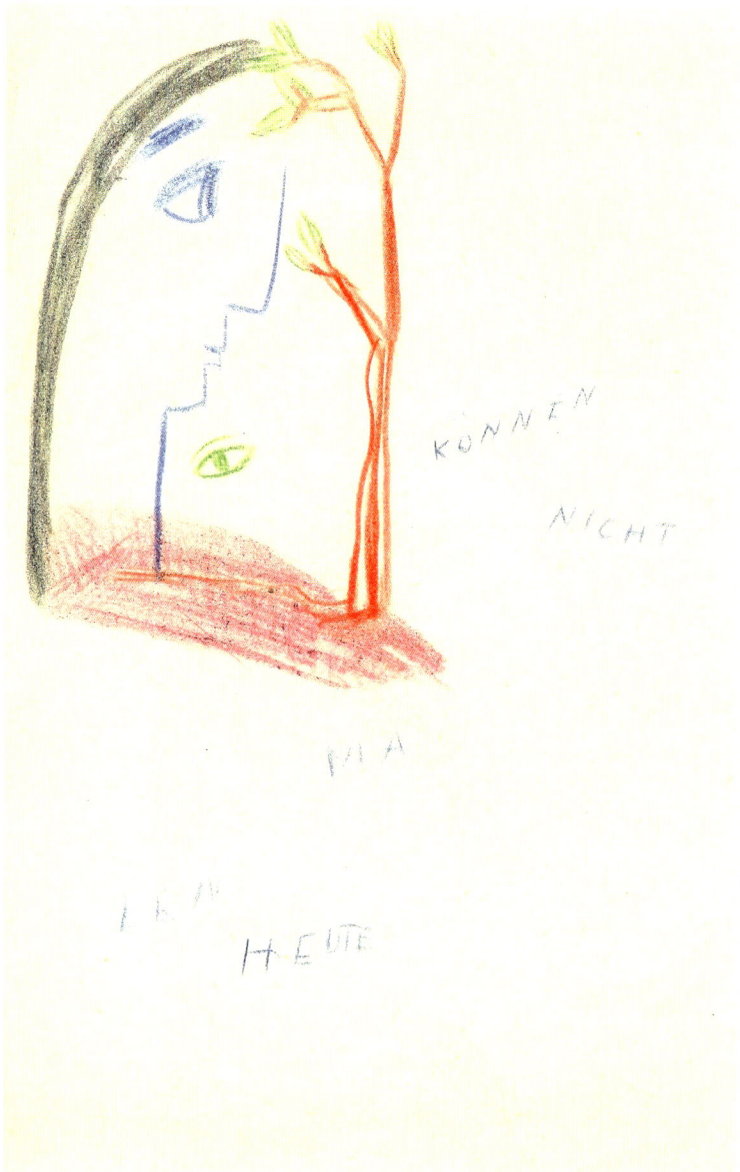

132 *A note to his pupil Helen Hoch, 1940s (We cannot paint today)*

Liebes Fräulein Hoch.

　　　　Soeben kommen diese

Einladungen, leider etwas spät.　　　Hoffentlich
können Sie sie doch unter Ihren Freunden
verwerten.　　　An Frl. Renner habe ich eine schon
geschickt.　Einen Gruss an Herrn Lichti, wenn Sie
ihn sehen.

　　Besten Grüssen
　　　　　g. wagner.

　　　　　　　　23. August. 1945.

133　An invitation to Helen Hoch to an exhibition, 1945

134 Picture sales in the back of Gerard Wagner's address book, 1940s/1950s

135 *Maria Koch and Elisabeth Koch, Haus Wundt, Dornach early 1950s*

136 Gerard Wagner before the 'Allgeyer Mural', Stuttgart 1955/56

DORNACH 1950–1969

137 Frida Lefringhausen, Haus Arild 1981

DORNACH 1950 – 1969

138 Gerard Wagner, 1963

DORNACH 1950–1969

139 Ernst Schuberth and Gerard Wagner, 1965

140 *Marie Keller, 1966*

DORNACH 1950 – 1969

141 Atelierhaus, Brosiweg 41, Dornach

DORNACH 1950-1969

142 *Erwin Thomalla, Elisabeth Koch and Gerard Wagner inspecting the Grafrath Mural, Bavaria September 1968*

143 *Gerard Wagner, 1973*

DORNACH 1970 – 1989

144 *Theodor Willmann, 1972*

DORNACH 1970–1989

145 Elisabeth and Rolf Adler, 1972

DORNACH 1970–1989

146 *'How feeling (orange) descends into the bodily organisation in the different ages of childhood', painted by Gerard Wagner during work with Rolf and Elisabeth Adler, 23.10.1975*

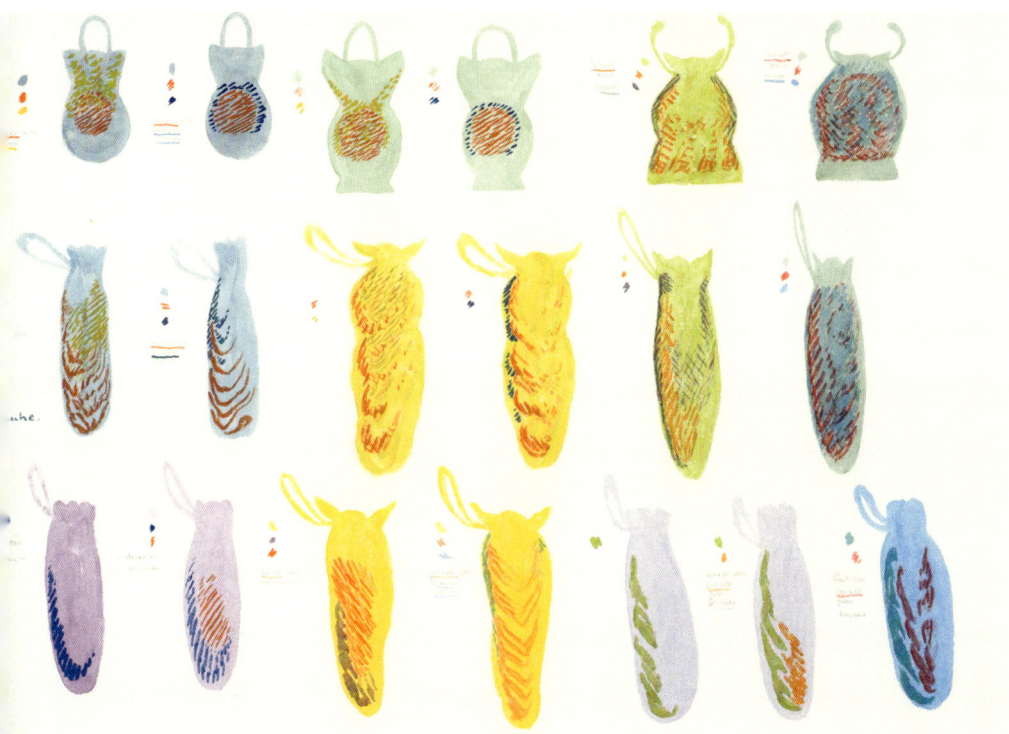

147 Bags, painted by Gerard Wagner, 1970s

148 *Hats, painted by Gerard Wagner, 1970s*

DORNACH 1970 – 1989

149 *Painting Smock, designed by Gerard Wagner for Erwin Thomalla, 1970s*

150 *Erwin Thomalla teaching in the 1970s*

DORNACH 1970–1989

151 *Gerard Wagner teaching at a weekend painting course
at the Arteum Painting School of Sonja Vandroogenbroeck, 1975*

152 *Gerard Wagner teaching at a weekend painting course*
at the Arteum Painting School of Sonja Vandroogenbroeck, 1975

153 *Gladys Mayer with her painting 'Call to Man', 1970s*

*154 Rengoldshausen Waldorf School, east-wing, painted summer 1981,
renovated 2009 by Alexander Winter, 2009*

*155 Rengoldshausen Waldorf School, east-wing, painted summer 1981,
renovated 2009 by Alexander Winter, 2009*

*156 Gerard Wagner painting at the Rengoldshausen
Waldorf School, west-wing, summer 1986*

*157 Rengoldshausen Waldorf School, mural painting,
summer 1986, Gerard Wagner with pupils*

158 Rengoldshausen Waldorf School, mural painting west-wing, summer 1986

159 *Gerard and Elisabeth Wagner with Hans-Bernhard Andrae
and pupils in Unterlengenhardt, 1988*

160 Dr Hans-Bernhard Andrae, ca. 1991

DORNACH 1970 – 1989

161 Gerard Wagner in Unterlengenhardt, 1988

DORNACH 1970–1989

162 Heilgart Umfrid, 1975

DORNACH 1970 – 1989

163, 163a Dining room murals at the Paracelsus Clinic Unterlengenhardt, by Gerard Wagner, 1987

164 Dining room murals at the Paracelsus Clinic Unterlengenhardt,
by Gerard Wagner, 1987
164a Paracelsus Clinic dining room. Gerard Wagner,
Dr Siegrun Andrae and Elisabeth Wagner, early 1990s

165 Gerard Wagner in his studio with Elisabeth Wagner, 1989

DORNACH 1970 – 1989

*166 Gerard Wagner with Elisabeth Wagner
painting the murals of the Foundation Stone Hall, 1990*

DORNACH 1990–1999

*167 Gerard Wagner with Elisabeth Wagner
painting the murals of the Foundation Stone Hall, 1990*

DORNACH 1990–1999

168 Murals in the Foundation Stone Hall

DORNACH 1990–1999

169 *Murals in the Foundation Stone Hall*

DORNACH 1990 – 1999

*170 Gerard Wagner and Eve Ratnowski
at the opening of the exhibition at Haus Ganna, July 1993*

DORNACH 1990–1999

171 The opening of the exhibiton at Haus Ganna, July 1993

172 Gerard Wagner, July 1995

DORNACH 1990‑1999

173 *Gerard Wagner, Witali Kovalenko and Elisabeth Wagner*
during the making of the film, August 1995

DORNACH 1990−1999

174 *Gerard Wagner teaching (filmed by W. Kovalenko), 1995*

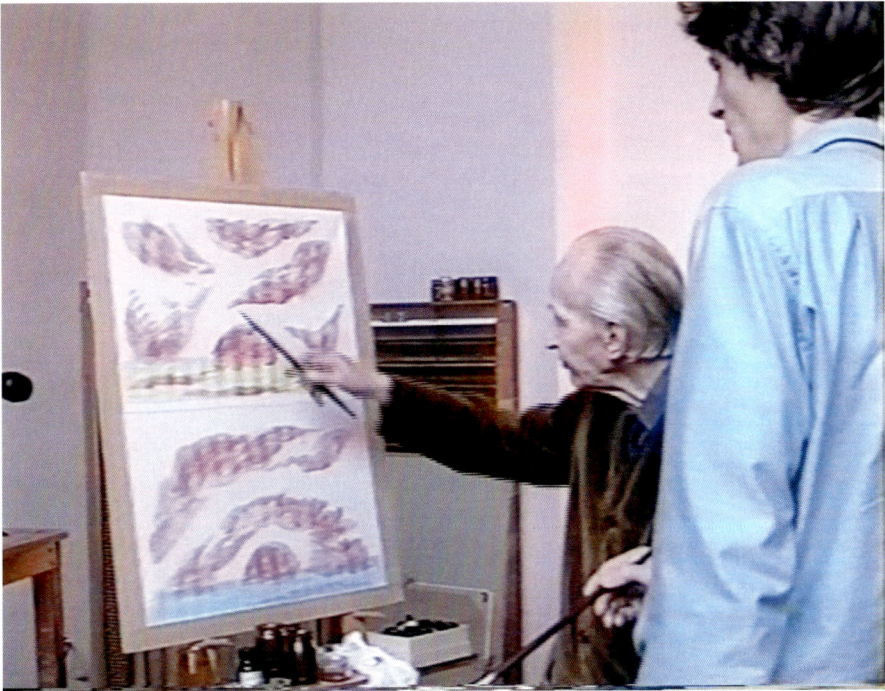

174a Gerard Wagner teaching (filmed by W. Kovalenko), 1995

175 *Gerard Wagner painting in his studio (filmed by W. Kovalenko), 1995*

DORNACH 1990–1999

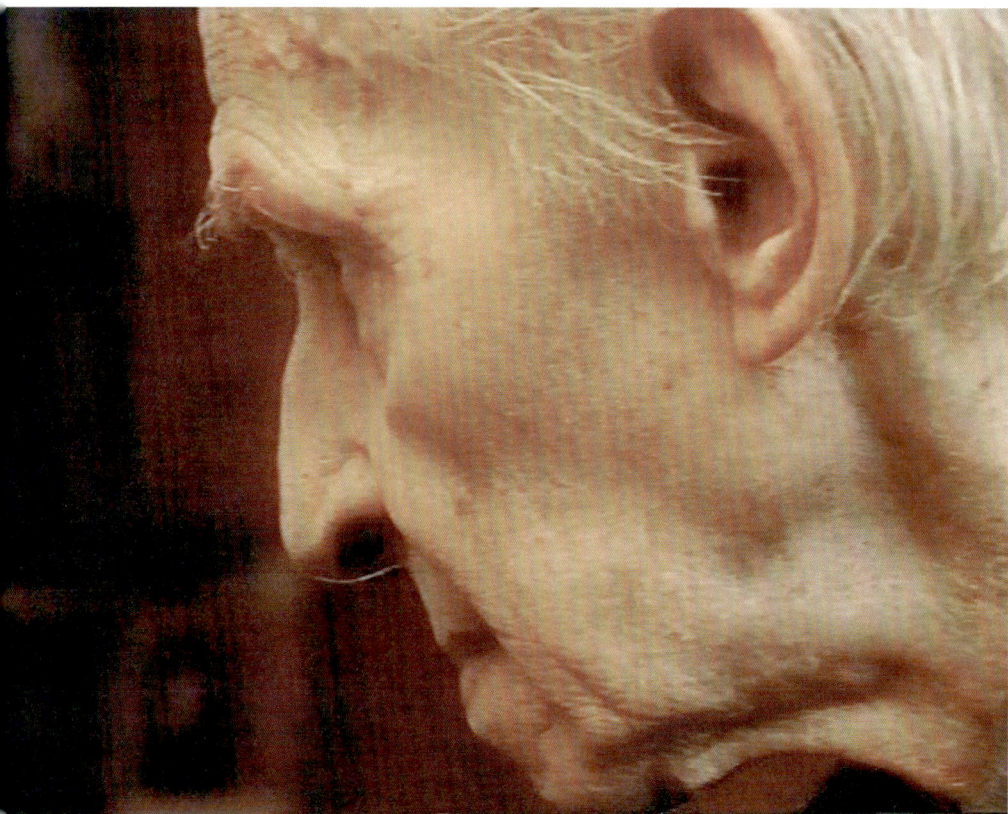

176 Gerard Wagner painting in his studio (filmed by W. Kovalenko), 1995

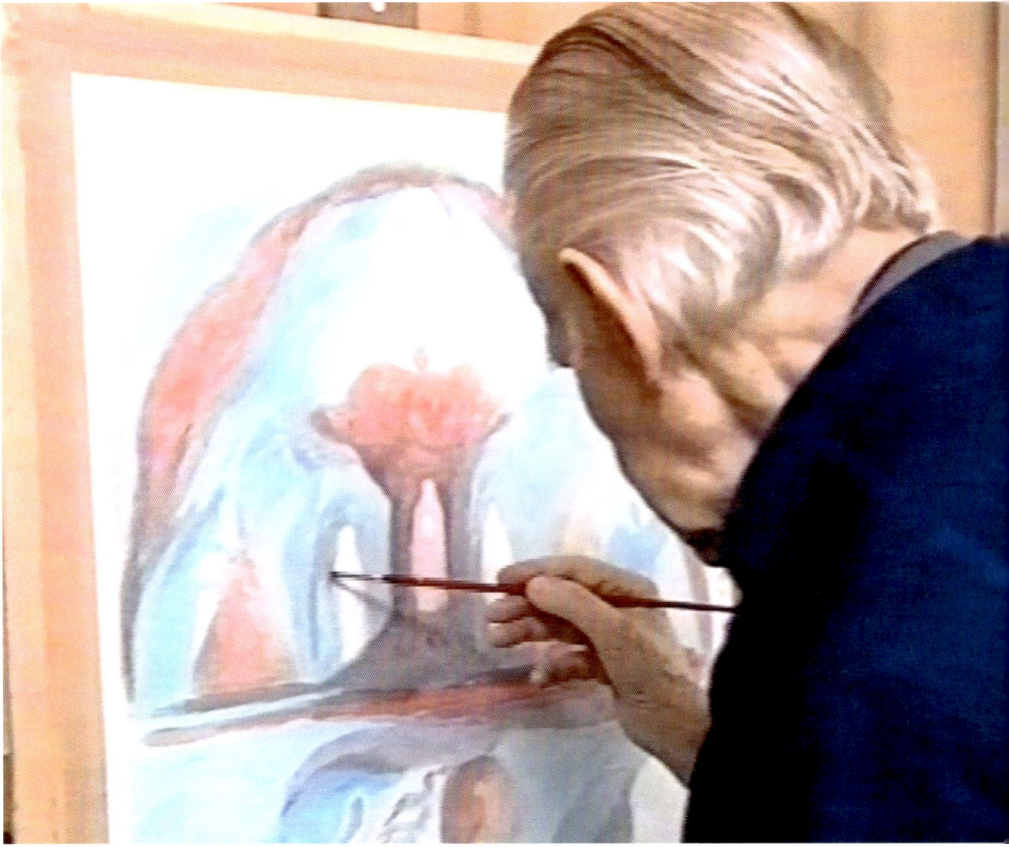

177 Gerard Wagner painting in his studio (filmed by W. Kovalenko), 1995

DORNACH 1990 – 1999

178 Gerard Wagner in his studio looking at paintings with visitors, 1997

179 Gerard Wagner and Caroline Chanter, 1998

DORNACH 1990–1999

180 Gerard Wagner in his studio, 1998

DORNACH 1990–1999

181 Gerard Wagner in his studio, 1998

DORNACH 1990–1999

182 Rex Raab and Gerard Wagner, November 1998

183 Jennifer Ware (Lang), Gerard Wagner and Mary Ingham (Wagner), May 1999

DORNACH 1990–1999

184 *Gerard Wagner painting in his studio, summer 1999*

DORNACH 1990 – 1999

185 Gerard Wagner, May 1999

DORNACH 1990 – 1999

186 *The Charioteer of Delphi, drawing by Gerard Wagner*

DORNACH 1990–1999

Ein Malerisches Werk, soll es zugleich Kunstwerk sein, wird ein ganz-
menschliches Erlebnis vermitteln, rein durch die künstlerischen Mittel von
Farbe und Form. Gesamtmenschliche = der dreigliedrige Mensch (Rudolf Steiners Skizze)

Das gesamtmenschliche lebt im Erlebnis des Farbkreises, in seiner Polarität und
seiner Steigerung. Gelb zum Warm rot, blau zum Kühlrot, und im Untersten - schwarz,
weiss, rot. Ausgewogenheit der Polaritäten von   *Anspannen - ausspannen,*
bin und Ansätzen, Festgin und
Lockerung, wärmen - kühlen, Bleiben - Abstreben usw.

Die verschiedenen Farben schon einzeln führen in verschiedene Schichten, der Natur und
des Menschen i. d. Kosmos. z.B. gelb - rot - blau, kühlrot in die vier
ätherarten Licht, Wärme, chem., Lebensäether. Braun und Schwarz
führen in Schichte die weit ab vom rein menschlichen liegen   *Unteres ä. (Schwarz/Weiss/Rot) oder im phys. leib interessiert bl.*

Der Maler bildet in sich aus im Erlebnis seiner eigenen Farbenganzheit.
Diese Farbenganzheits erlebnis will er mit dem Bilde vermitteln.
Nimmt er eine Farbe auf das weisse - oder gefärbte - Blatt, so ist diese Farbe
ein Glied, herausgenommen aus der inneren Farbenganzheit des Malers.   *oder der Natur.* Der
stellt die Notwendigkeit, diese eine Farbe durch eine Zweite - eine Steigerung   *erste*
oder eine Polarität - zu ergänzen, diese zusammen wiederum durch
eine Dritte, vierte usw Farbe, bis als Erlebnis des äusserlich Entstandenen
eine Entsprechung mit dem innerlich erlebten Farbenganzheit des eigenen Wesens
da ist.   Wie der Verlauf des Weges - des Prozesses - von der Einzelfarbe
bis hin zur harmonischen Ganzheit sich gestaltet - also das Motiv - hängt
weitgehend ab von der Wahl der ersten Farbe, oder der Beziehung der
ersten zwei Farben zueinander.   Das Ziel liegt also immer im Erreichen
der harmonischen Ganzheit. Der Anfang des Weges zum Ziel bestimmt die
erste gewählte Farbe.   Setzt man also ein Braun oder Schwarz als
erste Farbe hin, so hat man das Tote als Anfang, und das Folgende wird
dieses in die menschliche Ganzheit einzufügen haben.   Das kann auf
verschiedene Weisen geschehen.

Es gibt: "Künstler" deren Kunst darin besteht, sich von einem anderen Menschen
durch einen Stil fesseln zulassen, und sich dann von der Bindung zu befreien.
Der Maler bezieht sich, durch das wählen der ersten Farbe, in eine Situation

187 Text of 'A painting as a work of art' by Gerard Wagner, 1998

PAINTINGS

1 Mother and Child, ca. 1943

3 Trees/Golgotha 2, 1945

4 Rosecross motif, 1949

5 *The Pilgrim's Path, 'Curtain Motif'*
   for the Mystery Dramas, 1950

7 Baptism 1, 1955

9 *Above Blossoms, 1956*

10 Wolves, 1960

11 Plant Metamorphosis, 1967

*14 The Incarnation, from a series
of Baptism/Herod motifs, 1969*

*15 Motifs of the large cupola of the Goetheanum:
Man in Ancient Egypt; Man in Ancient Greece;
Jehova and the Luciferic Temptation/Paradise, 1976*

16 Motifs of the large cupola of the Goetheanum:
IAO – The Cosmic Image of Man;
I – The Wrath of God and the Yearning Grief of God;
A – The Dance of the Seven; O – The Cirlce of Twelve, 1976

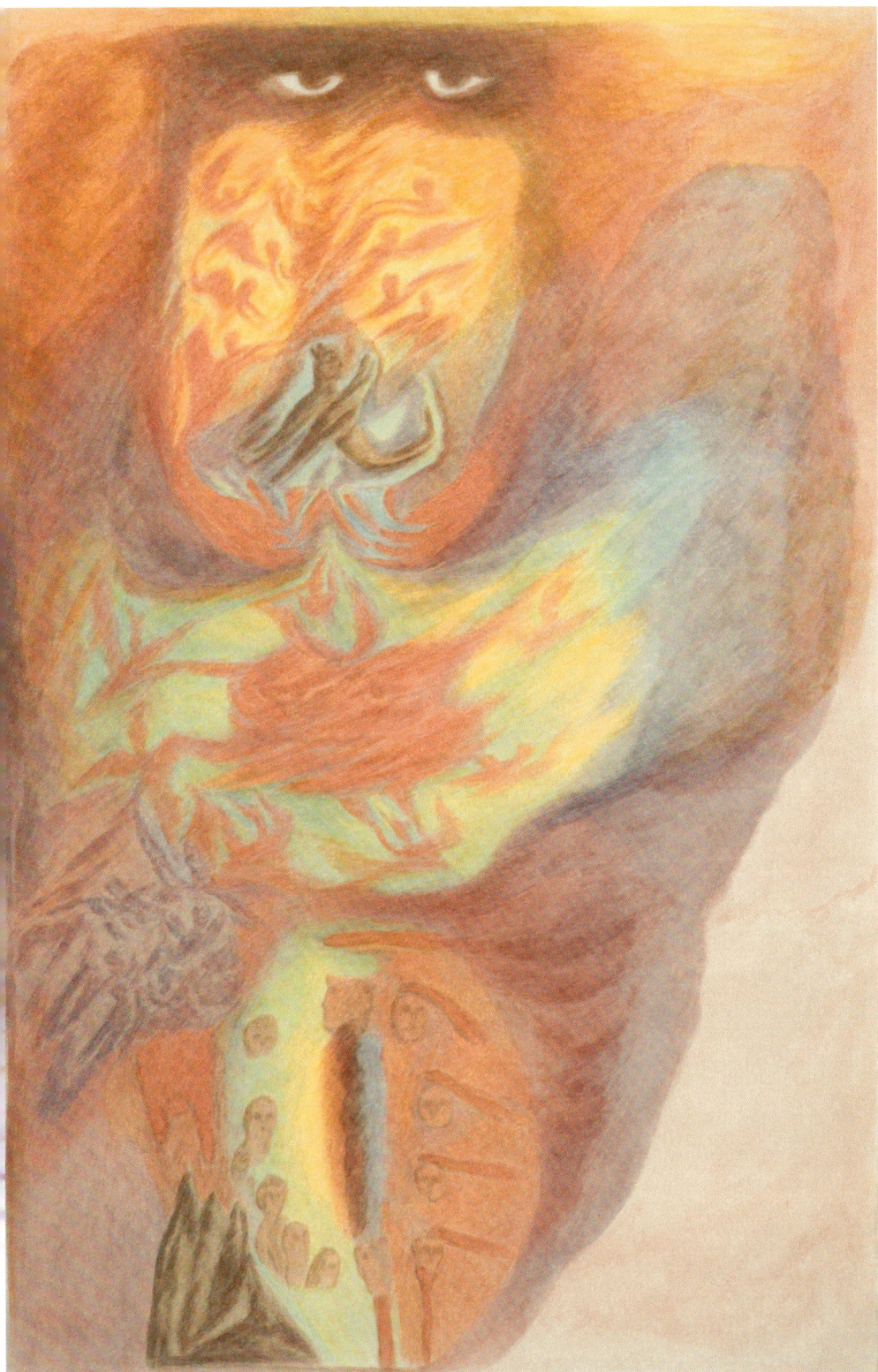

17 *Wonder of Death, 1978*

18 Madonna Motif, 1980

*19 A Plant Metamorphosis series:
blossom transformation, 1985*

*20   A Plant Metamorphosis series:
blossom transformation, 1985*

21 A Plant Metamorphosis series:
blossom transformation, 1985

23 Transformation of the Rose,
from the series 'God's Gardener', 1986

24 *Archetypal Plant, 1988*

25 Resurrection – consecrated earth-realm, 1989

26 Motifs of the small cupola of the Goetheanum:
The Representative of Humanity; the Slav Motif;
the Persian-Germanic Initiate; the Egyptian Initiate, 1989

*27 Motifs of the small cupola of the Goetheanum:
The Egyptian Initiate; Athena/Apollo; Faust, 1989*

29 Motif for a Chapel of Rest, 1992

30 *Three Kings Motif, 1993*

31 Archetypal Plant with Elemental Beings, 1993

*32 Transformation of the Goetheanum large
cupola motif 'God's Wrath and God's Sorrow', 1994*

33 *The Cross, 1994*

35 *Guardian Angel, 1994*

37 The Gardener, 1995

39 Motif for a Cupola, 1995

41 The Earth trembles, 1996

43 Archetypal Animal–Archetypal Human Being, 1996

45 *The Prodigal Son, 1997*

47 Behold!, 1997

51 *'Final Chord'*, 1998

LIST OF ILLUSTRATIONS
(PLATES) AND PAINTINGS

Illustrations (plates)

1   Cover image and dust jacket: Threefold Human Being, 1989, watercolour/plant-based pigments, 53 × 77 cm © Gerard und Elisabeth Wagner-Verein

2   Frontispiece: Gerard Wagner, 1983 © Gerard und Elisabeth Wagner-Verein

3   View of Plauen, 1850

4   Plauen, Market Place and Old Town Hall, 1908

5   Wagner and Lange Family Trees © Caroline Chanter

6   Heinrich Ernst Wagner (1827–1896), ca. 1883 © Mary Ingham (Wagner)

7   Plauen School Photograph, ca. 1870, Max Wagner 4th from right, sitting © Mary Ingham (Wagner)

8   Stephanie Beauharnais, Grand Duchess of Baden, by James R. Swinton, London 1852, oil on canvas, 80 cm × 68 cm © Helikon Kastély Museum, Hungary

9   Stephanie Mayerhöffer, Karlsruhe 1860 © Mary Ingham (Wagner)

9 a   Hermann Lange, Karlsruhe 1860 © Mary Ingham (Wagner)

10   Hermann Lange, Manchester 1890 © Mary Ingham (Wagner)

11   Stephanie Lange, Manchester 1890 © Mary Ingham (Wagner)

12   Julia Lange, ca. 1879/80 © Mary Ingham (Wagner)

13   Julia Lange and Siblings: Rose, Julia, Ernest, Gertrude and Emily, 1881 © Mary Ingham (Wagner)

14   Julie Lange, Manchester 1889, aged 21 © Mary Ingham (Wagner)

15   Max Wagner, Melbourne (Australia) 1889, aged 29 © Mary Ingham (Wagner)

16   Julie and Max Wagner, Hampstead 1895 © Mary Ingham (Wagner)

17   Wiesbaden, ca. 1908, by Hans Lack © Stadtarchiv Wiesbaden

18   Hot Springs, Wiesbaden 1905 © Hessische Landesbibliothek Wiesbaden

19   Kurhaus with Flower Garden, Wiesbaden 1905 © Hessische Landesbibliothek Wiesbaden

20   Uhlandstrasse 9, Wiesbaden 1899 © Mary Ingham (Wagner)

21   Max, Julie and Roland Wagner, 1899 © Mary Ingham (Wagner)

22   Julie, Roland and Max Wagner in the Black Forest, 1903 © Mary Ingham (Wagner)

23   Christmas 1903, Roland Wagner © Mary Ingham (Wagner)

24   Max Wagner, Wiesbaden 1904 © Mary Ingham (Wagner)

25   Max Wagner, 'From Max to Julie', Wiesbaden 1904 © Mary Ingham (Wagner)

56a Felix Wagner, Westholme June 1913 © Mary Ingham (Wagner)

57 Julie Wagner, October 1913 © Mary Ingham (Wagner)

58 Gerard and Felix Wagner, Michaelmas 1913 © Mary Ingham (Wagner)

59 School in Bowdon, Gerard Wagner first from right, sitting; Felix Wagner fifth from right, standing, 1914/15 © Mary Ingham (Wagner)

60 'In Lighter Mood', by Gerard Wagner, 1913/14 © Mary Ingham (Wagner)

61 'Pickles', Gerard Wagner, March 1916
    Dear (deer) Honey, I (eye) am (ham) so glad (G + lad) I owe you (I O U) half-a-crown – Ask (ass + k) me for (4) it on Sun-day – You (U) must be (bee) a … – Your uncle Pike (The last line still needs deciphering!) © Mary Ingham (Wagner)

62 Gerard Wagner aged nine with cousin Philip Sugden, August/September 1915 © Mary Ingham (Wagner)

63 Gerard and Felix Wagner with Ernest Lang's family, 22 April 1917 © Mary Ingham (Wagner)

64 Felix Wagner, Sheila Fleming and Gerard Wagner, August 1917 © Mary Ingham (Wagner)

65 4 Belfield Road, Didsbury, Manchester 2010 © Caroline Chanter

66 Julie Wagner, Belfield Road 1918 © Mary Ingham (Wagner)

67 Gerard Wagner, Belfield Road 1918 © Mary Ingham (Wagner)

68 Aldenham School, Hertfordshire 1970 © Aldenham School

68a Beevor's House, Aldenham School, 1910

69 Gerard Wagner, Aldenham School, Easter Term 1918 © Mary Ingham (Wagner)

70 'Daffodils', by Gerard Wagner, March 1918 © Mary Ingham (Wagner)

71 'Julie Wagner', by Gerard Wagner, August 1919 © Mary Ingham (Wagner)

72 Gerard and Felix Wagner, Belfield Road 1919/20 © Mary Ingham (Wagner)

73 Summer Holiday in Grenoble (France) 1921, Gerard Wagner first right sitting; Felix Wagner first right standing © Mary Ingham (Wagner)

74 'Mater Misericordiae', by Fra Marie Bernard, Abbaye Grande Trappe, Orne © Mary Ingham (Wagner)

75 Beevor's House 1922, Gerard Wagner, back row, third from right, Aldenham School © Aldenham School

76 Beevor's House 1922, Gerard Wagner back row, first left © Aldenham School

77 'Annecy in the Moonlight', by Gerard Wagner, summer 1921, oil on canvas © Private collection

78 Julie and Gerard Wagner, Penrhyn Bay summer 1922 © Mary Ingham (Wagner)

79 Felix Wagner, Belfield Road 1923 © Mary Ingham (Wagner)

79a 'Roland with his Chestnut Tree', Roland Wagner, Idstein ca. 1917 © Mary Ingham (Wagner)

173 Gerard Wagner, Witali Kovalenko and Elisabeth Wagner during the making of the film, August 1995 © Gerard und Elisabeth Wagner-Verein

174 Gerard Wagner teaching (filmed by W. Kovalenko), 1995 © Gerard und Elisabeth Wagner-Verein

174a Gerard Wagner teaching (filmed by W. Kovalenko), 1995 © Gerard und Elisabeth Wagner-Verein

175 Gerard Wagner painting in his studio (filmed by W. Kovalenko), 1995 © Gerard und Elisabeth Wagner-Verein

176 Gerard Wagner painting in his studio (filmed by W. Kovalenko), 1995 © Gerard und Elisabeth Wagner-Verein

177 Gerard Wagner painting in his studio (filmed by W. Kovalenko), 1995 © Gerard und Elisabeth Wagner-Verein

178 Gerard Wagner in his studio looking at paintings with visitors, 1997 © Caroline Chanter

179 Gerard Wagner and Caroline Chanter, 1998 © Caroline Chanter

180 Gerard Wagner in his studio, 1998 © Caroline Chanter

181 Gerard Wagner in his studio, 1998 © Caroline Chanter

182 Rex Raab and Gerard Wagner, November 1998 © Gerard und Elisabeth Wagner-Verein

183 Jennifer Ware (Lang), Gerard Wagner and Mary Ingham (Wagner), Mai 1999 © Caroline Chanter

184 Gerard Wagner painting in his studio, summer 1999 © Caroline Chanter

185 Gerard Wagner, May 1999 © Caroline Chanter

186 The Charioteer of Delphi, drawing by Gerard Wagner © Gerard und Elisabeth Wagner-Verein

187 Text of 'A painting as a work of art' by Gerard Wagner, 1998 © Caroline Chanter

Paintings

1 Mother and Child, ca. 1943, watercolour, 57.5 × 38.5 cm

2 Trees/Golgotha 1, 1945, watercolour, 31.5 × 55.5 cm

3 Trees/Golgotha 2, 1945, watercolour, 32.5 × 50 cm

4 Rosecross motif, 1949, watercolour, 78 × 57 cm

5 The Pilgrim's Path, 'Curtain Motif' for the Mystery Dramas, 1950, watercolour, 36 × 54 cm

6 Elemental World/Seed, 1954, watercolour, 65.5 × 47.5 cm

7 Baptism 1, 1955, watercolour, 101 × 68 cm

8 Baptism 2, 1956, watercolour, 55 × 76 cm

9 Above Blossoms, 1956, watercolour, 39.5 × 28.5 cm

10   Wolves, 1960, watercolour, 48 × 66.5 cm

11   Plant Metamorphosis, 1967, watercolour, 48.5 × 66.5 cm

12   Animal Metamorphosis: Archetypal Animal to Animal Forms, 1969, watercolour, 66.5 × 48.5 cm

13   Herod's Deed, from a series of Baptism/Herod motifs, 1969, watercolour, 48 × 66.5 cm

14   The Incarnation, from a series of Baptism/Herod motifs, 1969, watercolour, 46 × 66 cm

15   Motifs of the large cupola of the Goetheanum: Man in Ancient Egypt; Man in Ancient Greece; Jehova and the Luciferic Temptation/Paradise, watercolour/plant-based pigments, 1976, 66 × 99 cm

16   Motifs of the large cupola of the Goetheanum: IAO – The Cosmic Image of Man; I – The Wrath of God and the Yearning Grief of God; A – The Dance of the Seven; O – The Cirlce of Twelve, 1976, watercolour/plant-based pigments, 99 × 66 cm

17   Wonder of Death, 1978, watercolour/plant-based pigments, 66.5 × 48.5 cm

18   Madonna Motif, 1980, watercolour/plant-based pigments, 66.5 × 48.5 cm

19   A Plant Metamorphosis series: blossom transformation, 1985, watercolour/plant-based pigments, 53 × 77 cm

20   A Plant Metamorphosis series: blossom transformation, 1985, watercolour/plant-based pigments, 53 × 77 cm

21   A Plant Metamorphosis series: blossom transformation, 1985, watercolour/plant-based pigments, 53 × 77 cm

22   The Rose, from the series 'God's Gardener', 1986, watercolour/plant-based pigments, 77 × 53 cm

23   Transformation of the Rose, from the series 'God's Gardener', 1986, watercolour/plant-based pigments, 77 × 53 cm

24   Archetypal Plant, 1988, watercolour/plant-based pigments, 66.5 × 48.5 cm

25   Resurrection – consecrated earth-realm, 1989, watercolour/plant-based pigments, 77 × 53 cm

26   Motifs of the small cupola of the Goetheanum: The Representative of Humanity; the Slav Motif; the Persian-Germanic Initiate; the Egyptian Initiate, 1989, watercolour/plant-based pigments, 53 × 77 cm

27   Motifs of the small cupola of the Goetheanum: The Egyptian Initiate; Athena/Apollo; Faust, 1989, watercolour/plant-based pigments, 77 × 53 cm

28   Threefold Human Being, 1989, watercolour/plant-based pigments, 53 × 77 cm

29   Motif for a Chapel of Rest, 1992, watercolour/plant-based pigments, 77 × 53 cm

30   Three Kings Motif, 1993, watercolour/plant-based pigments, 77 × 53 cm

31   Archetypal Plant with Elemental Beings, 1993, watercolour/plant-based pigments, 77 × 53 cm

32 Transformation of the Goetheanum large cupola motif 'God's Wrath and God's Sorrow', 1994, watercolour/plant-based pigments, 77 × 53 cm

33 The Cross, 1994, watercolour/plant-based pigments, 77 × 53 cm

34 The Tree, 1994, watercolour/plant-based pigments, 53 × 77 cm

35 Guardian Angel, 1994, watercolour/plant-based pigments, 77 × 53 cm

36 Representative of Humanity 1, watercolour/plant-based pigments, 1994, 77 × 53 cm

37 The Gardener, 1995, watercolour/plant-based pigments, 77 × 53 cm

38 Transformation, 1995, watercolour/plant-based pigments, 77 × 53 cm

39 Motif for a Cupola, 1995, watercolour/plant-based pigments, 77 × 53 cm

40 Sophia, 1996, watercolour/plant-based pigments, 77 × 53 cm

41 The Earth trembles, 1996, watercolour/plant-based pigments, 77 × 53 cm

42 Representative of Humanity 2, 1996, watercolour/plant-based pigments, 77 × 53 cm

43 Archetypal Animal – Archetypal Human Being, 1996, watercolour/plant-based pigments, 53 × 77 cm

44 Plant World, 1997, watercolour/plant-based pigments, 77 × 53 cm

45 The Prodigal Son, 1997, watercolour/plant-based pigments, 53 × 77 cm

46 Battle for the Earth, 1997, watercolour/plant-based pigments, 53 × 77 cm

47 Behold!, 1997, watercolour/plant-based pigments, 77 × 53 cm

48 The Blue Flower, 1998, watercolour/plant-based pigments, 77 × 53 cm

49 Representative of Humanity 3, 1998, watercolour/plant-based pigments, 77 × 53 cm

50 New Life, 1998, watercolour/plant-based pigments, 77 × 53 cm

51 «Final Chord», 1998, watercolour/plant-based pigments, 77 × 53 cm

All paintings © Gerard und Elisabeth Wagner-Verein

ACKNOWLEDGEMENTS

I have many to thank for their help in the early and later days of researching and writing this book.

First and foremost Mary Ingham (Wagner) for the visits to her home. And other relatives of Gerard Wagner's: Jennifer Ware, Andrew Lang, Julie Gooch (Neild), Bernard Honey and Julian Clokie.

Rex Raab and Austin Wormleighton who gave such helpful advice on how to start writing a biography.

The occupiers of previous homes of the Wagner family in Wiesbaden: Herr Vinea, and on the Neroberg 'Gresser Architekten' who kindly allowed me into Nerobergstr. 15 to have a look around the basically unchanged house and garden.

Thorwald Thiersch, Diez Pohls, Roland Jeckelmann and Andrea Hitsch for their help with letters and texts written in German. Dear Lieselotte Strube who, with the old German alphabet in one hand and a magnifying glass in the other, deciphered Gerard Wagner's birth certificate and other Wagner/Lange/Mayerhöffer birth, marriage and death certificates.

Elisabeth Adler in Unterlengenhardt; Susanne Wulff; and the 'Dornachers': Jocelyn Walsh, Marie Keller, Hermann Koepke, Gabriele Kaiser, Ingeborg Maresca, Angela Kočonda, Michael and Beate Blume, Elisabeth Wagner-Koch and Jennifer Müller with whom I had special conversations.

My colleagues Ernst Schuberth and Anne Stockton as well as other former pupils who recounted or wrote down their memories: Heilgart Umfrid, Sonja Vandroogenbroeck, Alexander Winter, Beat Reinhard, Van James, Bernd Lutz, Angela Lord, Marianna Caluori, Ingrid Marl, Christa Bohnhorst (Dönges), Ans Groene, Gail McManus, Helga Bläuel (Raimund) and Angela Zbinden Wirz.

Helmut Raimund for his reminiscences of the 'Vienna Exhibition'; Raphaela Cooper for her memories of Gladys Mayer; Christian Thal-Jantzen for his assistance; and Graham Fradley, Michael Howard and David Adams, who shared their letters from Gerard Wagner with me.

There were vital contributions from various organisations. From: Neil Parkinson at the Royal College of Art; Jackie Wilkie at Aldenham School; the Victoria and Albert Museum. Ian Botting at the Rudolf Steiner House library; Christine Engels at the Albert Steffen Stiftung; Hans Schumm and

Peter Sagal at the Gerard Wagner Foundation US; the Goetheanum periodical 'Der Wochenschrift' for permission to use reviews and obituaries; Ekkehard Kurz of the 'Association of former co-workers of the firm 'Federal-Mogul/ Glyco e. V'; Frau Wüst at the Generallandesarchiv Karlsruhe who spent a few days with me looking for information about Stefan Mayerhöffer and his connection with Stephanie Beauharnais. Clemens Uhlig at the Stadt Archiv Plauen who kindly answered my questions and sent a rare old travel guide about Plauen: 'Plauen i. V. und die Vogtländische Schweiz' von A. Bruckmann, which I made use of for this biography.

Gerard & Elisabeth Wagner-Verein; Mary Ingham (Wagner); David Tovey; Silvana Gabrielli at the Rudolf Steiner Archiv Dornach; Dino Wendtland and Anna Pauli at the Goetheanum Archiv/Kunstsammlung Goetheanum; Tate Images and the Helikon Kastély Muzeum for supplying images of art works.

Matthew Barton for his editing of the English manuscript, and Sven Baumann for his editing of the German manuscript.

The Sampo-Initiative, the Turmalin Stiftung, Erika Umbricht Gysel, Steffen Gysel and other friends whose financial help made this publication possible.